THE POLITICS OF ACCOUNTABILITY IN THE MODERN STATE

For Charlie Flinders

The Politics of Accountability in the Modern State

MATTHEW FLINDERS
The University of Sheffield

LONDON AND NEW YORK

First published 2001 by Ashgate Publishing

Reissued 2018 by Routledge
2 Park Square, Milton Park, Abingdon, Oxon OX14 4RN
711 Third Avenue, New York, NY 10017, USA

Routledge is an imprint of the Taylor & Francis Group, an informa business

Copyright © Matthew Flinders 2001

All rights reserved. No part of this book may be reprinted or reproduced or utilised in any form or by any electronic, mechanical, or other means, now known or hereafter invented, including photocopying and recording, or in any information storage or retrieval system, without permission in writing from the publishers.

Notice:
Product or corporate names may be trademarks or registered trademarks, and are used only for identification and explanation without intent to infringe.

Publisher's Note
The publisher has gone to great lengths to ensure the quality of this reprint but points out that some imperfections in the original copies may be apparent.

Disclaimer
The publisher has made every effort to trace copyright holders and welcomes correspondence from those they have been unable to contact.

A Library of Congress record exists under LC control number: 2001093293

ISBN 13: 978-1-138-70288-2 (hbk)
ISBN 13: 978-1-138-63100-7 (pbk)
ISBN 13: 978-1-315-20695-0 (ebk)

Contents

List of Figures and Tables	xi
Preface	xiii
Overview	xv

PART ONE HISTORY AND THEORY

Chapter 1 Reinventing Accountability   **1**
- 1.1   Introduction   1
- 1.2   Ministerial Responsibility and the Theory of the British State: History, Permanence and Significance   2
- 1.3   Defining Accountability and Responsibility   9
- 1.4   Evolving Mechanisms of Accountability within the British Westminster Model   16
- 1.5   Conclusion   27

PART TWO ACCOUNTABILITY MODELS AND CASE STUDY ANALYSIS

Chapter 2 Parliamentary Accountability: Demoralised or Revitalised?   **41**
- 2.1   Introduction   41
- 2.2   The Origins of the Convention of Ministerial Responsibility   42
- 2.3   The Distinction between 'Ministerial Accountability' and 'Ministerial Responsibility'   47

2.4	Parliament and the 'Next Steps' Reforms of the Civil Service	52
2.5	The Crown Prerogative and the Absence of Law	55
2.6	Parliament and Politics	56
2.7	The Codification of Convention	60
2.8	Select Committees	64
2.9	Parliamentary Questions	71
2.10	Conclusion	76

Chapter 3 Parliamentary Accountability and the Home Office   93
3.1	Introduction	93
3.2	Parliamentary Questions	94
3.3	Select Committees	101
3.4	Party Accountability	115
3.5	Conclusion: Withering Parliamentary Accountability?	119

Chapter 4 Judicial Accountability   131
4.1	Introduction	131
4.2	The Constitutional, Historical and Theoretical Background	133
4.2.1	The Rule of Law and the Separation of Powers	134
4.2.2	Bureaucratic Reform and the Law	136
4.2.3	The Breakdown of the Relationship	137
4.2.4	The Judicial Protection of Fundamental Rights	140
4.2.5	Towards Formal Legal Regulation of Ministerial Action	142
4.3	Judicial Accountability and Central Government	145
4.3.1	Judicial Review	145
4.3.2	New Horizons? Judicial Accountability and Europe	155
4.3.3	Judicial Inquiries and Accountability	160

4.4	The Abdication of Responsibility Through Legal Advice	167
4.5	Conclusion	169

Chapter 5 Judicial Accountability in the Home Office — 187
5.1	Introduction	187
5.2	Judicial Review as a Mechanism of Accountable Government in the Home Office	188
5.3	Judicial Inquiries in the Home Office	203
5.4	The Home Office and the European Convention on Human Rights	212
5.5	The Abdication of Ministerial Responsibility Through Legal Advice	217
5.6	Conclusion	218

Chapter 6 Managerial Accountability and the Contract State — 229
6.1	Introduction	229
6.2	The Background to Managerialism	230
6.3	Managerialism	233
6.4	Accountability and Tensions in the Managerial Model	236
6.5	Conclusion	251

Chapter 7 Managerial Accountability and the Home Office — 265
7.1	Introduction	265
7.2	The Problems of Clarifying and Maintaining the Minister/Agency Distinction	267
7.3	Internal versus External Accountability within the Home Office	273
7.4	How Information Asymmetries are Avoided, The Role of Audit Mechanisms in the Accountability Relationship and the Degree to Which Home Office Ministers Remain 'Intelligent Customers'	278

	7.5	The Impact of Contracting Out on Accountability, Efficiency and Ministerial Control	287
	7.6	Conclusion: The Effect of Managerial Accountability on Ministerial Responsibility to Parliament	294

PART THREE   FREEDOM OF INFORMATION AND CONCLUSION

Chapter 8   The Executive Morality and Inverted Conventions: Ministerial Responsibility and Freedom of Information — 309

8.1	Introduction	309
8.2	The Code of Practice on Access to Official Information	310
8.3	The White Paper *Your Right to Know*	312
8.4	The Draft Freedom of Information Bill	315
8.5	The Difference between 'Open Government' and 'Freedom of Information'	319
8.6	The Rationale Underpinning the Draft Bill on Freedom of Information	320
8.7	Conclusion	327

Chapter 9   Understanding the Politics of Accountability — 339

9.1	Introduction	339
9.2	Research Findings and Future Research Agendas	340
9.2.1	Political Accountability	340
9.2.2	Judicial Accountability	342
9.2.3	Managerial Accountability	343
9.2.4	Future Research	345
9.3	Emerging Agendas for the Responsibility of the Core Executive	346
9.3.1	Risk	347
9.3.2	'Joined Up' Government	348
9.3.3	The Development of Information Technology	350

9.3.4	Innovations in Political Machinery	351
9.3.5	The Constitutional Reform Agenda	352
9.3.6	The Evolving State	356
9.4	Conclusion: Labour, Parliament and Power in the Modern State	359

Methodology	375
Bibliography	383
Index	431

List of Figures and Tables

Table 1.1	Comparing the Whig and Peelite strands of ministerial responsibility	6
Figure 1.1	Different Types of Accountability: Attempts at Categorisation	20
Figure 1.2	The Circuit of Accountable Government	22
Figure 1.3	Determinants of Accountable Government	24
Figure 1.4	Models of Accountability	25
Table 2.1	Government Defeats and Amendments Tabled to Government Bills 1851-1903	45
Table 4.1	Positive and Negative factors most commonly associated with the ability of Judicial Review to enforce accountable government	149
Table 4.2	Positive and Negative factors most commonly associated with the ability of judicial inquiries to enforce accountable government	162
Table 5.1	Number of Applications for Leave to Seek Judicial Review Against Selected Central Government Departments 1987-1991	189
Table 5.2	Judicial Review Applications Granted Leave in Selected Departments 1994-1997	189
Table 5.3	Judicial Review Challenges Against the Immigration and Nationality Directorate of the Home Office 1991-1999	190
Figure 6.1	Accountability Relationships: A Summarised Picture of Theoretical Insights	245
Figure 7.1	Home Office Departmental Aims 1999-2000	267
Figure 7.2	The Michael Howard/Derek Lewis Affair	268
Figure 7.3	Prison Service Key Performance Indicators 1998-1999	279

| Table 8.1 | Differences Between the Draft Bill on FOI and the Non-Statutory Openness Code | 317 |
| Table A1 | Case Study Tactics for Four Design Tests | 378 |

Preface

This book is my own work. I alone am responsible for its contents. Nevertheless, in completing it I have incurred a great many debts. I would particularly like to thank David Marquand, Ian Harden, Hugh McConnel, Sylvia McColm, Dave Richards, Martin Smith, Sandra van Thiel, Carsten Greve, Andrew Gamble, Tony Payne and Francesca Gains. Much of this research was conducted whilst working on the Economic and Social Research Council funded 'Whitehall Programme'. My thanks and gratitude is therefore extended to a great number of politicians and officials whose thoughts and opinions permeate the course of this book.

Finally, I would like to devote my deepest gratitude to my wife, Tamsin Ryder. There is little doubt this book would not have been completed without her love and support. Thank you.

Overview

The book examines: To what degree alternative forms of accountability have evolved to remedy the shortcomings commonly identified with ministerial responsibility to Parliament. It explores the accountability of the core executive and adopts a pluralistic perspective in an attempt to question the continuing centrality of ministerial responsibility to Parliament as the linchpin of the British constitution. The book concludes that alternative forms of accountability have not evolved to the point where they remedy the deficiencies associated with ministerial responsibility. Conversely, it is argued that, to some degree, these new mechanisms have undermined and complicated parliamentary accountability. The increasingly fragmented state has not in itself hollowed out the convention of ministerial responsibility to Parliament but markedly has exposed tensions that have always existed. Ministers have restricted their own spheres of responsibility while placing officials in an invidious position. The reformulation of ministerial responsibility is incompatible with the role and position of officials within the Westminster model. (The latter, it is suggested, creates an 'accountability gap'.) Whether this 'gap' has been plugged successfully by other accountability mechanisms is the topic of this book.

To examine this issue the study adopts a cross-comparative framework which is applied to a single case study. The cross-comparative framework provides an 'organising perspective' based upon three distinct models of accountability (parliamentary, judicial and managerial). The research acknowledges the existence of a range of processes which frequently compel the core executive to release information and account for actions and/or decisions, to the media for example. However, it is argued that these three models can be isolated as they provide formal, coherent and observable processes which could be subject to reform. Moreover, the three models facilitate a coherent methodological agenda whilst also maintaining the scope of the research within realistic boundaries. The study adopts a single case study as its primary tool of analysis. Critics have suggested that case studies are a 'soft' form of research, and in particular that single case studies offer a poor basis for generalisations. Only recently has the value of case study analysis been emphasised. As Rhodes stressed: 'It is possible to generalise based on a single case study - the heuristic case method - if the case study sets out to test a theoretical proposition'. The single case study *is* an appropriate design under several circumstances. Overall, the single-case study design is eminently justifiable under certain conditions - where the case represents a critical test of existing theory, where the case is a rare or unique event or where the case serves a revelatory purpose. It is argued that the Home Office represents a *critical* case, a *unique* case and a *revelatory* case.

The acknowledgement of a plurality of forms of accountability suggests the mechanisms are complex. Some forms of accountability - contractual and market models, for example - have been established by the core executive while other forms - judicial and quasi-judicial, for example - have been imposed externally. The British constitution is built, however precariously, on the political accountability of ministers to Parliament. The structure of the state and the responsibility of the core executive are inherently linked, but as the state diversifies away from the orthodox model of the ministerial department, the convention of ministerial responsibility appears increasingly untenable. In this environment the constitutional elasticity of the convention has been exploited. But the move from the traditional paradigm of public administration towards a more intricate model of new public management, emphasising networks rather than hierarchies, has clearly exposed the tensions and fault-lines that have always existed in the convention. In this context, both constitutional conservatives and reformers have emphasised the role of alternative mechanisms of accountability. The former have intended to undermine the need to introduce reforms and the latter to emphasise what alternative forms of accountability might be developed.

The adoption of a diversified approach offers a number of benefits. Examining the wider picture will allow the issue of political accountability to be located within broader discussions of public accountability. It will also highlight the interconnected nature of the British polity, in which reform in one area will inevitably have a (often unintended) consequence for other sections of the constitutional framework. Empirical research will reveal and contribute to the debate the views and opinions of the actors involved in the various processes and mechanisms. A pluralistic perspective also illuminates the fact that models of accountability shape relationships within the state, as well as expectations. Consequently, it could be suggested that certain forms of accountability are more or less compatible with specific areas of the central state.

Chapter One examines the history of ministerial responsibility and its centrality to the British constitution. It covers theoretical and defintional issues and introduces a pluralistic model of alternative methods of accountability. Chapter Two examines the ability of Parliament to ensure accountable government. It highlights the limitations commonly associated with ministerial responsibility and stresses critical trends, or changes in emphasis, that have arguably recast the convention in favour of the executive. Chapter Three explores the operation of parliamentary accountability in relation to the Home Office. It aims to determine to what degree the imperfections identified in the preceding chapter are present in reality and what factors and issues have been neglected by the wider literature. The evolution, scope and utility of judicial mechanisms of accountability are considered in Chapter Four. Chapter Five investigates the impact and influence of these mechanisms within the Home Office. The development of managerial forms of accountability (audit, charters, performance indicators, contracts, market mechanisms, etc.) are discussed in Chapter Six. A central tenet of the managerial revolution, encapsulated in new public management, has been that managerial and organisational reforms could improve accountability both upwards to ministers and downwards to consumers. This is tested in Chapter Seven in relation to the Home Office. Chapter Eight focuses on freedom of information legislation. It highlights how the imposition of restrictive measures by the executive exposes both the reality of power within the Westminster model and the inverted logic of ministerial responsibility to the derogation of public accountability. Chapter Nine draws together the findings of this research and offers concluding analysis. Key themes of this book include:

- What are the problems commonly associated with ministerial responsibility to Parliament?
- Is ministerial responsibility still appropriate as the primary mechanism of accountability in the modern state?
- If ministerial responsibility is no longer effective, how can it be made effective and who are the main actors controlling this process?

- What alternative mechanisms of accountability have evolved in the light of both concerns regarding parliamentary accountability and the increased fragmentation of the state?
- To what degree have these alternative mechanisms been shaped and moulded by the restrictions imposed by ministerial responsibility?
- Do these alternative forms of accountability complement and reinforce parliamentary accountability or do they undermine and complicate ministerial responsibility?
- How would the accountability, legitimacy and propriety of any new actors in the accountability processes be guaranteed?
- Has internal accountability (the accountability of officials to ministers) been improved at a cost to external accountability (the accountability of ministers to Parliament)?

PART ONE
HISTORY AND THEORY

1 Reinventing Accountability

1.1 Introduction

This book examines the accountability of the core executive in the United Kingdom from a pluralistic perspective which appreciates the existence of multiple and often conflicting processes of accountability.[1] The accountability of ministers and government as a whole has been the focus of intense attention in recent years. Advocates of the dominant paradigm of new public management have claimed enhanced accountability as one of their major objectives. At the same time, revelations involving political corruption have created cynicism regarding the processes of government and amplified demands for reform. Yet, there is a sameness within the literature on this topic. Not only are accountability and responsibility normally conflated, but also the Westminster model is employed as the only form of analysis. Ministers are often portrayed as irresponsible. This study adopts a more complex representation of accountability which acknowledges that within the framework of the Westminster model there are other competing forms of accountability operating.[2]

However, it is suggested that the development of alternative forms of accountability have been critically affected due to their evolution and implementation within a constitutional framework constructed upon the demands and processes of ministerial responsibility. This chapter examines the history of ministerial responsibility and its centrality to the British constitution. It then offers a definition of accountability and responsibility, whilst also emphasising that accountability is a multi-layered concept which can be informal or formal, can operate in a range of directions and can be conveyed through a number of 'codes of accountability'. The next section examines the evolving mechanisms of accountability within the British Westminster model. It also reviews the three models of accountability which form the basis of this book. First, it is necessary to examine the importance of ministerial responsibility within the British constitution.

1.2 Ministerial Responsibility and the Theory of the British State: History, Permanence and Significance

The convention of ministerial responsibility forms the cornerstone of the British constitution. Its importance cannot be overstated or ignored. It shapes the structure of government, the procedures of Parliament and the constitutional relationships on which the British conception of 'the state' stands.[3] The ideas of the ministerial department and ministerial responsibility continue to dominate the arguments of those who defend the constitutional *status quo* and those who call for radical reform. Ministerial responsibility is, nevertheless, a complex and enduring convention. Its influence underpins all spheres of government activity. The aim here is not to examine the utility of ministerial responsibility but to review the way in which modern British government developed and particularly how this evolution gave primacy to a convention that contained mutually supportive yet contradictory strands.

There were three major innovations in British governmental machinery in the nineteenth century: the creation of a meritocratic professional civil service recruited through open competition; the establishment of elected multi-purpose local authorities; and the ministerial department.[4] Of these, despite its fundamental importance, the latter has received least attention. The Reform Act of 1832 marks a fitting starting point to review the history of the ministerial department, as it marks a turning point in the relationship between the executive and Parliament.[5] After the Reform Act, Parliament's interest in controlling the administrative machinery increased. Up to the mid - nineteenth century, it was common practice to vest administrative powers in appointed boards. This continued up to the mid - 1850s as parliamentary appreciation of the virtues of individual ministerial responsibility grew, the ministries that existed became better equipped to take on new functions and the weight of tradition to give new functions to new boards waned.[6] Support for the ministerial department was engendered by the work of influential commentators such as Bentham, Mill, Bagehot and Toulmin-Smith.[7]

One board in particular aroused so much parliamentary attention that it played a central role in fostering support for the idea of the ministerial department. The Poor Law Commission was the subject of intense controversy. The Poor Law Commissioners formed a highly centralised agency independent of ministers and Parliament. The lack of an effective link between the Commission and legislature left Parliament devoid of control and the commissioners unable to explain their actions. The Commission was replaced by a ministry in 1847. The Poor Law Commission proved significant for two reasons: the controversy surrounding the Commission was used by commentators in support of wider reforms to the central administration; and it highlighted the benefit of having a recognised channel of communication between the administration and House of Commons.[8] The Poor Law Commission incident heightened and focused the Commons' awareness of its powers.[9] Between the first and second Reform Acts '...the House was the real arbiter of government fortune...it did not merely want to legislate, it was suspect of wanting to govern'.[10] Parliament resented the independence and insularity of boards, and from 1855 their numbers were drastically reduced and their functions placed in the hands of ministerial departments.[11] Those boards that continued to exist found their independence curtailed and encountered a far higher degree of ministerial involvement in their day-to-day activity. For example, the National Debt Commission did not meet at all after 1861, and its work was conducted by officials under the supervision of the Chancellor of the Exchequer.

These nineteenth-century innovations were premised on the belief that ministerial responsibility demanded departmental organisation and that ministerial responsibility and the department model should be applied throughout central government. By the middle of the nineteenth century, the demise of appointed boards - Bentham had been advocating the virtues of 'single-seatedness' for some time before 1832 - had been sealed by Parliament's faith in the individual responsibility of ministers. By the end of the Crimean War, both theoretical and practical factors had ensured the acceptance of individual ministerial responsibility as the normal administrative arrangement for central government.[12] In 1866, Todd gave an explicit formulation of the relationship of direct and universal ministerial responsibility to the structure of the central administration:

> It is no arbitrary rule which requires that all holders of permanent offices must be subordinate to some Minister responsible to Parliament, since it is obvious that without it, the first principles of our system of government - the control of all branches of the administration by Parliament - would be abandoned.[13]

Not only was the dominance of the convention buttressed by the reform of the civil service but also by procedural changes in the House of Commons. The Commons reformed its procedures to reflect its change from passivity to activity in relation to the administration of the state. The 1860s saw the creation of the Public Accounts Committee and the Comptroller and Auditor General. Supply debates became regular occasions for scrutinising the administration, and the old system of petitions was replaced by the Parliamentary Question. These procedural changes entrenched the convention of ministerial responsibility and emphasised the position of ministers as the focus of responsibility as opposed to the abstraction of responsibility to be found in a collegiate authority.

Despite the continued centrality of ministerial responsibility, after 1906 the dominance of the ministerial department as the building block of the state abated.[14] The legislation of the Liberal government expanded the horizons of the state rapidly, in social services and industry for example, and much of the new work was entrusted to boards rather than departments.[15] There was a reluctance to increase the amount of administrative power vested in the executive and a feeling that some of the functions would be best placed at a distance from party politics. As many of the functions were industrial and commercial, there was also a feeling that the orthodox administrative department might be too inflexible and its staff too cautious (factors which have fuelled the hiving-off of functions throughout this century).[16] So after 1906 there was a deliberate attempt to bypass the ministerial department in favour of appointed boards enjoying partial independence of ministerial and parliamentary control.[17] Despite this, the ideal of the ministerial department was canonised in The Haldane Report of 1918.[18]

A number of factors demand that the constitutional dexterity of the convention of ministerial responsibility to Parliament be unwrapped. First, it is clear that there was never any agreement as to either the exact boundaries of ministerial responsibility or the underpinning rules that upheld the convention. Jeremy Bentham was adamant that ministers should not be parliamentary, by which he implied they should have the right to speak in Parliament but not sit in Parliament or vote.[19] Lord Palmerston regarded a permanent civil service as a danger to, not a condition of, ministerial responsibility.[20] Secondly, the idea of the ministerial department never received the degree of universality as an organisational form that Bagehot demanded. Even during the second half of the nineteenth century boards existed, and there was a large degree of organisational deviation. After 1906, the growth of the state was largely administered by appointed boards, public corporations and non-departmental public bodies[21] (a trend that has continued throughout the twentieth century).[22] Finally, even the main proponents of the idea of the ministerial department accepted the limitations of the concept. Bentham acknowledged that ministerial responsibility was constrained by the realistic scope of ministerial vigilance: responsibility depended on directive and dislocative powers that could not usefully apply to subordinates so distant that an 'exercise' was effected before it was 'excluded'.[23] Sir Henry Taylor, though supporting Bentham, wrote: 'The far greater proportion of duties which are performed in the office of a Minister are and must be performed under no effective responsibility'.[24]

Post-war developments have presented doctrinal and practical challenges because they so markedly contrast with the normative and empirical assumptions of the theory of the ministerial state. However, as demonstrated above, the central problems and inconsistencies of the ministerial state were present from its beginnings. What then made the idea of the ministerial department so attractive and has, in turn, ensured its enduring influence within the British constitution? Beattie offers an answer to this question through an exploration of two distinct views of ministerial responsibility.[25] Both approaches explain the convention's adoption in the mid-nineteenth century, its fundamental inconsistencies and its enduring qualities. Beattie distinguishes two strands - a more representative 'Whig' view which stressed the need for political control to be paramount and for the government to be held responsible for state actions; and the 'Peelite' view, which defines ministerial responsibility as a way of limiting democratic control to ensure strong, coherent and stable government (see Table 1.1). (In 1964 A. H. Birch made a similar distinction with his observation of the 'liberal' view and 'Whitehall' view of the British constitution.)[26] In practice, the two views have combined to elevate the role of ministers and justify the unlimited notion of parliamentary sovereignty.

Table 1.1 Comparing the Whig and Peelite strands of ministerial responsibility

Whig	Peelite
Parliamentary Government	Strong Government
Representative	Responsible
Inclusion	Exclusion
Responsiveness	Distance
Participation	Stability
Accountability	Realism
Direction	Control
Exposure of Ministers	Insulation of Ministers

In the 'Whig' view, ministerial responsibility ensures that ministers use discretionary decision-making powers in accordance with the will of the House and are responsible for their decisions. The Whig view stresses representation, responsiveness and participation, while accepting that ministers must have some freedom to govern. The virtues of ministerial responsibility from this perspective are that responsibility is focused (on the minister), the line of accountability is clear (official/minister/Parliament) and that ministers are culpable. The Whig view clearly has a normative as well as empirical content - it specifies the paragon rather than the practice. Whereas the Whig view of ministerial responsibility emphasises *representative* government, the 'Peelite' view stresses *responsible* government. The Peelite doctrine favours executive control and stability. This view interpreted the decline of the monarch and the rise of Parliament as a threat to representative politics. The problem, as perceived by Sir Robert Peel in the 1830s and 1840s, was how to preserve stability. The aim was to preserve executive power; ministerial responsibility in that context ensured that the executive, rather than Parliament, was responsible for governing.[27] The convention insulated ministers and prevented Parliament interfering in the day-to-day operation of government. It formed a defensible balance between the responsibility of ministers to Parliament, while allowing them a degree of stability and tenure.[28] So for the Whigs in the nineteenth century, ministerial power was an insurance against the revival of monarchy; for Peelites, it was a pragmatic attempt at preserving executive power.[29] Peelism is thus best described as a doctrine of 'strong' government, rather than 'representative' government, with ministerial responsibility forming a buffer between politics and administration.[30]

Both Whig and Peelite views served, albeit from opposing standpoints, to rationalise and justify the ministerial state. Each approach involved the elevation of the ministerial role and involved centralisation, particularly the transfer of functions from appointed boards to ministerial departments, and the approval of the unlimited scope which the doctrine of parliamentary sovereignty conferred on the Commons and on ministers. The British constitution was moulded around the concept of ministerial responsibility because a strong case could be made that it ensured both the responsibility and responsiveness of ministers (Whig strand), while at the same time producing strong and stable government (Peelite strand). Accordingly, the constitutional rules that underpin the convention were designed with the need to stress the position of ministers and insulate the role of officials. Hence, officials are responsible to their ministers and can have no contact with Parliament without ministerial permission. Information is carefully guarded to ensure that individual officials do not become associated with a specific policy area and that internal department tensions remain hidden. Discussions within the Cabinet are also confidential so as to protect and ensure the collective responsibility of ministers to the House.

It is possible to trace a distinguished lineage of key constitutional texts that have sought to stress the dominance of the Peelite view and shift the balance back towards the Whig view through a range of reform proposals. In 1904 Sidney Low observed the growth of cabinet power and the diminishing role of Parliament; a theme taken on by Lowell in 1908. In 1929 Lord Hewart wrote of 'the new despotism' in which he suggested that the power of the executive had undermined the constitution. The authoritative texts of Muir (1930), Jennings (1934), Fell (1935), Ross (1943), Hollis (1949), Benemy (1965), Crick (1968) and Butt (1969), to name but a few, all charted the shifting of power from Parliament to the executive.

Appreciating both the history and the inherent tensions within the convention of ministerial responsibility is critical when exploring contemporary debates about the accountability of the core executive, parliamentary reform and alternative models of accountability. The wealth of literature that laments the demise of Parliament and offers proposals for reforming the constitution is addressed almost solely to the problems and values of the Whig version of ministerial responsibility. As Weir and Beetham stress: 'The Whig tradition has always been paraded as the public face of ministerial responsibility but the Peelite view has formed a strong undercurrent in governing attitudes'.[31] Thus, much of the reform literature contains a naivety which ignores the normative claims and practical influence of the Peelite view. The attraction to successive governments of the convention is that it offers both flexibility and a strong platform from which to implement their policies. The Whig strand has been repressed by the Peelite strand and the convention of ministerial responsibility has become a tool of 'strong government' to be employed against the participatory claims of reformers.[32] Arguments regarding the inversion of the logic of ministerial responsibility must therefore appreciate that the convention has always contained contradictory elements.[33]

As the state has become increasingly large and fragmented, the tensions within the convention have become more visible. Despite this, it retains both its centrality and importance for several reasons. First, the convention is culturally entrenched.[34] Post-entry socialisation, the 'culture' of Whitehall and personnel management procedures within the higher echelons of the civil service reinforce the constitutional theory.[35] Secondly, the importance of the convention does not only derive from the parliamentary hegemony it provides ministers but also its configuration of other constitutional relationships. Finally, the convention has a refreshing simplicity which, despite its shortcomings, is an enduring quality in an increasingly confused and fragmented state. Discussions regarding alternative forms of accountability or administrative reform, for example, must therefore be placed in the context of, and against, the restrictions imposed by the conventional framework of ministerial responsibility. The product of these two points is that ministers operate within a system with values and norms that justify and perpetuate their powerful position. The ministerial state was underwritten by both Whig and Peelite constitutional doctrines, but as the state grew, particularly away from the idea of the ministerial department model, the problems associated with ministerial responsibility became clear. But these problems were greater for the Whig strand of the convention than the Peelite alternative. The ascendancy of the Peelite strand is now complete. Ministerial responsibility has endured because it allows ministers to govern with a minimal level of parliamentary interference while also, in the main, delivering stability. The paradox is that reforms to increase the Whig strand of ministerial responsibility (parliamentary reform, freedom of information, etc.) are weak exactly because they would be inimical to that Peelite strand.[36]

1.3 Defining Accountability and Responsibility

The importance of accountability as the legitimating foundation of a liberal democracy cannot be overstated. As Pyper notes:

> The concept of accountability is often used as the benchmark against which systems of government can be judged. Accountable government is deemed to be good government and carries with it connotations of advanced democracy. Governments which can be characterised as unaccountable or not properly accountable are likely to prove fertile ground for the cultivation of authoritarianism, totalitarianism and every type of abuse of power.[37]

And yet the concept of accountability is complex and multifaceted. The creation of accountability relationships seeks to satisfy a range of aims. Most notably:

- *control* of abuse, corruption and misuse of public power;
- *assurance* that public resources are being used in accordance with publicly stated aims and that public service values (impartiality, equality, etc.) are being adhered to;
- *improvement* of the efficiency and effectiveness of public policies;
- the enhancement of the *legitimacy* of government.[38]

There is clearly, potentially at least, the possibility of some tension between the different goals. For example, the accountability system designed in order to single-mindedly achieve the first objective is likely to be very different from one designed to focus on the third objective. There are, therefore, many difficult trade-offs to be struck in the development of mechanisms of accountability. (An awareness of these tensions also raises questions regarding the impact of multiple mechanisms of accountability on the flexibility, creativity and operating conditions of civil servants.) It has been suggested that the contemporary salience of accountability issues stems from the Conservative governments' (1979-1997) emphasis on the third objective. As Sir Peter Kemp noted: 'In the 1980s nobody cared about accountability - they cared about value for money and efficiency. Accountability was rather a luxury which came after those two factors'.[39] A view echoed by the First Division Association:

> Until very recently, the arguments about reinventing government offered scant attention to the problems of accountability. Accountability has been regarded as a second order issue, well down the list of priorities behind efficiency and effectiveness in delivering services to the public or policy formulation to ministers.[40]

What then are the characteristics of good and reliable accountability? The Hansard Society's Scrutiny Commission identified the following indicators:

- that it should be based on clear and agreed criteria of success;
- that it should be consistently applied;
- that it should be self-critical;
- that it should be transparent;
- that its results should be communicated effectively to those on whose behalf it is exercised;
- that it should identify where responsibility lies for failure;
- that it should engender a culture of encouragement rather than blame;
- that it should be demonstrable that it has led to improved outcomes;
- that it should engage all participants actively in its processes.[41]

And yet it is clear from the wider academic literature and select committee reports that on none of these indicators can Parliament be seen as an overwelming success. Indeed the Hansard Society commented that 'on most of them its achievements fall between mediocrity and failure'.

Contemporary literature exhorts the primacy of accountability and the need to reformulate traditional approaches and mechanisms to the concept in theory and practice.[42] Propounding greater accountability always strikes a responsive chord but progress is often undermined by a lack of definitional clarity.[43] As Johnson noted: '...few would dispute that we now live in conditions in which it is difficult to say precisely what we mean in practice by "accountability" and even more difficult to assert with confidence that we know how to enforce it'.[44] Woodhouse states: '...despite its significance within the constitution, there is an elusiveness about the concept of accountability which makes it difficult to define and perhaps impossible to refine'.[45] Lello notes :

> Accountability involves reporting to other people voluntarily or compulsorily. It means having a conscience or a moral responsibility about what you are doing. It means being answerable to other people both junior and senior to yourself. It implies a dependence both on ideas, and on others. It is part of the essential administrative cement in a democratic society.[46]

Kernaghan and Langford state: 'Accountability is an enduring value not only in government but in society generally...accountability is often treated as an ethical principle, that is, a rule which provides for ethical behaviour'.[47] Lawton and Rose provide a sharper definition: 'Accountability is a process where a person or groups of people are required to present an account of their activities and the way in which they have or have not discharged their duties'.[48]

The most common error is to conflate accountability and responsibility.[49] As the government noted in response to the Treasury and Civil Service Committee's criticisms:[50]

> It may be that some of the difficulty the committee finds with the government's analysis is that the words 'accountability' and 'responsibility' have been used ambiguously and interchangeably in many authoritative constitutional texts.[51]

The difference between accountability and responsibility is culpability. Whereas accountability involves the obligation 'to give a reckoning or account'[52] responsibility also involves the 'liability to be blamed for loss or failure'.[53] The distinction has been most sharply delineated in relation to ministerial responsibility for executive agencies, but ministers and officials have increasingly stressed their 'accountability' obligations at the expense of their 'responsibility' requirements in all areas of government. For example, Sir Robin Butler utilised the distinction during the Scott Inquiry:

> I am using 'accountability' to mean that the minister must always answer questions and give an account to Parliament for the actions of his department whether he is 'responsible' in the sense of attracting personal criticism himself, or not. So I am using accountability, as it were, to leave out the blame element of it.[54]

In practice, accountability is a multilayered concept constructed of several constituent parts.[55] These can be identified as its redirectory, informatory, explanatory, amendatory and sacrificial elements.[56]

Redirectory accountability requires those charged with rendering an account to redirect questions to those best placed to answer them. This form of accountability is most prevalent in cases of devolved management, for example nationalised industries and executive agencies, when the request for information concerns routine or operational matters. Redirectory accountability is concerned with ensuring that information is provided by the person most suited to answer the question. Informatory accountability requires that an account is tendered to those to whom an account is due.[57] It does not involve an acceptance of blame for the information given and is therefore particularly relevant to matters of devolved management. It emphasises that a minister's duty is confined to acting as a conduit for the indirect accountability to Parliament of those managing devolved bodies. Explanatory accountability involves not just providing an account (informatory accountability) but also the duty to provide an explanation for the information contained within the account. It is therefore a more stringent level of accountability. Amendatory accountability requires that apology and action is taken for the shortcomings identified in the account.[58] This might take the form of an apology to the House, or the announcement of new guidelines to prevent a reoccurrence of the issue or the creation of an inquiry. The ultimate level is sacrificial accountability, which requires those responsible to resign due to information contained within the account. There are no guidelines which clarify exactly when the absolute form of accountability is necessary and Finer's conclusion that ministerial resignations are '...rare, arbitrary and unpredictable'[59] still remains true today.[60]

Dissecting the concept into its component levels is useful for many reasons. It particularly allows changes of accent within the wider convention of ministerial responsibility to be identified. Most notably an increased emphasis by ministers of the informatory, redirectory and amendatory strands while transferring the explanatory and sacrificial elements to their officials. Commentators have tended to examine these layers through a parliamentary perspective, thus failing to appreciate the range of non-parliamentary processes that also play a role in enforcing several of these layers.[61] Emphasising the various dimensions of accountability allows for specificity: '...calling for greater accountability is ambiguous unless it is specified who has to provide what information, to whom and what should be the consequences of providing or not providing it'.[62] It also demonstrates that there has been an unhelpful overconcentration on the sacrificial elements of the concept, which has led to an inadequate appreciation of the less severe but arguably more important levels of the convention (and which might also account for the defensiveness of ministers and officials). Finally, highlighting the various levels of accountability facilitates the suggestion that it is ministers who decide the level of accountability to be given. When a minister claims to have fulfilled their constitutional duty to account to Parliament through redirectory or informatory accountability, Parliament is inadequately equipped to demand a more exacting level.

For the purposes of this book 'accountability' is defined as 'the condition of having to answer to an individual or body for one's actions'. Accordingly, 'responsibility' is defined as 'the condition of having to provide and account to an individual or body for one's actions with the possibility of personal blame and/or sanction for the content of that account'.[63] Three related issues complement this discussion of accountability and responsibility: directional issues; formality versus informality; and codes of accountability.

The duty to provide an account is directional.[64] Ministers, for example, must account upwards to Parliament, laterally to the Cabinet and downwards to the media, wider public and constituents. Analysing the direction(s) of accountability is profitable as it allows changes of emphasis and procedure to be highlighted. For example, constitutionally civil servants may be accountable upwards to their minister but a strong case could be advanced that the form of their upwards accountability is changing as certain officials answer to Parliament for areas of government which are quite clearly their responsibility. (I have in mind particularly agency chief executives.) More generally, it could be suggested that a key component of the new public management agenda was, and is, to invert the public sector's traditional emphasis on upward accountability and introduce a greater thrust towards downward accountability. This is reflected in the 'customer' related rhetoric and manifested in the form of contracts, performance indicators, user surveys and charters.

Not only can accountability operate through a plethora of mechanisms and in a range of directions, but it can also be formal or informal. Formal mechanisms are official and recorded, for example ministerial answers to parliamentary questions (PQ). They are important not just because a minister must reply to a PQ as a central element of ministerial accountability to Parliament, but also because the information contained in the account is public property and is publicly accessible. Informal mechanisms of accountability are less certain and tangible but, arguably, they are processes of a purer and greater form of information. The problem for formal parliamentary mechanisms of accountability is that they are embroiled in the party political warfare of the House. Ministers are inevitably defensive when they know that the information they proffer ultimately will be used to attack them. Informal mechanisms enjoy an element of distance from the House. During confidential meetings, ministers and officials are often willing to provide a far more extensive account than they would in the House. The cost of that fuller account is that it is not attributable nor available to the wider public. The provision of such informal accounts, to academics and the press for example, could be criticised for undermining parliamentary accountability. In response, it could be argued that the practice was a symptom of the political immaturity of parliamentary politics.

A code of accountability is a system of signals, meanings and customs that binds the principal and the steward in the establishment, execution and adjudication of their accountability relationship.[65] Different codes affect different patterns of accountability. Thus, we need to understand their nature and variety if we are to understand accountability. Codes of accountability have traditionally been implicit rather than explicit in the British core executive. Expected standards of behaviour, codes and relationships between ministers and officials and officials and Parliament were transferred through a process of osmosis. Problems arise when one side of the accountability relationship makes an assumption which is not shared by the other party. As the state has become increasingly complex, traditional codes have become problematic. For example, there is a growing trend towards the codification and publication of expected codes in an attempt to clarify expected norms, in relation to the behaviour of officials before select committees, the behaviour of ministers and the outside interests of MPs.[66]

Accountability codes are not only political. Increasingly civil servants have to work within a complex structure of frequently competing codes. This can be seen by the way new public management has fostered the development of strict financial codes within Whitehall involving detailed record keeping. The public sector ombudsmen have also created a number of codes of good administration, as has the increasing influence of judicial review.[67] There are clear connections between codes of accountability, various mechanisms of accountability and the transformation of the state as outlined earlier. The promotion of one code of accountability by the executive will inevitably influence other codes, as it implies the promotion of certain values and rationalities at the expense of others - in recent years, for example, the emphasis on managerial and financial codes at the expense of traditional constitutional and political codes. But accountability codes are not simply a zero-sum equation. One code does not simply replace another; and this suggests that ministers and officials operate within a convoluted web or network of accountability codes. This, in turn, creates a number of questions: which codes are conflictual and which mutually supportive? At what point does too much accountability become pathological for an organisation? Where, then, does accountability become politically, managerially and economically inefficient?[68] The suggestion that ministers and their officials operate within a network of accountability codes provokes a discussion of the evolving mechanisms of accountability within the British Westminster model. This will be the topic of the next section.

1.4 Evolving Mechanisms of Accountability within the British Westminster Model

Accountability is a complex, fragmented and evolving concept within the British state. Debates inevitably focus on the utility of ministerial responsibility to Parliament as the fulcrum on which the constitutional structure of the state is constructed. New public management delivered fresh challenges to the convention, while exacerbating traditional tensions.[69] It also offered opportunities to rectify and remedy long-standing concerns, but progress in this direction was severely curtailed by the Conservative governments' (1987-1997) commitment to retaining ministerial responsibility while implementing bureaucratic and managerial reforms which made the convention increasingly untenable.[70] (It is almost a truism of British public policy that everything we do is somehow less effective and 'modern' than other countries. Several other Westminster democracies, New Zealand,[71] Australia[72] and Canada[73] for example, grasped the opportunity to reformulate ministerial responsibility while also strengthening other processes and mechanisms of accountability when implementing their respective brand of NPM).

The current situation is both circuitous and confused, as the core tenets of new public management sit increasingly uneasily with ministerial responsibility.[74] Despite the subtle reinterpretation of several aspects of the convention the attempt to reconcile devolved management with constitutional theory has proved problematic. Officials have been placed in a particularly invidious position, as their traditional anonymity has been weakened and responsibility deflected onto them, while their duty not to criticise their minister remains in place.[75] It has been argued, therefore, that a 'responsibility gap' has developed.[76] If the suggested responsibility gap is to be filled the convention of ministerial responsibility will have to be radically reconstituted, but this is something the executive has consistently refused to do.[77] Ironically, it is the executive's commitment to ministerial responsibility that is blocking moves designed to increase accountability. As concern increases that the accountability gap is widening those alternative methods of accountability which have long been largely invisible have become the focus of more attention. The Conservative governments were adamant that the public sector reforms they presided over had clarified accountability and made responsibilities more transparent, while 'domesticating the fiction' of ministerial responsibility.[78] The opposing camp, including journalists,[79] judges[80] and academics[81] see these reforms as far from increasing accountability but actually confusing, obscuring and making accountability more evasive and elusive.[82] While acknowledging these powerful critiques, it is possible to suggest some positive aspects of recent reforms, clarity of roles, transparency and increased information, for example.

As noted above, the aim of this book is to explore to what degree alternative mechanisms of accountability have evolved to remedy the shortcomings commonly identified with ministerial responsibility. Such an approach accepts that while specific mechanisms of accountability may be defective, if looked on as an agent of the total accountability process each has complementary strengths which, to a certain extent, may offset the others' weaknesses. Only through an appreciation of the virtues and vices of each model can new frameworks of accountability be suggested. But a serious challenge confronts those who advocate the construction of pluralistic accountability structures.[83] Reconciling the creation of 'fuzzy', or as Spiro terms them 'multicentric', accountability structures that reflect the increasingly diverse and fragmented state with a clear and effective bond of accountability between the governors and the governed is difficult.[84] The great quality of ministerial responsibility *was* its clarity and focus. Therefore, promoting a pluralistic perspective also risks making the overall system weaker, vacuous and more complex. Two interlinked issues flow from these concerns: first, if ministerial responsibility is no longer effective how can it be made effective and who are the main actors in this process? Secondly, if ministerial responsibility no longer provides clarity and focus, is the convention appropriate in the modern state and how can clarity be achieved through alternative processes?

Despite these uncertainties, examining the various mechanisms that play a role in enforcing accountable government is valuable for several reasons. The executive constantly lauds the existence and activity of these mechanisms as a justification for not enshrining new and stronger forms of accountability. Evaluating the actual impact of these mechanisms will not only allow the government's contention to be assessed but will also illuminate the potential of these mechanisms to play a more vigorous role. It will also allow widely held preconceptions to be challenged, particularly the suggestion that efficiency and accountability are inherently incompatible.[85] Inevitably the adoption of a pluralistic perspective will raise a number of questions about the role, influence and future of Parliament. As Riddell notes:

> The real challenge to Parliament is not the executive, but the growth of these alternative sources of power, such as the European institutions and law, judicial review, the proliferation of quangos and regulators and the shifting of the political debate to the media.[86]

During the Treasury and Civil Service Committee's inquiry into the role of the civil service the issue of 'non-parliamentary accountability' was examined briefly. The committee noted the existence and influence of judicial accountability and innovative new forms of downward accountability, such as charters, but was not persuaded that the existence of these forms of accountability could fill the void left by the poor performance of ministerial responsibility to Parliament.[87] (The committee did, however, agree to examine the topic of non-parliamentary accountability at some point in the future.) The inquiry by the Public Service Committee into ministerial accountability and ministerial responsibility adopted a markedly more positive approach to 'different sorts of accountability'.[88] Agreeing with the submission by David Faulkner that suggested that 'accountability should take multiple forms and operate through multiple and often reciprocal channels' the Committee, while asserting Parliament's centrality, welcomed the development of alternative forms of accountability.

> Recent changes in the management of the public service have had an impact, in many ways, on the extent to which it is publicly accountable. Delegation and privatisation are reducing the extent to which effective political accountability can be provided through Parliament. Accountability might be provided by some other mechanism, by Charters, through the Ombudsman, through the courts, even; to many different bodies. Accountability to Parliament should not preclude accountability to the public; and vice versa. Parliament needs to retain and protect its role; and to do so, it has to be more effective in fulfilling it.[89]

Categorising all the mechanisms that play a role in ensuring the accountability of the core executive is difficult. Romzek and Dubnick make useful distinctions between bureaucratic, legal, professional and political accountability.[90] The transferability of their model is fettered as their distinctions were based on the institutional arrangements of the American political system and yet they offer a valuable starting point. Figure 1.1 displays the subsequent work of Stone,[91] Oliver,[92] Pyper[93] and Lawton and Rose.[94] These authors have moved away from the traditional orthodoxies and have attempted to categorise the various processes and mechanisms of accountability.

It is immediately clear that there are major differences in categorisation (both between categories and within categories). The Parliamentary Commissioner for Administration appears in two of Pyper's categories (parliamentary and legal/quasi-legal),[95] in Oliver's administrative category and finally in Lawton and Rose's consumer/client model. Tribunals are also found in a variety of categories. Additionally some categories, while broadly similar, contain different elements. For example, it is clear that the judicial/legal categories are similar yet some are narrow in scope and others differ in what they include. (Pyper and Lawton and Rose include a European factor within their legal category whereas Stone does not.)[96] It is clear that, despite the diversity, links and correlations exist. This is most obvious among the parliamentary/political and judicial/legal categories. There are also less direct correlations between the categories on the third and fourth rows (as is true of the three categories on the bottom row).

Figure 1.1 Different Types of Accountability: Attempts at Categorisation

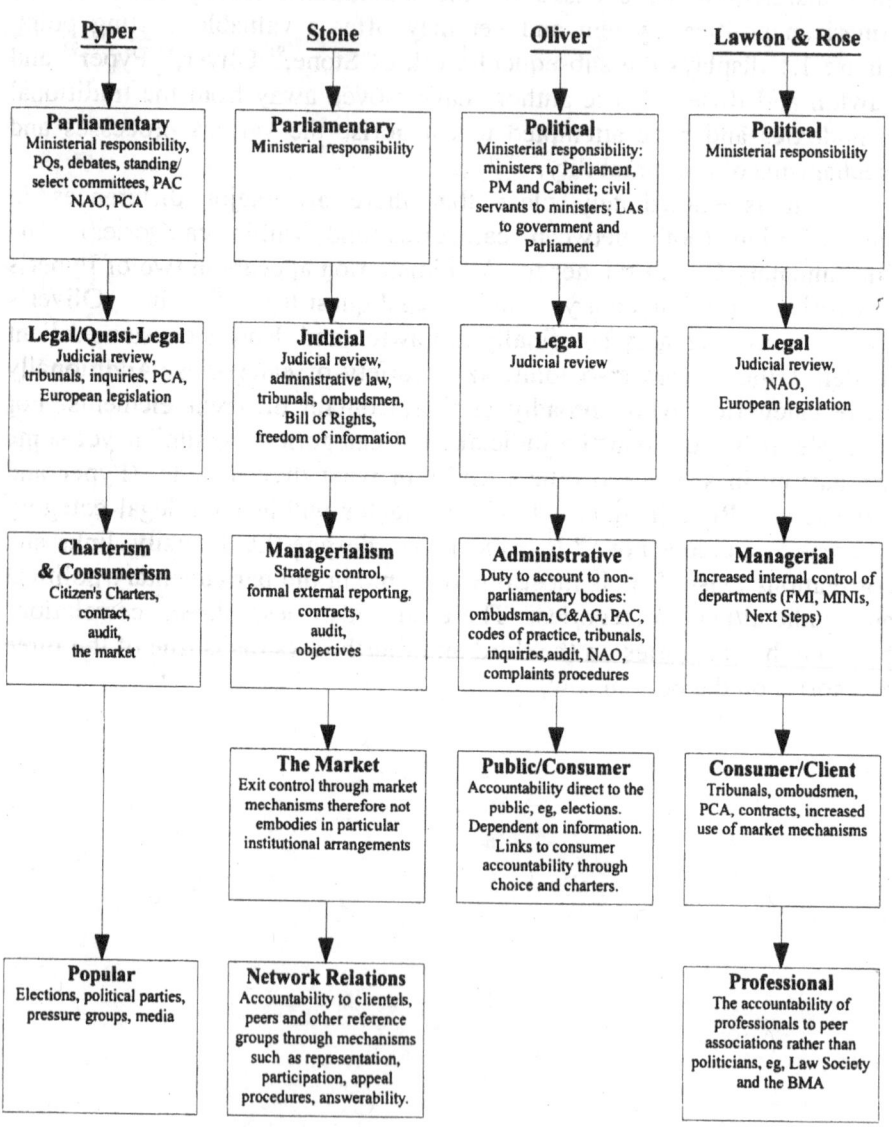

Figure 1.1 is a clear illustration of the diversity to be found in the pluralistic approach to accountable government. It indicates that in light of the problems commonly associated with ministerial responsibility a range of processes, actors and mechanisms have evolved both within and outside the traditional constitutional framework. As Barberis notes:

> There is now a quite widespread acknowledgement that the traditional notion of ministerial responsibility is itself no longer satisfactory and can no longer serve as the sole constitutional touchstone of accountability.[97]

That ministerial responsibility is so widely doubted suggests that there might be something to gain from comparing it with a range of other mechanisms. Some will be more suited to some areas of government rather than others, some methods may be conflictual whilst others are complementary. What is certain is that, since all the processes have evolved in an environment permeated by the norms and obligations of ministerial responsibility, conflicts and the need for compromises are inevitable, which will, in turn, necessitate what has so far proved impossible: '...freeing ourselves to some extent from an obsession with ministerial responsibility'.[98]

Accountability in a representative democracy is, in its strictest sense, linked to the revocability of a mandate. But electoral accountability on its own is a very crude form of democracy and as Madison noted: '...experience has taught mankind the necessity of auxiliary precautions'.[99] The degree to which a political system is said to deliver responsible government is dependent on a range of auxiliary precautions, of which Parliament is just one element. These are the mechanisms of accountability which, taken together, can be regarded as a complex circuit. Figure 1.2 attempts to display this circuit while also distinguishing which mechanisms are internal or external to Parliament.[100]

22 *The Politics of Accountability in the Modern State*

Figure 1.2 The Circuit of Accountable Government

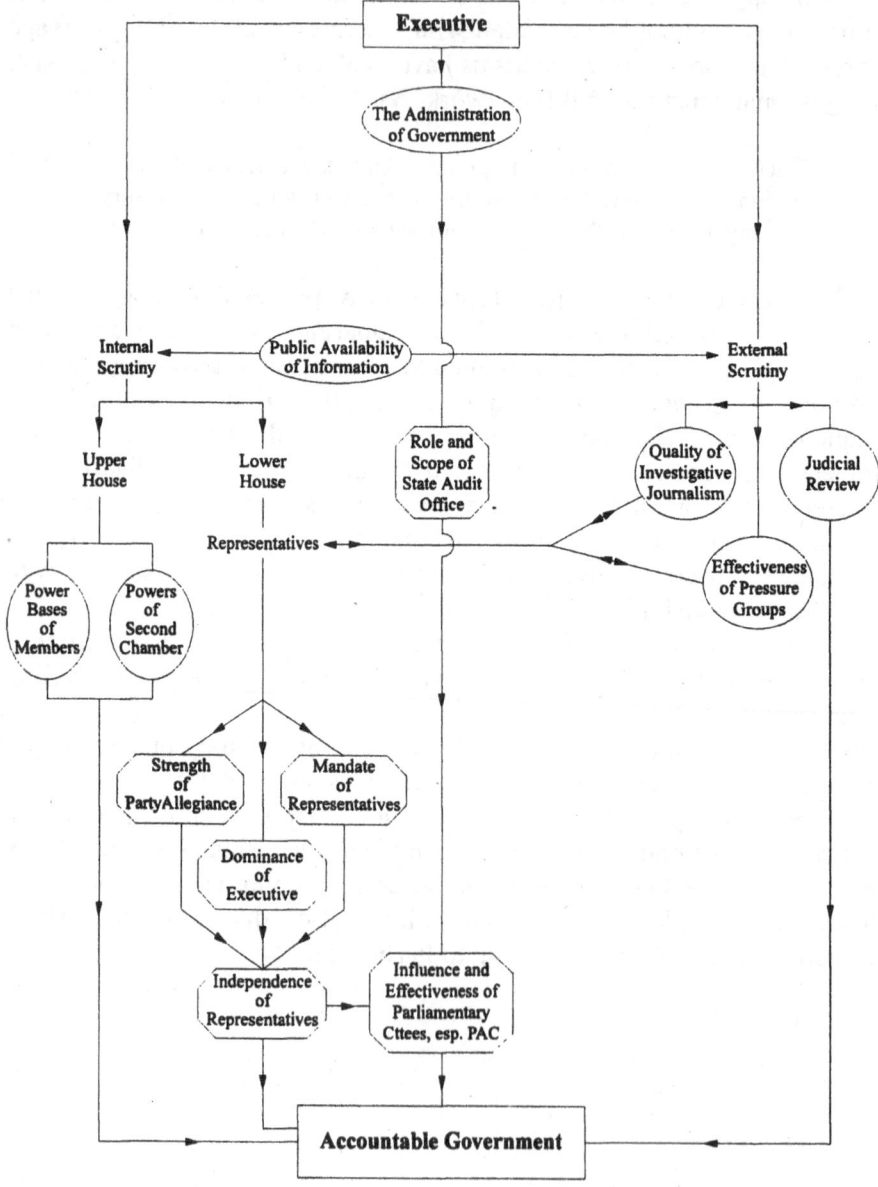

If figure 1.2 represents the paragon, figure 1.3 attempts to display the practice by refining the circuit with indications of effectiveness. The unbroken lines indicate accountability relationships that, while not unproblematic, are argued to be reasonably robust. The broken lines reflect relationships that, despite their strengths, possess inherent limitations. The question marks signify the contentious nature of some of these classifications, but it is argued that such categorisations facilitate debate and analysis. For example, the inability of the House of Lords to act as a significant check on the core executive is due to both its limited powers of oversight and revision and also its lack of democratic legitimacy.

Parliamentary accountability is largely dependent on the independence of its members and this is seen as a function of three tests: the strength of allegiance; the dominance of the executive; and the mandates of the representatives. (The borders of 'strength of party allegiance' and 'dominance of the executive' have been reinforced to signify the considerable, but dynamic, limit they place on MPs). Figure 1.4 highlights both the benefits and complexity of adopting a pluralistic approach. It suggests that the majority of the accountability mechanisms are severely limited in their utility. But this needs to be empirically tested, as does whether judicial review is the effective mechanism which the diagram implies. A key issue is also not just to test the efficacy of each model but also the interlinking relationships between the mechanisms.

Figure 1.3 Determinants of Accountable Government

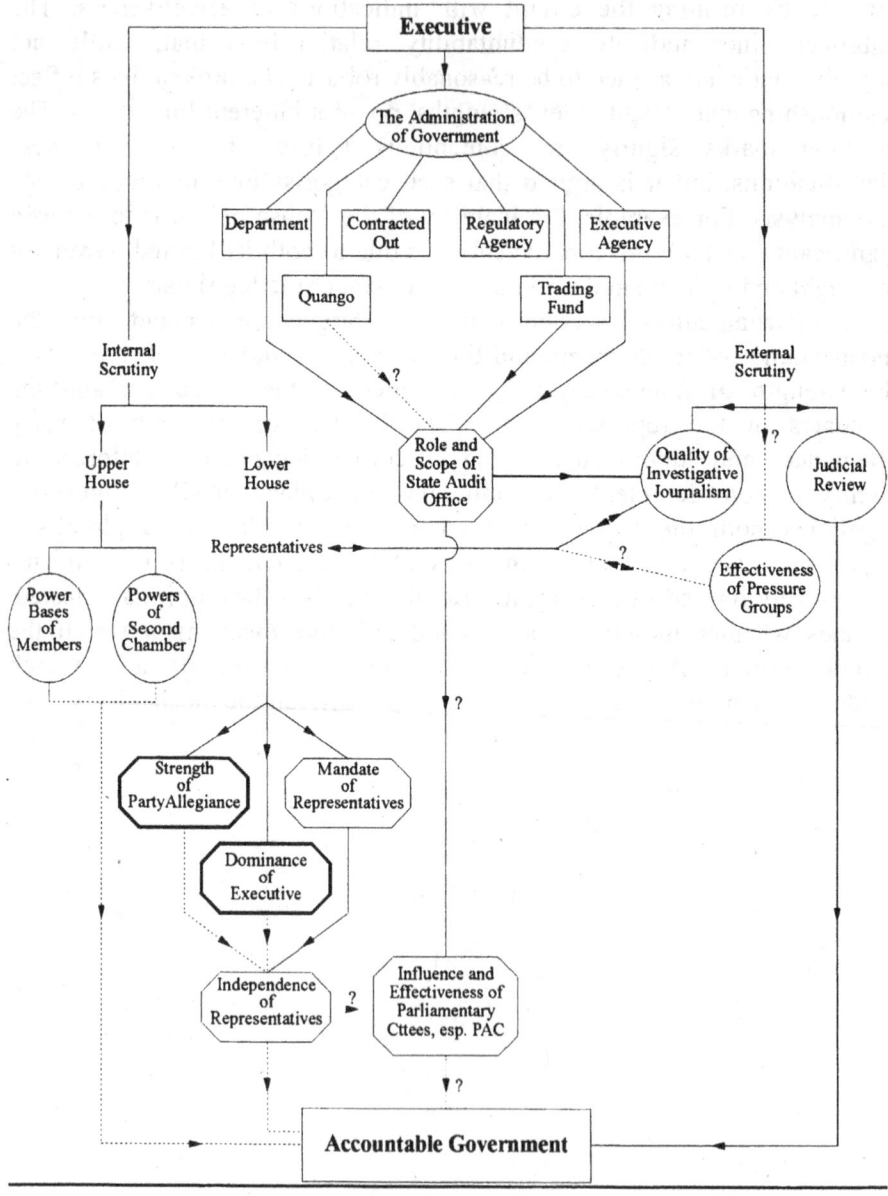

Building upon figure 1.1 and these circuit diagrams, this study is structured around three main models of accountability (see figure 1.4).

Figure 1.4 Models of Accountability

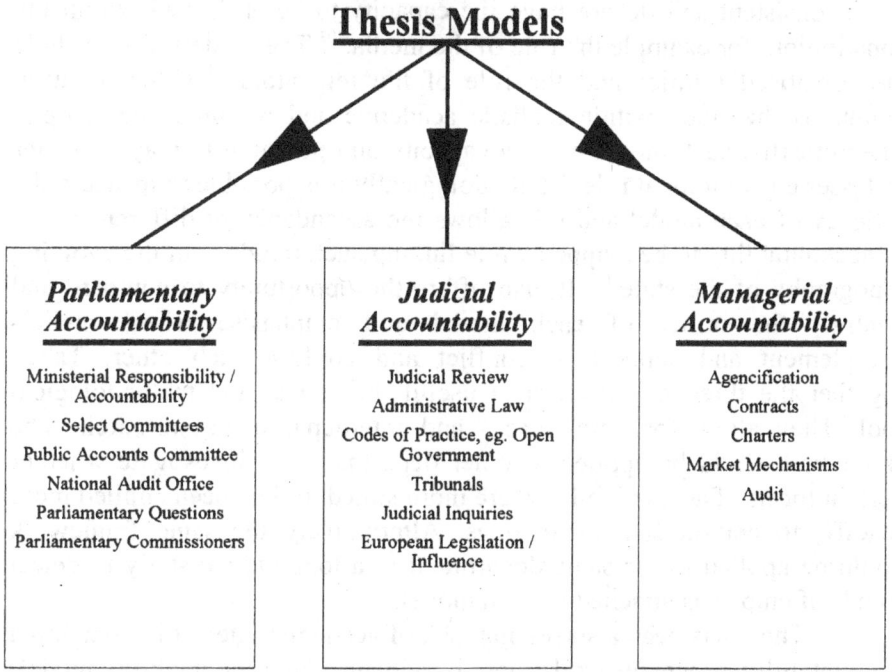

These three models provide an 'organising perspective'. That is '...a framework for analysis, a map of how things relate, or a set of research questions'.[101] It follows therefore that an organising perspective is always partial, it is not falsifiable, it never provides a comprehensive or even definitive account. However, the value of an organising perspective is that it provides a framework to explore complex issues, it identifies areas that are important and worthy of study. It also provides a basis for future refinement. The organising perspective outlined in figure 1.4 has been designed for several interrelated reasons. The three models allow a range of mechanisms and processes to be clearly encapsulated within defined areas. While the content of each model (or even the number of models) might be contested, the selection of three lucid models offers clarity in a complex area of research. The adoption of this organising perspective is not without precedent - Rhodes distinguishes between political, managerial and legal accountability in relation to sub-national government.[102]

The models exclude forms of accountability that, while important, are inconsistent and do not have the capacity to be enshrined within the constitution, for example the role of the media.[103] The models also exclude the privatised utilities and the role of the regulators.[104] (This, in turn, maintains the study within realistic academic and resource boundaries.) Theoretically, each model has the capacity and potential to play a greater or lesser constitutional role. Methodologically it is possible to measure the efficacy of each model and this allows the ascendancy of different forms of accountability to be mapped while linking such trends with the evolving topography of the state.[105] It also offers the opportunity to compare and contrast the utility of each model and emphasise where models complement and support or conflict and confuse each other. Taken together the three models form a useful theoretical and methodological tool. They allow for both intra - and interdepartmental research. The framework could be applied to other departments to investigate whether certain forms of accountability were more suited, or had been applied more readily, to certain functional areas. Alternatively the same framework could be applied to the same department in a longitudinal study to detect trends of emphasis attached to each model.

There has been a surprising lack of academic interest in competing accountability processes while there is evidence that accountability models are in fact being chosen and shaped by conscious choices to combine and trade off accountability mechanisms. In this climate, certain elements of the convention of ministerial responsibility have been elevated above others, notably its informatory, redirectory and explanatory elements. This has facilitated the development of alternative mechanisms by weakening public confidence in parliamentary accountability. However, the move towards a more pluralistic approach to accountability has been constrained by the executive's continuing commitment to ministerial responsibility. Ministers are content to diminish the sectors for which they are willing to accept personal responsibility but are unwilling to accept that the exercise of more autonomous authority and discretion by officials weakens their arguments for the need to restrict the exchange of information between those officials and the institutions to which an account is due. Stone notes that this is not a solely British phenomenon:

> It is noteworthy in all Westminster democracies in the 1980s and 1990s that the sponsors of the large scale programs of managerialist reform involving the devolution of power have typically argued that these innovations, including the creation of new semi-autonomous agencies, does not impair ministerial responsibility. The inconsistencies in this approach and its potential for creating confusion have been particularly noted by British academics discussing the Next Steps reforms. A doctrine offering government elites the prospect of control without responsibility is not likely to lack supporters.[106]

1.5 Conclusion

This chapter has introduced and unpacked some of the key themes and tensions surrounding contemporary debates regarding the accountability of the core executive. It has emphasised that the central question of this book is: to what degree have alternative mechanisms of accountability developed to remedy the shortcomings commonly identified with ministerial responsibility? A framework based on three models of accountability has been outlined as the research tool with which to answer this question. But what are the main shortcomings commonly associated with parliamentary accountability? The next chapter examines the ability of Parliament to ensure accountable government. It highlights the limitations commonly associated with ministerial responsibility and stresses critical trends, or changes in emphasis, that have arguably recast the convention in favour of the executive. This will be the topic of Chapter Two.

Notes

[1] The core executive being defined as ministers and their civil servants. See Smith, M (1999) *The Core Executive* (London : Macmillan) pp.1-8. See also Rhodes, R (1995) 'Introducing the Core Executive', in Rhodes, R & Dunleavy, P (eds.) *Prime Minister, Cabinet and Core Executive* (London : Macmillan).

2   The 'Westminster Model' is essentially an organising perspective that captures some essential features of the British system and, through sheer longevity, has become the conventional or mainstream view. Central features of the model include: the assumption that there is parliamentary sovereignty; strong cabinet government; accountability through elections; majority party control of the executive; a neutral civil service; elaborate conventions for the conduct of parliamentary business; and an institutionalised opposition. See Rhodes, R (1997) *Understanding Governance* (Milton Keynes : Open University Press); Gamble, A (1990) 'Theories of British Government' *Political Studies* Vol.38 pp.404-420; Judge, D (1993) *The Parliamentary State* (London : Sage); Mackintosh, J (1977) *The Politics and Government of Britain* (London : Hutchinson).

3   See Judge, D (1993) *The Parliamentary* State (London : Sage), Dyson, K (1980) *The State Tradition in Western Europe* (Oxford : Robertson).

4   The word board is used to describe an authority composed of more than one person that is not directly responsible to Parliament. The words ministry or department indicate a department of state headed by a single person who sits in and is responsible to Parliament. This clarifies the potentially confusing fact that several departments were still called boards after they had become ministerial departments, the Board of Trade for example.

5   For a discussion of the British administrative system before this time see: Finer, S (1952) 'Patronage and the Public Service; Jeffersonian Bureaucracy and the British Tradition' *Public Administration* Vol. 30 pp.329-360; and Hennessy, P (1989) *Whitehall* (London : Secker & Warburg) Ch. 1 'The Making of an Institution' pp.17-52. For a historical discussion of the development of models of accountability in relation to increasingly complex societies see: Day, P & Klein, R (1987) *Accountabilities: Five Public Services* (London : Tavistock); Bird, P (1973) *Accountability: Standards in Financial Reporting* (London : Haymarket).

6   See Willson, F (1955) 'Ministries and Boards: Some Aspects of Administrative Development Since 1832' *Public Administration* Vol.33 pp.43-58. It is significant that from 1845-1855 all the new boards, with the exception of the Civil Service Commission, had ministers among their members and/or had places open to MPs.

7   Bowring, J (1843) *The Works of Jeremy Bentham* (Edinburgh : Tait) Vol.III 'Plan of Parliamentary Reform of a Catechism' and Vol.IX 'Constitutional Code'; Mill, J S (1861) *Considerations on Representative Government* (London : Dent); Bagehot, W (1993 orig. pub. 1867) *The*

8. *English Constitution* (London : Fontana); Toulmin-Smith, J (1849) *Government by Commission: Illegal and Pernicious* (London). For a discussion of the contribution of each see Schaffer, B (1957) 'The Idea of the Ministerial Department: Bentham. Mill and Bagehot' *The Australian Journal of Politics and History* Vol.3 No.1 pp.60-78.

9. Bagehot, writing in 1867, quoted the experience of 'the three Kings of Somerset House' as the most prominent example of the weakness of '...conducting the administration of a public department by an independent unsheltered authority'. Bagehot, W (1867) *The English Constitution* (London : Fontana) p.189.

10. As Hanham noted: 'MPs began to feel dissatisfied with a form of administration [boards] which omitted to provide for what they regarded as acceptable ministerial representation in the House of Commons'. Hanham, H J (1969) *The Nineteenth Century Constitution* (London : Cambridge University Press) p.341.

11. Willson, F (1955) 'Ministries and Boards: Some Aspects of Administrative Development Since 1832' *Public Administration* Vol.33 p.51.

12. For example the Poor Law Commission in 1847, Railway Commission in 1851, Board of Works in 1851, Board of Health in 1854, Board of Ordnance in 1855, Emigration Commission in 1878, Patent Commission in 1883 and the Land Commission in 1889.

13. 'As a general rule, every executive function, whether superior or subordinate, should be the appointed duty of some given individual. It should be apparent to all the world who did everything, and through whose default anything was left undone. Boards, therefore, are not a fit instrument for executive business.' Mill, J S (1946 ed.) *Considerations on Representative Government* (London : Dent) p.289.

14. Todd, A (1866) *Parliamentary Government in England* (London).

15. Such was the dominance of the ministerial department that textbooks neglected non-ministerial departments in the second half of the nineteenth century. See, for example, Traill, H (1887) *Central Government* (London); Porritt, E (1893) *The Englishman at Home* (London); and Courtney, L (1905) *The Working Constitution of the United Kingdom* (London).

16. For example, The Development Commission, Road Board and Insurance Commission.

17. See Flinders, M V & Smith M J (1998) *Quangos, Accountability and Reform: the Politics of Quasi-Government* (London : Macmillan).

18. Although Bentham's writing had done much to engender support around the ministerial department it also provided a great deal of support for those who favoured the non-ministerial organisation. Bentham's work had suggested a range of mechanisms and models for increasing the accountability of boards

and he wrote: 'It would be an error if a conclusion was formed that there exists not any case in which government by bodies corporate or boards can be conducive to the legitimate ends of government'. Bowring, J (1843) *Works of Bentham* (Edinburgh : Tait) Vol. VI p.558.

[18] Cmnd 9230 (1918) *Report of the Machinery of Government Committee of the Ministry of Reconstruction* [The Haldane Report]. See Greenleaf, W (1983) *The British Political Tradition: Vol.I The Rise of Collectivism* London : Methuen) Ch.4.

[19] Bowring, J (1843) *The Works of Jeremy Bentham* (Edinburgh) Vol.III 'Plan of Parliamentary Reform of a Catechism' Section IV and Vol.IX 'Constitutional Code' Book II, Ch.VIII, Art.3-6 and 10 at p.206

[20] Benson, A & Viscount Esher (1908) *Letters of Queen Victoria 1837-1861* (London : Murray) Vol.1 pp.106-108, letter of the 25/2/1838.

[21] For example, the Wheat Commission, Livestock Commission, Marketing Boards, War Damage Commission and Arts Council.

[22] Wheare, K (1955) *Government by Committee: An Essay on the British Constitution* (Oxford : Clarendon); Willson, F (1957) *The Organisation of British Central Government* (London : Allen & Unwin); Cole, M (1999) 'Quangos: The Debate in the 1970s in Britain' *Twentieth Century History* forthcoming.

[23] Bowring, J (1843) *The Works of Jeremy Bentham* (Edinburgh) Book. II Ch..IX Section XXV Arts. 26, 27, 32, 35.

[24] Taylor, H (1883) *Works* (London) p.321.

[25] Beattie, A (1995) 'Ministerial Responsibility and the Theory of the British State' in Rhodes, R & Dunleavy, P (eds.) *Prime Minister, Cabinet and Core Executive* (Basingstoke : Macmillan) pp.158-181.

[26] Birch, A (1964) *Representative and Responsible Government* (London & Allen Unwin). More recently David Marquand has outlined the historical distinction between what he terms the 'republican vision' of British democracy based on an active citizenry and participatory government and a 'court vision' based on political realism and the need to get the business of government done. See Marquand, D (2000) 'Democracy in Britain' *Political Quarterly*, Vol. 71 No.3 pp.268-281.

[27] Mill noted that the job of Parliament was not to govern but to '...watch and control the government; then throw the light of publicity on its acts; to compel a full exposition and justification of all of them if found condemnable'. Mill, J S (1962 orig. pub. 1861) *Representative Government* (London : Dent) p.332.

[28] Marshall, G (1980) *Constitutional Theory* (Oxford : Clarendon) p.31.

[29] Hawkins, A (1989) 'Parliamentary Government and Victorian Political Parties 1830-1880' *English Historical Review* Vol.104 No.412 p.652.

30. As Bagehot noted the role of ministers was to bring 'outside sense and animation' into the 'inside' worlds of Whitehall departments and to prevent: '...the incessant tyranny of Parliament over the public offices'. Through the device of ministerial responsibility ministers stood between their departments and officials and '...the busy-bodies and the crotchet-makers of the House and the country'. (1993 orig. pub.1867) *The English Constitution* (London : Fontana).
31. Weir, S & Beetham, D (1998) *Political Power and Democratic Control in Britain* (London : Routledge) pp.338.
32. See Tant, A (1990) 'The Campaign for Freedom of Information: A Participatory Challenge to Elitist British Government' *Public Administration* Vol.68 pp.477-491.
33. Judge, D (1993) *The Parliamentary State* (London : Sage) pp.152-157.
34. 'So embedded is the convention within the psyche of ministers and civil servants alike that abstract principle comes to affect actual behaviour.' Judge, D (1993) *The Parliamentary State* (London : Sage) p.144.
35. See Chapman, R (1988) *Ethics in the Civil Service* (London : Routledge) pp.306-307; Wass, D (1984) *Government and the Governed* (London : Routledge); Administrative Staff College (1963) *The Accountability of Government Departments* (Henley - on - Thames : Administrative Staff College).
36. See Beattie, A (1998) 'Why is the Case for Parliamentary Reform in Britain so Weak?' *Legislative Studies* Vol.4 No.2 pp.1-16.
37. Pyper, R (1996) *Aspects of Accountability in the British System of Government* (Eastham : Tudor) p.1.
38. Adapted from Pollitt, C 'Accountability and Democracy: Answering to Political Authority and Citizen's Needs' Paper to the International Institute of Administrative Sciences Conference, 12-15/5/99, Civil Service College, Sunningdale.
39. Kemp, P (1996) *Delivering Public Services* Annual Lecture to the Centre for Socio-Legal Studies, Sheffield University, 12/11/96.
40. HC 313-II *Ministerial Accountability and Responsibility* Second Report by the Public Service Committee, Session 1996/97, HMSO, London. Memorandum submitted by the First Division Association, p.1.
41. Brazier, A (2000) *Systematic Scrutiny: Reforming the Select Committees* (London : Hansard Society) p.4.
42. As Hirst and Khilnani note: '...that this critical consensus should appear in the twilight years of a period of Conservative rule ostensibly dedicated to decentralisation and greater popular accountability is perhaps ironic'. Hirst, P & Khilnani, S (1996) *Reinventing Democracy* (Oxford : Blackwell) p.2. Examples of the contemporary literature include: Elcock, H (1998) 'The

Changing Problem of Accountability in Modern Government: An Analytical Agenda for Reformers' *Public Policy & Administration* Vol.13 No.3 pp.23-37; Barberis, P (1998) 'The New Public Management and New Accountability' *Public Administration* Vol.76 pp.451-470; Deleon, L (1998) 'Accountability in Reinvented Government' *Public Administration* Vol. 76 pp.539-558.

[43] For a theoretical discussion of the concept, see White, F , Harden, I & Donnelly, K (1994) *The Changing Constitutional Role of the Public Sector Audit: Audit and Government Accountability a Framework for Comparative Analysis* (Sheffield : University of Sheffield).

[44] Johnson, N (1974) 'Defining Accountability' *Public Administration Bulletin* No.17 p.3.

[45] Woodhouse, D (1994) *Ministers and Parliament; Accountability in Theory and in Practice* (Oxford : Oxford University Press) p.1.

[46] Lello, J (1993) *Accountability in Practice* (London : Cassel) p.10.

[47] Kernaghan, K & Langford, J (1990) *The Responsible Public Servant* (Halifax, Nova Scotia : Institute for Research on Public Policy and the Institute of Public Administration of Canada) p.160.

[48] Lawton, A & Rose, A (1991) *Organisation and Management in the Public Sector* (London : Pitman) p.19. For an analysis of several different definitions of accountability, see Stewart, J (1984) 'The Role of Information in Public Accountability' in Hopwood, A & Tomkins, C *Issues in Public Sector Accounting* (Oxford : Phillip Allan) pp.13-15.

[49] Day & Klein highlighted this as a particular problem in their research. See Day, P & Klein, R (1987) *Accountabilities: Five Public Services* (London : Tavistock) p.229. See also Johnson, N (1974) 'Defining Accountability' *Public Administration Bulletin* No.17 Dec. pp.3-14.

[50] HC 27 *The Role of the Civil Service* Fifth Report by the Treasury and Civil Service Committee, Session 1993/94, HMSO, London.

[51] Cm 2748 (1995) *The Civil Service. Taking Forward Continuity and Change* HMSO, London. p.27.

[52] Hawkins, M (1978) *The Oxford English Dictionary* (Oxford : Oxford University Press) p.5.

[53] Hawkins, M (1978) *The Oxford English Dictionary* (Oxford : Oxford University Press) p.548.

[54] Butler, R Evidence given to the Scott Inquiry on 9/2/94 Transcript pp.22-23. See HC 115 *Report of the Inquiry into the Export of Defence Equipment and Dual-Use Goods to Iraq and Related Prosecutions* Session 1995/96, HMSO, London. [The Scott Report] K8.2 Vol.IV p.1800.

[55] For insightful discussions of the concept, see Hinton, P & Wilson, E (1993) 'Accountability' in Wilson, J & Hinton, P (eds.) *Public Services in the*

1990s (Sevenoaks : Tudor) pp.123-142; Patton, J (1992) 'Accountability and Government Financial Reporting' *Financial Accountability and Management* Vol.8 No.3 pp.163-180.

[56] See Marshall, G (1986) *Constitutional Conventions: The Rules and Forms of Political Accountability* (Oxford : Clarendon); Turpin, C (1994) 'Ministerial Responsibility' in Jowell, J & Oliver, D (eds.) *The Changing Constitution* 3rd edition (Oxford : Clarendon) pp.109-151; McVicar, M, Judge, D & Hogwood, B (1998) 'Too much of a good thing?' *The Stakeholder* Vol.2 No.2 pp.10-11.

[57] Marshall termed this 'explanatory accountability'. Marshall, G (1978) 'Police Accountability Revisited' in Butler, D & Halsey, A (eds.) *Policy and Politics* (London : Macmillan) pp.61-62.

[58] See Turpin, C (1985) *British Government and the Constitution* (London : Weidenfeld) p.346.

[59] Finer, S (1956) 'The Individual Responsibility of Ministers' *Public Administration* Vol. 34 pp.377-396 at p.393.

[60] See Dowding, K & Kang, W (1998) 'Ministerial Resignations 1945-97' *Public Administration* Vol. 76 pp.411-429.

[61] For example, the courts can enforce informatory, amendatory and explanatory accountability on ministers while recent public sector reforms have attempted to strengthen informatory, amendatory and explanatory accountability, though mainly at the micro-level, through bureaucratic innovations such as Charters.

[62] McVicar, M, Judge, D & Hogwood, B (1998) 'Too Much of a Good Thing?' *The Stakeholder* Vol.2 No.2 pp.10-11.

[63] Adapted from Gagne, R (1996) 'Accountability and Public Administration' *Canadian Journal of Public Administration* Vol. 39 No.2 pp.213-223.

[64] See Elcock, H (1998) 'The Changing Problem of Accountability in Modern Government: An Analytical Agenda for Reformers' *Public Policy & Administration* Vol.13 No.3 pp.23-37.

[65] Gray, A & Jenkins, B (1993) 'Codes of Accountability in the New Public Sector' *Accounting, Auditing & Accountability* Vol.6 No.3 p.55. See also Baylis, R (1996) *Conflicting Modes of Accountability: A User Perspective* Newcastle Discussion Papers in Politics No.20, University of Newcastle.

[66] See Oliver, D & Drewry, D (1996) *Public Service Reforms: Issues of Accountability and Public Law* (London : Pinter). For a case study see: Rush, M (1997) 'Damming the Sleaze: The New Code of Conduct and Outside Interests of MPs in the British House of Commons' *The Journal of Legislative Studies* Vol.3 No.3 pp.10-28.

[67] For example, the Treasury Solicitor's Department has produced and distributed a guide of good practice in relation to judicial review entitled

68 'The Judge Over Your Shoulder'. See Oliver, D (1989) 'The Judge Over Your Shoulder' *Parliamentary Affairs* Vol.42 pp.302-316; Oliver, D (1994) 'The Judge Over Your Shoulder - Mark II' *Public Law* pp.514-515.

Hogwood, B, Judge, D & McVicar, M 'Too Much of a Good Thing? The Pathology of Accountability' paper presented to the Political Studies Association Annual Conference, University of Keele, 7-9/4/98; Hogwood, B 'The Quantitative Analysis of Agency Accountability: What Can It Tell Us and What Does It Miss Out?' Paper presented at the Conference of the Structure and Organisation Group (SOG) of IPSA on Taking the Measure of Government, Pittsburgh, USA, 30/11/97; McVicar, M, Judge, D & Hogwood, B (1998) 'Too much of a good thing?' *The Stakeholder* Vol.2 No.2 pp.10-11.

69 Debates about the structure of the state and the location of responsibility can be placed in the context of what Parsons has termed *'la malaise postmoderne'*. See, Parsons, W (1998) 'Fuzzy in Theory and Getting Fuzzier in Practice: Post-Modern Reflections on Responsibility in Public Administration and Management' in Hondeghen, A (ed.) *Ethics and Accountability in a Context of Governance and New Public Management* (Ohnsha : IOS Press). See also: Rhodes, R *Towards a Post-Modern Public Administration: Epoch, Epistemology or Narrative* paper given to the ESRC Whitehall Programme Conference on 'Understanding Central Government: Theory into Practice' University of Birmingham 16-18/9/96; Fox, C & Miller, H (1995) *Post-Modern Public Administration: Towards Discourse* (London : Sage); Clegg, S (1990) *Modern Organisations: Organisational Studies in the Post Modern World* (London : Sage); Smith, T (1994) 'Post-Modern Politics and the Case for Constitutional Renewal' *Political Quarterly* Vol.65 pp. 128-137.

70 The original Ibbs Report recommended a '...change in the British Constitution, by law if necessary, to quash the fiction that ministers can be genuinely responsible for *everything* done by officials in their name'. Quoted in Hennessy, P (1989) *Whitehall* (London : Secker & Warburg) pp.618-622.

71 Woodhouse, D (1994) *Ministers and Parliament: Accountability in Theory and in Practice* (Oxford : Clarendon) pp.266-271; Boston, J *et al.* (1997) *Public Management: The New Zealand Model* (Melbourne : Oxford University Press); Eagles, I, Taggart, M & Liddell, G (1992) *Freedom of Information in New Zealand* (Auckland : Oxford University Press).

72 Mascarenhas, R (1993) 'Building an Enterprise Culture in the Public Sector: Reform of the Public Sector in Australia, Britain and New Zealand' *Public Administration Review* Vol. 53 No.4 pp.319-328; Finn, P (1993) 'Public Trust and Public Accountability' *Australian Quarterly* Vol.65

73 pp.50-59; Mulgan, R (1997) 'Contracting Out and Accountability' *Australian Journal of Public Administration* Vol.56 No.4 pp.106-116; Mulgan, R (1997) 'The Processes of Public Accountability' *Australian Journal of Public Administration* Vol.56 No.1 pp.25-36; Kellow, A (1990) 'Changing Conceptions of Responsibility' in Power, J (ed.) *Public Administration in Australia: A Watershed* (Sydney : Hale & Iremonger).

73 Sutherland, S (1991) 'Responsible Government and Ministerial Responsibility: Every Reform is its Own Problem' *Canadian Journal of Political Science* Vol.24 No.1 pp.91-120; Hazell, R (1989) 'Freedom of Information in Australia, Canada and New Zealand' *Public Administration* Vol.67 pp.189-210; Gagne, R (1996) 'Accountability and Public Administration' *Canadian Journal of Public Administration* Vol. 39 No.2 pp.213-223.

74 The reinvention of government is not the only threat to the continuing validity of ministerial responsibility to Parliament. In the European context defining the responsibility of national ministers becomes increasingly difficult as responsibility is shared among a range of organisations and decisions are taken by collegiate authorities. For example, the Secretary of State for Defence's responsibility for recruitment to the British armed forces has been compromised by the decision of the European Court for Human Rights' ruling on the rights of homosexuals. See Lustig-Prean and Beckett v United Kingdom (Application Nos. 31417/96 and 32377/96), judgement of the European Court of Human Rights 27/9/99; and Smith and Grady v United Kingdom (Application Nos. 33985/96 and 33986/96), judgement of the European Court of Human Rights 27/9/99. Hence, not only is there a lack of clarity regarding responsibility within the state, but there is also imprecision about what that elected government is actually responsible for. For example, the Chancellor of the Exchequer has transferred responsibility for the setting of interest rates to an appointed Monetary Policy Committee. Yet the committee can be overruled in periods of emergency and is not insulated from informal public and political pressure. See Flinders, M (1998) 'Squaring the Circle: Parliamentary Accountability and the Bank of England' *The Stakeholder* Vol.2 No.1.

75 I have in mind particularly the *Memorandum on Guidance for Officials appearing before select committees* [The Osmotherly rules]. This is an issue that has arisen in other countries. See Sutherland, S (1991) 'The Al-Mashat Affair: administrative responsibility in parliamentary institutions' *Canadian Public Administration* Vol.30 No.4 pp.573-603. On the reformulation of the anonymity of officials see Cm 4310 (1999) *Modernising Government* HMSO, London.

[76] Barberis, P (1998) 'The New Public Management and New Accountability' *Public Administration*, Vol.76, pp.451-470.

[77] This recommendation was made by the Treasury & Civil Service Committee (HC 27 *The Role of the Civil Service* Fifth Report by the Treasury & Civil Service Committee, Session 1993/94, HMSO, London. Para.171) and by the Public Service Committee (HC 313 *Ministerial Responsibility and Ministerial Accountability*, Session 1996/97, HMSO, London. Paras.19-20 p.lxxxii) but was rejected both times in the subsequent government response. See HC 67 (1996/97) paras. 19-20 p.xii)

[78] A term used by Sir Peter Kemp. See HC 313-III (1996/97) p.108 para. 9.

[79] See Marr, A *The Independent* 17/10/95 p.14.

[80] See Judge Stephen Tumin *The Guardian* 19/2/95 p.20.

[81] O'Toole, B & Chapman, R (1995) 'Parliamentary Accountability' in O'Toole, B & Jordan, G *The Next Steps: Improving Management in Government?* (London : Dartmouth) pp.118-141.

[82] There is a wealth of information on this argument, some of the best examples include;. Greer, P (1994) *Transforming Central Government: The Next Steps Initiative* (Milton Keynes : Open University Press); Jowell, J & Oliver, D (1994) *The Changing Constitution* (Oxford : Clarendon); Massey, A (1995) 'Civil Service Reform and Accountability' *Public Policy & Administration* Vol.10 No.1 pp.16-33.

[83] See Parsons, W (1998) 'Fuzzy in Theory and Getting Fuzzier in Practice: Post-Modern Reflections on Responsibility in Public Administration and Management' in Hondeghen, A ed. *Ethics and Accountability in a Context of Governance and New Public Management* (Ohnsha, Japan : IOS Press) pp.87-104.

[84] By 'multicentric' Spiro means: '... to different authorities, for different purposes, to different degrees and in terms of different, though mutually complementary standards'. Spiro, H (1969) *Responsibility in Government: Theory and Practice* (New York : Van Nostrand Rheinhold) p.98.

[85] See Roth, D (1996) 'Finding the Balance: Achieving a Synthesis Between Improved Performance and Enhanced Accountability' in OECD *Performance Auditing and the Modernisation of Government* (Paris : OECD) pp.249-259; Bellone, C & Goerl, G (1992) 'Reconciling public entrepreneurship and democracy' *Public Administration Review* Vol.52 No.2 pp.130-134; Moe, R (1994) 'The "Reinventing Government" Exercise: Misinterpreting the Problem, Misjudging the Consequences' *Public Administration Review* Vol.54 No.2 pp.111-122.

[86] Riddell, P 'Putting Parliament to rights' *The Times* 21/10/96 p.20. See also Riddell, P (1998) *Parliament Under Pressure* (London : Victor Gollancz).

[87] HC 27 (1993/94) para. 135 p.xlii.

88 HC 313 (1996/97) para.173.
89 HC 313 (1996/97) para. 174 p.lxxix.
90 Romzek, B & Dubnick, M (1987) ' Accountability in the Public Sector' *Public Administration Review* May/ June Vol.47 p.228.
91 Stone, B (1995) 'Administrative Accountability in "Westminster" Democracies: Towards a New Conceptual Framework' *Governance* Vol.8 No.1 pp.505-525.
92 Oliver, D (1991) *Government in the UK: The Search for Accountability, Effectiveness and Citizenship* (Milton Keynes : Open University Press).
93 Pyper, R (1996) *Aspects of Accountability in the British System of Government* (Eastham : Tudor).
94 Lawton, A & Rose, A (1991) *Organisation and Management in the Public Sector* (London : Pitman).
95 Robert Pyper's is an edited collection and it would appear that there has been some overlap between contributors.
96 It should be noted that Bruce Stone is talking about 'Westminster' democracies and therefore is not specific to Britain in his categories. This explains his inclusion of Freedom of Information Legislation and a Bill of Rights under his Judicial model.
97 Barberis, P (1998) 'The New Public Management and New Accountability' *Public Administration* Vol.76 p.452.
98 Johnson, N (1982) 'Accountability, Control & Complexity: Moving Beyond Ministerial Responsibility' in Barker, A (ed.) *Quangos in Britain* (London : Macmillan).
99 Madison, J (1788) *The Federalist Papers* No.51 quoted in Weir, S & Hall, W (1994) *EGO Trip: Extra-Governmental Organisations in the UK and their Accountability* Democratic Audit Paper No.2 (London : University of Essex/Scarman Trust) pp.10-12.
100 Adapted from Lovell, A (1996) 'Notions of Accountability and State Audit: A UK Perspective' *Financial Accountability & Management* Vol.12 No.4 pp.261-280.
101 Rhodes, R (1997) *Understanding Governance: Policy Networks, Governance and Accountability* (Buckingham : Open University Press) p.5. See also: Greenleaf, W (1983) *The British Political Tradition Vol.1: The Rise of Collectivism* (London : Methuen) pp.3-8; Gamble, A (1990) 'Theories of British Politics' *Political Studies* Vol.38 p.405.
102 Rhodes, R (1988) *Beyond Westminster and Whitehall* (London : Unwin - Hyman) pp.402-406.
103 See, Riddell, P (2000) 'The Media' in Riddell, P *Parliament Under Blair* (London : Politicos) pp.160-181.

[104] On this topic see, McHarg, A (2000) *Accountability and the Public -Private Distinction* (Buckingham : Open University Press), Doyfield, K (2000) *The Politics of Regulation* (London : EPF), Mather, G (2000) *Making Decisions in Britain* (London : EPF), The Hansard Society (2000) *Regulation of Privatised Utilities* (London : Hansard Society).

[105] Methodology.

[106] Stone, B (1995) 'Administrative Accountability in "Westminster" Democracies: Towards a New Conceptual Framework' *Governance* Vol.8 No.1 pp.523.

PART TWO
ACCOUNTABILITY MODELS AND CASE STUDY ANALYSIS

PART TWO

2 Parliamentary Accountability: Demoralised or Revitalised?

> The executive is no longer monolithic and centralised. It comprises instead a great many bodies, of varying size, structure and legal status. The scrutiny of these bodies, and the securing of effective accountability, is one of the great challenges which Parliament must face over the next few years (Lord Nolan, Warwick University 1996).

2.1 Introduction

The preceding chapter outlined the theoretical and general debates surrounding the accountability of the core executive. This chapter examines the particular issues surrounding the parliamentary accountability of ministers and officials. In a political system founded on parliamentary sovereignty ministerial responsibility to Parliament is crucial as the legitimating foundation of the constitution. In the post-Scott era much has been written about ministerial responsibility and Parliament.[1] The key argument of this chapter stresses trends, or changes in emphasis, that are recasting the convention increasingly in favour of the executive. Ministers portray this as strengthening the structure of accountability and modernising the convention in line with reality. Conversely, it is suggested that the reformulation is making accountability and responsibility more opaque largely due to the existence of a 'responsibility gap'. This lacuna emerges from ministers restricting their own sphere of responsibility whilst they uphold the constitutional constraints on those to whom responsibility is deflected. This chapter is critical for the whole book. Should the concerns and deficiencies it highlights be supported by the empirical research of the subsequent case study chapter then this places added emphasis on the role of the alternative models of accountability to be explored later in the book. It would also raise questions of whether parliamentary accountability had actually been weakened and complicated because of the existence of these alternative models.

While there is currently much concern regarding the ability of Parliament to scrutinise the executive, the issues raised are not particularly new. They are variants of long-standing concerns, which predate the Thatcher years and reflect, among other things, the lack of a codified constitution and the nature of a public sector without statutory authority.[2] It is fundamental to understand three important tenets that will permeate and influence the whole course of this chapter: ministerial responsibility is a convention without statutory force; there has never been universal agreement about the terms of that accountability; and there is no independent source of authority that can determine whether the convention has been observed in a given circumstance.[3]

However, as a result of structural reforms and specific incidents the utility of ministerial responsibility is a salient topic. (I have in mind the Lewis/Howard affair in the Prison Service;[4] the 'Cash for Questions' scandal;[5] the Scott Report,[6] the activity of the Committee on Standards in Public Life;[7] the inquiry into ministerial responsibility and accountability by the Public Service Committee;[8] the subsequent government response;[9] the limited achievements of the Modernisation Committee since 1997; and the caustic relationship between the Liaison Committee and the Labour government.)[10] If the suggested accountability gap is to be filled the convention of ministerial responsibility will have to be radically reconstituted, but this is something the executive has consistently refused to do.[11] Ironically, it is the executive's commitment to ministerial responsibility that is blocking moves designed to increase accountability. It has become an accountability shield rather than a sword.[12] The continuing centrality of the convention therefore lies not in the fact that it necessarily ensures accountable government but that it is employed by the executive as a legitimating tool to justify the refusal to introduce reform. To explain both the centrality and the longevity of the convention it is necessary to examine its origins.

2.2 The Origins of the Convention of Ministerial Responsibility

The convention of ministerial responsibility antedates the modern party system and was designed in a period when the role of government was limited and it was reasonable to assume that a competent minister would have personal control over a small department. The mid-Victorian state was modest in both size and ambition. There was no pretence that government could do much on its own to remedy or compensate for social ills. The minimalist character of the state was underpinned by the constraints of Gladstonian finance and reinforced by its inaccessibility. The traditional duties of government were not concerned with the regulation of everyday life but with quite different issues, such as defence, law and foreign affairs. Departments of state were small and vicarious responsibility was accepted as ministers had no excuse for not knowing everything that was happening in their department. As Young noted: 'The most striking feature of British administration in the first quarter of the nineteenth century was the extent to which the work of government departments was performed by ministers'.[13] The minimalist size of the state is reflected in the fact that in 1876 the Department of Trade and Industry employed only 6 clerks and in 1884 it had only 30.[14] The staff of the department were little more than a ministerial secretariat of clerks and porters who aided the minister in carrying out their limited duties.[15]

The contemporary problems exist because it is this convention, designed to suit the state of two centuries ago, that still forms the foundation of the British constitution. It underpins the beliefs people hold about how ministers should act and it shapes the procedures of Parliament. That we use this outdated convention to control a modern executive has contributed to the current problems: 'The true offences Scott found were not those of individuals but the failure of a system, principally because of the decline of old conventions, which had achieved a tolerable accountability most of the time when government was simpler'.[16] Even when departments were small the utility of ministerial responsibility was widely doubted. In 1823 William Cobbett wrote:

> Socks that pinch a pair of ankles are like ministerial responsibility; a thing to talk about, but for no other use; a mere mockery; a thing laughed at by those whom it is intended to keep in check.[17]

Doubts were being expressed long before most academics acknowledge, certainly long before Crichel Down or Finer's seminal 1956 article.[18] By the 1850s, due to the progressive extension of the franchise, departments began to evolve as parties developed and acted in an increasingly interventionist manner. From being little more than private offices, the departments were quickly becoming administrative entities of increasing size and complexity. A large constitutional bureaucracy was developing. With the increased size of departments, it seemed obvious that new forms of accountability would have to be introduced. Parliament resisted any such reforms due to its strong faith in and commitment to ministerial responsibility, a belief fostered during the crucial period between the two Reform Acts of 1832 and 1867. The Reform Act of 1832 enlarged the electorate by 50%. The House of Commons was liberated from the discipline of Crown influence and, with parties in an embryonic stage, the House entered into more than three decades of making and unmaking governments. As late as 1893 Lord Hartington noted:

> Parliament makes or unmakes our ministries, it revises their actions. Ministries may make peace and war, but they do so at pain of instant dismissal by parliament from office; and in affairs of internal administration the power of parliament is equally direct. It can dismiss a Ministry if it is too extravagant or too economical...It does actually and practically in every way directly govern England, Scotland and Ireland.[19]

The House was free of Crown influence, not yet constrained by strict party discipline; departments were still small enough for ministerial responsibility to be strictly applied without dispute; and MPs felt empowered to play a more active role in government due to their popular support in the country. Parliament demonstrated a determined ability to hold ministers to account and '...exercised a constant supervision of all governmental affairs'.[20] It was expected that ministers would have to work to maintain the confidence of the House. More importantly, the government accepted the right of Parliament to hold ministers to account. Forced resignations were common.[21] MPs collaborated in shaping government measures as well as heavily amending and rejecting legislation: 'The existence of numerous individuals and earnest members with a great deal to say and the right to say it meant that no government could, with any certainty, plan any legislative programme'.[22]

Table 2.1 Government Defeats and Amendments Tabled to Government Bills 1851-1903[23]

Parliamentary Session	No. of Govt. Defeats	No. of Amendments to Govt. Bills
1851-1855	59	29
1856-1861	52	24
1862-1867	60	26
1868-1873	50	27
1874-1879	8	1
1880-1885	26	11
1886-1891	13	5
1892-1897	9	2
1898-1903	2	1

The mid-nineteenth century can be interpreted as the zenith for the convention of ministerial responsibility. After the second Reform Act the relationship between parliament and the executive shifted in the latter's favour. Within and beyond parliament, party control of its members became much tighter. In 1867, for example, the National Union of Conservative and Constitutional Associations was formed in order to organise the party outside of Westminster. Three years later Conservative Central Office was established to provide a central base. Moreover, the procedural reforms within Parliament in the early 1880s considerably strengthened the position of the executive and restricted the opportunities for backbenchers to table amendments (as indicated by table 2.1). Reforms including the closure motion and the guillotine allowed the executive to dictate the length of most debates, the right of MPs to raise adjournment debates was curtailed and the powers of the speaker were strengthened. These, along with other rule changes, reduced the power of the individual MP and consolidated the control of the executive. By the end of the nineteenth century most votes were whipped and party discipline strong.[24]

The success of the convention may well have been overstated by constitutional writers at the time, such as Bagehot, Dicey and Maitland, who needed to demonstrate a workable theory of accountability to accommodate a constitution in which Parliament was supreme, both as a legislature and check on the executive. A constitution based on convention as a method for ensuring accountability also reassured the ruling elite that the government of the country would remain in its hands - for the essence of conventions is that they are developed and controlled by those who operate the system and are not imposed externally. (A fact contemporary governments are well aware of.)

Crucially, this period convinced Parliament that ministerial responsibility was a workable convention through which accountable government could be enforced. Parliament severely underestimated the subsequent effect that the evolving state and mass parties would have on the convention and the convention became the political rationale and procedural logic around which an expanding system of government was structured. Crucially, the perceived success of ministerial responsibility in the 1832-1867 period cultivated the belief that it was practically and constitutionally superior to other forms of accountability. Woodhouse notes:

> ...so while on the continent administrative courts were being established to police the administrative functions of the state, and in the USA the foundations of a regulatory system centring on agencies were being laid, in Britain ministerial departments were established and began to absorb the responsibility.[25]

It is this British exceptionalism which explains the organisation of departments in this period.[26] As Chapter One noted, before then, in common with most other European states, it was the practice to establish independent boards to regulate social functions, but concerns about the accountability of these boards led to their functions being transferred into departments headed by a minister.[27] The period 1832-1867 is crucial to an understanding of the contemporary situation. It was during this period that, due to a number of short-lived factors, ministerial responsibility became entrenched as the primary mechanism for ensuring accountable government. The effect of the growth of parties and the state was seriously miscalculated. By the time the problems associated with the convention were apparent the dominant position of the executive had been established.[28] The convention of ministerial responsibility provided the critical link in the Westminster/Whitehall model, and yet the executive's majority within the House insulated ministers from effective scrutiny. Moreover, the position of the executive allowed it to dictate the rules, resources and information flows through which it would be held to account. This has been particularly visible in relation to the evolving state which has led to an increasingly formalised differentiation between ministerial 'accountability' and 'responsibility'.

2.3 The Distinction between 'Ministerial Accountability' and 'Ministerial Responsibility'

The Conservative governments of the 1980s and 1990s sought to accentuate the distinction between a minister's 'accountability' and 'responsibility'. A minister was accountable to Parliament for his or her department: '...but is not responsible for all the actions in the sense of being blameworthy'.[29] Although Sir Robin dislikes the term, this is known as the 'Butler doctrine'.[30] It follows that if responsibility does not reside with ministers it must lie with officials, a point the distinction goes on to recognise: '...a civil servant is not directly accountable to Parliament for his actions but is responsible for certain actions and can be delegated clearly defined responsibilities'.[31]

Ministers have sought to limit their respective spheres of responsibility since the Crichel Down affair.[32] So while an unofficial distinction between policy and operations has gradually evolved in the last 40 years its formal recognition, enshrined in documents like *Questions of Procedure for Ministers* and agency framework documents, is a more recent development. Although unsupported by precedent, the convention dictated that the minister, and only the minister, should accept vicarious responsibility for the work of his or her officials.[33] This strict interpretation died in the aftermath of the Crichel Down affair. Sir Thomas Dugdale on the eve of his resignation spoke of his responsibility for the vicarious actions of his officials: 'So far as they are persons, and most of them are, for whose conduct I am responsible as a minister of the Crown, the responsibility I wholly accept'.[34] This statement was followed by a strict restatement of the convention by Sir Edward Bridges, then permanent secretary to the Treasury.[35] So extreme a doctrine of ministerial responsibility would have been accepted by Palmerston or Gladstone, but in 1954 it raised concerns and a reformulation was swift.[36] In July 1954 Sir David Maxwell-Fyfe, then Home Secretary, restated the convention but in a way that absolved the minister of vicarious responsibility and introduced the first distinction between accountability and responsibility:

> Where action has been taken by a civil servant of which the minister disapproves and has no prior knowledge, and the conduct of the official is reprehensible, then there is no obligation on the part of the minister to endorse what he believes to be wrong, or to defend what are clearly shown to be errors of his officers. The minister is not bound to defend action of which he did not know, or of which he disapproves. But of course, he remains constitutionally responsible to Parliament for the fact that something has gone wrong, and he alone can tell Parliament what has occurred and render an account of his stewardship.[37]

This was an important refinement of the antique and fanciful fiction - long overtaken by the development of a modern interventionist state and the vast bureaucracy that grew up with it - that a minister should take the blame for everything that happens in his or her department.[38] However, the statement is confusing and ambiguous as to the requirements of ministerial responsibility where operational fault is concerned.[39] As a result the convention has been subject to the vagaries of interpretation and remains 'at best elastic'.[40]

Ministers seeking to narrow their sphere of responsibility have employed the distinction between 'policy' and 'operations', a ploy first used by James Prior after the escape of 38 prisoners from the Maze Prison in 1983.[41] A similar defence was mounted by Kenneth Baker in 1984 after the Brixton Prison break out.[42] More recently, Michael Howard employed the distinction to absolve himself of responsibility after prison escapes.[43] Few could defend the strict Bridges statement in times when the state has reached such high levels of size and complexity, and the distinction has its supporters.[44] The consequences of a minister accepting complete vicarious responsibility would be absurd. The Conservative government was confident that the distinction has improved accountability. William Waldegrave stated:

> The old myth of personal ministerial responsibility for every action undertaken by each government department was, in Herbert Morrison's words 'the minister is responsible for every stamp stuck on an envelope' or as Nye Bevan more colourfully had it 'If a bedpan is dropped the minister will hear of it'. As Sir Robin Butler has recently said, this was not only a myth - it was a dangerous myth. What we have done is to make a clear distinction between, responsibility which can be delegated, and accountability, which remains firmly with the minister.[45]

But, as the Public Service Committee emphasised: '...to the extent that it [the distinction] protects ministers from being seen as personally to blame for minor failings (an incorrect social security payment for example), it is no more than a statement of the obvious'.[46] The distinction would seem, therefore, to serve a doubtful constitutional purpose, and there are concerns that the distinction, far from being a statement of the obvious, actually represents a more fundamental refinement of the convention and that 'ministerial responsibility for departmental acts has been defined away to almost nothing'.[47] Critics argue that the use of a demarcation that is imprecise blurs responsibility.[48] In the context of departments it suggests that a minister can disclaim personal responsibility for serious departmental fault, even if he or she knew or should have known of the problems, simply on the basis that the fault was administrative. Taken to its logical conclusion the notion of a minister being negligent in the administration of his or her department therefore disappears. As the First Division Association noted: '...does such *reductio ad absurdum* mean that a Secretary of State is relieved of the responsibility for the way in which the department operates?'.[49]

The concerns surrounding the policy/operations distinction have been amplified with the rapid establishment of agencies. Despite the greater clarity provided by framework documents responsibilities remain blurred, particularly in sensitive agencies. The Treasury and Civil Service Committee noted: 'The theoretical separation of accountability and responsibility is nowhere more untenable than in the operation of agencies'.[50] Rather than framework documents improving accountability they may provide the opportunity for ministers to '...pass the buck for policy failures and disclaim responsibility for operational activities'.[51] The Public Service Committee criticised the distinction: 'It is not possible absolutely to distinguish an area in which a minister is personally responsible, and liable to take the blame, from one in which he is constitutionally accountable'.[52] The government subsequently confirmed its commitment to the distinction:

> ...highlighting those matters for which a minister bears a direct responsibility from amongst all the matters for which he remains obliged to give an account describes modern practice and so provides Parliament and the public with a broad, practical framework against which to judge the Government's continuing endeavours to remain properly accountable.[53]

That government ministers should attempt to limit the parameters of their responsibility is understandable. While a distinction between accountability and responsibility emerged long before Next Steps the formal delegation of powers and responsibilities to chief executives reinforces the Butler doctrine. The distinction attempts to resolve the outdated nature and limitations of the traditional convention. Sir Peter Kemp has pointed out that one of the key aims of the Next Steps was to deal with the 'bed pan' issue:

> Patently this was a fiction. The object of the Next Steps was to domesticate, as one might say, this fiction and to provide a regime whereby those who were responsible for the bedpans could be held to be so, recognisably; while ministers retained ultimate answerability and of course responsibility...the problem as ever is making it work satisfactorily.[54]

The attacks on the distinction can be reversed and it can be seen as an opportunity to enhance rather than undermine accountability. The separation of roles, in a quasi-contractual document, has the potential to increase clarity, transparency and responsibility for specified tasks. In effect the distinction and the reforms bring the structures more into line with reality. While this 'domestication of the fiction' is a welcome advance for accountability the fact that other elements of the fiction exist have caused acute concerns in Parliament and Whitehall.[55] The distinction demands the ability to separate policy and operational boundaries. In reality this is problematic and critics regard this as allowing ministers to decide what they will be responsible for:

> I do not believe the Butler doctrine to be a helpful development or interpretation of the historical texts because it dramatically reduces the scope for allocating defined responsibility. It is a doctrine that allows the guilty or the incompetent to escape their responsibility, whether they are ministers or officials.[56]

The problems stem from the fact that while the convention has been altered to limit the areas for which a minister is personally responsible there has been no concomitant alteration for the provision of information to allow Parliament, first, to decide whether the minister is legitimately deflecting responsibility, or; secondly, to hold accountable the civil servant to whom responsibility has been delegated. Sir Richard Scott captured the issue succinctly:

> If ministers are to be excused blame and personal criticism on the basis of the absence of personal knowledge or involvement, the corollary ought to be an acceptance of the obligation to be forthcoming with information about the incident in question. Otherwise Parliament (and the public) will not be in a position to judge whether the absence of personal knowledge and involvement is fairly claimed or to judge on whom responsibility for what has occurred ought to be placed.[57]

Sir Richard's observation raises a number of issues. First, from a structural perspective it is ministers and not Parliament who define their own sphere of responsibility. The operation of ministerial responsibility reflects both a dominant value system and the predilections of the most powerful actors in the House and so supports the existing distribution of power.[58] Secondly, the crucial questions when ministers distance themselves from responsibility are: Why didn't they know of the issue under consideration? Why did the structure not inform the minister? Was the minister negligent? Were officials acting on the perceived wishes of the minister and, if so, who is responsible? Vicarious responsibility always remains with the minister.

Yet the reinvention of government contains a responsibility gap. Constitutional rules that underpin the convention, especially those concerning the civil service have not been amended. When an incident occurs the minister can deflect blame as operational but the convention blocks Parliament's access to the civil servants involved and the Osmotherly rules allow the minister to control the information a civil servant can give, should they be allowed to attend.[59] No one is responsible to Parliament. Ministers declare themselves only accountable and the constitution dictates that officials are not responsible to Parliament, only their minister. Therefore an unsatisfactory equilibrium exists. The executive has remoulded the convention as it applies to ministers (an act that is not without some degree of wider support) but have refused to implement additional reforms that would allow Parliament to hold to account those to whom responsibility is deflected.

This section has described how as the state has grown ministers have sought to limit the scope of their own personal culpability. This process has been accelerated and formalised by the adoption of devolved management within Whitehall in the late 1980s, known as the 'Next Steps' reforms. While this programme of structural reform cannot be blamed for the fundamental tensions within the British constitutional system, it has illuminated and exacerbated certain pressures. Not least due to the executive's insistence on introducing the reforms within a framework of ministerial responsibility.

2.4 Parliament and the 'Next Steps' Reforms of the Civil Service

The Efficiency Unit report *Improving Management in Government: The Next Steps* built on earlier attempts, such as the MINIS and FMI, to increase the efficiency and effectiveness of the civil service.[60] The report concluded that the civil service was simply too large to be reformed as it was and recommended the creation of separate agencies. These agencies would be directed by a chief executive, appointed from either inside or outside the civil service, and would operate under a policy and resources agreement, known as a framework document, devised by a minister.[61] The Next Steps represents more than administrative adjustment but a fundamental reappraisal of the role and working of the state. It links into wider theories of new public management and represents a shift from direct to strategic control.[62] The aims of the Next Steps programme included increasing efficiency, introducing private sector management techniques and reducing ministerial overload.[63] Its central objective involved changing the culture of the civil service '...to establish a quite different way of conducting the business of government'.[64]

Sir Robin Ibbs recognised that such a fundamental reform would have an obvious effect on accountability and sought to dispel the fiction that ministers can genuinely be held responsible for everything that happened in their department. Ibbs blamed ministerial responsibility for causing ministerial overload and recommended placing '...responsibility for performance squarely on the manager of an agency. We believe it is possible for Parliament, through ministers, to regard managers as directly responsible for operational matters'.[65] Margaret Thatcher refused to alter the convention of ministerial responsibility and maintained that '...each agency will be accountable to a minister, who will in turn be accountable to Parliament for the agency's performance'.[66] When pressed on the topic, Thatcher replied: '...there will be no changes in the arrangements for accountability. Ministers will continue to account to Parliament for all the work of their departments, including the work of their agencies...I repeat there will be no change in the arrangements for accountability'.[67] Although Thatcher received formal support from Sir Peter Kemp[68] and Sir Robin Butler[69] they both caused concern and confusion by reiterating how ministerial responsibility would not be changed without being able to describe how this would work with any clarity.[70]

The Treasury and Civil Service Committee stressed from the outset the need to address the question of accountability directly. In its first report it argued that parliamentary accountability should not be regarded '...as a cost which must be weighed in the balance against the benefit of executive management'.[71] Sir Peter Kemp has argued that accountability was not a forgotten concept at the outset of the Next Steps: 'It is of course a myth...that at the start accountability was overlooked, and that in the later stages it was not cared about'.[72] He notes:

> We did quite a lot of work for Next Steps on what the implications might be for accountability. We came, rather to our surprise, to the reluctant conclusion then that, as far as one can see, technically it was difficult to argue other than that the position would remain unchanged.[73]

(This begs the question why did other countries believe it necessary to overhaul their accountability structures while implementing similar reforms?) Despite considerable concern,[74] the transfer of functions and staff into agencies was swift;[75] a process assisted by all-party support.[76] The adoption of the agency model raises two critical issues. The first is a question of whether agencies have increased the internal accountability of officials to ministers. While managers have a greater capacity for freedom and innovation, ministers also have a clearer picture of responsibilities within departments and therefore the capacity to hold specific areas 'to account' for performance. But while the Next Steps may well have created a civil service that is more accountable to ministers, has this achievement been at the cost of a reduction of external accountability to Parliament and the public? The government thinks not:

> The further delegation of authority to managers inherent in the Next Steps concept concerns internal accountability within departments and does not conflict with the external accountability of ministers to Parliament.[77]

But external accountability to Parliament has been affected. Agencies have changed the relationship between ministers, officials and Parliament, arguably to the benefit of ministers. The traditional anonymity of senior officials has been removed without the corollary of the removal of the Osmotherly rules. Therefore the minister is simultaneously able to deny personal responsibility and also withhold from a civil servant the information that would enable the select committee to make an assessment of the veracity of the minister's denial. Ministers have therefore freed themselves from the restrictions of the convention while the agency chief executives remain bound by the traditional requirements of loyalty and confidentiality, but unlike traditional civil servants, they are no longer anonymous or protected from public blame.[78]

Secondly, the introduction of agencies dramatically illustrates the Crown prerogative powers of the executive as highlighted in the preceding section. The Next Steps reforms were introduced without formal parliamentary approval and Parliament was unable to impose measures which it believed would remedy the perceived responsibility gap. For example, the Treasury and Civil Service Committee recommended that chief executives should give evidence to select committees on their own behalf about their actions as the heads of agencies.[79] But the government has consistently rejected this proposal, and the formal position remains that agency chief executives appear before parliamentary committees according to the wishes of their minister.[80]

How can the Conservatives' adoption of radical bureaucratic reform while remaining constitutionally conservative be explained? Smith highlights that the Conservative government was never solely dominated by the New Right. Many of their perceptions were influenced by traditional conservatism, especially in relation to Parliament and the civil service. Consequently their attitude to the civil service always remained confused and ambiguous.[81] The rationale of Next Steps is one which contains a central dilemma: does managerial delegation entail reduced ministerial accountability and therefore require fundamental changes to the arrangements for parliamentary scrutiny?[82] The government has consistently maintained that it does not, but procedures and practices have changed and new forms of accountability are evolving. As the state has evolved, both in size and complexity, away from the model around which ministerial responsibility was deemed appropriate, the deficiencies of the convention have become more obvious. In this respect, agencies represent the latest stage of a historical problem. Nevertheless, agencies appear unproblematic in many areas of government. However, problems exist where the policy/operations dichotomy is imprecise, and the convention's bias in favour of ministers is seen at its crudest. This tension is symptomatic of two critical factors that underpin the core executive. First, the executive has the capacity to reform the central state without encumbrance. Secondly, the constitutional position of officials derives from the executive's power of Crown prerogative and is not bolstered by a comprehensive public law system.

2.5 The Crown Prerogative and the Absence of Law

Due to Britain's constitutional history the executive wields tremendous powers under the authority of Crown prerogative. The government is 'the Crown' and a significant aspect of this is the doctrine of indivisibility. Thus the civil service lacks any legal personality of its own. This makes it theoretically impossible for agencies to legally contract with their ministers. (This is known as the Carltona doctrine.)[83] This dates back to the Northcote-Trevelyan reforms which were not enshrined in legislation because civil servants were seen as part of the executive and their appointments were authorised by Order in Council. (Civil servants are still employed directly by the Crown.)[84] The executive and civil service are therefore constitutionally indivisible. This historical anachronism has important ramifications for any contemporary discussion of accountability. It ensures that the civil servants are not personally responsible to Parliament, that ministers are accountable for everything that happens in their departments, and also that agencies cannot be put on a statutory footing as the legal position would be that the minister was contracting with himself or herself.

A second legal consideration is the fact that civil service reforms are carried out by government using common law powers. Constitutionally, the civil service is purely the administrative arm of the executive and the executive can restructure itself however it deems appropriate. There is no formal requirement whatsoever for Parliament to play a role. The Next Steps programme was launched without parliamentary approval or discussion. The House has played no formal role in drafting framework documents nor in ratifying senior appointments. Parliament has played a largely reactive role with certain select committees attempting to oversee crucially important reforms in an area in which Parliament has few formal rights. As Freedland notes:

> In substance the Next Steps programme assumes an unrestricted power to turn the civil service into a small policy making core and a large fragmented periphery, and to constitute the relationship between the centre and the periphery in any way thought fit. However well-schooled one is in the understanding that Parliamentary supremacy is more of a constitutional theory than a day to day reality, this still comes as something of a shock.[85]

The legal position of the civil service ensures agencies are administrative creations within departments rather than legally separate entities.[86] Consequently, the functions that agencies fulfil are not vested directly in them but in the departments of which they are part. As a result, agencies lack any legally enforceable guarantees of autonomy. The arms-length relationship they enjoy from the department is purely at the behest of the minister resisting the temptation to intervene. This has led many commentators to suggest that agencies need to be put on a statutory footing to achieve a degree of autonomy from the minister. Indeed, the original architect of the Next Steps programme noted how legislation might be necessary to enable agencies to operate with sufficient independence.[87] Trusting ministers not to intervene is particularly problematic in politically salient agencies,[88] but the experience of the nationalised industries, which experienced ministerial interference despite a statutory basis, suggests that a simple legal basis would not be a panacea for the problems of accountability.[89] The lack of a legal basis for public administration in the United Kingdom reflects the fact that most of the limits that have been placed on the executive have traditionally been conventional rather than legal. This has rested on the theory that politicians should regulate their own behaviour and the courts should play no role.[90] And yet the ability of Parliament to control the executive is limited by the fact that it is a political body in which party loyalties dominate.

2.6 Parliament and Politics

Parliament is a political body. This rather obvious statement is often overlooked. Parliament has two inherently contradictory roles - first, to sustain the executive, which it would appear to do well, and secondly, to hold the executive to account, which it does rather less well. The impact of this constitutional contradiction should not be underestimated and forms the context against which more specific debates about accountability should be considered. Take, for example, the effect of ambition on the average backbench MP.[91] Backbenchers are inclined to see themselves as 'embryonic front benchers' and this will ensure the deference of most MPs to the whips.[92] Over 100 MPs are ministers or parliamentary private secretaries and will be opposed by a similar number of 'shadows'. Together this means that around a third of all MPs are either in executive office or on the ladder. As Lord Nolan noted:

> The role of sustaining the government does not sit well with the task of challenging it and holding it to task. Party political considerations inevitably enter into the process. Of course they should and must do, and issues of policy are quite properly debated on a political basis. But instances do occur where the function of Parliament appears to suffer as a result.[93]

The constitutional system which has developed has, either implicitly or explicitly, ascribed to Parliament a quasi-judicial role which it simply cannot perform. This fact has been recognised for some time. For example, in the 1936 budget leak affair the inability of a select committee to investigate such a party political incident was accepted by both sides.[94] Clement Attlee, the Leader of the Opposition, was isolated when he stood up for constitutional theory by stating:

> Members of this House may be involved, and this House, after all, is the High Court of Parliament, yet the Chancellor says that this House is unfit to act as a court because of its partiality.[95]

The mechanisms that are used to achieve accountability are also used as the weapons of party warfare.[96] As Giddings noted: '...the process of scrutiny is mixed with that of discrediting government'.[97] Constitutional theory assumes that our modern day parliamentarians will examine dispassionately the case made by a minister, take into account all the relevant evidence (that the 'good chap' will have provided) and pronounce whether they have faith in the minister or not. However, this is a distant reality. Unless the partisan dimension can be somehow eradicated from the accountability process its effectiveness will always be limited by this inhibition. A Cabinet minister noted, 'There is always, and always will be, the intrusion of political events and political niceties so you cannot have a pure doctrine of ministerial responsibility that would be objective'.

Such a scenario ignores crucial factors including the existence of highly organised political parties, party discipline and the pre-eminent position of the Prime Minister. To view Parliament as a neutral arbiter of accountability would necessitate the ability to take the politics out of Parliament. As Sir Michael Quinlan told Sir Richard Scott:

> ...it is unrealistic to suppose that information will be provided and used, on either side, in the same manner and spirit as if the actors were participants in a court of law. And although participants may sometimes be blameworthy, the fact that the competition can work to the detriment of balanced public understanding rests less with individuals than with the dynamics of the Westminster system itself.[98]

Although select committees arguably have been successful in mellowing these partisan tendencies they operate within an environment in which the whips can normally steer the committee, via the government's majority, away from controversial issues.[99] Moreover, this constant yet subtle coercion will often affect the topic of inquiry, as the chairman will aim to investigate issues that lack political salience. This is known as the 'Rossi doctrine' after Sir Hugh Rossi the Environment Committee's longstanding chairman who stated:

> 'We decided, as an act of conscious policy, not to become involved in topics which are the subject of major political controversy or which are likely to be debated fully on the floor of the House in any event'.[100]

Ambition and party related influences have significant ramifications for accountability. Several witnesses before the Public Service Committee's inquiry into ministerial accountability and ministerial responsibility stated that while some structural reforms might benefit the system, the most valuable changes would aim to affect the culture of backbench MPs and inject a greater degree of independence. As Philip Norton pointed out, Next Steps brings with it the opportunity to enhance accountability, as has been achieved in other countries. The fact that problems still exist is not specific to Next Steps but to the fundamental nature of the House:

> On the face of it, the changes therefore do not challenge the doctrine of individual ministerial responsibility and, if anything, bring procedures into line with what has been the practice. If there are weaknesses, or potential weaknesses, then they are weaknesses inherent in the system.[101]

Real progress necessitates a change of culture not just by Parliament but by the executive itself. Ministerial responsibility allows the executive to control the supply of witnesses and information to Parliament. As Woodhouse noted: 'There is no overarching reform, other than a fundamental change in attitude by government, that will guarantee better accountability'.[102]

This section has stressed that the underlying realities of power within the Whitehall/Westminster framework must be understood as the context against which the limitations of parliamentary accountability have evolved and currently exist. As Judge notes: 'The paradoxes of the constitution have to be addressed and cannot be resolved by simply asserting the principles of the parliamentary state'.[103] The executive mentality cannot be ignored. Accountability and power are inherently linked. Therefore discussions on the shortcomings of parliamentary accountability and reforms to remedy those deficiencies must take into account the hierarchical configuration of power within Parliament.[104] Parliament is largely a creature of the executive and all the reforms that could be implemented to change the balance of power do not happen because of this fact. As Hennessy noted: '...we sit here and devise these improvements...but in the end it is really rather like expecting ministers not to behave like politicians'.[105] Yet changes have happened. The subtle, yet crucial, issue is that changes have taken place in the accountability process. Mechanisms and relationships have changed but always within the context and against the limitations imposed by the convention of ministerial responsibility. One such change is the codification of relationships and expected standards of behaviour.

2.7 The Codification of Convention

One attempt to overcome perceived deficiencies in ministerial responsibility has been the increasing codification of roles and responsibilities in relation to both ministers and their senior civil servants. Consequently many tacit understandings and rules have now been written down and published.[106] Although not legally enforceable, in a nation that prides itself on the flexibility of its unwritten constitution this is an important development. It is also important for facilitating a change both of culture and working relationships between ministers and their officials.[107] The codification of expectations has also been about maintaining or restoring public confidence in government.[108] Hence it has been as much about reaffirming and clarifying existing standards to allay the scepticism of reformers as about laying down new and more exacting standards.[109]

These documents attempt to specify expected standards of behaviour and dictums which were previously passed down between generations of ministers and officials through a process of osmosis.[110] For example, the rules governing the conduct of ministers are detailed in Questions of Procedure for Ministers (revised and published since June 1997 as the Ministerial Code),[111] the conduct of civil servants in the Civil Service Code[112] and the interaction of civil servants and select committees in the Osmotherly rules.[113] These documents represent a 'normativisation of politics and administration with a view to establishing standards and enhancing accountability'.[114]

For the first time once fluid relationships and tacit understandings are being defined and relative responsibilities outlined. Several commentators have stated that without a legal basis these documents are worthless, but the publication of these documents marks a positive departure from the traditional unwritten nature of British constitutional relationships.[115] As Drewry and Oliver note: 'There are strong pressures to normativize political, managerial and administrative processes, and even non-statutory, extra-legal normativization through the use of quasi-legislation can serve to enhance responsibility and accountability'.[116]

Although the Civil Service Code is not justiciable it does provide a powerful statement of the civil servant's duties against which ministerial behaviour and instructions can be judged. It also empowers an aggrieved official with the right to approach the Civil Service Commissioner.[117] The First Division Association viewed its publication as a 'substantial' advance.[118] It is another, admittedly modest but important, contribution to a new Whitehall in which relationships are increasingly formalised. The proliferation of these documents marks a silent acknowledgement by the executive of the limitations of ministerial responsibility in light of recent bureaucratic reforms and the need to clarify relationships and expected standards of behaviour in an increasingly fragmented state.

But the power relationship between Parliament and the executive has not changed that markedly. When recommendations have been made to make the codes more rigorous and reflective of political realities they have been blocked by the need to uphold ministerial responsibility. For example, the most significant piece of this codification in relation to ministers is Questions of Procedure for Ministers (QPM). For Peter Hennessy this is the 'central strand of DNA which determines the proper conduct of central government' from which the other documents flow.[119] Although its paragraphs dictate a set of honourable principles the problems lie in making the threat of censure a real one. The Committee on Standards in Public Life recognised that as the House was party dominated it is the Prime Minister, as the leader of the majority group, who holds the key to ensuring the accountability to Parliament of ministers. The committee recommended that QPM be amended to reflect this fact and should have the Prime Minister as the central figure. It advocated a revision to the sentence: 'It will be for individual ministers to judge how best to act in order to uphold the highest standards' by adding '...it will be for the Prime Minister to determine whether or not they have done so in any particular circumstance'.[120]

This was the only rejected recommendation contained in Lord Nolan's first report. The spectre of ministerial responsibility descended again with the government arguing: '...it would not reflect the responsibility that ministers should have to justify their conduct to Parliament'.[121] The Public Service Committee took up the issue and sought to emphasise the Prime Minister's responsibility to ensure that ministers accounted to Parliament.[122] They endeavoured to link Prime Ministerial power with the responsibility to ensure that 'ministers live up to the standards required of them' and for the decision as to 'whether their performance is good enough' noting '..the Prime Minister hires and fires them. No one else can'. The government was unmoved:

The government notes this conclusion but continues to believe that the current wording of QPM provides a balanced statement of the proper relationship between a Prime Minister and his ministerial colleagues.[123]

It would seem that neither Parliament nor the Prime Minister is willing to accept responsibility for upholding ministerial standards.[124] Both have attempted to distance themselves from any such obligation, Parliament on the grounds of political reality and the Prime Minister on grounds of constitutional principle. Thus, the codification of ministerial responsibility in QPM seems nonsensical as, without a means of enforcement, the behaviour of ministers remains dependent on their integrity, political circumstances and their relationship with the Prime Minister.

Other documents mark a more stark departure from traditional norms. Framework documents are increasingly prominent and the quasi-contractual public management approach could improve on the traditional position of the senior civil servant who is regulated by anachronistic forms of control by ministers. Indeed:

> It is a fundamental claim of the market based, private sector-derived school of 'new public management' that a well designed managerial analysis of the public service in question can clarify responsibilities and so improve public accountability...[contracts] give organisational and practical form to answering the question of who is responsible for what and on what terms.[125]

Not only is a framework document an attempt to clarify respective responsibilities but it is also a shield that chief executives might use to insulate themselves from ministerial interference. An agency chief executive noted, '...the framework document is the most important document in the relationship. It tells me what my responsibilities are and can be held up, politely, to any minister'. As Derek Lewis proved, officials in the Whitehall no longer have to do the honourable thing and silently disappear. They can attempt to hold the minister to account for failings for which they have been blamed.

Several commentators interpreted the public debacle between Michael Howard and Derek Lewis as a negative incident which underlined the accountability gap existing between ministers and their officials.[126] Conversely, the incident could be interpreted positively: as it entered the public domain, ministerial 'blame shifting' proved problematic and the Home Secretary could not deny his residual responsibility. The significance of this codification of relationships for accountability was clear as Derek Lewis used the framework document to launch a legal challenge to his dismissal. This had dramatic implications for both future agency/minister relations and parliamentary accountability. The court found that Mr Lewis, using his framework document as a formal contract, had the right, subject to the court's supervision, to 'discover' Home Office internal papers relating to Mr Lewis' claims of constant ministerial interference. If the case had not been settled out of court the dispute would have moved from Parliament and into the High Court. In this scenario not only would the incident have been examined in an arena free of party politics but Mr Howard would not have enjoyed the guarantee of party support. Nor would Derek Lewis have been constrained by civil service rules on disclosure.

If the government's modernisation agenda progresses and results in more external appointments to senior civil service positions the traditional relationship between ministers and officials may alter. Senior officials who have not been imbued with the culture of Whitehall, via formal training and career experience, may be less deferential to ministerial pressure. This tendency may be encouraged by the increased use of personal and administrative contracts. In this situation although the limits of ministerial responsibility will theoretically apply their practical force will diminish and chief executives will become more like the semi-independent heads of non-departmental public bodies. As Barker notes:

> This informal political acceptance and the quasi-contractual relationship which flows from it may make some agency chiefs as able to criticise ministers or their departments as the heads of the department's sponsored quangos.[127]

This process of codification or 'normativisation' is in line with the approach to regulating the standards of conduct taken recently in a number of liberal professions.[128] It can be an effective way of introducing strong formal standards into anti-legalistic environments. If a non-statutory approach is to be introduced 'then a set of principles and a Code built around precedents establishes a sound foundation'.[129] While the introduction of rules governing accountability where previously no agreed rules existed is a positive development, its value is undermined without effective parliamentary mechanisms of scrutiny to enforce and uphold the boundaries. The introduction and development of the select committee system was a response to the challenges of enforcing ministerial responsibility in an increasingly large and complex state. It is to the efficacy of these committees that we now turn.

2.8 Select Committees

The fact that the utility of ministerial responsibility had been severely compromised by the emergence of professional political parties and the development of the state had not gone unnoticed by Parliament. From the mid - 1960s onwards discussions raged about the inability of Parliament to hold the executive to account. The solution was seen in the creation of a new committee structure to allow a degree of specialism, increase Parliament's ability to investigate departments and allow for discussion in a constructive and non-partisan way.[130] A number of objections were raised to their creation. Not least that the committees were based on the American model and were therefore not transferable to the Westminster model, that committees would distract attention away from the floor of the House,[131] that they would encourage independence and reduce party discipline,[132] and that committees would undermine the convention of ministerial responsibility to the House.[133] Arguments of this kind were powerful for their emotive force rather than their procedural logic as they negate many of the reasons the committees were being recommended in the first place. Nevertheless, both Labour and Conservative ministers alleged in the 1950s and 1960s that the setting up of select committees was 'incompatible with ministerial responsibility'.[134]

The victory of Harold Wilson in 1966 created the conditions necessary for the modernisation of Parliament and the first system of committees was established. Richard Crossman stated: '...it is a cautious advance in the revival of continual parliamentary control over the executive'.[135] Unfortunately, such comments proved to be overoptimistic as the committees made only limited advances and struggled against departmental obstruction, strict party discipline and tight control of information. As Judge noted: 'The experience of select committees had demonstrated their essential powerlessness in the face of executive recalcitrance'.[136] The creation of the Procedure Committee in 1976 was a recognition of the deep felt concerns of MPs about the poor public reputation of Parliament and the power of the executive.[137] The Procedure Committee noted the extreme nature of the problem:

> ...the essence of the problem...is that the balance of advantage between Parliament and the executive in the day to day working of the constitution is now weighted in favour of the government to a degree which arouses widespread anxiety and is inimical to the working of Parliamentary democracy...a new balance must be struck with the aim of enabling the House as a whole to exercise effective control and stewardship over ministers and their expanding bureaucracy of the modern state for which they are answerable.[138]

The 1978 Procedure committee recommended the select committee structure be reformed and empowered. The select committee structure was duly reformed but no new powers were granted. When Norman St. John Stevas announced the reforms he stated: 'We are embarking upon a series of changes that could constitute the most important parliamentary reforms of the century'.[139] When Gavin Drewry gave evidence to the Procedure Committee a decade later he remarked:

> I have often wondered when I have read and re-read Norman St John Stevas's original speech in setting up the committees, whether his tongue was in his cheek when he spoke about redressing the balance of power.[140]

One of the main limitations on the effectiveness of the committees has, ironically, been the convention of ministerial responsibility. The executive has consistently stressed the convention as the basis on which the relationship between ministers, civil servants and select committees are built: 'Select committees exercise their formal powers to inquire into policies and actions of departments by virtue of the accountability of ministers to Parliament'.[141] In response Parliament stressed that it, and not the executive, is sovereign: 'Select committees exercise their formal powers to inquire into policy and actions of departments because Parliament is sovereign and has established the select committees to monitor government departments on its behalf'.[142] The differences are fundamental and represent the negative executive mentality using a convention that is supposed to secure accountability to limit accountability. The executive is implying that the committees are defined by the convention and can only call ministers and officials to account within the conventional framework of ministerial responsibility. The committees are stressing the sovereignty of Parliament and its inherent right to scrutinise and control the government. As Woodhouse notes:

> This suggests a paradoxical situation in which the conventional mechanism through which ministers account to Parliament also acts to restrict that accountability which is exercised before committees.[143]

As noted above, the advent of agencies did not formally alter the convention of ministerial responsibility and, therefore, the position of ministers and civil servants appearing before select committees. This has proved problematic, and committees have consistently called for accountability to follow responsibility rather than being separated from it. The Public Service Committee noted: '...we recommend that the Osmotherly rules are amended to indicate that agency chief executives should give evidence to select committees on matters which are delegated to them in the framework document'.[144] Without such a move Bogdanor believes: 'Agencies will serve to obscure, not to clarify, the true chain of accountability'.[145] Sir Peter Kemp, the Next Steps project manager who was opposed to such a reform, has stated:

> Let agencies loose from their parent departments...and turn them into free-standing units accountable to ministers and Parliament in their own right...a new form of delegation from ministers, recognised by Parliament, would allow chief executives to be held directly accountable to select committees for delegated authority.[146]

The government has refused to yield and legitimates this stance through recourse to the convention of ministerial responsibility.[147] Ministers are adamant that independent account giving by officials is unconstitutional (as well as politically hazardous). Chief executives are bound by the Osmotherly rules which allow them to be publicly questioned by select committees but may render them unable to defend themselves against implicit or explicit criticism.[148] Without ministerial approval they cannot reveal the impact of underresourcing or the effect a switch in policy priorities had on the ability of the agency to achieve its targets. Ministerial intervention may be extensive, especially in politically sensitive fields. Indeed, Roger Freeman highlighted that the obligation to account to

Parliament obliged ministers to '...look and question and even to intervene in the operation of the agency if public or parliamentary concerns justify it'.[149] Intervention is therefore '...the right - indeed, the responsibility - of ministers'.[150] He accepted that with extensive ministerial intervention the operations of an agency '...may become his [the minister's] responsibility and not the chief executive's and therefore the minister might have to resign due to operational failings'.[151] But the point at which responsibility changes hands is uncertain, especially without a procedure for recording and monitoring intervention.[152]

The Conservative government argued that far from improving accountability the appearance of civil servants on their own behalf would confuse accountability. Parliament will not know who to blame when accountability is inadequate and '...the direct accountability of ministers to Parliament will not be as comprehensive and clear as it should be'.[153] But such an argument is grounded in the rather suspect premise that ministerial responsibility is at present comprehensive and clear. There is one distinguished precedent for making civil servants directly accountable to Parliament for clearly specified aspects of their work. Accounting officers are directly responsible for the regularity and propriety of their organisation's expenditure before the Public Accounts Committee.[154] The ability to issue notes of reservation about value for money as well as about the legality of expenditure, most famously in the Pergau Dam affair, introduces a new dimension into the civil servant/minister relationship.[155] It also increases Parliament's influence as it implies that incumbents who fail to issue a note may later be held to account. The example of accounting officers highlights that that the relationship between ministers, civil servants and Parliament have changed with a move towards a *de facto* form of direct accountability appearing to work effectively.

The government's arguments for refusing to allow accountability to follow responsibility are unconvincing, fuelling suspicions that they are designed to protect ministers from the repercussions of a more comprehensive accountability. But the theory needs to be separated from the practice. The rules that underpin the convention are often overlooked.[156] Lord Howe believes that the gulf between theory and practice is such that 'Ministerial responsibility has been diminished and a new form of accountability, between the head of the executive agency and Parliament or society, has been created'.[157] A view the Public Service Committee concurred with:

> The practice of the House in relation to agencies has already moved a good distance from the conventional position...what happens in practice has evolved considerably in advance of the theory enshrined in the Osmotherly rules.[158]

Peter Kemp noted: 'Whatever the formalities of a chief executive answering "on behalf of the minister" or otherwise, in practice a good chief executive will answer the questions that are put to him or her'.[159] Research suggests that external appointees may be reluctant to be constrained by the rules of the traditional civil service.[160] Despite extensive academic literature on the theoretical limitations of the Osmotherly rules, the practical limitations deserve examination.[161] A stark variance between theory and practice would undermine the status and authority of ministerial responsibility. It also would raise questions concerning why the executive is so reluctant to bring theory into line with reality which, in turn, perpetuates the notion that the convention is simply a facade behind which the executive can retreat in times of difficulty.

The convention of ministerial accountability also dictates that officials appear before committees only with the consent of the minister: '...it is customary for ministers to decide which officials should represent them'.[162] Sir Richard Scott found this an obstacle when he tried to secure the attendance of two retired Department of Trade and Industry officials.[163] In relation to Next Steps it is doubtful whether a minister could prevent the appearance of a chief executive as the heightened visibility of the position and clear delegation of power would make it impossible for the minister to argue that operational issues were not their responsibility. Indeed, since the creation of agencies no chief executive has been stopped from appearing in front of a select committee. The Treasury & Civil Service Committee, in its 1990 report on the Next Steps initiative, declared itself satisfied that chief executives were accountable to the committees.[164] Despite this, commentators vigorously advocate that the formal position of chief executives should be changed to officially recognise this direct accountability to Parliament.[165] But a general direct accountability would mark a radical departure from the traditional constitutional minister/civil servant relationships and raise fundamental questions which have, as yet, hardly been considered. Should officials become directly accountable for operational affairs, ministers may be relieved of the need to keep a close eye on the day-to-day operation of the agency, but would this not lead to them becoming divorced from the operational considerations that ought to shape policy formulation? As Bogdanor eloquently states: 'Would not the Cabinet, as a result, be in danger of becoming merely a collection of disembodied wraiths brooding in glorious and isolated impotence in a void, and quite removed from political realities?'.[166]

The First Divisions Association has warmed to the idea of direct accountability, largely since Scott, but urges caution: 'What we are saying is that the *status quo* cannot be allowed to prevail because it is profoundly unsatisfactory. What does that [direct accountability to Parliament] do to the political neutrality of the Civil Service? What does it do to the relationships with ministers?'.[167] Would the chief executive be able to criticise the minister in defence of their agency? As Lord Nolan noted: 'For a civil servant to criticise a minister in that way would be heretical; but then again chief executives are not intended to be conventional'.[168]

In opposition the Labour Party implied that they would both abolish the Osmotherly rules and introduce direct accountability.[169] Ann Taylor outlined this to the Public Service Committee:

> I think there is a very specific problem so far as agencies and quangos are concerned, because they are said by ministers to be arms-length and to be free standing. Therefore, I think they should have some degree of direct accountability, not just to a minister but to a select committee. I think that the head of any such quango should, in fact, be making an annual report, or an annual appearance before a select committee, so that they can be questioned directly, without the head of the quango or that chief executive of an agency having to get ministerial approval and following the ministerial line. We cannot have a situation where the minister is saying that there is an arms-length responsibility and then not have direct accountability from the executive head to the select committee.[170]

Just as it would be wrong to conclude that the disparity between the practice and the neo-Diceyan doctrine of accountability is a recent phenomenon, it would also be wrong to believe that the capability of select committees to enforce accountable government has been undermined solely by the reinvention of government. New public management has simply highlighted the inherent weaknesses that have always existed. Committees operate in a unique environment that is replete with restrictions and obstacles to their effectiveness (political, procedural, constitutional and resource issues). They are also inadequately assimilated into the parliamentary process. For example, Gregory found that between

1979 and 1995 the departmental select committees produced over 500 reports, only 4 of which were debated on the floor of the House and subsequently voted on.[171]

Some of these deficiencies could only be removed or diminished with the support of the government, while many theoretically could be addressed by the committees independently. For example, committees have few resources in terms of support staff and research capabilities. It has been suggested that the effectiveness of committees to scrutinise ministers and officials would be enhanced if either the research capacity provided by the National Audit Office to the Public Accounts Committee were extended to all committees[172] or they had their own substantial research budgets.[173] But to increase the budgets of the committees would necessitate a vote in the House that would be unlikely to receive government, and therefore majority, support. The government is unlikely to make its job of governing any harder.

Some obstacles could be lifted independently of the government if the committees employed the powers they already have. For example, committees have expressed a desire to play a role in appointments to agencies,[174] others have suggested they play a role in the drafting of framework documents.[175] Although time constraints may prevent committees taking on these extra roles, in practice ministers are reluctant to surrender powers to backbenchers but, as the Treasury Select Committee has proved, Parliament and not the executive is sovereign.[176] Many of the advocated reforms are already well within the formal powers of committees. The barrier to their use is that MPs are loyal to their party before Parliament. As one former Leader of the House noted: '...committees could do virtually all the things I am asked about if that is what they wanted to do'.[177] For example, Sir Richard Scott has urged committees to make more use of their contempt proceedings.[178] Peter Hennessy and Philip Norton have stressed that the Osmotherly rules are Whitehall and not parliamentary rules and therefore committees should refuse to be bound by them.[179] But this would require an unrealistic shift in the mentality of backbench MPs, involving a transfer of primary allegiance from party to Parliament. This section has highlighted a number of limitations connected with the ability of select committees to enforce ministerial responsibility. If the case study supports the existence of these deficiencies, then the operation of other mechanisms of parliamentary accountability assumes a greater weight. One such mechanism is parliamentary questions.

2.9 Parliamentary Questions

The debate over parliamentary questions encapsulates the challenges associated with reconciling the conflicting tensions associated with balancing the centrifugal pressures of devolved management with the centripetal pressures of ministerial responsibility. With the announcement of the Next Steps programme a central concern was how exactly it would affect the accountability of the executive through the medium of parliamentary questions.[180] (This fact is intriguing given that surveys suggest that MPs do not hold PQs in high regard and that larger constitutional issues were left unresolved.)[181] When Mrs Thatcher made the original statement in the House, several supplementary questions examined the issue of PQs on areas of government which were to be delegated to agencies. Mrs Thatcher insisted there would be no changes. It quickly became apparent that this was not the case.

When MPs had an operational grievance they were encouraged to direct their question, in the first instance, directly to the agency: '...members of Parliament may wish to approach agencies directly about enquiries concerning operational matters'.[182] This quickly became the established practice and was written into the framework documents. (Evidence, according to some, that the Efficiency Unit regarded parliamentary accountability largely as a disbenefit in the administrative process.)[183] The trend towards the devolution of explanatory and informatory accountability is in line with the original aims of Next Steps.[184] But this development may bring certain dangers in that ministers may seek to remove themselves from operational affairs altogether although the right to take the issue to a minister may prevent this. Written questions, and parliamentary correspondence, provide ministers with a constant indicator of salient issues and problems. 'A minister's mailbag may therefore serve as a form of barometer, alerting ministers to problems that are building up.'[185]

A particular concern was that the answers to written PQs which were redirected to chief executives were not included in Hansard.[186] The Treasury and Civil Service Committee asked the government to examine this issue.[187] The government provided assurances that in future all answers by chief executives would be placed in the Commons library but due to a number of administrative and resource issues this process proved unsatisfactory.[188] Critics argued that Hansard was available and utilised by a large number of external research bodies and academics and that as ministers no longer answered these specific questions and the chief executives' replies were not placed in Hansard there was an overall reduction in public accountability.

In 1992 the government accepted the House Administration Committee recommendation that answers from chief executives be published in Hansard.[189] They appear under a standard form of reply by the relevant minister thus maintaining the constitutional rule that Hansard is only for ministerial replies. This maintains the chimera of ministerial responsibility, when in fact a new form of direct written accountability has developed.[190] The fact that answers appear 'through ministers' is typical of the unresolved tension between a new line of direct accountability and the executive's commitment to traditional notions of ministerial responsibility.[191] Not everyone is satisfied with the present arrangements.[192] Rose noted:

> Where once ministers took responsibility for the actions of their departments with their signatures on letters and answers in Parliament, now they leave it to the mysterious and proliferating cadre of agency chief executives...even in Hansard, the chief executives' letters have usurped ministerial replies to written questions.[193]

Although Rose overlooks the right to demand a ministerial answer, he is right to highlight that uncertainties remain about the way in which the system operates. It is not known whether a particular reply has come directly from the chief executive or has been approved or amended by the minister; the practice varies from agency to agency.[194] The Conservative government refused to adopt measures that would introduce transparency to the system.[195] This flexibility and opaqueness means that a wrong assumption may be drawn about the responsibility for a reply, especially where a chief executive's answer is amended by the minister without recognition. The refusal of the last government to clarify the system highlights the nature of the constitutional power relationship in which the executive decides the rules of the game. It also 'suggests that its interests are served by imprecision rather than clarity'.[196]

Jack Straw has announced that in future a Home Office minister and not the Director General of the Prison Service will answer all written questions. He told the House: 'I regard it as essential that ministers should answer personally to the House for what is done in our prisons and not leave the matter to their civil servants'.[197] But the Home Secretary has been careful to add: 'This should not be taken as a trigger for resignation when there has been a problem or you would get through five or six Home Secretaries in the space of a week'.[198] This acknowledges the current confusion. It concedes that the agency model with accountability along the lines of the Waldegrave model (where the informatory, explanatory and even sacrificial elements of ministerial responsibility are delegated to identified civil servants) is inadequate and that the system, as currently conceived, cannot operate with any new form of direct accountability for civil servants. Jack Straw's decision also highlights the incoherence and *ad hoc* nature of the accountability processes in central government. Other agencies have been as, if not more, problematic since their creation, for example the Child Benefit Agency, yet they continue to answer written questions on behalf of the minister. It is also disputable whether the reform will actually increase the level of accountability, as, paradoxically, emphasising ministerial responsibility may well make the answers more defensive and incomplete. It would simply be replacing the constitutional veneer that has failed so spectacularly in the past.

Although written questions are heavily employed by MPs, a common criticism is that answers are rarely extensive, consequently necessitating multiple questions and the piecing together of information through a series of questions. Norman Baker MP, one of the most prolific tablers of questions in the current Parliament (averaging five each parliamentary day) noted:

> Questions are one of the only ways MPs have of calling the executive to account. It is not a very effective way because they obfuscate and you have to keep going back again. If they want me to ask fewer questions then they should stop stalling.[199]

But the perceived need of backbenchers to table a high volume of written questions creates important financial, resource and structural questions especially for those departments and agencies that receive a high degree of parliamentary attention. Either directly or indirectly, accountability costs. According to the most recent Treasury estimate researching and drafting replies to a written question or oral question costs £112 and £260 respectively.[200] (On this basis Norman Baker's inquisitiveness, tabling 859 written questions between May 1997 and March 1998, cost slightly under £100,000.) The costs are largely borne by the organisation under investigation and although the financial costs are substantial the overall burden, in terms of staff time and senior management involvement, can become excessive to the point of having a pathological impact on the organisation. For most organisations answering questions and parliamentary correspondence is unproblematic. Where responding does not impact on the core aim of the body nor consume large resources then parliamentary attention can be positive.[201] Agencies subject to intense and regular parliamentary attention will need to develop a structural capacity to respond to this external interest. Several of the larger and politically sensitive agencies have created parliamentary groups or correspondence units, the Benefits Agency[202] and the Child Support Agency, for example.[203] These 'pathological organisational effects' represent the clash between the downward accountability these bodies were supposed to create and the traditional upward accountability to ministers and Parliament which was never formally or coherently adapted in line with the arms - length principle.[204]

Oral questions in the House epitomise the relationship between the mechanisms for ensuring accountable government and the adversarial context in which those mechanisms are used.[205] As Sir Richard Scott noted:

> Disentangling is the key to the problem. It surprised me when witnesses described PQs as a game - that is the antithesis of democratic accountability. On the other hand it would be naive not to see some realism in the point.

The scarcity of literature on oral questions reflects the general impression that oral questions are little more than part of the theatre of Parliament, a game of 'political knockabout'.[206] Lord Howe listed the true aims of oral PQs: '...to secure damaging admissions, to secure damaging refusals, to secure damaging denials, to contrast the response of the minister with that which we wanted to offer, and so on, and very seldom were we actually after facts'.[207] Such observations about the purpose of oral questions are not new, but the fact that such politically aggressive questioning receives limited, defensive and largely uninformative replies impacts upon the overall level of accountability and further undermines the status of the House.[208]

Questions in the House do have one key value in that they are non-negotiable in terms of ministerial responsibility. While ministers might seek to deconstruct their own responsibility in their answers, it is ministers, and ministers only, who must stand at the despatch box and account to Parliament for their departments. But oral questions, like other processes, are often not used by Parliament to force an account but by ministers to make a statement or put new issues on the agenda. They are frequently a tool of the executive rather than Parliament.[209] In 1990 stringent rules were introduced to outlaw the 'syndication'[210] of oral questions but within a year the principal clerk responsible for questions reported that 'syndication is alive and well'.[211] When the former Trade and Industry minister Nigel Griffiths was discovered writing his own parliamentary questions for 'safe' MPs to put to him coverage centred on the foolishness of the minister in getting exposed rather than there being anything wrong with what he had been doing.[212] Reforms have been advanced to increase the effectiveness of oral questions: the establishment of a parliamentary commissioner to monitor both refusals to answer and replies,[213] or the secondment of civil servants to the opposition to help draft questions,[214] for example, but they have not received, and are unlikely to receive, the executive's support. Yet it would be wrong to give credence to the view that oral questions are irrelevant. Woodhouse has demonstrated that questions in the House can be troublesome for ministers, especially unsolicited questions from a minister's own party.[215] Therefore the utility of oral questions might be defined by a minister's standing in their party rather than the power of Parliament. This suggestion raises an innovative and under-researched perspective on the accountability of ministers to Parliament - the relationship between the executive and their parliamentary party. Do the channels and processes through which ministers communicate with their backbenchers, to ensure and retain their confidence, undermine or support the parliamentary mechanisms of scrutiny?

2.10 Conclusion

This chapter has traced the origins of the convention of ministerial responsibility and stressed its influence on both the structure of the state and the procedures of Parliament. It has suggested that although concerns regarding the utility of the convention are long standing they have become particularly acute in recent years. This is due both to the evolution of the state and the dominance of the executive within the House of Commons. The increasingly complex configuration of central government combined with the widespread adoption of devolved management has become increasingly hard to reconcile within a credible framework of ministerial responsibility. Consequently, a distinction has emerged between ministerial accountability and ministerial responsibility. While this refinement can be interpreted as an attempt to modernise a convention that was designed to regulate a far simpler system of government it has been criticised for obscuring responsibility and facilitating ministerial 'blame shift'. Moreover, it is possible to construct a body of evidence that supports Judge's thesis that the principles of ministerial responsibility - openness and accountability - have been inverted.[216] The executive mentality manipulates the convention to legitimate the maintenance of an arcane and closed system of government. Other aspects of the British constitution, particularly Crown prerogative powers and the lack of an effective system of public law, sustain this equilibrium.

The enduring centrality of ministerial responsibility within the British constitution is explained by reference to the fact that it ensures the maintenance of the executive's dominant position between elections. Indeed, this book will demonstrate how a range of reforms have been introduced within an increasingly tenuous framework of ministerial responsibility to retain this advantage. This chapter has been largely critical of the mechanisms of parliamentary oversight. A number of factors combine to reduce the effectiveness of these processes and yet it would be wrong to assume that Parliament did not matter. Parliament is critical as the focus of political power in the Westminster model due to its provision of a framework for legitimate state action. Ministerial responsibility is a central element of this framework. And yet the executive's *de facto* control of the efficacy of the convention allows the executive to define the boundaries of legitimate action. (Conversely, this orthodoxy allows recommendations that challenge the convention of ministerial responsibility to be interpreted and rejected as constitutionally illegitimate.) Indeed, a central claim of this book is that the development of alternative forms of accountability has been circumscribed by the executive's insistence on the centrality of ministerial responsibility.

It is, however, necessary to provide evidence and verify the suggestions made within this chapter. Do the shortcomings in parliamentary accountability which have been identified really exist in practice? Are they as acute as the wider literature would suggest? Do certain mechanisms of parliamentary scrutiny have powers and advantages which have been overlooked? Are there critical processes which have been ignored or overlooked by legislative research? These questions are examined in Chapter Three, which provides a case study of parliamentary oversight of the Home Office.

Notes

[1] See, for instance, the special editions of *Public Law* (Autumn 1996) *Parliamentary Affairs* (Vol.50 No.1 1996) and *Public Administration* (Vol.74 No.4 1996) on the topic.

[2] As Peter Barberis notes: 'New Public Management, while not itself the root cause of such disparity, has nevertheless both exacerbated and further exposed existing fault lines'. (1998) 'The New Public Management and New Accountability' *Public Administration* Vol.76 p.451.

[3] Lord Nolan, Second Radcliffe Lecture, University of Warwick 21/11/96.

[4] Landers, B (1998) 'Of Ministers, Mandarins and Managers' in Flinders, M V & Smith, M J (eds.) *Quangos, Accountability and Reform: The Politics of Quasi-Government* (London : Macmillan).

[5] Harding, L, Leigh, D & Pallister, D (1997) *The Liar* (London : Penguin).

[6] HC 115 *Report of the Inquiry into the Export of Defence Equipment and Dual-Use Goods to Iraq and Related Prosecutions* Session 1995/96, HMSO, London. [The Scott Report].

[7] Cm 2850 (1995) *First Report of the Committee on Standards in Public Life* HMSO, London. [The Nolan Report].

[8] HC 313 (1996/97).

[9] HC 67 *Government Response to the Second Report from the Committee (Session 1995-96) on Ministerial Responsibility and Accountability* First Special Report by the Public Service Select Committee, Session 1996/97, HMSO, London.

10   HC 300 *Shifting the Balance: Select Committees and the Executive*, First Report of the Liaison Committee, Session 1999-2000, HMSO, London; Cm 4737 (2000) *The Government's Response to the First Report from the Liaison Committee on Shifting the Balance: Select Committees and the Executive*, HMSO, London; HC 748 *Independence or Control?* Second Report of the Liaison Committee, Session 1999-2000, HMSO, London.

11   This recommendation was made by the Treasury & Civil Service Committee (HC 27 *The Role of the Civil Service* Fifth Report by the Treasury and Civil Service Committee, Session 1993/94, HMSO, London. para. 171) and by the Public Service Committee (HC 313 (1996/97) para.19-20 p.1xxxii) but was rejected both times in the subsequent government response. See HC 67 (1996/97) para.19-20 p.xii.

12   See Lewis, N & Longley, D (1996) 'Ministerial Responsibility: The Next Steps' *Public Law* pp.490-508.

13   Quoted in Parris, H (1969) *Constitutional Bureaucracy* (London: Allen & Unwin).

14   Greenleaf, W (1987) *The British Political Tradition Vol.3 'A Much Governed Nation'* (London : Methuen) p.131.

15   See Cole, M (forthcoming) 'Quangos: The Debate of the 1970s in Britain' *Twentieth Century British History*.

16   Foster, C (1996) 'Reflections on the True Significance of the Scott Report for Government Accountability' *Public Administration* Vol. 74 No.4 pp.567-592.

17   Cobbett, W (1823) *Rural Rides* Everyman No.66 (Harmondsworth : Penguin), quoted in Greenleaf, W (1987) *The British Political Tradition: Vol.III A Much Governed Nation* (London : Methuen) p.814. In 1920 Sidney and Beatrice Webb wrote the convention was 'illusory as an instrument of democratic control'. *A Constitution for the Socialist Commonwealth of Great Britain'* (London : Longmans) p.170 quoted in Barberis, P (1998) 'The New Public Management and a New Accountability' *Public Administration* Vol. 76 p.453.

18   Finer, S (1956) 'The Individual Responsibility of Ministers' *Public Administration* Vol.34 pp.377-396. Finer's work has recently been validated by Dowding, K & Kang, W (1998) 'Ministerial Resignations 1945-97' *Public Administration* Vol. 76 pp.411-429.

19   H.L. Debs. 5/9/1893, Vol.17. Cols. 33-34.

20   Maitland, F (1908) *The Constitutional History of England* (Cambridge : Cambridge University Press) p.380.

21   For example, Lord John Russell in 1855 and Lord Ellenborough in 1858.

22   Swinhoe, K (1971) *A Study of the Opinion About the Reform of the House of Commons Procedure 1945-68* Unpublished PhD Thesis, University of Leeds.

[23] Taken from Birch, A. (1964) *Representative and Responsible Government* (London : Unwin) p.75.
[24] Power, G (2000) *Creating a Working Parliament* (London : Hansard) pp.6-7
[25] Woodhouse, D (1994) *Ministers and Parliament: Accountability in Theory and Practice* (Oxford : Oxford University Press) p.12.
[26] Marquand, D (1995) *The State in Context: Travails of an Ancien Regime* (Swindon : ESRC/RSA).
[27] See Parris, H (1969) *Constitutional Bureaucracy* (London : Allen Unwin) p.82.
[28] Fraser, P (1960) 'The Growth of Ministerial Control in the Nineteenth Century House of Commons' *English Historical Review* Vol.75 pp.444-463.
[29] HC 27-II (1993/94) Memorandum by the Cabinet Office.
[30] HC 313-III (1996/97) Evidence by Sir Robert Butler, p.151 Q.872.
[31] HC 27-II (1993/94) Memorandum by the Cabinet Office.
[32] The modern interpretation of Crichel Down suggests that, despite the rhetoric at the time, Sir Thomas Dugdale's resignation owed more to his adherence to a policy which was unpopular with his party than to an acceptance of vicarious responsibility. See Nicholson, I (1986) *The Mystery of Crichel Down* (Oxford : Clarendon); Griffith, J (1987) 'A Commentary on Crichel Down' *Contemporary Record* Vol.1 No.1 pp.35-40.
[33] 'No post-war case has involved such an assumption and it can be said with confidence that the convention of ministerial responsibility contains no requirement of any such vicarious responsibility' Marshall, G (1986) *Constitutional Conventions* (Oxford : Clarendon) p.65.
[34] Brown, R (1955) *The Battle for Crichel Down* (London : Bodley Head) p.113.
[35] 'Under our constitutional practice, executive powers are conferred by Parliament on ministers of the Crown. Both in regard to these powers and to others which derive from the prerogative and not from statute it has long been the established constitutional practice that the appropriate minister of the Crown is responsible to Parliament for every action in pursuance of them.' PRO, CAB 130/102 (Gen 471/3).
[36] Note how, in evidence to the Public Service Committee, the Office of Public Service rewrites these texts but adds in brackets when the author wrote 'responsible' they really meant 'accountable'. HC 313-III (1996/97) pp.187-191.
[37] Hansard HC Debs. 20/7/54, cols. 1286-7.
[38] Oliver, D & Drewry, G (1996) *Public Service Reforms: Issues of Accountability and Public Law* (London : Pinter) p.7.
[39] Although this pronouncement is often cited as evidence that the distinction is not new but has always existed: 'In the government's view, a minister is accountable to Parliament for everything which goes on within his department, in the sense that Parliament can call the minister to account for

it, but a minister cannot sensibly be held responsible for everything which goes on in his department'. Cm 2748 (1995) *The Civil Service. Taking Forward Continuity and Change* HMSO, London. pp.27-28.

40 HC 313-II (1996/97) Memorandum by Prof. Rodney Brazier, p.1.

41 Hansard, HC Debs. 24/10/83 cols. 23-24. Sir Douglas Wass was under no doubts as to the beginning of the problems with ministerial responsibility: 'The watershed seemed to be Jim Prior's abdication of responsibility after the Maze escape in 1983. That was an unfortunate landmark'. Interview with the author, June 1996.

42 Woodhouse, D (1994) *Ministers and Parliament: Accountability in Theory and Practice* (Oxford : Clarendon) pp.153-161.

43 Claiming such a division had: '...been recognised for years, indeed generations' Hansard, HC Debs. 10/1/95. See Barker, A (1996) *Political Responsibility for UK Prison Security: Ministers Escape Again* Essex papers in politics and government. No.106.

44 'The kernel of Sir Robin's point, I think, is that the conduct of government has become so complex and the need for ministerial delegation of responsibilities to and reliance on the advice of officials has become so inevitable as to render unreal the attaching of blame to a minister simply because something has gone wrong in the department of which he is in charge. For my part I find it difficult to disagree.' HC 115 Vol.IV, K8.15 & K8.16, pp.1805-6. See also: HC 313-III (1996/97) Evidence by Lord Howe, Q266 and; HC 313-ll (1996/97) Memorandum by Prof. Rodney Brazier, p.12 para. 7.3, who notes: 'The distinction should be accepted between ministerial accountability and ministerial responsibility.'

45 Quoted in Marr, A (1995) *Ruling Britannia: The Failure and Future of British Democracy* (London : Michael Joseph) pp. 259-260.

46 HC 313-I (1996/97) para. 21.

47 Mather, G (1996) 'Clarifying Responsibility and Accountability' in CIPFA *Government Accountability* (London : CIPFA) p.21.

48 A problem associated with the nationalised industries from where this division was imported.

49 First Division Association (1996) *Accountability in Government: An FDA Discussion Paper* (London : FDA).

50 HC 27-I (1993-4) para.171.

51 HC 27-III (1993/94) Memorandum by Dr Patricia Greer.

52 HC 313 (1996/97) p.IXXX para.1 & para. 21.

53 HC 67 (1996/97) p.VI para.1. See also Cm 2748 (1995) p.28.

54 HC 313-III (1996/97) Evidence by Sir Peter Kemp, p.108 para.9.

55 Sir Peter later apologised for using this term and defined it as meaning: '...the aim of reconciling in practical terms the long - standing constitutional theory that ministers are ultimately responsible for everything that happens within the Civil Service with the realities of the complexity of today's public administration'. HC 313-lll (1996/97) p.120 Q725.
56 HC 313-III (1996/97) Evidence by Mr Graham Mather p.121.
57 HC 115 (1995/96) K8.16 p.1806.
58 See Judge, D (1983) 'Considerations on Parliamentary Reform' in Judge, D (ed.) *The Politics of Parliamentary Reform* (London : Heinemann) p.190.
59 In 1982 Hugo Young and Ann Sloman wrote that the Osmotherly rules ensure that civil servants: '...told the truth and nothing but the truth, but certainly not the whole truth'. *No, Minister* (London : BBC) p.64.
60 Cabinet Office (1988) *Improving Management in Government: The Next Steps* [The Ibbs Report]
61 This idea was remarkably similar to Lord Fulton's recommendation made 20 years earlier when he had advocated the creation of 'management units'. Cmnd 3638 (1968) *The Civil Service. Vol.1 Report of the Committee 1966-68* HMSO, London. [The Fulton Report] para.150.
62 Lewis, N (1994) 'Reviewing Change in Government: New Public Management and the Next Steps' *Public Law* pp.105-113.
63 Cabinet Office (1988) *Improving Management in Government: The Next Steps* para.7.
64 Cabinet Office (1988) *Improving Management in Government: The Next Steps* para.44.
65 Cabinet Office (1988) *Improving Management in Government: The Next Steps* para.23.
66 Hansard HC Debs. 1988 Vol.127 col. 1149.
67 Hansard HC Debs. 1988 Vol.127 col. 1151.
68 HC 494-II *Civil Service Management Reform: The Next Steps* Eighth Report by the Treasury & Civil Service Select Committee, Session 1987/88, HMSO, London. pp.10-11.
69 HC 494-III (1987/88) p.60.
70 Sir Peter Kemp stated rather curiously that '...the mechanics may change' (HC 494-I [1987/88] Q.36) and Sir Robin Butler confused matters by commenting: 'I think that the structure of accountability remains; its operation will be changed'. (HC 494-II [1987/88] Q.277).
71 Judge, D (1993) *The Parliamentary State* (London : Sage) p.150 . See HC 494 (1987/88) p.xvii.
72 HC 313-III (1996/97) Evidence by Sir Peter Kemp p.108 para.6.
73 HC 313-III (1996/97) Evidence by Sir Peter Kemp p.115 Q703.

[74] See RIPA (1991) *The Civil Service Reformed: The Next Steps Initiative* (London : RIPA).

[75] By February 1992 some 57 agencies, along with 32 Executive Units in Customs and Excise, together employing 230,360 officials were already in existence.

[76] See HC 494 (1987/88) p.ix; Smith, J (1991) 'The Public Service Ethos' *Public Administration* Vol.69 No.4 pp.515-523; Hansard HC Debs. 20/5/91 cols. 668-696.

[77] Cm 524 *Civil Service Management Reform: the Next Steps: Government Reply to the Eighth Report from the Treasury & Civil Service Committee (1987-88)* HMSO, London. para. 9.

[78] Sir Ivor Jennings noted that ministers cannot blame their civil servants when things go wrong because '...if the minister could blame the civil servant, then the civil servant would require the power to blame the minister'. Jennings, I (1966) *The British Constitution* 5th ed. (Cambridge : Cambridge University Press) p.149.

[79] The recommendation was originally made by the Treasury & Civil Service Committee. At HC 494 (1987/88) p.xxii.

[80] See Cm 1761 (1991) *The Next Steps Initiative: Government Reply to the Seventh Report from the TCSC* HMSO, London. p.11.

[81] Smith, M (1996) 'Reforming the State' in Ludlam, S & Smith, M (eds.) *Contemporary British Conservatism* (London : Macmillan).

[82] HC 313-II (1996/97) Memorandum by Dr Philip Giddings p.27 para.3.5.

[83] The Carltona doctrine will be discussed further in Chapter 4. See Freedland, M (1996) 'The rule against delegation and the Carltona doctrine in an agency context' *Public Law* pp.19-31.

[84] See Lord Nolan, Second Radcliffe Lecture, University of Warwick 21/11/96.

[85] Freedland, M (1994) 'Government by Contract and Public Law' *Public Law* p.94.

[86] In this respect they differ from NDPBs which are legally separate from the departments that sponsor them. See HC 313-II (1996/97) Evidence by Prof. Alan Page pp.34-35.

[87] Cabinet Office (1988) *Improving Management in Government: The Next Steps* para.29. According to Peter Hennessy, Sir Robin Ibbs had wanted, in the original unpublished report, '...a change in the British constitution, by law if necessary, to quash the fiction that ministers can be genuinely responsible for everything done by officials in their name'. Quoted in Hennessy, P (1989) *Whitehall* (London : Secker & Warburg) p.620.

[88] Dudley, G (1994) 'The Next Steps Agencies, Political Salience and the Arms Length Principle' *Public Administration* Vol.72 pp.219-240.

89   A point made by Richard Mottram. See HC 313-III (1996/97) Q967 p.166.
90   Peter Hennessy has termed this the 'good chaps theory of government'. See Hennessy, P (1996) *The Hidden Wiring: Unearthing the British Constitution* (London : Victor Gollanz) p.57.
91   For light relief, see Riddell, P (1993) *Honest Opportunism: The Rise of the Career Politician* (London : Hamish Hamilton).
92   Piper, J (1991) 'British Backbench Rebellion and Government Appointments' *Legislative Studies Quarterly* Vol.26 No.2 pp.24-28. See also: Hennessy, P (1996) 'Teething the Watchdogs: Parliament, Government and Accountability' in Hennessy, P (1996) *Muddling Through* (London : Indigo) pp.63-80.
93   Lord Nolan, First Radcliffe Lecture, Warwick University, 7/11/96.
94   Hansard HC Debs. 5/5/36 col.1552. See Winetrobe, B (1997) 'Inquiries after Scott: The Return of the Tribunal of Inquiry' *Public Law* pp.61-75.
95   Hansard HC Debs. 5/5/36 col.1554.
96   See Turpin, C (1989) 'Ministerial Responsibility: Myth or Reality?' in Jowell, J & Oliver, D *The Changing Constitution* (Oxford : Clarendon).
97   Giddings, P (1997) 'Parliament and the Executive' *Parliamentary Affairs* Vol.50 No.1 p.84.
98   HC 115 (1995/96) 15/2/96 at D4.61.
99   Anthony King has suggested that British politics struggles under the weight of a 'surfeit of partisanship'. King, A (1996) *Is Britain a Well Governed Country?* Paper given to the Lloyds TSB Forum 5/6/96.
100 Quoted in Butler, D, Adonis, A & Travers, T (1994) *Failure in British Government* (Oxford : Oxford University Press) p.230
101 HC 313-II (1996/97) Memorandum by Prof. Philip Norton p.74.
102 HC 313-II (1996/97) Memorandum by Dr Diane Woodhouse p.60.
103 Judge, D (1993) *The Parliamentary State* (London : Sage) p.215.
104 See Judge, D (1981) *Backbench Specialisation in the House of Commons* (London : Heinemann) pp.186-203; Judge, D (1983) 'Considerations on Parliamentary Reform' in Judge, D (ed.) *The Politics of Parliamentary Reform* (Heinemann : London) pp.186-195; Judge, D (1989) 'Parliament in the 1980s' *Political Quarterly* Vol.60 No.4 pp.400-412.
105 HC 313-III (1996/97) Evidence by Prof. Peter Hennessy p.17 Q.68.
106 I have in mind particularly: *The Code of Practice on Access to Official Information; Questions of Procedure for Ministers;* the Osmotherly Rules (*Departmental Evidence and Response to Select Committees*); the *Guidance on Answering Parliamentary Questions: Basic Do's and Don'ts,* the *Civil Service Code;* and the *Parliamentary Resolution on Ministerial Accountability to Parliament.* See House of Commons Library (1997) *The*

[107] *Accountability Debate: Codes of Guidance and Questions of Procedure for Ministers* Research Paper 97/5.
Indeed, such has been the proliferation of written standards and codes of conduct that the Cabinet Office has produced *Guidance on Guidance* (1996).
[108] Page, A (1998) 'Controlling Government from Within: A Constitutional Analysis' *Public Policy & Administration* Vol.13 No.4 p.89. See also: Foster, C & Plowden, F (1996) *The State Under Stress* (Buckingham : Open University Press) p.229.
[109] David Willetts MP, the Chancellor of the Duchy of Lancaster, in 1996 when the process of codification began denied that the impetus was public concern at a perceived lack of implicit shared rules in central government. On the contrary he argued that in: '...a far more open society' it was 'right that all citizens should be able to have access to the rules by which their politicians and public servants are expected to behave'. Willetts, D (1996) 'Public Service Reform' Speech delivered at the Civil Service College, Sunningdale, 17/7/96.
[110] HC 313-III (1996/97) Memorandum by Prof. Dawn Oliver & Prof. Gavin Drewry p.18.
[111] Cabinet Office 1992. The document had been in existence for much longer.
[112] Cabinet Office 1996. Replacing but reiterating the Armstrong Memorandum: *The Duties and Responsibilities of Civil Servants in Relation to Ministers*, 1987. See HC 27-II (1993/94).
[113] Cabinet Office (1994) *Departmental Evidence and Response to Select Committees*.
[114] Oliver, D & Drewry, D (1996) *Public Service Reforms: Issues of Accountability and Public Law* (London : Pinter) p.3.
[115] See Massey, A (1995) 'Civil Service Reform and Accountability' *Public Administration* Vol.10 pp.16-33.
[116] Oliver, D & Drewry, D (1996) *Public Service Reforms: Issues of Accountability and Public Law* (London : Pinter) p.83.
[117] At the time of writing this post was held by Sir Michael Bett.
[118] HC 313-III (1996/97) Evidence by the First Division Association pp.11-12 Q35.
[119] HC 313-III (1996/97) Evidence by Prof. Peter Hennessy p.16 Q66.
[120] Cm 2850 (1995) *First Report of the Committee on Standards in Public Life* HMSO, London. [The Nolan Report].
[121] Cm 2931 (1995) *The Government's Response to the First Report of the Committee on Standards in Public Life* HMSO, London. See also HC 313-III (1996/97) p.19 Q82, p.207 Q1141.
[122] HC 313 (1996/97) para.32.
[123] HC 67 (1996/97) p.viii para.6.

[124] In February 2001 the Select Committee on Public Administration once more called for a greater role to be played by the Prime Minister in enforcing the Ministerial Code. The Committee noted, 'Its Prime Ministerial ownership should be clearly acknowledged and tied to responsibility'. HC 235 *The Ministerial Code: Improving the Rule Book*, Third Report of the Select Committee on Public Administration, Session 2000/01, HMSO, London.

[125] Barker, A (1996) *Political Responsibility for UK Prison Security: Ministers Escape Again* Essex papers in politics and government. No.106. p.3.

[126] O'Toole, B (1995) 'Accountability and the Civil Service Now' *Public Policy and Administration* Vol.10 No.4 pp.1-3.

[127] Barker, A (1996) *Political Responsibility for UK Prison Security: Ministers Escape Again* Essex papers in politics and government. No.106. p.7.

[128] For example, the Code of Conduct of the Bar of England and Wales.

[129] Oliver, D (1995) 'The Nolan Committee' in Ridley, F & Doig, A *Sleaze: Politicians' Private Interests and Public Reaction* (Oxford : Oxford University Press) p.47.

[130] For an in-depth analysis of the history of the select committee structure see Woodhouse, D (1994) *Ministers and Parliament* (Oxford : Clarendon); Drewry, G (1989) *The New Select Committees* (Oxford : Clarendon).

[131] Michael Foot was particularly associated with this view. He admits his misgivings were wrong and that select committees have made a positive contribution to Parliament in *New Statesman* 11/1/97 pp.30-31.

[132] See John Mackintosh quoted in Theakston, K (1992) *The Labour Party and Whitehall* (London : Routledge) p.170.

[133] A particular belief of Herbert Morrison, reference in Giddings, P (1994) 'Select Committees and Parliamentary Scrutiny: *Plus Ca Change' Parliamentary Affairs* Vol.47 No.4 pp.669-689.

[134] HC 313-II (1996/97) Memorandum by Dr Geoffrey Marshall p.33.

[135] Hansard HC Debs. 14/12/66. See Crick, B (1968) 2nd ed. *The Reform of Parliament* (London : Weidenfeld) pp.212-234.

[136] Judge, D (1993) *The Parliamentary State* (London : Sage) p.79.

[137] House of Commons Public Information Office, Fact Sheet No.6 *The Post-1979 Departmental Select Committee Structure*.

[138] HC 588 *Reports* First Report by the Committee on Procedure, Session 1977-78, HMSO, London. pVIII.

[139] Hansard, HC Debs. 25/6/79, Vol.969 col.35.

[140] HC 19 *The Working of the Select Committee System* Second Report by the Committee on Procedure, Session 1989/90, HMSO, London.

[141] Cm 9916 (1986) *The Government's Response to the Fourth Report from the Defence Committee on 'Westland Plc: The Defence Implications for the*

142   *Future of Westland Plc: The Government's Decision Making'* HMSO, London. p.9 para.41.

143   HC 62 *Accountability of ministers and civil servants to select committees of the House of Commons* First Report of the Liaison Committee, Session 1986/87, HMSO, London.

144   Woodhouse, D (1994) *Ministers and Parliament* (Oxford : Clarendon) p.186.

145   HC 313 (1996/97) p.IXXXII para.20. This reform was advocated by the majority of those giving evidence to the committee. See, for example HC 313-III (1996/97) Evidence by Sir Richard Scott p.74 Q428; HC 313-III (1996/97) Evidence by Prof. Norman Lewis p.99 Q643; HC 313-III (1996/97) Evidence by Lord Howe p.52 Q268; HC 313-III (1996/97) Evidence by Prof. Peter Hennessy p.21 Q92.

146   Bogdanor, V (1994) 'Ministers, Civil Servants and the Constitution' *Government and Opposition* Vol.29 p.680.

147   Kemp, P (1993) *Beyond the Next Steps: A Civil Service for the 21st Century* (London : Social Market Foundation) paper 17 p.22.

148   'The government is not prepared to breach the long-standing basic principle that civil servants, including chief executives of Next Steps Agencies, give an account to Parliament on behalf of the ministers whom they serve.' HC 67 (1996/97)p.VII (response to the PSC). Lord Butler also remains loyal to convention: 'If a minister refuses to give information to Parliament then that is the minister's right and the civil service cannot subvert that and it is then up to Parliament to pursue the minister'. Interview with the author, March 1999.

149   'Where a Select Committee is investigating matters which are delegated to an agency in its Framework Document, evidence will usually be given by the chief executive. Like other officials, Agency Chief Executives give evidence on behalf of the Minister to whom they are accountable and are subject to the minister's instructions' Cabinet Office (1997) *Departmental Evidence and Response to Select Committees.*

150   Hansard, HC Debs. 12/2/96 col.680.

151   Hansard, HC Debs. 12/2/96 col.681.

152   Hansard, HC Debs. 12/2/96 col.681.

153   The adoption of a procedure similar to that of the accounting officer could be established. The chief executive could write a formal letter should they feel their responsibility for the day to day management of the agency is being compromised by ministerial intervention. Should the performance of the agency decline or a specific incident occur, the documentation could be supplied to the relevant select committee.

  HC 313-III (1996/97) Evidence by Mr Roger Freeman Q19.

[154] Permanent secretaries in departments and chief executives in agencies. See Barberis, P (1996) *The Elite of the Elite: Permanent Secretaries in the British Higher Civil Service* (Aldershot : Dartmouth).
[155] Harden, I (1994) 'Audit, Accounting Officers and Accountability: The Pergau Dam Affair' *Public Law* pp.526-534.
[156] Prof. Philip Norton suggests '..these have not been rigidly adhered to by civil servants appearing before select committees, indeed not all officials appearing before the committees have been aware of them'. At HC 313-II (1996/97) p.76-77. See also Pyper, R (1995) *The British Civil Service* (Hemel Hempstead : Prentice Hall) p.125.
[157] HC 313-III (1996/97) Evidence by Lord Howe p.52 Q268.
[158] HC 313-I (1996/97) para. 110.
[159] See HC 313-III (1996/97) Evidence by Sir Peter Kemp p.109 para.16. In a lecture he noted: 'The Osmotherly rules will never be officially removed - they will simply wither on the vine' Centre for Socio-Legal Studies, University of Sheffield 12/11/96.
[160] 'I'll answer any questions I want to. If the minister asked me why I answered a certain question I'll say that if I hadn't I'd still be there now! There was never a problem until the Lewis/Howard affair...a good chief executive has to learn to manage his minister - that's what Lewis failed to do!' Agency Chief Executive interview with the author, September 19/96.
[161] Hennessy, P & Drewry, G (1996) 'Critics of the Osmotherly Rules' in Barberis. P (ed.) *The Whitehall Reader* (Milton Keynes : Open University Press) pp.230-234.
[162] Cabinet Office (1994) *Departmental Evidence and Response to Select Committees* para.38.
[163] See Scott, R (1996) 'Ministerial Accountability' *Public Law* pp.410-426.
[164] HC 481 *Progress in the Next Steps Initiative*, Eighth report from the Select Committee on the Treasury and Civil Service, Session 1989/90, HMSO, London. p.xviii, para.65.
[165] These views are common though see in particular - HC 313-III (1996/97) Evidence by Prof. Peter Hennessy pp.16-23.
[166] Bogdanor, V (1994) 'Ministers, Civil Servants and the Constitution' *Government and Opposition* Vol.29 p.683.
[167] HC 313-III (1996/97) Evidence by the First Division Association p.12 Q38/39.
[168] Lord Nolan, Second Radcliffe Lecture, 21/11/96 University of Warwick.
[169] Taylor, A *New Politics, New Parliament* paper presented at the Charter 88 seminar on the Reform of Parliament. 14/5/96.

170 HC 313-III (1996/97) Evidence by Ann Taylor MP p.180 Q1058. An important point to note about the statement is that she conflates agencies with quangos despite their different legal and constitutional status.

171 Gregory, D (1999) 'Style over Substance? Labour and the Reform of Parliament' *Renewal* Vol.7 No.3 pp.42-50.

172 See Harden, I, Donnelly, K & White, F (1994) *Should the NAO Serve Departmentally Related Select Committees?* (Sheffield : PERC/Department of Law). This proposal has been strongly advocated by several committees. See HC 313-II (1996/97) Memorandum by the Welsh Affairs Committee p.92. The Public Service Committee recommended that the Liaison Committee examine the relationship between the PAC, NAO and committees (at HC 313 [1996/97] p.IXXII para.27).

173 See Banham, J (1994) *The Anatomy of Change* (London : Orion) p.50.

174 For example see HC 313-II (1996/97) Memorandum by the Environment Committee p.86. Ann Taylor noted: 'One of the things that I have suggested is that senior appointments...be ratified by the appropriate select committee'. HC 313-III (1996/97) Evidence by Ann Taylor MP p.180 Q1058.

175 HC 313-III (1996/97) Evidence by Sir Peter Kemp and Ms Kate Jenkins p.113 Q693; HC 313-III (1996/97) Evidence by Mr Michael Bichard p.161 Q932.

176 With the increased independence given to the Bank of England, the Treasury Select Committee petitioned the government to be given the power to formally oversee appointments to the powerful new Monetary Policy Committee. Despite the government's refusal to grant the committee such powers they have undertaken the role anyway. See HC 82 *The Monetary Policy Committee of the Bank of England: Confirmation Hearings* Sixth Report by the Treasury Committee, Session 1997/98, HMSO, London.

177 HC 313-III (1996/97) Evidence by Mr Anthony Newton MP p.212 Q1164.

178 HC 313-III (1996/97) Evidence by Sir Richard Scott p.73 Q419.

179 HC 313-III (1996/97) Evidence by Prof. Peter Hennessy p.20 Q91; HC 313-II (1996/97) Memorandum by Prof. Philip Norton p.77.

180 Evans, P (1995) 'Members of Parliament and Agencies: Parliamentary Questions' in Giddings, P (ed.) *Parliamentary Accountability: A Study of Parliament and Executive Agencies* (Basingstoke : Macmillan) p.119.

181 Franklin & Norton found that in their research 85% of respondents did not judge PQs as performing well. See Franklin, M & Norton, P (1993) *Parliamentary Questions* (Oxford : Clarendon).

182 HC494-I (1987/88) Memorandum of evidence by the Project Manager (Sir Peter Kemp) para.15.

183 See Winetrobe, B (1995) 'Next Steps and Parliamentary Scrutiny' in Giddings, P (ed.) *Parliamentary Accountability: A Study of Parliament and Executive Agencies* (Houndmills : Basingstoke).

184 Hogwood, B & McVicar, M (1997) 'The "Pondlife" of Executive Agencies: Parliament and 'Informatory' Accountability' *Public Policy and Administration* Vol.12 No.2 pp.95-115.

185 Norton, P (1982) 'Dear Ministers.....The Importance of MP-to-Minister Correspondence' *Parliamentary Affairs* Vol.35 No.1 p.65.

186 Although they could be placed in the Commons library by request.

187 HC 481 (1989/90) p.XX para.70.

188 See Woodhouse, D (1994) *Ministers and Parliament: Accountability in Theory and Practice* (Oxford : Oxford University Press) pp.239-240.

189 Hansard, HC Debs. WA, 16/7/92 col.941.

190 See HC 481-II (1989/90) Q104.

191 It is also an example of how sustained parliamentary pressure, in this case over three years, can force the government to accede to demands for changes to the accountability process to which they were at first hostile.

192 Gerald Kaufman has called the development: '...the creeping abnegation of ministerial accountability' Gerald Kaufman *The Guardian* 7/12/93 p.19. See also Hansard, HC Debs. Vol. 236, cols. 1289-90.

193 Rose, D 'A dangerous state of irresponsibility' *The Observer* 30//1/94.

194 Weir, S & Wright, A (1997) *Power to the Backbenches?* Democratic Audit paper No.9 (London : Scarman Trust).

195 The government stated in response to the Public Service Committee:'...a chief executive may conclude that a particular issue requires discussion with the minister, or a ministerial answer; and it is open to ministers to arrange to be consulted on a more regular or routine basis if they consider it necessary'. HC 67 (1996/97) p.XI.

196 Woodhouse, D (1997) 'Ministerial Responsibility: Something Old, Something New' *Public Law* p.272.

197 Hansard, HC Debs. 19/5/97 col. 396.

198 Richards, S 'Interview: Jack Straw' *The New Statesman* 23/5/97 pp.16-17.

199 McSmith, A 'OK, answer this one: just how inquisitive is your MP?' *The Observer* 17/5/98 p.27.

200 Hansard, HC Debs. WA 11/12/97 Q20721 col.641. The Chancellor revised these figures to £115 and £267 respectively in March 1999. See Hansard, HC Debs. WA 11/3/99 col.363 Q76588.

201 'It is actually quite a good mechanism for staff to be made aware that people are actually caring and looking at their actions.' Lawrie Haynes, chief executive of the Highways Agency at HC 313-V(1996/97) p.86.

202 See HC 313-III (1996/97) p.160 Q925.
203 Child Support Agency *Annual Report 1994* p.14.
204 Hogwood, B, Judge, D & McVicar, M 'Too Much of a Good Thing? The Pathology of Accountability' paper presented to the Political Studies Association Annual Conference, University of Keele, 7-9/4/98.
205 Sir Michael Quinlan noted: '... the provision of proper information to the public is the primary function of parliamentary answers but in the real world it is unreal to forget that they will be shaded by considerations of the adversariality of the context in which they are delivered'. At HC 313-III (1996/97) p.36 Q.174.
206 HC 313-II (1996/97) Memorandum by Mr David Lipsey p.30 para.9.
207 HC 313-III (1996/97) Evidence by Lord Howe p.54 Q.281.
208 See Chester, D & Bowring, N (1962) *Questions in Parliament* (Oxford : Clarendon) esp. pages 238-239.
209 This recently annoyed Andrew Mackinlay so much that he asked the Prime Minister: 'Does the Prime Minister recall that, when we were in opposition, we used to groan at the fawning, obsequious, softball, well-rehearsed questions asked by Conservative members? Will my right honourable friend distinguish his period in office by discouraging such practices...during this Parliament. Furthermore, in view of the rather depleted official opposition will he encourage rather than discourage without fear or favour...loyal Labour backbenchers who wish to seek and provide scrutiny and accountability in this place'. Hansard HC Debs. PMQs 3/6/98 Q1[42525] col.359.
210 The practice adopted by parliamentary private secretaries and by whips of distributing pre-arranged favourable PQs to compliant backbenchers.
211 HC 379 *Oral Questions* First Report from the Select Committee on Procedure, Session 1989/90, HMSO, London. p.vi. See also HC 178 *Parliamentary Questions* Third Report by the Select Committee on Procedure, Session 1990/91, HMSO, London. p.16.
212 Pierce, A 'Minister caught writing questions for tame MPs' *The Times* 24/3/98 p.2.
213 See Scott, R (1996) 'Ministerial Accountability' *Public Law* pp.410-427. Especially to validate the refusal of ministers to answer questions on 'public interest' grounds.
214 This relates back to Sir Douglas Wass' discussion in his Reith Lectures about the benefits of creating a Department of the Opposition. See Wass, D (1984) *Government and the Governed* (London : RKP) pp.76-80. The idea was supported by Labour in opposition but quickly dropped in office: 'The secondment of a limited number of civil servants for up to two years at a

time to the offices of senior opposition frontbenchers would ensure that oppositions were better prepared for government and civil servants better understood the wider mechanics of the relationship between Parliament and Whitehall'. Taylor, A *New Politics, New Parliament* speech to the Charter 88 seminar on the Reform of Parliament, 14/5/96.

215 Woodhouse, D (1994) *Ministers and Parliament: Accountability in Theory and Practice* (Oxford : Oxford University Press).

216 Judge, D (1993) *The Parliamentary State* (London : Sage) pp.152-157.

3 Parliamentary Accountability and the Home Office

> Things are not going to change under Labour. You can change the machine but you cannot change the culture of Parliament, the ambience of the House and the ambitions of its members. Parliament is a balance between the lazy and the idle - the lazy don't do anything and the idle don't believe that anything needs to be done (Labour MP, April 1998).

3.1 Introduction

The previous chapter highlighted three interconnected themes:

- the convention of ministerial responsibility forms the foundation of the British constitution yet concerns about its practical utility are longstanding;
- the creation of agencies has exposed tensions in the convention which have always existed, but ministerial statements and specific events create concern that a 'responsibility gap' has emerged;
- finally, due to a number of factors, not least the government's majority, the balance of power is weighted (heavily) in favour of the executive, consequently the wider literature suggests that the main mechanisms of parliamentary scrutiny suffer from serious deficiencies.

This chapter examines the degree to which the shortcomings identified in the preceding chapter exist in reality. It focuses on the relationship between the Home Office and Parliament. Areas of interest include: Are the flaws associated with parliamentary mechanisms of scrutiny as severe as the wider literature suggest? What strengths does Parliament possess? What processes and mechanisms has the wider literature neglected? What impact does parliamentary accountability have on the Home Office? On what issues do the views of the actors in the accountability networks converge or differ? This chapter is critical to the overall book because if ministerial responsibility is confirmed as little more than a chimera then the alternative models of accountability that this book examines become increasingly important. Such a conclusion would also weaken arguments supporting the *status quo* by questioning the ability of Parliament to provide legitimate government between elections. On the contrary, should the research support the view that the deficiencies have been overstated then not only might Parliament be vindicated but the role of the alternative forms of accountability becomes less acute.

The first section of this chapter examines the usefulness of parliamentary questions, written and oral, as a tool of parliamentary scrutiny. The next section focuses on the work of the Home Affairs Committee in an attempt to gauge its capacity to enforce parliamentary accountability over the Home Office. Several interviewees suggested that the shortcomings associated with the formal mechanisms of parliamentary accountability are somewhat appeased by the existence of informal and/or party mechanisms of accountability. The third section examines these claims and describes the processes and channels involved. The final section offers concluding comments. As noted above, the next section is concerned with parliamentary questions and the Home Office.

3.2 Parliamentary Questions

Section 2.9 stressed how uncertainties and tensions still existed in relation to PQs, especially with regard to the answering of written questions by chief executives. This section explores the argument that in the case of the Home Office PQs are not an effective mechanism of scrutiny and suffer from a number of shortcomings. It examines the impact of PQs on the department and the manner in which the Home Office approaches its duty to answer PQs. In turn, the veracity of the answers received is considered and in particular whether the Home Secretary's decision to answer all PQs concerning the Prison Service personally has improved or impaired this mechanism of accountability.

The Home Office is the target for a large number of written questions, the vast majority of which concern the Prison Service. In 1995 613 questions were tabled involving the Prison Service making it, by nearly three times, the most popular agency for written questions.[1] In the light of the two prison breakouts during 1995, and the subsequent dismissal of Derek Lewis, the number of questions rose dramatically in 1996 to 1137, falling back to 602 in 1997.[2]

The majority of MPs interviewed were of the general opinion that written questions were a useful mechanism for achieving informatory accountability but that their utility depended on the type and topic of the information being requested. Several members of the Home Affairs Committee (HAC) referred to the Home Office as a traditionally 'defensive' department and suggested that this was often apparent when questions sought information on policy issues or in relation to certain incidents.[3] As one MP (April 1998) noted:

> If you want to know how many prisoners are being held in a prison then a written question is fine but if you want to know why a certain prison has an exceptionally high suicide rate then the shutters come down and the defensiveness begins and the process degenerates into a game.

Despite this HAC members felt that written questions had clandestine powers and stressed the need for persistence and detail. Robin Corbett MP noted that it would often take him 20 or more written questions to get the information he sought. He likened the process to a 'war of attrition' as he would have to reword the question carefully each time to try and prevent the Home Office circumnavigating the real issue. But he found the process '...useful for letting the Home Office know that you are on the warpath and are not going to give up and also building up a case to go and see the minister in person'.

The link between the informal and formal mechanisms of accountability emerged frequently as MPs noted how pertinent written questions often resulted in useful unofficial contact. Beverly Hughes MP, a former member of the HAC, noted (March 1998):

> Most of the answers I have received have been very good...and I've often followed them up with more subtle forms of accountability like an informal meeting with a minister or even just a coffee with an official so I can discuss the issue in more depth.

This experience supports my earlier suggestion that party accountability undermines ministerial responsibility to Parliament. MPs should not be thankful for unofficial meetings with representatives of the

Home Office because that department has answered their formal PQs in a defensive and obstructive manner. PQs are important exactly because they are public statements. The term 'defensive' was frequently used by MPs discussing the Home Office, and the analogy of PQs being a 'game' was common. This reflects both the underlying power relationship and the context in which questions are tabled. If the Home Office does not want to answer a written question there is very little Parliament can do. As one HAC member suggested:

> If the Home Office decides to avoid answering a question it can follow one of two options: it can either answer the question so as to include no information whatsoever; or it can avoid answering at all by claiming to answer it would involve disproportionate costs, would be against the public interest or against the national interest. Whichever option they pick there is damn all Parliament can do!

This fact puts the emphasis on those who dominate the power relationship to be forthcoming with information, but evidence suggests that within the Prison Service the need to protect ministers is ingrained in officials - with adverse consequences for Parliament.[4] A former Home Office official noted:

> The key consideration when answering PQs was to avoid anything that might embarrass ministers. This is absolutely ingrained in civil servants. In my experience nobody ever proposed an untrue answer but it was not at all unusual to deliberately hide information which the MP had clearly been seeking if it might prove embarrassing. If the question was not specific enough then we would respond in harmless generalities. If it was too specific we would answer only the precise point raised ignoring any side issues.[5]

On assuming office Jack Straw announced that all written question concerning the Prison Service would be answered by a minister and not the director general as they had been in the past.

> This change will put right what many in Parliament have long regarded as bad practice. I regard it as essential that ministers answer personally to Parliament for what is done in our prisons and do not leave it to their civil servants. This is the first step I am taking to ensure proper ministerial responsibility for the running of the prison service.[6]

This marks an isolated reversal of the delegation of responsibility to civil servants and therefore an acceptance of the responsibility gap within the reinvention of government. This, in turn, creates questions of why this move should be so isolated and highlights the incoherence of current frameworks for accountability. The restoration of ministerial responsibility for answering questions does address a number of concerns but, paradoxically, it may also lead to the diminution of accountability.

The change in procedure certainly solves the uncertainty noted in Chapter Two regarding the responsibility for a reply. Gone is the suspicion that a ministerially amended reply may be despatched under the chief executive's name. It also addresses the concern that with operational questions being answered by the chief executive ministers may become isolated from administrative matters. The move might also be expected to lessen the accountability burden on the chief executive and solve the problem highlighted by the Learmont Report: 'The problem of the director general's preoccupation with parliamentary matters must be overcome'.[7]

Although Prison Service officials supported the Home Secretary's decision, senior officials thought the move was largely cosmetic. The issue of parliamentary attention has never been satisfactorily resolved and the pathological impact of this burden is considerable. In addition to the written questions there is an equally exhaustive, if not greater, level of parliamentary correspondence.[8] For example, in addition to written PQs in 1995 the Prison Service attracted 2546 letters from MPs requesting information, 2911 in 1996 and 2008 in 1997.[9] This considerable level of parliamentary correspondence raises three issues: first, it highlights a form of informatory, explanatory and amendatory accountability that has largely escaped academic study; secondly, this provokes a consideration of why MPs choose to seek information through a letter rather than a written question; and finally, it exposes the true extent of parliamentary interest in certain areas of departments.[10]

In an attempt to manage this informatory demand efficiently the Prison Service has established a dedicated Parliamentary Unit. Not only does parliamentary attention impose a substantial financial burden on the Prison Service (costing over £450,000 in 1996 and nearly £300,000 in 1997)[11] it also distracts senior managers away from the day-to-day management of the service.[12] The Home Secretary's decision was designed to reduce this pressure and allow managers get on with running the service. My research suggests this has not happened. In March 1998 a senior Prison

Service official noted: 'In reality nothing has changed...if anything things have got worse. The Director still reads and signs every reply the only difference is that they are now signed by a minister after him'. Senior officials are adamant that the demands of parliamentary accountability have not been lifted off their shoulders and that in fact the restoration of ministerial responsibility has increased the weight. Although no reply has ever been rejected by the minister it is common for replies to be returned to the agency for rewriting, confirmation or supporting material so that the minister is prepared for subsequent questioning; and this increases the overall burden. One senior official estimated that he spent in excess of 30 hours a week on parliamentary work making 90 hour weeks the average.

Not only would it appear that the reimposition of ministerial responsibility for PQs concerning the Prison Service has failed to free up managers but it may also have impaired the effectiveness of written PQs as a form of scrutiny. Specialists in legislative studies, notably Philip Norton, have suggested that replies by chief executives on behalf of ministers tended to be significantly more extensive and helpful than those by ministers.[13] Ironically, senior officials within the Prison Service implied that since ministers had resumed signing answers the quality of those replies had fallen. One official from the Prison Service's Parliamentary Unit supported this view:

> If anything this has lead to a reduction in the quality of answers. Ministers know they are accepting responsibility for the information contained in the reply and are careful to limit risks whenever and wherever possible.

The perception among MPs that written PQs are not an effective method for obtaining information, and may well have become less useful since the Home Secretary resumed signing all replies, might provide an answer as to why so many MPs write letters to the Home Office rather than tabling PQs. While the replies to MPs' letters are unequivocal they are viewed as being less 'political' than PQs. The replies are not public documents nor are they recorded in Hansard. It might be suggested that as letters from MPs are not a formal parliamentary mechanism they receive a less defensive reply from the Home Office.[14] If true this would be a further example of a channel of accountability that is undermining the accountability of ministers to Parliament. Not only does this demonstrate the executive defining the method and scope of its own accountability, but also when MPs receive unsatisfactory replies to their letters they are, as with written PQs, essentially powerless to compel a full account from the executive.

Ministers, however, have less freedom to manoeuvre with regard to oral questions. The previous chapter suggested that oral questions in the House have a poor reputation as a mechanism of accountability, but on this issue there is an acute contrariety between MPs and ministers. The majority of MPs interviewed supported the proposition that oral questions were a 'sycophants paradise'. Several members of the HAC emphasised how orals had little to do with accountability but were simply a tool of party warfare. As Robin Corbett noted:

> If I want to make a political point I'll ask a question in the House but if I want some information I'll write to the minister or go and see the relevant official in the department.

There was an all - party consensus among MPs who were sceptical that oral questions could ever force a reluctant minister to provide an account to the House. A Conservative member of the HAC stated:

> Opposition questions will receive guarded and uninformative replies whilst it is likely that those from a minister's side of the House will usually have been prepared by that minister's office.

However, past and present Home Office ministers disagreed. For them oral questions represented the undiluted reality of a minister's responsibility to Parliament. Question Time was important and was frequently an occasion for providing informatory, explanatory and amendatory accountability. But the importance of the occasion and the accountability were not necessarily linked. Successive ministers (David Waddington, Douglas Hurd, Ann Widdecombe, Michael Howard) recounted how departmental questions were never underestimated. Question time was important because it embodied the reality of ministerial responsibility as only ministers could appear and once they were at the despatch box responsibility was focused. Officials outlined how ministers would clear at least one and a half days before departmental questions to prepare. A senior Home Office official noted (April 1999): 'Ministers don't like departmental questions...they are isolated, they cannot hide and they know that a bad performance could end their career'.

Ann Widdecombe described oral questions as a game of '...see if you can catch me out and I'll show you that you can't'. She felt they were a vital mechanism forcing ministers to pay attention to key issues of parliamentary concern. It might therefore be suggested that oral questions are a consequential element of ministerial responsibility as ministers are well aware of the need to take into account pugnacious questioning, particularly from members of their own party. Perversely, the significance given to questions in the House is frequently not due to the fact that Parliament can force a minister to provide an extensive account. Ministers will often use Question Time as a platform from which to make an announcement, offer information or account for a specific incident. In this respect oral questions are a component part of ministerial responsibility but, like so many other parts, it is controlled by the minister not Parliament. When an answer is incomplete or inadequate, unless it can be categorically proven that the minister knowingly misled the House, there is little Parliament can do to improve the level of ministerial responsibility.

In the case of the Home Office PQs appear to support the underlying argument that the executive, and not Parliament, dictates the effectiveness of this mechanism. It has highlighted that ministerial responsibility inevitably bears a political cost. Jack Straw's restoration of ministerial responsibility delivers clarity in respect of responsibility for the content of the answer but at a cost that the answer may not be as informative, precisely because the minister has accepted responsibility. Arguably, restoring ministerial responsibility may have been a guise to evade and restrict accountability (through tighter control of previously delegated informatory accountability) for an area of government in which delegation had clearly proved unsatisfactory, disguised as a move to increase it. It is clear that a satisfactory solution to the demands of parliamentary accountability has yet to be found. The theoretical restoration of ministerial responsibility has, if anything, increased the burden with the associated pathological effects, particularly in terms of senior management distraction, which did so much to frustrate the early years of the agency. With the clearly identified weaknesses of PQs the need for an effective and rigorous system of select committees becomes paramount. If select committees are also found to be ineffective then the whole system of parliamentary accountability becomes questionable.

3.3 Select Committees

The evolution of the select committee system epitomises Parliament's attempts to redress the scales of power between the legislature and the executive. Since their creation in 1966, select committees have encountered a range of obstacles. New public management cannot, therefore, be blamed for incapacitating Parliament's scrutiny committees. It has, however, delivered new challenges, arguably made their duties more difficult and has crudely highlighted their fundamental weaknesses. This section examines the ability of the HAC to enforce the neo-Diceyan doctrine of ministerial responsibility. Against the critique of the inverted logic of ministerial responsibility and the underlying power relationship within Parliament it examines just how large the gulf is between theory and practice.

The HAC is appointed under Standing Order No.130 to examine the expenditure, administration and the policy of the Home Office and associated public bodies. It consists of 11 members and has the power to:

- send for persons, papers and records, to sit notwithstanding any adjournment of the House, to adjourn from place to place, and to report from time to time;
- appoint specialist advisers either to supply information which is not readily available or to elucidate matters of complexity within the Committee's order of reference;
- communicate to any other committee appointed under the same Standing Order (or to the Committee of Public Accounts and the Deregulation Committee) its evidence and any other documents relating to matters of common interest;
- meet concurrently with any other such committee for the purposes of deliberating, taking evidence, or considering draft reports.

It has always been an active committee.[15] The committee plays a central role in ensuring the accountability of Home Office ministers to Parliament although the depth and standard of that accountability is questionable. In the 1992-1997 Parliament the committee questioned a Home Office minister 13 times and ministers from other departments on several occasions. No Home Office minister has ever declined an invitation from the committee to appear.[16] Committee attendances also tend to be high when a minister is giving evidence. The committee has taken evidence from a very wide spectrum of groups and individuals, as well as ministers and their officials. Thus allowing each witness to have their views taken into account, collecting information with which to challenge the minister and in so doing contributing to the overall level of public accountability and knowledge.

The effectiveness of the HAC is determined by a complex range of interconnected factors. These can be divided between political and practical issues (although it would be naive to believe that many of the practical constraints on committees do not have political foundations, for example membership, resources and time.) One of the main constraints faced by the HAC is time. The committee meets for an average of two to four hours per week during parliamentary sessions, although the chair will spend an average of five additional hours per week on committee business. Most current and former members of the committee emphasised the lack of time as the biggest problem facing the committee. The following statement from a member of the HAC is typical:

> The Home Office is a massive and complex department operating with a wide range of policy responsibilities all of which have a direct impact upon the public, but you have to be realistic about what we can achieve in the time we have available.

Time was highlighted not only as a quantity issue but also as a quality issue. Most committee members admitted that they rarely have time to prepare in advance for committee meetings, for example by reading the background briefs provided by the two clerks of the committee. Consequently members are frequently ignorant about the topic under discussion. Sir Ivan Lawrence, chairman of the committee 1992-1997, noted (April 1998): 'There is a difference in quality amongst the members and in this regard I include in that not necessarily intellectual ability but propensity to master the subject before they come along and ask questions'.

During interviews a distinction emerged between what were known as 'lazy' and 'busy' members within the committee. Lazy members simply lack enthusiasm and commitment. They are, as one member of the HAC put it, the members who 'wander in late and meander out early between which they have usually asked a couple of questions which reflect an embarrassing lack of knowledge'.[17] 'Busy' members have other parliamentary or extra-parliamentary commitments that distract their attention away from committee work.[18] As Chris Mullin noted:

> One problem is that sometimes a committee member will be on two or three committees in the House at the same time. It's a ridiculous situation which means they might come in and out of our session three or four times in an afternoon which is obviously disruptive.[19]

The inability of the HAC's members to devote more time to committee work is a severe constraint on both the scope and depth of its inquiries. Time considerations have important ramifications for arguments over parliamentary reform. As Robin Corbett noted: '...the one thing that select committees really need is the one thing that nobody can give them - more time'. But is time really the key issue? Given more time would committees really become more effective in enforcing accountable government? Such a belief overlooks the underlying power relationship in Parliament and the influence the government's inbuilt majority, and particularly the power of the chair, has on the committee.

Continuity of membership is another practical issue that impacts upon the committee. It was argued that the new post-1979 committee structure would provide a sense of security and encourage members to build up a cumulative body of wisdom and expertise. But the development of a corporate memory depends to some degree upon continuity of membership. The HAC has lacked continuity and is characterised by fluidity rather than permanence.[20] Membership turnover has been a problem for the HAC since its formation. For example, the average turnover rates for the 1979-1983 and 1992-1997 Parliaments was 55%. Membership instability has continued to be an issue in the current Parliament. After only two full parliamentary sessions over half the original members had left, for example Chris Mullin, Beverly Hughes, Richard Allan, Ross Cranston and Douglas Hogg. Membership continuity is also an inter-parliamentary problem. Of the previous committee (1992-1997) only Chris Mullin continued to serve on the HAC in the current Parliament. Broader research confirms membership turnover as an important issue. For example, between 1997 and November 1999 the Social Security Committee had a turnover of 64% and the Treasury Committee had a turnover of 42%.[21]

Some degree of turnover is inevitable but there is a suspicion that political factors have also ensured a degree of instability. Committee members were adamant that continuity was important. Chris Mullin (April 1998) noted that: 'This turnover of membership reduces our ability to scrutinise the executive, as, effectively, every five years our collective memory is wiped away'. Robin Corbett, who is currently on the committee but also served on it between 1983-1987 noted: 'I think looking back on it it does pay to have some long-serving members on the committee who cannot easily be fooled'.

Frequently the most effective and active committee members leave. Several commentators have emphasised the value of former ministers on committees due to their knowledge of the procedures and practices of Whitehall.[22] Douglas Hogg, one of the few ministers from the previous administration to serve on any committee, sat on the HAC until March 1988 when he left to concentrate on outside interests. Richard Allan, although not a former minister, was an enthusiastic member of the committee until he left in June 1998 to become chairman of the Information Committee. In March 2000 the Liaison Committee recommended reforms to reduce the degree of committee membership.[23] The Government's reply was unsympathetic and the recommendations were not accepted. It stated that of the 121 MPs who had served as ministers in this government, only nine had done so on leaving a select committee.[24] This response is economical with the truth. Far more members left select committees to take Principal Parliamentary Secretary (PPS) positions than became ministers. As the Hansard Society were quick to note, 'In total, members leaving select committees to become ministers and PPS has had an enormous impact'.[25]

Conversely, a clerk to the committee suggested that a regular turnover promoted a healthy committee: 'I think there is a case for getting new people in with fresh ideas'. In his experience long term committee members tended to become uninterested and apathetic while a constant flow of 'fresh blood' helped keep the committee active and enthusiastic. Several interviewees suggested that the turnover of members was politically calculated and that the membership of the current committees had been carefully engineered by the whips to displace the independent members and ensure 'safe' committees.[26] Gerald Bermingham believed his case represented an example of this issue. A member of the HAC between

1992-1997 he had expressed an interest in remaining on the committee but was not selected by the Committee of Selection. He noted:

> There is a planned lack of continuity which means that the build up of expertise has been wasted. They have put on members who either have no experience or who are safe. They put on people who are ambitious and are not going to rock the boat and they have kept the nasties and the hard hitters away. They took off the old lags like me who would give ministers a hard time.

An official in the Leader of the House's office (then Ann Taylor) rejected these accusations: 'She has not replaced the independent members at all. The role of the select committees is to keep the government on its toes and avoid being caught out'. Nevertheless, he added, she had previously been a whip and 'understood the benefits of party discipline'.[27] This highlights a key issue - it is the executive, through the whips influence on the Committee of Selection, that decides who will sit on each committee.[28] It is ministers, once again, who control both the membership and resources of the parliamentary committees charged with holding them to account. Selective membership reinforced by party discipline ensures that the power relationship is not threatened.[29] Tony Wright MP (April 1998) developed this line of thought:

> The whips have vast control over the membership of these committees and will decide the members in consultation with the departmental ministers. They will not appoint people who they know will be extremely troublesome; this has always been the case but sometimes people who think they will be safe will go native.

(The downfall of Nicholas Winterton crudely highlighted that even when a committee member becomes unexpectedly vexatious the government can conspire to remould Parliament's procedures to remove the individual.)[30] However, the engineering of innocuous committees by the government does not seem to sit comfortably with the appointment of Chris Mullin as the chairman of the HAC in 1997. The answer may well be linked to the fact that Chris Mullin was offered a ministerial post shortly after the 1997 general election. Mullin had not divulged this information previously but thought it had direct links with his chairmanship of the committee. He declined the ministerial post as far too obvious a ploy to restrain him through collective ministerial responsibility.[31] (In light of this fact the chairmanship might be considered an attempt both to pacify and overburden him).[32]

But how important are the chairs of committees and what powers do they possess? Research suggests that their personality, ambition and view of the role of the committee will heavily shape the standard and depth of the committee's activities:

> The chair shapes the agenda, controls the questions and sets the environment within which the committee will operate (Sir Ivan Lawrence, April 1998).

> The role and personality of the chairman is crucial and in many ways facilitates or impedes the committee's ability to scrutinise the government (Chris Mullin, April 1998).

Douglas Hurd concurred with the above views and stressed how important it had been when he was Home Secretary that the chairman of the HAC had been a 'sensible man'.[33] First, the chair, to a considerable extent, controls the agenda of accountability. Possible topics for inquiry are suggested by a range of sources (committee members, clerks, pressure groups, events, etc.). The committee considers the options and a series of inquiries is selected. Votes are rare and a process of negotiation and compromise usually leads to agreement, but the chair is far more than *primes inter pares*. A parliamentary clerk noted, 'In reality the chairman will choose the agenda for the committee and present it to the members. Although there may be some disquiet the chair is rarely defeated'.

Although substantial the powers of the chair are not absolute. Votes can be called and inquiries chosen against the wishes of the chairperson. Sir Ivan Lawrence highlighted how he never wanted to examine the funding of political parties but gave way to committee pressure.[34]

Members of the previous HAC attacked Sir Ivan Lawrence for consistently protecting ministers and curtailing questioning. Robin Corbett captured the general mood: 'He was a lickspittle of the Conservative Party who thought he was part of the government'.[35] Sir Ivan makes no apology for his close relationship with Mr Howard: 'It used to be said that I was his only friend in Parliament'. But the fact that the chairperson controls the questions and agenda for each session effectively allowed Sir Ivan, in the view of other members, to limit the degree of accountability the committee could achieve. An extract from the committee's inquiry into the management of the Prison Service highlights this issue. Derek Lewis was appearing before the committee - and, as he had left the civil service, was no longer bound by the Osmotherly rules - when Chris Mullin invited him to contribute to the debate that information which the rules had prevented him from disclosing to the committee previously:

> Mr Mullin: Now that you are not constrained by the burden of office, would you like to add anything to the evidence you gave then?
> Sir Ivan Lawrence (Chairman): I think, Mr Lewis, that we do not wish to go down that line. We are here just to consider views on the management. We are not here to go over...
> Mr Mullin: Chairman, I do think you ought to permit questions to be asked. What the witness chooses to answer is up to him.
> Sir Ivan Lawrence (Chairman): No, I do not think the witness ought to be tempted by going down a branch line.
> Mr Mullin: Let the record show that the Chairman is throwing his cloak over a puddle on behalf of the Home Secretary, and not for the first time.[36]

Sir Ivan defended his interruption by stating that the aim of the inquiry was not to go over well-trodden ground but to examine management issues: 'I said that he had indulged the bee in his bonnet long enough and that it was time to get on with some other questions and he responded that I was covering up for the government which was total nonsense'. Sir Ivan stressed that a key function of the chair was often to protect witnesses from intimidation especially where they were being drawn into commenting on topics they were uneasy with and that were peripheral to the inquiry. But in this instance neither was the topic of the question peripheral to the inquiry nor was Lewis reluctant to discuss the issue. Indeed further research suggests the true nature of the intervention was political. Immediately after his dismissal Derek Lewis had contacted the HAC and offered to reappear in front of the committee to discuss his dismissal and outline the true state of the Prison Service.[37] The Conservative majority on the committee rejected this offer with Sir Ivan Lawrence using his casting vote to ensure that the committee heard no more.[38]

The issue of time slots and questions emerged as an important topic in the course of interviews with committee members. Areas of questioning are divided between members in advance of committee sessions to avoid overlap and ensure that all the main issues are covered. The chairman plays a key role in ensuring that all members receive the opportunity to ask their questions. Evidence from the HAC suggests that in practice the procedure is far from satisfactory. MPs who had served on the HAC under both Sir John Wheeler and Sir Ivan Lawrence were adamant that the chairmen had often moved the questioning on prematurely to prevent the discomfiture of the minister to the detriment of parliamentary accountability. Secondly, members of the committee and witnesses highlighted that members rarely shared information. Consequently when a member of the committee uncovers a serious issue but the questioning moves on no other members of the committee have the information with which to pursue that line of inquiry.[39] Brian Landers, director of finance at the Prison Service 1993-1996, stressed how this was not a problem unique to the HAC:

> I twice witnessed Westminster's most feared committee, the Public Accounts Committee, in action. What was notable in both cases is that they missed the fundamental issues due to an evident lack of effective briefing, the rather mixed quality of the committee membership and their own procedures.[40]

At the time the Prison Service had serious and long term financial control problems. One member of the Public Accounts Committee, Alan Williams, had received a leaked memo that Landers had written to ministers highlighting the severity of the situation.[41] Although the MP asked some questions on the topic the questioning moved on before the issue could be examined in any depth. As Williams had not shared the information with the rest of the committee no other member had the ability to follow up the issue. Landers concluded: '...at the end of the day we were adjudged to have won because the real issues remained uncovered and our minister had not been embarrassed'.[42]

If, for a variety of reasons, committees are unable or unwilling to ask insightful questions this will have an obvious and marked impact on their capacity to enforce ministerial responsibility. Research uncovered a severe divergence of opinion on the standard of questioning. Members of the HAC consistently rated the standard of their questions as high. Beverly Hughes's statement was typical: 'If we've read our briefs there is no question that the standard of questioning is high'. Witnesses before the committee disagreed. Douglas Hurd described the general standard of questioning in his time as 'moderate'. Ann Widdecombe stated: 'I never felt I was put under any real pressure by the committee'. A senior Prison Service official and a director of a company managing a contracted out prison described the standard of questioning as 'very poor'. That serving members of the HAC talk up their capacity to demand a full and extensive account through questions in committee is not surprising. The paradigm of parliamentary accountability is maintained at all costs. What is stark is the gap between theory and practice. An apathetic MP noted,

> Committee members will always talk up their role, power and influence. Few backbenchers believe what they say but they are trapped into upholding a front which thinly veils their impotence.

Despite the imperfections and constraints noted above, ministers and officials place the upmost importance upon their duty to account to Parliament via select committees. Witnesses described how appearing before a committee often involved the temporary abdication of habitual responsibilities and the restructuring of working procedures to release those called to appear to prepare. Ann Widdecombe recounted how the Home Office would set up a mock committee and hold extensive sessions, over several days, until she and her senior officials were satisfied she would be able to 'adequately defend the department'. A senior Prison Service official described a process in which he would delegate 95% of his duties in the week before an appearance so that he could absorb a large briefing folder that two or three officials would have spent a month preparing solely for the appearance. Brian Landers describes how seriously a select committee appearance is taken:

> A full - time defence team worked for weeks preparing briefings for us. The permanent secretary cleared his diary and waded through enormous quantities of paper. I received special one to one training at the Civil Service College from a former permanent secretary. We rehearsed with a host of Home Office and Treasury advisers.[43]

Although ministers have never blocked the appearance of a named official before the committee there is evidence that when it comes to the rules concerning civil servants appearing before select committees the gap between theory and practice may not be as large as is commonly thought.

There have never been any overt instances when an official has refused to answer a question invoking the Memorandum of Guidance as the basis for declining to co-operate but several interviewees emphasised the contemporary importance of the Osmotherly rules. Derek Lewis recalled how he had been made aware of the Osmotherly rules by the Home Office and how he had abided by them. (Hence his offer to reappear before the committee after his dismissal.) A senior Prison Service official noted: 'Yes, I'm aware of the rules, everyone here is. They've caused me to tiptoe along a very fine line on occasions but I think they're necessary.' Current members of the HAC were also aware that these rules prevented agency officials rendering a full account. Robin Corbett noted: 'With the agency heads you get the impression that there is a lot more they could tell you but they are not going to'.

A committee inquiry culminates in the publication of a report, which in the majority of cases will contain recommendations.[44] The government's response to these reports is a telling reflection of the balance of power in Parliament. How frequently does the government accept the recommendations of the HAC committee? What powers does the committee have to force the government to take its report into account? A systematic survey of HAC reports and the government's subsequent response and action since 1979 exemplifies the weakness of the committee. It is, of course, difficult to calculate the direct impact of a committee's report. Indirect consequences are just as important as direct ones but much harder to measure. The causal connection between a particular report and action taken is further obscured by the fact that reports themselves are not discrete entities but the products of cumulative committee activity. Wider social, economic and media factors may also have an equally important influence on the executive's response to the report.

Where a direct correlation can be made between a report and subsequent reform evidence would suggest that only recommendations that coincide with the opinion of the executive are accepted. The Committee's investigation into the 'sus' law is frequently cited as a success story.[45] It highlighted the harm done to race relations by the perceived discriminatory use of Section 4 of the Vagrancy Act 1824. The committee denounced 'sus' as a fundamentally unsatisfactory law. When the report was debated in Parliament the Home Secretary, Willy Whitelaw, refused to take immediate action stating that he preferred to wait for the results of a Law

Commission inquiry into the topic.[46] Sir Graham Page, the Conservative HAC chairman, argued against the Home Secretary and voted with the opposition. The committee then published a supplementary report in which it threatened to introduce a Private Members Bill if the government refused to legislate. In the next session the government repealed the 'sus' law with the Criminal Attempts Act and the Home Secretary acknowledged that '...the inclusion in the Bill of a provision to repeal the offence obviously owes a great deal to the committee's report'.[47]

Gavin Drewry noted that some civil servants had privately told him that the committee had '...merely anticipated something that would have happened anyway - a claim which is not very convincing but is, by its nature, hard to refute'.[48] But a rigorous survey of reports and government replies reveals a strong tendency towards acceptance only when the recommendations are in line with government thinking. For example, the government accepted the majority of the recommendations contained in the HAC's report on computer pornography.[49] Most had been anticipated by the government and included in the Criminal Justice and Public Order Bill and the revision of the Obscene Publications Act 1959 and Computer Misuse Act 1990. The government also accepted the recommendations of the committee's inquiry into video violence and young offenders.[50] The committee inquiry was established shortly after the James Bulger murder and recommended a tightening of the law, a new classification system and increased powers for the British Board of Film Classification.

The HAC's inquiry into the 'year and a day' rule in relation to murder is often cited as a success. The committee recommended that the rule be abolished,[51] which the government duly accepted.[52] But the committee's report had not been published in isolation. The rule had been debated during the passage of the Criminal Justice and Public Order Act 1994 and the Law Commission had examined the issue in detail.[53] The HAC was aware that the government intended to legislate on the issue in the near future and the Home Secretary had acknowledged that the conclusions of the committee would be of great value.[54] It could therefore be argued that the committee was a vehicle for the expression of the executive's views rather than a force in shaping them. In October 2000 the government accepted the vast majority of the recommendations contained in the HAC's report on firearms.[55] The government had introduced a complete ban on handguns in 1997 and the Home Office had already indicated its intention to introduce further statutory controls on firearms.[56]

The work of the committee therefore complemented the stated intentions of the government.

When the recommendations do not fit in with the government's thinking there is very little the committee can do to force the government to take its views into account. Many of the HAC's inquiries (for example domestic violence; juvenile offenders; and racial attacks and harassment) have been very broad. In these cases the government's response was sympathetic, but the vast majority of the specific recommendations were politely rejected.[57] On narrower issues the government is free to simply reject the committee's recommendations - the legal aid and private security industry reports for example.[58] Often the convention of ministerial accountability is used as a justification for rejecting proposals that have been designed by the HAC to increase accountability and openness. For example, the committee recommended that the security service should be responsible to the committee.[59] But the government rejected this proposal on the basis that the director general was responsible to the Home Secretary who was in turn responsible to Parliament.[60] Not only was the government defining the committee's sphere of oversight but ministerial responsibility was employed as a justification for preventing reforms that sought to remedy concerns about the failure of ministerial responsibility in the first place.

A similar situation occurred in response to the HAC's report on the mandatory life sentence and the proposal that responsibility for setting the tariff and making decisions about the release of prisoners sentenced to life be removed from the Home Secretary.[61] The recommendation was made due to concerns that politicians may be tempted to take political considerations into account and that they were inadequately accountable at present for their decisions. The government based its rejection of the proposals on the need to maintain ministerial responsibility to the House. 'The Home Secretary is himself in a unique position. No other authority, either judicial or independent, can be held directly to account by Parliament.'[62] But the committee was suggesting that the Home Secretary's responsibility to the House was not enough. (The government concluded it was 'disappointed' with the recommendation of the committee.)[63]

Several interviewees raised concerns that the relationship between the current HAC and the Home Office had lapsed into an unhealthy over-intimacy since May 1997. The government responded positively to the committee's reports on freemasonry and police discipline.[64] In the case of the freemasons the recommendations were in line with the evidence given by the Labour party while in opposition and therefore it is unsurprising that they were readily accepted.[65] But it would have been unlikely that the recommendations would have been accepted if the Conservatives had remained in power. The power relationship allows the executive to decide what proposals to accept. There is little the committee can do to force the executive to take its views into account. The police discipline and complaints inquiry was, again, an area in which the Home Secretary had signalled his intention to reform the system.[66] As one senior Home Office official noted:

> That is a good example of his [Jack Straw's] attitude to Parliament. He thought there were issues around the topic which needed to be dealt with and was happy to use the Home Affairs Committee as the vehicle around which a new policy can be designed.

But the role of Parliament is not to be employed as a policy-making vehicle for the executive. Several current members of the committee thought that the cordial relationship between the Home Office and committee had lapsed into an unhealthy intimacy: '...the committee is not there to make policy, it is there to challenge and scrutinise the actions of ministers and the administration and management of the Home Office'.[67] MPs suggested that 'the Office' was using the committee to foster support for policies decided in Queen Anne's Gate. Chris Mullin, the committee chairman at the time, defended his committee:

> I don't agree that we are now too close. I think that we have a more mature relationship based on trust and mutual respect which has not been present in the past but that does not mean that ministers will not get a hard time if they deserve it or that we will become policy makers rather than scrutineers.

Comparing committee reports with government replies highlights the frailty of Parliament when faced with an unsympathetic executive.[68] Only when the recommendations of the committee are in line with the broad thrust of government thinking, and/or heavily supported by external media and public support, are they likely to be accepted. It is hard for committees to generate parliamentary momentum behind a report due to the limited opportunities to debate reports on the floor of the House. For example in the 1979-1983 Parliament only one Home Affairs Committee report was debated on the floor (race relations and the 'sus' law),[69] and in the 1992-1997 Parliament only two reports were debated (domestic violence and the private security industry) with another being 'tagged' as relevant to another debate (legal aid).[70]

It could be suggested that the HAC is ineffectual. This is due to a wide range of political and practical issues that are inevitably interlinked. The fundamental power relationship within the House ensures that there is little the committee can do when faced with government obduracy.[71] When the recommendations of a report are in line with the evidence of the Home Office the committee can expect a favourable response,[72] and vice versa.[73] Who chairs the committee and how is a key ingredient to the political chemistry of the committee, a fact overlooked in the wider literature. For example, earlier chairmen, like Sir Graham Page and Sir John Eden, were widely felt to have been fair and even-handed. Despite them both being Conservative ex-ministers they were praised by interviewees for their neutrality and fairness. (This may be linked to the fact that they were Heath-men, rather than Thatcherites.) As the committee structure settled and became more competent it appears that the whips appointed chairs more carefully. Sir John Wheeler and especially Sir Ivan Lawrence were famed for their partisanship. The crucial point for accountability is that the chair has the power to nullify the committee - protecting witnesses, avoiding issues and employing their casting vote to protect the government.

The HAC struggles with the breadth of its remit. Its scope is too wide and it should not be strictly regarded as a departmental committee.[74] This affects the depth of its inquiries and the ability of its members to master its activities. And yet research failed to detect any enthusiasm among backbench MPs for parliamentary reform. MPs have been consistent in their reluctance to employ special advisers, fearing that the advisers may disguise well-honed prejudices among their evidence and that the committee might become 'staff' rather than 'member' driven. The Hansard Society have criticised this reluctance to increase the number of special advisers and support staff.

> The assumption that the current system is overwhelmingly member-driven, and that further staff would jeopardise this position, is something of a polite fiction. Furthermore, it says a lot about the potential

management skills of MPs that faced with an increase of staff, their first reaction is to fear that they would lose control of the work.[75]

Nevertheless, no interviewee, minister or backbenecher, thought that the challenges faced by select committees could be resolved by an increase in either staff or resources.[76] Such recommendations were viewed as naive: they failed to appreciate the executive's mentality and dominance, which would eviscerate reforms to increase Parliament's capacity for government scrutiny. That MPs should espouse such depressing basic beliefs locates specific hurdles faced by parliamentary mechanisms within the wider context of the realities of parliamentary politics. Several interviewees suggested that the shortcomings associated with the formal mechanisms of parliamentary accountability are somewhat appeased by the existence of informal and/or party mechanisms of accountability. The next section examines these claims and describes the processes and channels involved.

3.4 Party Accountability

Party accountability refers to the duty of ministers to account to their parliamentary party in order to retain their confidence and support. This relationship raises a number of questions: As party accountability involves ministers accounting to a section of the House can it be viewed as an element of ministerial responsibility? Does party accountability support or undermine ministerial responsibility to the House? Through what channels and processes does it operate? How do ministers perceive party accountability compared to their duty to account to the House? A discussion of party accountability is also important as it suggests that the wider academic literature may have overlooked a number of vital processes and constitutional relationships.[77] It also adds weight to the contention that the traditional dichotomy between government and opposition is too simplistic and might suggest that the irrelevance of backbenchers is a myth. Ronald Butt's (1967) scholarly analysis of the ways in which MPs have always scrutinised and influenced ministers in more subtle and informal ways than by outright revolts has been neglected by academics in recent decades.[78] Butt's extensive explication about the informal influence of government backbenchers on ministers is too often ignored.

During interviews MPs, and particularly those with ministerial experience, stressed the importance of these informal channels and suggested that their existence to some extent mitigated the problems associated with the formal mechanisms of parliamentary accountability. Ministers especially emphasised that their accountability to Parliament was far more complex than commonly recognised. Parliament matters to ministers. It matters because the phrase 'government majority' is inaccurate. The executive consists of up to 95 ministers out of a total of 659 MPs.[79] The government is always in the minority in the House and it is this fact that ensures that ministers account to the House to ensure the support and confidence of the majority. (But the government and the majority party are not synonymous.) Ann Widdecombe remarked:

> Accountability to the party was crucial. It operated through the backbench Home Affairs Committee, the 1922 Committee, informal meetings and a whole range of channels. Party accountability was in many ways harder to deal with than PQs and select committees and all that because it was not a game, you could not fob them off...you relied on their support and if you lost that you lost everything.

The locus of accountability in Parliament is therefore dynamic. A divided opposition may not signify a diminution of accountability it might just mean that with a dominant majority adversarial politics returns to the shadows.[80] It may also add credence to the view that those who can really enforce ministerial responsibility sit behind rather than in front of the minister in the House.[81] Too large a majority can in itself encourage backbench questioning and unrest as not only does it diminish the opportunities for ministerial office but is also allows backbenchers a degree of independence without seriously endangering the government. One MP noted (April 1999):

> The accountability in Parliament comes from the government's own side and not from Parliament itself. The accountability that the Major government had was not to Parliament but to its own backbenchers. Similarly here with a majority of this size what matters is what your own people think.

Former Home Office ministers stressed that the nature of their accountability to their parliamentary party differed from their constitutional duties under ministerial responsibility to Parliament. Ann Widdecombe suggested that it tended to be much more constructive as those challenging you were 'in the same family' and therefore the questioning was not tainted by party political point scoring. Douglas Hurd noted: '...it did not require any great wisdom on my part to realise that there was an important need to keep in touch with backbenchers'.

Members of the Home Affairs Committee (HAC) also verified the importance of the informal channels of accountability.[82] Unofficial meetings with ministers and officials, letters, telephone calls and even chance meetings in the corridor were all advanced as important aspects of the accountability relationship between the Home Office and Parliament.[83] Interviewees suggested that because the contact existed externally to the adversarial nature of Parliament, it often delivered a more comprehensive and helpful response from ministers. Indeed, there is an unwritten convention that these processes are not abused for party political gain. A member of the HAC noted:

> In my experience most ministers will always agree to meet an MP, or group of MPs, of any party, informally to discuss an issue or event. Safe in the comfort of their department, and without the media or minutes, most ministers will discuss most issues freely. The quid pro quo is that the minister will not expect to see what they have said on the front page of the next morning's papers.

Formal and informal mechanisms of accountability often interact. One member of the HAC described tabling a number of parliamentary questions to the Home Office but receiving defensive and partial answers. He raised this issue during a chance meeting with a minister who proceeded to tell him exactly how to frame the question. The MP followed this advice and duly received the information he had been seeking. Other members of the committee recounted that after questioning ministers and/or officials during a formal HAC session they would subsequently receive a phone call either offering them the explanation or information or offering them an informal meeting. One HAC member stressed how these subtle lines of accountability had always been the most powerful:

> They have always been the most important and there is nothing new about that. It is what lubricates the system...it is much less the formal

mechanisms as they are conditioned by the party system. The informal ones are conditions of power, policy and so on.

Two former chairmen of the HAC, Sir Ivan Lawrence and Chris Mullin, agreed that the informal mechanisms of accountability were crucial and tended to operate in an apolitical fashion. In their cases this took the form of regular, often weekly, informal meetings with the Home Secretary. Previous and current members of the committee were surprised to learn of these meetings. Even the committee clerks were unaware of them, and yet both Lawrence and Mullin stressed the importance of these meetings as a way of collecting 'pure' information which could then be relayed back to the committee.

Labour members of the HAC linked the importance of internal mechanisms of accountability to Labour's prolonged period in opposition. Gerald Bermingham noted: 'The old Labour MPs from the 1979 and 1983 intakes have gone through the Parliaments of minority and have learnt to take a more diplomatic approach to accountability'. This might explain criticisms that the Labour party's desire to maintain a united face has undermined backbench vitality.[84] A united face may have been achieved by strengthening the informal processes of accountability. One member of the committee noted:

> The executive, only under this government, has said that the backbench committees have to be consulted before a major policy initiative is made. That is an attempt to develop a system of strong internal accountability within the party and not to depend on those formal parliamentary routes which are very different.[85]

The emphasis placed upon these informal processes of accountability is crucial for a number of reasons. Ministerial responsibility is a duty to account publicly and officially to the House and can never therefore be abrogated through informal channels. Likewise, although the need to maintain the support of their parliamentary party may ensure ministers account to Parliament via backbench committees this should be regarded as a distinctly separate process to their duty to uphold the convention of ministerial responsibility to the House as a whole. Ministers are not accountable to their parties in a constitutional sense and therefore their constitutional duties cannot be absolved through rendering an account to one section of Parliament.

Informal accountability is, once again, accountability defined and dictated by the executive. It displays the fundamental power relationship and the failure of parliamentary accountability to enforce ministerial responsibility. We should not be happy democrats because a minister may decide to release unofficially information that they chose not to disclose to a select committee. Parliamentary accountability is crucial to democracy exactly because it is transparent and therefore contributes to a wider public accountability and knowledge. If parliamentary accountability worked effectively these informal processes would be unnecessary. The language employed by former Home Office ministers when discussing party accountability may provide an insightful glimpse of their true opinion of Parliament. (Ann Widdecombe's phrases 'it was not a game' and you 'could not fob them off', for example.)

A robust argument can be advanced that party accountability undermines ministerial responsibility to the House. It forms a conduit through which ministers can privately sustain and foster support within the House without using those procedures and mechanisms that have been designed to do that publicly. Party accountability cannot constitutionally legitimate the actions of ministers, yet emphasising informal channels of accountability offers benefits to backbench MPs who are keen to rebut accusations of parliamentary impotence and executive control. But when a minister fails to provide a satisfactory account through parliamentary channels and is also unhelpful when approached informally the fundamental problems of parliamentary scrutiny remain. The next section places the findings of this case study within this wider picture and teases out it implications for the wider thesis.

3.5 Conclusion: Withering Parliamentary Accountability?

The discourse used to discuss an issue is often indicative of the underlying attitude and value system attached to the topic. The rhetoric employed by ministers, officials and parliamentarians might be interpreted therefore as reflective of their intrinsic beliefs. Overwhelmingly interviewees referred to parliamentary accountability as a game. 'Politics as a game is a recurring theme in Whitehall.'[86] This, in turn, might explain the common accusation that the Home Office is a defensive department. The sensitivity of the issues with which the Home Office is concerned might, by their nature, cause officials to expect blame rather than praise.[87] But the language perpetuates a defensive approach to Parliament: a 'them and us' mentality according to which the department is judged to have 'won' if the main issues remain uncovered. A constitution in which officials owe their primary allegiance to their minister, rather than Parliament, cements the system.

This chapter has essentially confirmed and substantiated the existence of a range of serious deficiencies with the mechanisms of parliamentary scrutiny. Moreover, it has demonstrated the degree to which the balance of power within the House is weighted heavily in favour of the executive. Ministerial responsibility is an elusive paragon - and yet it remains the cornerstone of the British constitution.[88] There are occasional glimpses of parliamentary independence. For example, the Foreign Affairs Committee's inquiry into Sierra Leone[89] and the Treasury Committee's scrutiny of the Monetary Policy Committee.[90] But these infrequent events do not threaten the fundamental power relationships and the dominance of the executive.[91] Parliament does, of course, play a central role in calling ministers and their officials to account. But the content and depth of the account is defined by the executive rather than Parliament. Faced with an obdurate minister with party support Parliament is largely impotent. The constitution ascribes Parliament a quasi-judicial role that it simply cannot fulfil.

Nevertheless, the research findings contained within this chapter suggest that Parliament is far from insignificant.[92] Home Office ministers and officials take their duty to account to Parliament extremely seriously.[93] Why then, if Parliament is such a toothless watchdog, is it, undoubtedly, taken so seriously?[94] Three mutually reinforcing explanations can be advanced using constitutional, conspiratorial and egoistic explanations.

Britain is a parliamentary democracy. Parliament is the locus of political and media attention. Although ministers may provide information and answers to a range of bodies it is to Parliament that they are constitutionally and regularly responsible. Often it is a very pure and focused form of accountability. Ministers must treat Parliament with respect because they need to retain the support of their parliamentary party. An unprepared minister would appear contemptuous. It is also necessary for ministers to appear to take Parliament seriously to uphold the facade that Parliament really is enforcing parliamentary accountability. By paying lip service to ministerial responsibility, which serves them so well, they undermine calls for new methods of accountability or parliamentary reform. Finally, individual self interest ensures that Parliament is taken seriously. Ministers know full well that careers are won and lost at the despatch box; and this ensures that parliamentary appearances are given paramount attention. Officials understand too that being caught unprepared in front of a select committee may damage their minister and therefore, indirectly, their own career.

The findings of this chapter are critical to the overall book. If the parliamentary model of accountability is failing then the managerial and judicial models of accountability become increasingly significant. If research suggests that they are comprehensive and robust this may, to some extent, mitigate the deficiencies of parliamentary accountability which have been identified in this chapter. On the contrary, should evidence suggest that these alternative forms of accountability are also incapable of enforcing an acceptable degree of accountability over the core executive it will be clear that a serious constitutional lacuna exists with regard to responsibility in the contemporary state. New models of accountability are 'path dependent' on the extant forms of accountability. Therefore it is important to explain and understand the influence of ministerial responsibility as determined by the executive, in creating the legitimate framework within which these new models have evolved.

Earlier chapters have described how the British constitution is a political constitution in which ministers are responsible not to the courts but to Parliament.[95] Nevertheless concerns surrounding the dominance of the executive within Parliament have fostered a burgeoning literature considering the merits of the mechanisms of judicial accountability and the possibility of the courts adopting an increased role in enforcing the accountability of the core executive.[96] As Sir Richard Scott noted:

> It must be recognised that if the obligations of accountability are not accepted by ministers, both in theory and in practice, as binding, and are not, where necessary, enforced by Parliament, the remedy can only lie in reducing at least that part of our written constitution into statutory form.[97]

Sir Richard admitted that he was 'crying to the moon' when he provocatively suggested that the requirements of ministerial responsibility be codified in statute and enforced by the courts.[98] Yet the idea raises a number of questions and issues regarding the evolving relationship between the judiciary and the executive and what implications this has for both parliamentary accountability, in particular, and public accountability, in general. This topic will be the focus of Chapter Four.

Notes

1   See Judge, D. Hogwood, B. & McVicar, M (1997) 'The "Pondlife" of Executive Agencies: Parliament and Informatory Accountability' *Public Policy and Administration* Vol.12 No.2 p.99.
2   Statistics from the Prison Service Secretariat, correspondence with the author, 20/5/98.
3   Ken Livingstone MP observed: 'The Home Office is the most difficult department to prise information out of. You have this broad defensive mentality and they see everything as a threat'. Radio 4 *The Matrix of Power* broadcast 14/10/99.
4   'I think I have been a judge long enough not to be shocked by many things but I was getting on for being shocked at how the process for accounting to Parliament through answering questions was regarded by officials as something to be got rid of by the convenient answer rather than as any sort of opportunity to be informative about what the government was doing.' Sir Richard Scott interview with the author, March 1998. See also HC 115 *Report of the Inquiry into the Export of Defence Equipment and Dual-Use Goods to Iraq and Related Prosecutions*, Session 1995/96, HMSO, London. [The Scott Report] Vol.1 D4.25-D4.63.
5   Landers, B (1998) 'Of Ministers, Mandarins and Managers' in Flinders, M V & Smith, M J (eds.) *Quangos, Accountability and Reform: the Politics of Quasi-Government* (London : Macmillan) p.129.
6   Home Office (1997) 'Jack Straw Announces Ministers to Answer Prison Service PQs' press release no.118/97 8/5/98.
7   Cm 3020 (1995) *Review of Prison Security in England and Wales and The Escape from Parkhurst Prison on Tuesday 3rd January 1995*, HMSO, London. [The Learmont Report] p.93.
8   See Hansard, HC Debs. 17/6/97 Vol.296, cols. 107-110.
9   Prison Service Secretariat, correspondence with the author 20/5/98.
10 An extensive literature review found just one piece of work on MP to minister correspondence. This was Norton, P & Wood, D (1993) 'Back from Westminster: British Members of Parliament and Their Constituents' (Lexington : University of Kentucky Press) chapter 3.

11   Calculated using the Treasury's estimate of the cost of answering a written question (£112) and using the same figure for the cost of answering a piece of parliamentary correspondence.
12   See HC 313-V *Ministerial Accountability and Responsibility* Second Report of the Public Service Committee, Session 1996/97, HMSO. London. Evidence by Derek Lewis p.99 Q641. For Derek Lewis the problem was never solved and he was left to: '...groan every morning when confronted by the heap of letters' Lewis, D (1997) *Hidden Agendas* (London : Hamish Hamilton) p.69. Landers noted: '...even the totally potty had to be answered. Religious peers consumed hundreds of hours of very senior time with questions on the accuracy of our computer records on Buddhist inmates or our policy on scientology'. Landers, B (1998) 'Of Ministers, Mandarins and Managers' in Flinders, M V & Smith, M J (eds.) *Quangos, Accountability and Reform: The Politics of Quasi-Government* (London : Macmillan) p.129.
13   See, for example, HC 313-II (1996/97) Memorandum by Prof. Philip Norton p.74.
14   This suggestion is supported by the work of Norton & Wood who wrote: 'A letter invites a considered, often detailed response, usually free of the party pressures that prevail in the chamber; by being a private communication, it avoids putting a minister publicly on the defensive. Ministers are thus more likely to respond sympathetically in the use of their discretion than is the case if faced with demands on the floor of the House'. Norton, P & Wood, D (1993) 'Back from Westminster: British Members of Parliament and Their Constituents' (Lexington : University of Kentucky Press) p.76.
15   In total the Home Affairs Committee completed 45 inquiries or evidence sessions in the 1992-1997 Parliament. For a full list see HC 323-II *The Work of Select Committees* First Report of the Liaison Committee, Session 1996/97, HMSO, London. pp.66-73.
16   Apart from one instance in the Committee's first parliamentary session when a debate regarding the remit of the committee led to the Attorney General declining to appear. The Attorney's role as the government's principal and confidential legal adviser makes this a special case: though a member of the government, he is not a minister. See HC 434 *Proposed New Immigration Rules and the European Convention of Human Rights* First Report of the Home Affairs Select Committee, Session 1979/80, HMSO, London. para 6.
17   Sir Ivan Lawrence noted: 'I would often take them to one side in the bar or the corridor afterwards and urge them to buck up or leave and make way for someone who wanted to do the job'. Interview with the author, April 1998.

18   'Competing pressures' was an important impediment to the 1992-1997 Home Affairs Committee noted by Sir Ivan Lawrence in his end of Parliament report. See HC 323 (1996/97) Appendix 14 pp.46-47 para. 7.
19   Interview with the author April 1998. Examples include Beverley Hughes, in the current Parliament, who missed most of the committee's inquiry into police complaints due to standing committee commitments and in the last Parliament Gerald Bermingham who was an infrequent member due to his extra-parliamentary commitments as a barrister.
20   The first Home Affairs Committee, created on 25 June 1979, had no continuity of membership with its predecessor the Education, Arts and Home Office sub-committee of the expenditure committee.
21   See Brazier, A (2000) *Systematic Scrutiny: Reforming the Select Committees* (London : Hansard Society) p.8.
22   See Riddell, P (1998) *Parliament Under Pressure* (London : Victor Gollancz) p.232; See also HC 323-I (1996/97) Appendix 'Reports of the committee chairman' p.3 para 17.
23   HC 300 *Shifting the Balance: Select Committees and the Executive*, First Report, Session 1999-2000, HMSO, London.
24   Cm 4737 *The Government's Response to the First Report from the Liaison Committee on Shifting the Balance: Select Committees and the Executive*, HMSO, London.
25   Brazier, A (2000) *Systematic Scrutiny: Reforming the Select Committees* (London : Hansard Society) p.9.
26   A common complaint in relation to committees. See HC 19 *The Working of the Select Committee System* Second Report by the Committee on Procedure, Session 1989/90, HMSO, London. p.xliii; Cremin, M (1993) 'The setting up of the Departmental Select Committees after the 1992 election' *Parliamentary Affairs* Vol.46 No.3; Judge, D (1992) 'The Effectiveness of the Post - 1979 Select Committee System' *Political Quarterly* Vol. 63 No.1 pp.400-420; Weir, S & Beetham, D (1998) *Political Power and Democratic Control in Britain* (London : Routledge) p.408.
27   Ann Taylor was a Labour whip between 1977 and 1979.
28   HC 19 *The Working of the Select Committee System*, Second Report from the Procedure Committee, Session 1989-1990, HMSO, London. Para.178.
29   See Cremin, M (1993) 'The setting up of the Departmental Select Committees after the 1992 election' *Parliamentary Affairs* Vol.46 No.3; Weir, S & Beetham, D (1998) *Political Power and Democratic Control in Britain* (London : Routledge) pp.407-408.
30   Conservative chairman of the Health Committee 1991-1992. Party managers implemented a new rule to the effect that no Tory MP could serve on a committee for more then three consecutive Parliaments. While

this allowed them to remove Nicholas Winterton it also meant they had to remove a number of loyal Tory committee members including Sir John Wheeler, Chairman of the Home Affairs committee. See Dawnag, I & Atkins, R 'Parliament and Politics: Winterton anger at committee move' *Financial Times* 9/7/92 p.11; Owen, D & Atkins, R 'Senior Tories' angry at committee ruling' *Financial Times* 14/7/92 p.10.

[31] '...they wanted me on the inside throwing bombs out rather than on the outside throwing them in.' Interview with the author, April 1998.

[32] Mr Mullin did leave the Home Affairs Committee to become a Junior Minster in the Department of the Environment, Transport and Regions in September 1999.

[33] Interview with the author, April 1998. Talking about Peter Wheeler MP (Con. Westminster North) Chairman of the Home Affairs Committee 1987-1992).

[34] Interview with the author 21/4/98. HC 301 *Funding of Political Parties* Second Report of the Home Affairs Select Committee, Session 1993/94, HMSO, London.

[35] Interview with the author, March 1998. A view reinforced in the media who labelled him a 'ministerial poodle'. See 'A nasty turn for Mr Howard' *The Guardian* 30/3/96 p.24.

[36] HC313-II (1996/97) p.128 Q1173. See also HC 313-II (1996/97) p.129 Q1179.

[37] He had appeared once before but had been bound by the Osmotherly rules. See HC 144 *The Operation and Performance of the Prison Service* minutes of evidence, Home Affairs Committee, 18/1/95, Session 1994/95, HMSO, London.

[38] Derek Lewis interview with the author, June 1996. See also Cohen, N 'Power without responsibility: does being a minister mean never having to say that you're sorry?'. *The Independent* 22/10/95 p.20.

[39] An issue raised by Tom King in relation to his appearances before select committees. King, T, Jenkin, P & MacGregor, J (1997) 'Ministers and Parliament' *The Journal of Legislative Studies* Vol.3 No.4 pp.1-24.

[40] Landers, B (1998) 'Of Ministers, Mandarins and Managers' in Flinders, M & Smith M (eds.) *Quangos, Accountability and Reform: The Politics of Quasi-Government* (London : Macmillan).

[41] For an in-depth and insightful discussion of the interaction between the Home Office and the Public Accounts Committee see: Landers, B (1999) 'Encounters with the Public Accounts Committee: A Personal Memoir' *Public Administration* Vol. 77 No.1 pp.195-213.

[42] Landers, B (1998) 'Of Ministers, Mandarins and Managers' in Flinders, M & Smith, M (eds.) *Quangos, Accountability and Reform: The Politics of Quasi-Government* (London: Macmillan) p.130.

126 *The Politics of Accountability in the Modern State*

[43] Landers, B (1998) 'Of Ministers, Mandarins and Managers' in Flinders, M V & Smith M J (eds.) *Quangos, Accountability and Reform: The Politics of Quasi-Government* (London : Macmillan) p.130.

[44] Where issues are particularly party political and it is likely that the committee will split down party lines it is common for committees to hold inquiries and place the evidence on the public record without making recommendations. For example, see HC 301 (1993/94); HC 46 *Racial Attacks* Second Report of the Home Affairs Committee, Session 1981/82, HMSO, London.

[45] Sir John Eden stated in his end of Parliament report: 'In the case of the "sus" law our Report was instrumental in bringing about the repeal of that provision through the Criminal Attempts Bill the following session'. HC 92 *The Select Committee System* First Report of the Liaison Committee, Session 1982/83, HMSO, London. p.84 para.7.

[46] Hansard HC Debs. 5/6/80 cols. 1963 *et seq*.

[47] Hansard HC Debs. 19/1/81 cols.21 *et seq*.

[48] Drewry, G (1989) 'The Home Affairs Committee' in Drewry, G (ed.) *The New Select Committees* (Oxford : Clarendon) p.199.

[49] HC 126 *Computer Pornography* First Report of the Home Affairs Select Committee, Session 1993/94, HMSO, London.

[50] HC 514 *Video Violence and Young Offenders* Fourth Report of the Home Affairs Select Committee, Session 1993/94, HMSO, London.

[51] HC 111 *Murder - The Mandatory Life Sentence* First Report of the Home Affairs Select Committee, Session 1995/96, HMSO, London.

[52] Cm 3346 (1996) *The Government Reply to the First and Second Reports from the Home Affairs Committee, Session 1995/96 HC 111 and HC 412: Murder and the mandatory life sentence* p.27.

[53] The Law Commission 'Legislating the criminal code: the year and a day rule in homicide' Report No.230.

[54] HC 111 (1995/96) p.v para.2.

[55] Cm 4864 (2000) *The Government's Reply to the Second Report from the Home Affairs Committee, Session 1999-2000, HC 95, Controls Over Firearms*, HMSO, London.

[56] Clark, J 'Gun lobby attacks Straw over curbs on teenagers' *The Sunday Times* 1/11/00 p.7.

[57] For example 'The government agrees with the committee that this is an extremely important issue...'. 'The government is grateful for the committee's views.' Cm 2269 (1993) *The Government Reply to the Third Report from the Home Affairs Committee, Session 1992/93 HC 245: Domestic Violence* p.23.

58 HC 17 *Legal Aid - The Lord Chancellor's proposals* Fifth Report of the Home Affairs Committee, Session 1992/93, HMSO, London. HC 517 *The Private Security Industry* First Report of the Home Affairs Committee, Session 1994/95, HMSO, London.
59 HC 265 *Accountability of the Security Service* First Report of the Home Affairs Committee, Session 1992/93, HMSO, London. p.xi para. 28.
60 Cm 2197 (1993) *The Government's Reply to the First Report from the Home Affairs Select Committee, Session 1992/93, HC 265 Accountability of the Security Service* HMSO, London. para. 5 section C.
61 HC 111 (1995/96) p.vii para. 14.
62 Cm 3346 (1996) p.2 para. 6.
63 Cm 3346 (1996) p.5 para. 30.
64 HC 192 *Freemasonry in the Police and the Judiciary* Third Report of the Home Affairs Select Committee, Session 1997/98, HMSO, London. HC 258 *Police Discipline and Complaints Procedures* First Report of the Home Affairs Select Committee, Session 1997/98, HMSO, London.
65 See HC 192-II (1997/98) Appendix 25 p.139. See HC 577 *Government Reply to the Third Report from the Home Affairs Select Committee, Session 1996/97: freemasonry in the police and the judiciary* First Special Report of the Home Affairs Committee, Session 1997/98, HMSO, London.
66 HC 258 (1997/98). HC 683 *Government Reply to the Home Affairs Committee (First Report) Police Disciplinary and Complaints Procedures* Second Special Report of the Home Affairs Committee, Session 1997/98, HMSO, London.
67 Labour MP, interview with the author, April 1998.
68 Wider research supports my case study findings in relation to select committee reports and executive action. See Adonis, A (1990) *Parliament Today* (Manchester : Manchester University Press); Weir, S & Beetham, D (1998) *Political Power and Democratic Control in Britain* (London : Routledge) pp. 404-440. See also Hawes, D (1993) *Power to the Backbenches?* (Bristol : School for Advanced Urban Studies, University of Bristol).
69 Hansard, HC Debs. 5/6/80, cols. 1963 *et seq.*
70 See HC 323-II (1996/97) pp.66-72.
71 This fundamental power relationship is thinly veiled by the positiveness of the end of Parliament reports. See HC 92 (1982/83) pp.83-87. HC 323-II (1996/97) pp.66-72.
72 For example in the case of the committee's inquiry into the Representation of the People Acts. HC 21 *Representation of the People Acts* First Report of the Home Affairs Select Committee, Session 1982/83, HMSO, London.

128 *The Politics of Accountability in the Modern State*

73 As in the case of the committee's inquiry into miscarriages of justice where the committee supported the evidence of the pressure group Liberty in opposition to the Home Office's evidence and consequently had its recommendations rejected by the government. HC 421 *Miscarriages of Justice* Sixth Report of the Home Affairs Select Committee, Session 1981/82, HMSO, London.

74 One clear lacuna in the committee's work has been its inability to enforce the accountability of the Lord Chancellor to Parliament. Despite the department falling under the HAC's remit it has received scant attention. Sir Ivan noted this in the committee's end of Parliament report and called for the creation of a new committee: 'The Lord Chancellor's and the Law Officers' Departments have been inadequately scrutinised' at HC 323-II (1996/97) Appendix 14 para.4. An issue raised by the committee as far back as 1983. See HC 92 (1982/83) p.87 para. 13.

75 Brazier, A (2000) *Systematic Scrutiny: Reforming the Select Committees* (London : Hansard Society) p.18.

76 This is in line with wider surveys of Parliament. See, for example, HC 323 (1996/97) p.xiii.

77 King, A (1976) 'Modes of Executive-Legislative Relations' *Legislative Studies Quarterly* Vol.1 pp.13-32.

78 Butt, R (1967) *The Power of Parliament* (London : Constable).

79 The *House of Commons Disqualification Act 1975* (section 2) provides that no more than 95 sitting MPs may hold ministerial office at any one time.

80 See Parris, M 'The end of opposition?' *The Times* 1/5/98 p.12.

81 A view supported by wider literature. Ministers from the 1980s have emphasised the power of the 1922 committee. Patrick Jenkin remembers a sharp phone call with Edward du Cann after one particular incident while he was Secretary of State for the Environment (1983/1985) which left him in no doubt that his job was at risk: 'My colleagues and I think you should come and try and explain yourself to the committee this afternoon.' King, T, Jenkin, P & MacGregor, J (1997) 'Ministers and Parliament' *The Journal of Legislative Studies* Vol.3 No.4 pp.1-24.

82 A Labour MP noted: 'I think, in a sense, there are informal and party systems of accountability that are obviously not transparent but nevertheless are important and powerful forms of accountability. One of the problems for the new intake is that there is no introductory training on how best to use either the formal or informal mechanisms of accountability. Clearly the informal methods are not written down anywhere and you have to learn them almost through an osmotic process but when you do get round them they are really important and effective'. Interview with the author, March 1998.

83   Plans for parliamentary reform may have unintended consequences for these informal processes of accountability. For example, proposals to replace lobby voting with electronic voting from MPs' offices have been attacked by backbenchers for reducing their opportunities to 'collar' ministers.

84   See: Hencke, D 'Blair defends his "babes" on charges of toadying' *The Guardian* 18/4/98 p.12; Purves, L 'Silence of the babes' *The Times* 31/3/98 p.18.

85   Interview with the author, April 1998. There are 26 Labour backbench committees. See House of Commons, Public Information Office list No.4 *Labour Party Departmental Committees and Regional Groups* May 1998.

86   Landers, B (1999) 'Encounters with the Public Accounts Committee: A Personal Memoir' *Public Administration* Vol. 77 No.1 p.195.

87   Roy Jenkins suggested Home Officials have a 'slightly defensive expectation that whenever the Home Office attracted attention it would also attract blame'. Jenkins, R (1975) 'On Being a Minister' in Herman, V & Alt, J (eds.) *Cabinet Studies - A Reader* (London : Macmillan) p.212.

88   Judge asserts: 'In this sense conventions serve to delineate the flow and strength of political power that ought to pertain in constitutional relationships'. Judge, D (1993) *The Parliamentary State* (London : Sage) p.139.

89   HC 760 *Sierra Leone: Exchanges of Correspondence with the Foreign Secretary* First Report of the Foreign Affairs Select Committee, Session 1997/98, HMSO, London. HC 852 *Sierra Leone: Further Exchanges of Correspondence with the Foreign Secretary* Second Special Report of the Foreign Affairs Select Committee, Session 1997/98, HMSO, London. See Watt, N 'MPs defy Cook over inquiry into arms deal' *The Times* 1/7/98 p.10.

90   HC 82 *The Monetary Policy Committee of the Bank of England: Confirmation Hearings* Sixth Report by the Treasury Committee, Session 1997/98, HMSO, London.

91   Disagreeing with Patrick Wintour. See Wintour, P 'The New Opposition' *The Observer* 28/6/98 p.32.

92   Richardson, J & Jordan, A (1979) *Governing Under Pressure; The Policy Process in a Post Parliamentary Democracy* (Oxford : Blackwell).

93   This is clear by the literature and biographies of former ministers. See, for example King, T, Jenkin, P & MacGregor, J (1997) 'Ministers and Parliament' *The Journal of Legislative Studies* Vol.3 No.4 pp.1-24; Waldegrave, W (1995) 'The Future of Parliamentary Government' *The Journal of Legislative Studies* Vol.1 No.2 pp.173-177; King, T, Jenkin, P & MacGregor, J (1997) 'Ministers and Parliament' *The Journal of Legislative Studies* Vol.3 No.4 pp.1-24; Hurd, D (1997) 'The Present Usefulness of the House of Commons' *The Journal of Legislative Studies* Vol.3 No.3 pp.1-9.

[94] Hennessy, P (1996) 'Teething the Watchdogs: Parliament, Government and Accountability' in Hennessy, P (1996) *Muddling Through* (London : Indigo) pp.63-79.

[95] Griffiths, J (1979) 'The Political Constitution' *Modern Law Review* Vol.42 pp.1-21.

[96] Laws, J (1993) 'Is the High Court the Guardian of Fundamental Rights?' *Public Law* pp.59-79; Laws, J (1994) 'Judicial Remedies and the Constitution' *The Modern Law Review* Vol.57 pp.213-227; Laws, J (1995) 'Law and Democracy' *Public Law* pp.72-93; Sedley, S (1994) 'The sound of silence: constitutional law without a constitution' *Law Quarterly Review* Vol.110 pp.270-291; Sedley, S (1995) 'Human Rights and a Twenty First Century Agenda' *Public Law*; Leigh, I & Lustgarten, L (1996) 'Five Volumes in Search of Accountability: The Scott Report' *Modern Law Review* Vol.59 p.697; Oliver, D (1996) 'Comment: The Scott Report' *Public Law* pp.357-368; Foster, C (1996) 'Reflections on the true significance of the Scott Report for Government Accountability' *Public Administration* Vol.74 No.4 pp.567-592.

[97] Scott, R (1996) 'Ministerial Accountability' *Public Law* p.426.

[98] Interview with the author, March 1998.

4 Judicial Accountability

> There is considerable public support for judicial control of an otherwise unaccountable executive. Administrations of all colours may have themselves to blame for a popular consciousness which, at least occasionally, casts them in the role of dragons and the judiciary in the role of St George.[1]

4.1 Introduction

The commonly identified shortcomings of ministerial responsibility have engendered a debate about the United Kingdom's reliance on political mechanisms of accountability. A central strand of this considers the increased use of legal regulation and judicial forms of accountability. These discussions are increasingly important for a number of reasons. First, unlike in the United Kingdom, several Westminster democracies established strong frameworks of public law as a counterweight to the centrifugal pressures of new public management. This involved more legal regulation within the state to remedy the obvious challenges devolved management presented to ministerial responsibility to Parliament.[2] Moreover, the fragmentation and devolution associated with new public management has arguably initiated a reformulation of the state, so that it increasingly resembles Harden's 'contract state'. The increased use of contracts and legal or quasi-legal agreements (framework documents, private finance initiative agreements, civil service contracts, etc.) is likely to increase recourse to the courts to settle issues which previously had been constitutional/political rather than legal in nature. Second, the wider literature suggests that during the last decade the relationship between the executive and the judiciary has changed markedly.[3] At the heart of this shift is the perception that the judiciary attempted to rectify what they identified as an inadequate framework of accountability and extended judicial creativity to new levels in an attempt to increase judicial oversight of the core executive. As Stone notes: 'Developments have been sufficiently distinctive, extensive and important for us to describe them as creating a new system of accountability in Westminster democracies'.[4] Finally, several aspects of the Labour government's constitutional reform programme (devolution, freedom of information, incorporation of the European Convention on Human Rights, etc.) will increasingly draw the senior judiciary into the political sphere. In this context the balance of power between politicians and the judiciary may change dramatically as judicial scrutiny of executive action may become more frequent and cases decided much quicker, with the judgement resting on a clearer and more legitimate foundation than in the past.

This chapter examines the role of the courts, law and judiciary in relation to central government and the complex interrelationships on which these linkages are constructed. The central question is: *To what degree have judicial mechanisms of accountability evolved to remedy the shortcomings commonly identified with ministerial responsibility to Parliament?* This is clearly a complex question involving an analysis of a range of secondary questions: How can the impact of judicial review on the core executive be measured both quantitatively and qualitatively? Does the literature on an increasingly active judiciary reflect reality? What would life be like without ministerial responsibility for public administration? Does judicial accountability complement or undermine parliamentary accountability? How available are judicial forms of accountability to the public? To what degree has ministerial discretion been fettered by legal regulation? Is there a correlation between European integration and judicial accountability? To what degree has the convention of ministerial responsibility affected the development of mechanisms of judicial accountability? How effective are judicial inquiries as mechanisms of accountability in central government? Is there a trend towards ministers avoiding responsibility through recourse to the law or legal advice? Can predictions be made, with any certainty, regarding the future equilibrium between politics and the law?

This chapter does not examine the responsibility of ministers for the legal system.[5] It examines to what degree judicial mechanisms facilitate responsible government in the United Kingdom.[6] Judicial mechanisms of accountability are vital and potentially powerful for a range of reasons. First, they provide a core *auxiliary precaution* to prevent the abuse of power and to ameliorate the accountability of ministers and officials.[7] Second, judicial mechanisms, like judicial review, are non-parliamentary. In court, ministers are not protected by a party majority, their parliamentary privileges are absent and issues rarely become entwined in party political point scoring.[8] Third, judicial mechanisms are powerful due to their wider ramifications. They possess the potential to elucidate wider notions of public accountability by empowering the public with formal rights and clarifying procedures. Finally, the courts have coercive powers that empower them with the capacity to deliver explanatory, informatory and amendatory accountability.[9] The courts can compel any public body to perform certain duties, release information or refrain from acting in a certain way. However, like Parliament's, their powers are discretionary and a distinction must be drawn between theory and practice. This chapter aims to fill the academic void highlighted by Drewry when he noted how political scientists appear to have underestimated the effects of the law on both public policy and politics.[10] (This divide is being bridged increasingly by journals publishing special editions examining the relationship between politics and the judiciary[11] and publications jointly authored by political scientists and public lawyers.)[12]

The impact and utility of judicial accountability is difficult to measure.[13] Some commentators are keen to inflate the role of judicial oversight of the executive.[14] Others suggest the role of the judiciary has been exaggerated.[15] This chapter is important to the central thesis of this book as it examines through what channels the executive is compelled to provide an account to judicial processes. It is divided into three sections. The first examines constitutional, historical and theoretical issues. The second section examines the impact of judicial accountability on the core executive. Exploring three distinct processes (judicial review, European legislation and judicial inquiries), it evaluates the positive and negative aspects of each mechanism with the aim of developing pertinent questions and hypotheses to explore in the following case study chapter. The final section concludes the chapter with a synopsis and a review of the main issues and questions that deserve empirical research.

4.2 The Constitutional, Historical and Theoretical Background

One of the most striking characteristics of the British constitution is that its structures and procedures for accountability are not based on statute. In contrast to continental Europe, Britain lacks both a strong system of administrative law, which controls the actions of the administration, and constitutional law, which controls the actions and behaviour of the executive.[16] This means that ministers have few limitations on their actions and are free to do anything that is not explicitly illegal. The United Kingdom has a constitution that places a heavy burden upon a sense of tradition, propriety and good form, but which is marked by an absence of legal mechanisms to enforce these standards.[17] And yet at the heart of the British Constitution lies the rule of law.

4.2.1 The Rule of Law and the Separation of Powers

The rule of law is a fundamental doctrine of the British constitution.[18] As Dicey noted:

> It means...equality before the law, or the equal subjection of all classes to the ordinary law of the land administered by the ordinary law courts; the "rule of law" in this sense excludes the idea of any exemption of officials or others from the duty of obedience to the law which governs other citizens.[19]

Dicey examined the development of administrative law in other countries and objected to the way the state was given a privileged position, as he believed, as it could only be challenged in special courts. Dicey therefore argued that the state should be subject to the same laws as the ordinary citizen and as a consequence in the British legal system there is no formal separation between private and public law.[20] Thus executive and public bodies are subject to the same laws as private citizens, and will be tried in the same courts. De Smith and Brazier see the main tenets of the rule of law as: that the powers exercised by politicians and officials must have a legitimate foundation (i.e. they must be based on authority conferred by law); and that the law should conform to certain minimum standards of justice, both procedural and substantive.[21] The aim is to guard against the arbitrary exercise of power by making everyone subject to the same impartially enforced rules.

The importance of the rule of law is that, unlike our European neighbours, Britain has failed to develop a strong system of public law, resulting in an over-reliance on outdated and problematic parliamentary conventions and a reluctance to move towards legally based accountability systems. Dicey's ideas looked back to the minimalist *laissez faire* state and this led to a restricted view of public law which struggles to accommodate the size and complexity of the large interventionist twentieth - century state.[22] The modern state now carries out such a large array of functions that Parliament has conferred wide discretionary powers on the executive. Yet it is widely acknowledged that the legislature is now much less capable of controlling the executive. The judiciary, through judicial review, has sought to fill this constitutional vacuum and tried to ensure that the executive does not abuse those powers conferred upon it by Parliament.[23] In Lord Bingham's words: 'The courts have reacted to the increase in the powers claimed by the government by being more active themselves'.[24]

The 1932 Donoughmore Committee on Ministers' Powers rejected William Robson's scheme for introducing a separate system of administrative courts using Diceyan arguments that the *droit administratif* is incompatible with '...a flexible unwritten constitution under which there is no clear cut separation of powers'.[25] The lack of a clear separation of powers in Britain has important implications for accountability and in many ways puts extra emphasis on the role of the courts. This doctrine of the separation of powers is usually portrayed positively, as a central feature of good government, but a formal separation of powers has never been at the centre of the British constitution. As Stephens wrote: 'Nothing underlines the atheoretical nature of the British constitution more than the casualness with which it approaches the separation of powers'.[26] Britain lacks a strict constitutional divide. The executive is drawn from the legislature; the highest ranks of the judiciary sit in the legislature; the Lord Chancellor is head of the judiciary, sits in the legislature and is even a member of the executive. As Chapter Three clearly demonstrated this has significant implications for the accountability of the executive, as Parliament's capacity to enforce accountable government is effectively curtailed by the executive's control of the House, thus exerting extra pressure on the judiciary to fulfil this role. As Wade noted 'The separation of powers means little more than an independent judiciary'.[27] In the British state sovereignty lies in Parliament and the courts therefore can only uphold the will of Parliament as stated in statute; but as Chapter Two discussed, the executive is free to remould the state without recourse to statute. This has important ramifications for the ability of judicial forms of accountability to scrutinise central government.

4.2.2 Bureaucratic Reform and the Law

Ministers are free to restructure and reorganise central government without the need for legislation. Reforms, such as the Next Steps, have been introduced under a combination of Orders in Council, Royal Prerogative, and administrative fiat. It is a principle of administrative law that discretionary powers should only be exercised by those to whom those powers have been entrusted. This is known as the rule against delegation (*delegatus non potest delegare*). It would appear then that where there is an official devolution of discretionary powers this would need to be accompanied by empowering legislation. But with regard to government agencies this legal rule is qualified by the Carltona doctrine.[28] This states that the principle is not breached where discretion conferred upon ministers is exercised by civil servants within their departments, as constitutionally the actions of the civil servants are those of their ministers.[29] The protagonists of the Next Steps programme did not see the creation of executive agencies as constituting a reform that fettered the Carltona principle. It has been argued, however, that the delegation of responsibility involved in the Next Steps has clearly breached the rule against delegation and therefore demands legislation.[30] The suggestion being that functions have, in practice, been devolved so far out of the department decision-making structure that the Carltona principle should no longer apply.

In recent years the civil service has been the topic of several Acts. These have facilitated the commercialisation and privatisation involved in new public management. For example, the Civil Service (Management Functions) Act 1992 empowers agency chief executives to take control of pay and conditions of service. The Deregulation and Contracting Act 1994 expedited the deregulation of functions previously performed by government departments.[31] Freedland uses the existence of these acts to argue that if it is accepted that legislation was necessary for these purposes it must be needed for the more all - encompassing devolution of power involved in the Next Steps.[32]

The significance of the Carltona doctrine and the rule against delegation in the agency context is twofold. First, the absence of a need for legislation has effectively taken Parliament out of the process and evaded parliamentary accountability. For example, agency framework documents are not laid before Parliament for debate nor are appointments laid before the House for ratification. Second, the substantial powers exercised by agency chief executives are not derived from statute, and this insulates them from direct oversight by the courts. The fact that agencies are non-statutory creations hampers judicial accountability as there are no explicit criteria against which behaviour can be judged. The courts cannot rule that an agency has acted *ultra vires* because there is no legal statement of the powers within which the agency was supposed to be acting. As Drewry and Oliver noted: 'There is commonly nothing for the British Courts to bite on in the institutional arrangements of British central government'.[33]

The constitutional position that agencies are still parts of their parent departments also prevents them using recourse to the law to protect themselves from what they might see as unnecessary ministerial interference. While it is common for local authorities to bring judicial review against central government, this is not an option for agencies because in law they have no separate legal identity from their parent department. A reform proposal involves putting agencies on a statutory footing, or at least setting agencies up under legal contracts.[34] So far this has been resisted by an executive that has upheld the constitutional position that the Crown is indivisible.[35] This questionable, but politically convenient, argument has meant that the vast majority of the contractualisation associated with new public management, at the central government level, has been quasi-contractual rather than legal. Parliament has had a minimal role to play in what have been fundamental structural reforms to central government. The executive has considered bureaucratic reform as a managerial and not a constitutional issue. This belief is erroneous. The shift from hierarchical to increasingly fragmented departmental structures, an emphasis on managerial style rather than administrative rigour, the burgeoning growth of public/private partnerships and a devolution of control and responsibility away from ministers are challenges that are clearly constitutional in nature. But it is not only the structure of the state that has changed markedly: so have relationships between key actors within the state, not least between the executive and the judiciary.

4.2.3 The Breakdown of the Relationship

The constitutional position of the judiciary is awkward. Its role in upholding the rule of law produces an inevitable friction between the judiciary and ministers.³⁶ This constitutional tension grows from the fact that judges, through the process of judicial review, are involved in reviewing the actions of ministers, and that their decisions can have substantial administrative, financial and political repercussions.³⁷ Traditionally this potential has been contained through a process of non-provocation. Parliamentary sovereignty involves the subordination of the courts to Parliament. In return Parliament was deferential to the views of the courts and did not impede upon judicial independence.³⁸ The traditional *quid pro quo* between politics and law has always been one of mutual respect and acceptance of clear boundaries. Drewry summed up the traditional relationship: 'The lip service paid by the courts to the sovereignty of Parliament is reciprocated by Parliament's own traditional deference to judicial independence'.³⁹ The delicate equilibrium is maintained as *ultra vires* enables the judiciary to claim that it is simply upholding the will of Parliament by ensuring that ministers have not acted beyond the powers Parliament has ascribed to them.⁴⁰ Although judges have dabbled with the concepts of fairness and reasonableness in the past, they have been careful to do so by justifying their decision as acting in line with the will of Parliament. In this way, judges on the whole managed to avoid political controversy until the mid-1980s.

Oliver notes that in the post-war period the courts accepted ministerial responsibility as an effective constitutional principle.⁴¹ This was due to that fact that it was widely seen to be functioning adequately, but it also provided a legitimate excuse for the courts not to have to intervene in political issues. The attitude of the judges to politicians was one of deference, demonstrated most famously in the case of *Liversidge v Anderson* in which the law lords found in favour of the executive and stressed the fact that the minister involved was responsible to Parliament and not the courts.⁴² (In a dissenting opinion Lord Atkin decried the decision of the court and stated: 'I view with apprehension the attitude of judges who show themselves more executive minded than the executive.')⁴³

The degree of judicial activism or deference is difficult to gauge and there are opposing opinions on it. Will Hutton believes: 'The long standing tradition of Britain's judiciary being more executive minded than the executive, in Lord Atkin's famous dictum, came into its own in the 1980s'.⁴⁴ But Lord Bingham spoke of Hutton's passage in disbelief and thought that Conservative ministers '...would find this description of the judges' role hard to match up to the world they live in'.⁴⁵ However, two issues are clear: by the mid-1990s the judiciary had significantly extended the sphere of executive action that it was willing to rule on; and the relationship between the judiciary and the executive had deteriorated markedly (and often publicly).[46] Not only was this a new and potentially worrying development for the constitutional equilibrium but it also challenged previously understood theories about the relationship between the judiciary and governments of different political complexions (especially Griffiths' thesis that judges were conservative with a small 'c' and were more likely to have a harmonious coexistence with Conservative governments).[47]

The demise of the relationship has been well-documented.[48] According to Woodhouse, the judiciary were increasingly concerned about six main issues: the domination of the executive; its encroachment into the administration of justice; the perceived arrogance of some ministers with regard to the law and judiciary; an underlying concern that rights were being eroded; a concern that concepts such as fairness and reasonableness were being sacrificed in the drive for efficiency; and the rise in judicial suspicion that ministers were hiding behind the defence of 'public interest' when they were in fact acting in the government's interest.[49]

At the same time, ministers became anxious about a perceived tide of judicial activism and the rapid increase in judicial review applications. Judicial decisions were seen as undermining executive discretion and challenging the sovereignty of Parliament. Ministers were increasingly concerned as in a series of articles senior judges seemed to call for an increased constitutional role and laid claim to being the protectors of fundamental rights.[50] In 1995 a series of legal challenges against the government, notably the Home Secretary, were upheld in the domestic courts, the European Court of Justice (ECJ) and the European Court of Human Rights (ECHR). The media portrayed these cases as personal attacks against the ministers involved. Ministers resented the growing activism of the courts, especially when public confidence in the government was already low.

Against this background the old relationship of non-confrontation appeared mythical. At the 1995 Conservative conference Michael Howard marked a clear foray into the traditional grounds of the judiciary by announcing the increased use of both mandatory and minimum sentences without consultation with the judiciary - a clear move by the executive into areas traditionally left to the judiciary. The judges feared their independence was being eroded and that if the proposed reforms were introduced sentencing would become based on electoral imperative and not an objective consideration of the public good by the judiciary. The debate raged in the media and even deteriorated into a dirty tricks campaign in which Conservative Central Office leaked a bogus speech by Lord Mackay warning judges not to challenge an elected government.[51] (Lord Mackay denied that he was ever going to deliver the speech in question.)[52] The relationship between ministers and the judiciary has changed from one of mutual respect and non-provocation to one in which the two parties involved have consistently moved into each other's traditional spheres: judges have sought to control and limit the powers of ministers, while ministers attempt to undermine the traditional discretion enjoyed by the judiciary.[53] There lies, at the heart of this tension, a fundamental constitutional challenge. Judges increasingly have decided cases by reference to 'fundamental rights' rather than upholding the will of Parliament.

4.2.4 The Judicial Protection of Fundamental Rights

Accountability to whom? Accountability for what? These simple questions are often the hardest to answer when discussing accountability. The first question is refreshingly simple to answer in this context - this chapter explores the accountability of the core executive to the courts and judiciary. The second question is more problematic - against what criteria, rules and standards should the judiciary hold ministers to account? The British Constitution is (in)famous for lacking clearly formulated rules and standards against which the behaviour of ministers can be judged.[54] The traditional justifications for judicial review are developed from the Diceyan model of the constitution. The role of the judiciary is to uphold the rule of law and the supremacy of Parliament by ensuring that ministers and their officials do not exceed or abuse the powers given to them by Parliament. The judges' function rests on the limitation of executive power which is inherent in a parliamentary democracy and is therefore a central part of our representative democracy.[55] However, in the last decade senior judges have decided cases through recourse to their role as protectors of 'fundamental freedoms' that need to be safeguarded in any democratic society,[56] thus creating the situation in which judges are no longer holding ministers to account for the lawful exercise of powers conferred upon them by Parliament. Instead also holding them accountable against judicial interpretations of very abstract rights which became a form of judge-made law in so far as such interpretations are regarded as binding precedents. Sir John Laws summed up the stance: '...a democratic constitution is in the end undemocratic if it gives all power to its elected government'.[57] This clearly challenges the basic principles of our parliamentary democracy and goes beyond the rule of law.[58] (That an unelected, unrepresentative and largely unaccountable elite should seek to constrain the elected in this way obviously raises a number of constitutional issues.)[59] Such creativity cannot be legitimated through the traditional defence that the courts are simply upholding the original intention of Parliament.[60] Several senior judges have given up the facade of the 'will of Parliament' and called for the constitutional fiction to be scrapped:

> They are categorically judicial creations. They owe neither their existence nor their acceptance to the will of the legislature. They have nothing to do with the intentions of Parliament, save as a fig leaf to cover their true origins.[61]

Sir John Laws believes that for a democracy to flourish there must be some constraints on elected politicians due to the imperative of higher-order law.[62] If Sir John's position is accepted it would fuel the idea that, despite lacking a written constitution, we have *de facto* the beginnings of a constitutional court; this in itself raises fundamental questions about the powers and position of ministers as well as parliamentary sovereignty. Several judges now believe that parliamentary sovereignty is in truth an absolute rule, which is a dangerous situation to have in a constitution in which the public lacks any protected fundamental freedoms. 'I am not impressed with a constitution in which the freedoms of the people are in the end protected only by the expectation, however confident, that the government will behave decently.'[63] Lord Woolf has echoed the beliefs of Sir John:

> I myself would consider there were advantages in making it clear that ultimately there are even limits to the supremacy of Parliament which it is the courts' inalienable responsibility to identify and uphold.[64]

Lord Woolf has also suggested that in certain circumstances the courts may declare statutes passed by Parliament invalid, arguing that the courts could refuse to recognise and give effect to legislative action that sought to undermine the rule of law by restricting the powers of review by the High Court.[65] Ministers have interpreted such statements as a threat to their position. Lord Irvine has warned against judges adopting the role of the guardians of fundamental rights believing this would 'lead judges into dangerous territory'.[66] Denying that he is simply protecting a Labour government from judicial obstruction, he has set out his defence against judicial activism many times - from a legal/constitutional perspective[67] and from a moral/philosophical perspective[68] - culminating in his assertion '...it is both wrong and politically stupid for judges to challenge Parliament's sovereignty'.[69] Yet there are clear examples of an increase in legal regulation over ministerial activity.

4.2.5 Towards Formal Legal Regulation of Ministerial Action

There are clear examples of the imposition of legal regulation on ministerial discretion which suggests that mechanisms of political accountability have been found unsuitable in several areas. This sets an important precedent and invites the question why could the law not be employed so effectively in more areas and especially in central government?

With the advent of post-war social democracy and the growth of a large welfare state the need arose for discretion to be devolved to officials, in the area of benefit entitlement for example. This started a gradual process in which the decision-making powers and discretion enjoyed by both ministers and civil servants were placed under a stronger system of legal regulation than had previously existed. A system of tribunals was established to deal with the complaints of aggrieved citizens. These are independent adjudicatory bodies established by statute to deal with disputes in their area of specialism. Theoretically, ministerial responsibility could have remained as the sole political channel of accountability with MPs taking their constituents grievances to the minister. But Parliament could not have coped with the volume of cases and it was seen as preferable to have them dealt with by a structure of specialist, independent and accessible tribunals.[70]

The increased use of public inquiries is another example of a degree of legal regulation involving and constraining the actions of ministers which has been developed in recent years. Public inquiries can be set up by a minister before a decision is taken, to gauge and take into account the opinions of all interested parties, or after an incident, to examine a particular issue or episode. This 'before or after' capability of inquiries suggest they possess the ability to exert both *ex post* and *ex ante* accountability. In addition there is a provision for an appeal to the courts against a minister's decision should the inquiry generate suspicions of illegality or procedural impropriety. As with tribunals, theoretically these decisions could have been taken by ministers and subject only to the scrutiny provided by ministerial responsibility to Parliament. Oliver notes how this was not considered acceptable due to the limited time available to Parliament and the lack of expertise in the areas to be examined by MPs.[71]

In addition to the development of tribunals and inquiries there have been several pieces of legislation which have slowly increased the amount of legal regulation over government activity. These have reduced the discretion of ministers and exposed them to being held accountable judicially should they be found to have breached these statutes. These Acts are important as they define the limits to ministerial freedom and provide criteria against which ministerial action can be judged - they provide something for the courts to 'bite on'. For example, the Interception of Communications Act 1985 placed the authorisation of phone tapping on a statutory footing, where before it had operated under the convention that the Home Secretary or Attorney General authorised tapping. The Act also facilitates an independent element of accountability in the creation of a Commissioner for the Interception of Communications whose role is to scrutinise the actions of the executive in this sphere of work.[72] In addition, the Security Service Act 1989 and the Intelligence Services Act 1995 have been passed in response to public concern. Once again they place areas that were previously under the control of ministers purely responsible to Parliament, on a statutory foundation, and therefore open to judicial scrutiny. (The Acts also fostered the development of new quasi-parliamentary accountability controls such as the cross-party Intelligence Service Committee which shadows the operations of the secret services and reports privately to the Prime Minister.)

The Law Commission has proposed new laws to prevent bribery and corruption in public life.[73] Prompted by the 'Cash for Questions' affair the commission, chaired by the High Court judge Dame Mary Arden, has proposed a new single offence of corruption.[74] In a linked development and in response to recommendations made by the Nolan committee,[75] the Home

Office has produced an internal paper[76] and published a consultation paper[77] which both discuss clarifying the outdated and confusing common and statute laws on bribery, which date back to 1551. These documents examine the options and effects of an extension of the scope of the current law or any new law to include MPs. One of Jack Straw's first initiatives when he became Home Secretary was to sign the European Convention on Corruption in Paris in May 1997[78] and he is said to be determined to incorporate this into UK law through Home Office legislation.[79] But the introduction of a new and fortified law on corruption which included MPs would increase the jurisdiction of the courts over MPs. It would represent another example of the growing sphere of judicial accountability in recognition of the inadequacies of political mechanisms. Such a move would be important for two reasons: first, it would not replace parliamentary accountability but simply complement the convention of ministerial responsibility; secondly, by definition the inclusion of MPs in laws relating to corruption would be an admission of both the deficiencies of parliamentary accountability and the inability of Parliament to rectify those shortcomings internally.[80]

This section has examined the increased use of legal regulation. This creates an important precedent for the increased use of judicial or legal forms of accountability. In each area it was recognised that, for various reasons, ministerial responsibility to Parliament was not an adequate check against the abuse of power and more legally based and formalised controls were established. This, in turn, may add weight to the arguments of public law proponents who emphasise the potential offered by legal regulation to a system trembling under the weakness of its traditional commitment to political rather than legal forms of accountability. Conversely, stressing a change of emphasis from political to legal regulation invites questions about the nature of power in the constitutional system, in particular identifying which actors control to which areas of the political spectrum legal regulation is applied. That power resides in Parliament explains why legal regulation has been so minimal and applied so selectively with ministerial responsibility forming the legitimating foundation.

4.3 Judicial Accountability and Central Government

4.3.1 Judicial Review

> Ultimately, this country's checks and balances are no longer here. They are in the courts and they are called judicial review.[81]

Judicial review is the principal means by which the courts exercise supervision over the conduct of central and local government in the United Kingdom.[82] Since the late 1970s, the perceived willingness of the courts to sit in judgement over the actions of the executive has given them a reputation for legal and political activism, even supremacism. However, it is crucial to place the process of judicial review in perspective. That Rozenberg describes judicial review as the 'theatre of war' rightly implies that the process inevitably creates friction between law and politics.[83] There have been several high profile cases in which the courts have found against ministers, most notably in the Pergau Dam affair.[84] (In 1992 the Conservative government was threatened when judicial review was successfully invoked against Michael Heseltine's coal pit closure policy.)[85] The historic growth in the use of judicial review continued almost unabated throughout the 1990s. In the first quarter of 1991 applications for leave were running at an annual rate of just over 1800, and this had increased to over 3200 by a similar period in 1994/1995, a growth of 78%. Figures from the Crown Office review indicate that in the latter half of the decade growth in judicial review applications continued, albeit at a lower rate of just over 40% for the period from 1994-1999.[86] The total number of applications reached over 4500 in 1998, falling back slightly to 4437 in 1999.[87] The rapid increase in judicial review applications has been linked by many observers to an attempt by the judiciary to rectify the shortcomings commonly identified with parliamentary accountability.[88] Lord Irvine noted:

> Let me begin with a recognition that the consequences of the 'democratic deficit', the want of parliamentary control over the executive in recent years, has been, to an important degree, mitigated by the rigours of judicial review... It has so often rightly held the executive to account and improved the quality of administrative decision making.[89]

Liberal judges, enjoying the relaxation of the Kilmuir Rules by Lord Mackay,[90] have embellished the role of judicial review stating that: 'Parliament is too weak to vindicate to the just satisfaction of the citizen its historic power to control the executive in the name of the people'.[91] As Woodhouse notes:

> Senior judges have recognised the inadequacy of political accountability and the shortcomings of Parliament in bringing ministers to account, and see judicial activism as a response to the increase of the powers claimed by government and to the confrontational style of politics practised by the Thatcher governments.[92]

The reasons for the rapid growth in judicial review applications are numerous but stem from the extensive 1977 reforms which '...transformed the face of administrative law and rapidly increased the number of cases brought against government bodies'.[93] James summarises the other factors as: the dramatic decline of public deference towards public bodies and politicians; the growth of government activity; an increasing awareness of Parliament's limitations; a gradual but important shift in judicial attitudes; the growth in the number of High Court judges who have made assertions to fundamental rights; and the impact of European law and Charters.[94] Woolf, Jowell and De Smith add one important impetus to this list: '...pressure against public bodies which had previously seemed immune from accountability or control'.[95]

An application for judicial review must be made on one of three grounds: illegality (the minister acted *ultra vires*); irrationality (that no reasonable person could have reached the final decision); or procedural impropriety (that prescribed rules were not followed or the rules of natural justice were breached).[96] Traditionally the courts have mainly concentrated on issues of illegality. Thus their decisions and powers have been legitimated against the courts' role of upholding the rule of law and ensuring that ministers act only within the powers conferred upon them by Parliament. Increasingly the courts' focus on *ultra vires* has shifted to irrationality and procedural propriety. This change of emphasis is crucial because: any decision which is not based on illegality is difficult to legitimate constitutionally; it also allows the courts to take into account a much wider range of factors (e.g. 'irrelevant considerations' under irrationality have included fear of political embarrassment); an increase in considered factors, combined with the discretion and differing value systems of individual judges, makes the whole process much less predictable. The *Wednesbury* test of reasonableness exemplifies the dangers of the judiciary holding ministers to account for decision/actions.[97] Governments are not voted into office to act unlawfully or disregard due process. Therefore judges can justify striking down executive action on the grounds of illegality or fair process by reference to the rule of law. But judges have invented the 'reasonableness' principle. There is no political or legal consensus about what constitutes 'irrational' ministerial behaviour. The judiciary's answer has been to apply incoherent criteria and set the threshold high. Without a clear and universally agreed statement of what constitutes 'reasonableness' the courts have no democratic or constitutional foundation for their action. This lays them open to accusations of acting undemocratically, undermining Parliament, and fuels suspicions that judges may strike down a decision as 'irrational' simply if they do not like it.

How can the impact of judicial review on the core executive be classified? James, building on the earlier work of Rawlings[98] and Feldman,[99] offers a fourfold categorisation of the impact of judicial review which distinguishes between *cancelling, corrective, restrictive* and *inhibitive* effects.[100] Each category has a direct relationship with accountability, as the minister is in effect having to account for their actions against judge - made standards. The *cancelling* effect negates a ministerial decision and forces the minister to reconsider the decision. If the decision was deemed procedurally unfair or irrational the minister need only repeat the decision-making process (following the correct procedures and/or dismissing irrelevant considerations) and may arrive at the original decision. If the minister was found to have acted *ultra vires* the decision or policy may have to be cancelled. The cancelling effect is crucial to accountability as the knowledge that the final decision may well be challenged will weigh against arbitrary government (therefore having an *ex ante* and *ex poste* effect).

The *corrective* impact applies when the deficiency the court recognises lies not just in the individual case but in the underlying policy or procedural practice. The impact of the decision will vary, but it is not unknown for an adverse judgement to destroy a policy.[101] This is important as it re-emphasises the need for ministers to stay within the powers conferred upon them by Parliament.[102] There is also evidence that departments with knowledge that legal aid or leave has been granted for judicial review will review their procedures or amend a decision before the case reaches court. (This might explain the high number of cases granted leave that fail to reach a full hearing.) Ministers may also shy away from policy decisions that are likely to become nullified by review applications.[103]

The *restrictive* impact extends further than the case in question and creates procedures and standards to which the core executive must adhere in the future. For example, a common law creation is the principle of legitimate expectations. This arose from the 1985 GCHQ case in which the Law Lords noted that if national security had not been a factor the government would have lost the case because as the staff had been consulted about wages and conditions in the past a legitimate expectation had been created that they should have been consulted on this occasion.[104] This decision set an important precedent with significant ramifications for accountability. The scope of public law was advanced by the principle of 'legitimate expectation' which empowered those who had been consulted over a decision to be consulted over similar future decisions. It forces the core executive to take into account the views of those stakeholders whom they had communicated with in the past. Such a significant ruling with wider implications underlines the potential impact of judicial review for the central administration, policy-making process and executive-judicial relations.[105]

James notes that the *inhibitive* impact of judicial review requires a jettisoning of previous misconceptions. The first of these is that judicial review is rarely more than a mere irritation. It compels ministers, and more frequently their officials, to account for decisions, provide information, it upsets their policies, causes great delay and may potentially generate publicity and embarrassment. Nor are judicial and political accountability mutually exclusive. A sudden increase in leave applications in a specific area can often focus parliamentary attention (select committees, parliamentary questions) and/or highlight flaws in subordinate legislation.[106]

The issues so far considered may create the perception that judicial review plays a major role in enforcing the accountability of ministers and civil servants in the United Kingdom. (The massive increase in review applications, a number of high profile cases which have struck down ministerial action, a number of statements by judges and politicians apparently vindicate this view, and there is a judicial shift of emphasis away from *ultra vires* towards judge-made law.) Such a perception may be wrong. A range of issues suggests that judicial review remains 'sporadic and peripheral'.[107] (See Table 4.1.)

Table 4.1 Positive and Negative factors most commonly associated with the ability of Judicial Review to enforce accountable government

Positive	Negative
• Takes place in an environment free of party politics in which the minister is not protected by party support. • Coercive powers can force the attendance of witnesses and the release of information, or overturn decisions. • A surge of judicial review applications in a specific area can focus parliamentary attention on an issue. • The threat of judicial review may provide a constant counterweight to arbitrary government. • The procedures for applying for judicial review have been simplified. • Judicial review may well be a facilitator of 'good administration' (although this is not the same as accountable government).	• Constitutionally the judiciary has a weak foundation on which to enforce accountable government beyond upholding the rule of law. • The executive can overturn any judicial decision through legislation or remaking the decision following prescribed guidelines. • Judicial review is rarely used as a challenge to the core executive. • When an application is against a department it rarely involves ministerial actions. • The vast majority of review applications fail at the first (leave) stage. • Of those granted leave the executive wins the vast majority (80%+) of cases. • Judges are still deferential to Parliament and are unlikely to rule in areas involving economic policy, defence or national security. • Judges rarely overturn Public Interest Immunity Certificates or even examine the documents covered. • Practical (financial, delays, backlogs) and procedural (need to prove 'sufficient interest' and obtain leave) obstacles. • It is a reactive and secondary mechanism of accountability. • Democratically the judiciary has a weak foundation on which to enforce accountable government as judges are not elected or accountable. • Judicial review is a very uncertain and discretion based process.

The first issue is methodological. There is a severe lack of information in relation to judicial review. The fact that judicial review applications have increased since the late 1970s is often used as evidence of the increasing importance of judicial review but it is an incomplete statistic. There is no capacity for knowing the proportion of applicants, those seeking leave to appeal, that never get to court and therefore the accessibility of judicial review to the public. We cannot therefore know what proportion of disputes between the core executive and the public are being dealt with by the courts. For example, how many people cannot utilise judicial review as a mechanism of accountability due to inadequate advice and/or funding? (There is also a dearth of information regarding specific subject areas and the types of bodies most commonly under challenge.) The statistics that are available highlight how rarely judicial review is invoked against the core executive. In June 1996 Margaret Hodge MP tabled a trawling parliamentary question asking each department how often they had been challenged by judicial review in the previous five years.[108] Five departments, including the Home Office, gave no answer on the grounds that they did not keep records or that the answer would involve disproportionate cost. The answers indicate that for the vast majority of departments judicial review challenges are rare, happening only once or twice a year. The Department of Health and the Department of Social Security were by far the biggest targets with an annual average of 11 cases. The Ministry of Agriculture, Fisheries and Food and the Department for Education and Employment were typical with averages of two and four cases respectively. Moreover, the statistics indicate that review challenges are unsuccessful in the vast majority of cases. According to the Public Law Project's research over three-quarters of all judicial review cases concerning central government are directed against the Home Office.[109] Margaret Hodge tabled the same question to the Home Office in July 1997 with the Home Office stating that they had received several thousand review challenges since 1991 and that its decisions had been upheld in over 90% of cases.[110] In 1999 alone the Home Office received 2170 review challenges against asylum decisions, with less than 10% of these challenges being upheld by the courts.[111]

For the great majority of departments, judicial review challenges happen only once or twice a year. This fact undermines the common recitals of burgeoning figures as evidence of an increased impact on central government. They weaken the media imagery of an over-mighty judiciary usurping Parliament's role of enforcing ministerial responsibility and emphasise that while judicial review challenges may be common against local government and other public bodies they are used infrequently to challenge the core executive. Sunkin concluded: '...it appears to have played a minimal role in the redress of grievances and to have provided the community with a very partial and limited check upon government illegality'.[112] (That the vast majority of challenges are targeted at the Home Office is significant for this study as its conclusions on the Home Office case study are likely to represent the zenith of judicial review's influence on the core executive.)

Selective media reporting has contributed to the perception of judicial activism. The courts are not considering the merits of the policy but only the way the policy decision has been reached and whether ministers have the authority to launch the policy. 'All too often the fundamental point that the courts are judging the legal basis, not the substance or merits, of a decision is virtually suppressed in favour of presenting the judges as an alternative government.'[113] To address this the courts have increasingly stressed their constitutional position.[114] In the vast majority of cases the courts continue to display a great deference to Parliament and the executive, but selective media coverage paints a false picture of judicial activism and creates '...a real danger of false perceptions giving rise to mistrust and cynicism'.[115] Le Seuer concludes:

> I believe that much of the current critical polemics about judicial review rest on weak factual foundations. The reality is different, more subtle and certainly less newsworthy: judges are doing little that is new and, as before, often hold contentious government policy to be entirely lawful.[116]

Judicial review as a mechanism of accountability also suffers from a number of financial, administrative and procedural obstacles. Although reforms have been implemented to increase the accessibility of judicial review it is not widely available.[117] It is a procedure of the last resort, is highly centralised and there are many procedural obstacles (time, sufficient interest, major backlogs of cases, etc.). Applicants must obtain 'leave', more recently known as 'permission', to proceed with their case but a significant proportion of cases are dismissed at this early stage without the opportunity to present the case.[118] Of the 4539 applications for leave to apply for judicial review in 1998, less than 23% were allowed.[119] Designed to allow judges to filter out hopeless cases, thereby speeding up the process for successful litigants, it is a highly discretionary process with substantial variances in refusal rates between individual judges,[120] making this mechanism of accountability both inconsistent and uncertain.[121] Weir & Beetham subsequently concluded that: 'Obtaining leave to apply for judicial review is something of a lottery'.[122] The high financial costs of judicial review also form a major obstacle to this mechanism, with legal aid being discretionary and only available to those with extremely low incomes.[123]

Unless European legislation has been fettered, parliamentary sovereignty dictates that judicial review is a secondary form of accountability. Any adverse court ruling can be overturned by a minister introducing new legislation or guidelines.[124] A case study of this is provided by Prosser's work on how the victories achieved by the Child Poverty Action Group's test case strategy in the 1970s were reversed by retrospective legislation: 'Any judicial decision producing change which causes administrative difficulty or increased expense is likely to face legislative nullification'.[125] A more recent example is the Conservative government's reversal of the judgement declaring illegal its new criminal injuries compensation scheme with the Criminal Injuries Compensation Act 1995.[126] More recently, the Labour government has announced its intention to press ahead with its performance related pay scheme for teachers despite the High Court's ruling that it is illegal on the grounds that the Secretary of State had acted beyond the powers conferred on him by Parliament.[127] The possibility of judicial review being overturned by subsequent legislation has obvious implications for judicial accountability and led Rawlings to pessimistically conclude:

> In these circumstances judicial attempts to 'control' government through the process of judicial review are capable of being swept away, and their corrections of 'deviant' government behaviour are doomed.[128]

Judicial review is a reactive form of accountability. The constitutional position of the courts, their reliance on litigants, their inability to control the range of issues and standard of evidence available to them all have implications for the quality of their scrutiny and their ability to make ministers accountable. Judicial review has also failed to permeate every sphere of central government. National security and economic policy are still eschewed by the courts on the grounds that they are 'non-justiciable' and are concerns of Parliament rather than the courts.[129] Despite the landmark case of *Conway v. Rimmer* (1968) in which the House of Lords overturned a ministerial public interest immunity certificate (PII) the courts rarely challenge PIIs.[130] Informatory accountability is obviously reduced by the courts' unwillingness to challenge the confidentiality conferred on documents by PIIs.[131] In the absence of statutory guidance or agreed criteria for determining whether the documents deserve PII protection much depends on the discretion of individual judges - which causes severe uncertainty that hampers aggrieved citizens and form a substantial impediment to judicial accountability. (The Law Commission has criticised the judiciary for being too reluctant to grant applicants 'discovery of documents'.)[132]

What does the wider literature suggest has been the response towards this perceived growth in judicial review from the perspective of the core executive? Adapting the work of Harlow and Rawlings, two distinct responses can be proposed - firewatching and firefighting.[133] Firewatching emphasises prevention by increasing legal awareness and establishing internal mechanisms to reduce the potential challenges of judicial review. Examples include increased legal training and ouster clauses. In 1987 the Treasury Solicitor produced a booklet 'The Judge Over Your Shoulder' (JOYS).[134] It aimed '...to give guidance as to the principles involved and to highlight the danger areas where you are particularly at risk of laying your minister open to a challenge in the courts'.[135] JOYS summarised the main elements of administrative law and gave officials guidance on how to avoid review challenges. Overall the tone of the original JOYS was negative, portraying judicial review as an administrative nuisance with the emphasis on demonstrating how officials could 'judge proof' their decisions. The 1995 revised edition of JOYS ('Judicial Review - Balancing the Scales') was a much less hostile document.[136] It states: 'Judicial review is all about allowing us to carry out the job Parliament has given to us, but ensuring that we do so fairly and not in an over zealous or wrong headed manner'.[137] The publication and distribution of JOYS around Whitehall is but one example of the core executive attempting to increase the awareness of officials in an attempt to avoid challenge in the courts. A second example is the insertion of ouster clauses in legislation. Ouster clauses seek to protect the policy from judicial challenge by stating that 'a decision shall not be called into question in any court'. The courts have always regarded these clauses as constitutionally objectionable as they are in direct challenge to the rule of law.[138] But the courts' disregard towards clauses in legislation approved by Parliament challenges parliamentary sovereignty.[139] Despite this the courts have consistently found ingenious ways to circumvent ouster clauses; but as Oliver notes: 'The battle continues, however, and parliamentary draftsmen devise even more subtle ways of preventing the courts from exercising their jurisdiction'.[140]

Firefighting is a more aggressive and proactive strategy. Le Sueur states that the Conservative government adopted this strategy in the 1990s as a *modus operandi* to control judicial accountability.[141] Le Sueur's thesis emphasises a perceived change of attitude on the part of Conservative ministers rather than judges. He refutes theories of judicial activism and states that the real change involved ministers who were more willing to ignore legal advice and risk challenge in the courts only to deride adverse decisions in an attempt to intimidate what they perceived as nothing more than a sectional interest.[142] (The convention which prevented ministers criticising the judiciary or judicial decisions certainly appeared to wane in the 1990s.) Le Sueur is supported by Ward and Newman who also place the emphasis not on the judiciary but on the attitude and behaviour of ministers: '...the government has passed laws which erode human rights, brought in sloppily drafted legislation and attempted to use laws for things for which they were not intended'.[143] There is limited empirical evidence to support the firefighting theorists. However, Barker's research found that 'Whitehall's deference to the courts has declined... In particular ministers have more often wanted to fight in the courts'.[144]

It may have been an oversanguine statement when Lee wrote: '...the great legal success of the past thirty years has been the remorseless march of administrative law calling governments to account'.[145] It is clear that judicial review is a rarity in central government. The vast majority of petitions fail at the leave stage. Where leave is granted, issues such as cost, backlogs, discretion and judicial deference create difficult obstacles. The Home Office is the most likely department to be challenged and otherwise ministers are infrequently required to account to the courts. It might be argued that the importance of judicial review should not be measured by the direct influence of judicial rulings but by a more subtle impact on public administration (e.g. changes in culture and operating procedures). Such an approach may suggest that judicial review has a strong *ex ante* impact in that the core executive must take into account the demands of judicial review constantly. Although there is no empirical evidence to substantiate this statement of faith, there is evidence of a heightened legal awareness throughout Whitehall. Whilst the above discussion regarding judicial review provides a rich range of pertinent issues to explore in the case study chapter it is possible to make two critical observations. First, the constitutional structure dictates that accountability through judicial review is a secondary form of accountability, as Parliament is supreme. The fact that parliamentary sovereignty is a euphemism for executive hegemony leads to the second point that those commentators who petition for the introduction of a codified system of administrative and public law fail to appreciate the dominance of the Westminster model.[146] Although a codified system may well introduce clarity into a system built upon discretion and uncertainty such reforms are unlikely to be favoured by ministers who are served so well by the current system. Yet there is an increasingly important legitimating foundation for judicial decisions which allows the judiciary to reconcile parliamentary sovereignty with wider notions of fundamental rights: Europe.

4.3.2 New Horizons? Judicial Accountability and Europe

Although the Human Rights Act 1998 is purported to reconcile the protection of human rights with the sovereignty of Parliament it represents an unprecedented transfer of political power from the executive and legislature to the judiciary.[147] A critical restructuring of our 'political constitution' with potentially fundamental consequences for traditional notions and mechanisms of accountability.[148] Although it was the post-war Labour government which in 1951 ratified the treaty and the Labour government of Harold Wilson, which accepted the right of individual petition the Labour party has traditionally had an ambiguous relationship with the European Convention of Human Rights (ECHR).[149] Although keen to support the protection of rights abroad, it was reluctant to entrust the protection of human rights to the judiciary.[150] A prolonged period in opposition, the dominance of an executive backed by a large majority, an increasing concern with the mechanisms of parliamentary accountability and a reappraisal of traditional socialist views of the judiciary arguably changed this.[151] Labour's 1997 manifesto contained a commitment to incorporate the ECHR which duly happened with the Human Rights Act 1998.[152]

Incorporation of the ECHR is crucial to judicial accountability as it empowers members of the public with a broad range of positive rights (life, liberty, expression, assembly, etc.).[153] As the white paper 'Rights Brought Home' clearly states, the aim of incorporation is to make it easier, cheaper and quicker for members of the public to launch legal challenges against public bodies should they feel their human rights have been breached.[154] The public has greater formal rights, ministers have more responsibilities and the courts are the mechanism through which these competing tensions will have to be balanced. Guided, but not bound, by convention, case law and jurisprudence, the judiciary's position in the constitutional structure is greatly enhanced, especially vis-à-vis ministers. Judges will no longer have to create innovative legal reasons to legitimate their commitment to fundamental human rights.[155]

The act does not empower the courts to strike down legislation.[156] Thus it theoretically protects the sovereignty of Parliament. Instead, higher courts can issue a 'declaration of incompatibility' where they are unable to interpret legislation in a way that is consistent with the ECHR.[157] The courts cannot, therefore, invalidate legislation but simply highlight incompatibility. Confusion surrounds the status of an act that has been declared incompatible with the ECHR. The Human Rights Act states that the act continues to apply until the government amends it. A number of issues arise. Ministers have not relinquished any formal power to the courts. Parliamentary sovereignty and ministerial responsibility to Parliament are triumphed as reasons not to adopt the alternative models in which the courts can strike down legislation.[158] The white paper naively suggests that to do otherwise would 'draw the judiciary into serious conflict with Parliament', but conflict is likely where the executive does not agree with a declaration of incompatibility, which ministers have already admitted is likely.[159] In September 2000 the Lord Chancellor, Lord Irvine, caused controversy by stating that 'In some cases, government and Parliament could take the view that there was some sort of over-riding reason not to change the law to make it compatible'.[160] An unsatisfactory situation would exist but the dominant position of the executive would not be threatened. As the Home Secretary noted: 'The default setting is the *status quo*'.[161]

Where the executive does decide to address the declaration of incompatibility the act provides ministers with new powers which alter the relationship between the legislature and executive and challenge traditional notions of parliamentary accountability. The Act allows the appropriate minister to utilise a 'fast-track procedure' for introducing new legislation.[162] The ability of ministers to bypass Parliament's usual procedures led Jim Garnier to state:

> It is just one more facet of the government's attack on our constitution, aimed at increasing the power of the executive and diminishing the power of the people, through elected representatives in Parliament, to hold the government to account.[163]

Concern centres on the fact that neither the Human Rights Act nor the white paper clarifies exactly under what circumstances ministers will be able to use the fast-track procedure. No definition of the 'compelling reasons' ministers must have has been advanced by the executive as a benchmark against which Parliament can assess ministerial action. Parliament, not the executive, creates legislation, yet the act will allow ministers to decide when their legislation should avoid full and proper parliamentary scrutiny.[164]

Another important issue revolves around the government's refusal to underpin human rights with a Human Rights Commission.[165] This stands in stark contrast both to earlier rights legislation, which was buttressed by new bodies, for example the Equal Opportunities Commission and Commission for Racial Equality, and the creation of new bodies to foster the use of the Human Rights Act in specific areas (for example, the Northern Ireland Human Rights Commission and the Disability Rights Commission). In opposition the Labour front bench was firmly committed to creating a Human Rights Commission as a powerful independent body to support human rights cases, investigate specific issues and incidents and monitor the operation of the act.[166] The Labour government has reneged upon this commitment (based on concerns regarding cost and remit issues)[167] and has suggested that Parliament create a Human Rights Committee.[168] This volte-face encapsulates power within the constitutional framework. The move away from an external independent body to a parliamentary committee ensures the executive's control. Not only would a parliamentary committee suffer from a range of practical impediments but it would also lack the political will and independence that an independent commission offers.[169]

Incorporation of the ECHR therefore raises a number of issues for public accountability in general and parliamentary accountability in particular. First, despite the formal commitment to parliamentary sovereignty and ministerial responsibility in the Human Rights Act, it is obvious that in reality both tenets of the British constitution have been compromised to some degree. Incorporation shifts the balance of power in favour of the judiciary. (This provokes questions regarding the appointment, accountability and suitability of judges to wield this power in a representative democracy.) The fast track procedure for legislation that is declared incompatible represents a weakening of Parliament's established procedures for scrutiny; while the executive's preference for a parliamentary committee to police the act rather than an independent commission might be seen as indicative of the executive's regard for parliamentary accountability. Judicial accountability will certainly become more immediate with incorporation. Currently cases take an average of five years to reach Strasbourg but with incorporation ministerial decisions will be examined in the High Court within weeks.

There is, however, a very real danger that incorporation might undermine and weaken parliamentary accountability. Judges increasingly will make the final decisions about issues and disputes which were previously under the final jurisdiction of ministers. This may absolve ministers of responsibility and allow them to deflect responsibility onto the courts which are, of course, free from parliamentary oversight. The abdication of ministerial responsibility due to judicial decisions may become an increasingly common scenario.

Ironically a reform which is designed to protect citizens from arbitrary government and increase accountability might actually cloud and weaken parliamentary accountability while at the same time transferring power to individuals who are unarguably far less accountable than ministers. However, the impact of incorporation will depend on a range of unpredictable factors (volume of cases launched, the attitude and approach of the judiciary, the level of training and preparation within Whitehall, etc.).

Within Whitehall there is no single authority with over-riding authority for dealing with incorporation of the Human Rights Act; no dedicated unit has been established within the Cabinet Office and the government has refrained from creating a 'Minister of Human Rights'. Although the Home Office is the lead department, individual departments have been given responsibility for ensuring that their procedures and proposed policies are compatible. The experience in Scotland, where convention challenges were presented in over 500 cases by the beginning of May 2000, has been carefully analysed in Whitehall.[170] Despite a few high-profile cases, the main lesson from Scotland appears to be that while there will be a large number of cases, very few will be upheld by the courts (currently only around 3% of challenges in Scotland are successful). The government's own estimate is that when the ECHR comes into force on 1 October 2000 the number of judicial review challenges is likely to double, but it is confident that there will be relatively few areas of government business vulnerable to challenge. There is also, however, a degree of realism, particularly amongst officials, that no preparatory process is watertight. Unanticipated challenges are likely, even in areas thought compatible with the Convention, and some policy areas are known to be vulnerable to challenge because there is no settled opinion on what could be done and therefore a court judgement is needed to clarify the issue.

Although the number of successful ECHR cases against the government is likely to be limited it is possible that incorporation may well affect other mechanisms of judicial accountability. For example, in July 2000 the High Court, in a landmark decision, ruled that the Secretary of State for Health had acted 'irrationally' and breached article 10 of the ECHR (the right to freedom of expression) when he decided that the judicial inquiry, under Lord Laming, into the serial killer Harold Shipman should be held in private.[171] The Secretary of State chose not to appeal against this decision.[172] The case may have far reaching implications for future official inquiries into significant matters of public concern and could significantly limit the scope for ministers to hold inquiries behind closed doors. This interaction between incorporation of the ECHR and judicial review also exposes wider themes and issues for the future of British democracy. The courts will have to delineate the necessary qualities of a constitutional democracy and, that zone in which individual democratic rights are immune from government intervention.[173] Thus we are moving significantly from a majoritarian model of democracy to one based upon limited government.

What is certain is that the Home Office is likely to be the focus of the majority of cases brought under the ECHR due to the nature of its functions. Yet there is a final mechanism through which the judiciary often plays a critical and central role in enforcing the accountability and responsibility of the core executive.

4.3.3 Judicial Inquiries and Accountability

> Such inquiries are from time to time essential mechanisms of accountability and reassurance in a system where the investigative will and capability of an executive-dominated House of Commons is so very weak.[174]

Judges are not only involved in enforcing the accountability of ministers and their officials through the courts but also through their involvement in inquiries.[175] The inquiries in question are those triggered not by some broad policy issue but by a specific event that would be inappropriate for investigation by Parliament. Paradoxically, the original impetus behind the legislation on which the most powerful form of inquiry was founded (a statutory tribunal of inquiry) was the failure of Parliament to enforce ministerial responsibility in 1916. The Marconi scandal involved allegations of corrupt financial speculation by ministers.[176] The select committee that investigated the affair split along party lines. The realisation that incidents involving ministers could not be investigated satisfactorily by Parliament, combined with the public disquiet surrounding the affair, led to the Tribunals of Inquiry (Evidence) Act 1921. Inquiries established under this act have all the powers of the High Court including the right to examine witnesses under oath, demand papers and subpoena witnesses with contempt of court.[177] The establishment of an inquiry can be seen as a complement to the convention of ministerial responsibility to Parliament as the inquiry is charged with obtaining informatory and explanatory accountability. So the use of inquiries is not a recent phenomena. As Drewry wrote in 1975:

> It is almost a reflex action at times of dire political emergency for judges to be rushed to the scene to extinguish the blaze of concern (often by retrospectively legitimating official actions) and to spread calm and reassurance.[178]

Inquiries can be established under statute (either the Police Act 1964,[179] Railway Act 1974,[180] Merchant Shipping Act 1970[181] or the Tribunals of Inquiry [Evidence] Act 1921) or under the prerogative powers of any Secretary of State. The legal or political foundation of an inquiry is crucial.[182] The most powerful and formal inquiries are established under the 1921 act. Between 1921 and 2000 only 24 inquiries have been established under the 1921 Act.[183] In recent decades governments have preferred to establish inquiries under Crown prerogative therefore allowing ministers to tightly dictate and control the terms, scope and powers of the inquiry.[184] Although the 1921 act arose from an incident involving ministers there is a clear correlation between the use of statutory and non-statutory inquiries. Where ministers are involved statutory inquiries are rarely used, whereas when an incident is unlikely to involve ministerial culpability the executive is more willing to establish a statutory inquiry under the 1921 act.[185] For example, the Scott Inquiry was a non-statutory inquiry established under the auspices of the Department of Trade and Industry.[186] By contrast the two subsequent inquiries, which were unlikely to involve ministers, into the Dunblane massacre[187] and the North Wales child abuse allegations,[188] were statutory inquiries.[189]

Although Lord Salmon's 1966 Royal Commission on Tribunals of Inquiry recommended that the chairperson should always be someone holding high judicial office there is no legal or constitutional requirement that the chairperson is a judge.[190] That the prefix 'judicial' is used in relation to inquiries owes little to Lord Salmon and more to the qualities possessed by the judiciary which encourages ministers to appoint judges.[191] As Woodhouse notes:

> A judicial appointment, presumed to be apolitical, acts to reinforce the independence and impartiality of the inquiry and to enhance its credibility and legitimacy. Judges also lend dignity and authority to the proceedings and symbolise the serious nature of the investigation.[192]

Ministers are keen to exploit the apolitical image of judges and the 'borrowed authority' they confer on inquiries.[193] By bringing the judiciary into the accountability process they fulfil a legitimating function through which politicians aim to increase their own legitimacy and restore public confidence.[194] But just how great is the capacity of judicial inquiries to enforce the accountability of the core executive? What positive attributes might they possess and, conversely, what are the main limitations on inquiries? Table 4.2 attempts to draw together the wider literature to clarify the positive and negative factors associated with the capacity of judicial inquiries to enforce accountable government.

The positive column clearly includes some valuable factors. A case can be constructed that members of the judiciary do possess a range of personal qualities and professional skills that mitigate against partisanship while also having the capacity to unravel complicated incidents. When compared with the practical constraints faced by select committees it is clear that inquiries enjoy far greater time, personnel and staff resources.[195] While some witnesses may appear reluctantly it is unlikely that an individual would refuse to appear. If they did a statutory inquiry could order attendance more easily than a select committee as the inquiry could subpoena a witness while the committee would have to go to the floor of the House, at which point the executive may well employ its majority to protect the individual(s) concerned.

Table 4.2 Positive and Negative factors most commonly associated with the ability of judicial inquiries to enforce accountable government

• Judges are crucially able to deal in/with abstract qualities (fairness, equality, reasonableness, objectivity). • Judges possess important professional skills (process and understand vast amounts of information). • The inquiry will be conducted in a non-party political arena. • Practical advantages (time, resources, staff, specialist assistance). • Constitutional limitations may be lifted (the Osmotherly rules for example). • Unlikely that called witnesses could/would refuse to attend.	• Judges lack an in-depth knowledge of Whitehall. • Inquiries are established by the executive not Parliament (therefore ministers dictate the remit, scope, powers and resources of the committee). • Inquiries report to the executive not Parliament (therefore ministers decide when and in what form to publish the report). • Inquiries tend to be very expensive and take a long time to report. • The establishment of an inquiry distances the issue from ministers and provides a political buffer between the minister and incident. • Inquiries tend to focus on operational issues rather than policy issues with obvious consequences for ministerial responsibility. • Inquiries may be subject to informal and subtle political influence. • Although a judicial inquiry may provide important informatory and explanatory accountability about an incident, only Parliament can enforce ministerial responsibility. When the report is debated in the House a minister is likely to be protected by their party's majority.

In his autobiography, John Major recalls that his appointment in 1992 of Sir Richard Scott to conduct the Arms to Iraq Inquiry 'was a mistake...it became clear that when he began work he did not have the grasp of the workings of government necessary to put the issue at stake into context'.[196] However, the lack of an in-depth understanding of Whitehall could also be deemed a positive fact facilitating objectivity.[197] One characteristic of the Scott Inquiry was the removal of the constitutional rules that restrict the flow of information between civil servants and select committees. The Attorney General informed ministers that they must attend if summoned and officials were told that the Memorandum of Guidance for Officials appearing before Select Committees (the Osmotherly rules) would not apply to their appearances.[198] That a rule which forms the foundation of the relationship between officials and Parliament could be temporarily lifted underlines the ad hoc and cosmetic nature of accountability arrangements in central government. It exemplifies how accountability arrangements are dictated by the executive and undermines the executive's arguments for maintaining such constitutional limitations between officials and Parliament's committees. (The first judicial inquiry under Labour followed this precedent.)[199]

There are, however, a number of factors that suggest that far from being a tool of accountable government judicial inquiries are a poor facilitator of accountable government and may be a mechanism employed by ministers to evade and deflect responsibility. Judicial inquiries are not a form of parliamentary accountability but an instrument of executive accountability. It is ministers and their officials, and not Parliament, that decides whether to establish an inquiry. This is critical. There have been many occasions when the executive has refused Parliament's demands to establish a judicial inquiry into an incident. For example, in October 1996 Tony Blair and Paddy Ashdown demanded a judge - led inquiry under the 1921 Tribunals of Inquiry (Evidence) Act into the 'Cash for Questions' affair, believing that Sir Gordon Downey, parliamentary commissioner for standards, neither had the powers nor the will to investigate the affair adequately.[200] Lord Nolan supported their demands stating: 'Parliament could never have resolved satisfactorily the conflict involving ex-minister Neil Hamilton, the only solution would have been a tribunal of inquiry chaired by a Law Lord'.[201]

Similarly, the Labour government rejected parliamentary demands for a judicial inquiry into the Sierra Leone affair.[202] During an opposition motion calling for the inquiry to be held in public and presided over by a judge Mr Howard highlighted what he thought was an inconsistency between the BSE inquiry and the Sierra Leone affair:

> What is the difference between that inquiry and this? It is simply that when the government wants an inquiry into events that took place under its predecessors, it holds a public inquiry presided over by a judge. But when it is forced to hold an inquiry into events for which it is responsible it holds an inquiry in private behind closed doors and presided over by a Whitehall insider who spent his whole working lifetime as a civil servant.[203]

The Foreign Secretary legitimated his decision claiming that the small number of documents to be examined did not warrant the delay and costs involved in appointing a judge - thus exemplifying the key issue that it is the minister under suspicion and not Parliament who decides which mechanism of accountability to employ. The House of Commons has the power to establish its own inquiries but the reliance on the executive's support is indicative of both Parliament's weakness and the power of party solidarity within the House. For example, the opposition motion to force the establishment of a judicial inquiry into the Sierra Leone affair was defeated by the government. In May 2000 the Labour government rejected demands for an independent judicial inquiry into the Millennium Dome. In December 2000 the government successfully resisted demands, following a Public Accounts Committee report, for an independent inquiry into the Chinook helicopter disaster of June 1994 in which 29 people died.

Second, ministers and not Parliament control the remit, resources and powers of the inquiry through their powers of appointment and establishment.[204] Ministers create a buffer zone between themselves and the incident in question by establishing an inquiry. It may well remove the issue from the political agenda completely as with a statutory inquiry the matter may become *sub judice* thus undermining parliamentary accountability and providing ministers with a useful excuse when asked awkward questions.[205] It distances the minister from the incident because the establishment of an inquiry to discover what went wrong implies that the minister could not have been personally involved. Some commentators have also challenged the assertion that judges have the professional skills necessary to explore issues in central government. Thus Woodhouse believes that the adversarial training that judges receive does not prepare them well for the inquisitorial nature of inquiries.[206] The tendency for judicial inquiries to take a long time to report is a common criticism. Lord Phillips inquiry into BSE lasted three years, whereas Lord Saville's inquiry into the 1972 Bloody Sunday incident, established January 1998, is expected to last until 2005.[207] The final reports are often condemned as bland and unreadable. The Scott report into arms to Iraq was criticised for its lack of both conclusions and summaries. The Phillips report into BSE consisted of 16 volumes and over 4000 pages.

The creation of an inquiry delays the need for the minister to provide a full account to the House, allowing parliamentary and public interest to abate and culpable ministers to be reshuffled if necessary.[208] For example, in January 2001 the Home Secretary, Jack Straw, caused controversy in the House of Commons by refusing to answer questions regarding the Hinduja Passport affair. The Home Secretary stated, 'The Prime Minister has asked Sir Anthony Hammond QC to conduct an inquiry, it would be wrong of me to pre-empt the outcome of his review'.[209] Several MPs complained to the Speaker of the House, Michael Martin, that the existence of an inquiry did not prevent the issue being explored in Parliament. The Speaker agreed, adding that the matter was not *sub judice*, but proceeded to explain that the Speaker was not responsible for ministers' answers and 'it is up to MPs to keep persevering and putting down questions'.

The nature of inquiries means they are likely to concentrate on matters of detail with regard to the specific incident in question rather than wider matters of strategy or policy which may well have been a critical factor.[210] This helps the minister attach blame to civil servants whilst limiting their own responsibility to matters of high policy.[211] This happened for the first time in 1972 with the final report by Justice James into the collapse of the Vehicle and General Insurance Company. The report contained the explicit assignment of various degrees of blame to named civil servants in the DTI and exonerated ministers who should, in strict constitutional theory, have been responsible for the actions of those officials.[212]

Inquiries report to ministers not Parliament. This allows the executive to present the account in a way which favours them rather than how the inquiry might have preferred.[213] This may involve publishing the report at an opportune moment,[214] altering the format to the government's advantage or omitting particularly damaging sections in the 'public interest'.[215] It has been suggested that Sir Richard Scott bowed to informal political pressure and retreated from initial conclusions that had been included in the draft report and that politically sensitive papers were omitted from the supporting material published in July 1996.[216] This led Woodhouse to conclude 'It would seem that a government, so used to getting its own way in Parliament, cannot countenance being held to account either by the courts or a judicial inquiry'.[217]

Several select committees have made recommendations that would combine the strengths of judicial inquiries with parliamentary mechanisms. The Trade and Industry Committee has recommended the creation of 'parliamentary commissions', created sparingly, and as an adjunct to the select committee system. The crucial difference with such a commission would be that 'The House or its committees rather than the government would be responsible for initiating the investigation, defining the terms of reference and establishing the arrangements for the conduct of the inquiry and for its publication'.[218] The Public Service Committee supported this recommendation suggesting a tribunal of inquiry under the 1921 act should be the model to adopt,[219] a proposal supported by the Liaison Committee.[220] Such suggestions fail to recognise the underlying power relationship in Parliament. The constraints that fetter select committees would also affect a commission, as the executive is unlikely to offer its support to a powerful mechanism of accountability which may threaten the position of ministers. Parliament is not weak by accident.

So are judicial inquiries an effective mechanism of ensuring the accountability of the executive or a mechanism employed by the executive to restrict and limit ministerial responsibility? The wider literature would suggest the latter. Two key issues underpin this. First, from a structural perspective the utility of a judicial inquiry is critically linked to the fact that it is a creation (or non-creation) of the executive rather than Parliament. Second, judicial inquiries are an aid to parliamentary accountability rather than a separate and distinct form of accountability. Ministers are free to ignore their findings. Indeed, Lord Cullen's inquiry into the Paddington rail disaster took the unprecedented step of asking for a guarantee from the Deputy Prime Minister that its recommendations would not be ignored. If culpable ministers are identified it is only Parliament that has the power to enforce amendatory, explanatory or even sacrificial accountability. Yet political realities dictate that Parliament is largely unable to do this. As Thompson wrote: '..the judge may provide the ammunition but does not shoot himself - only Parliament has the power to pull the trigger and too often it cannot even muster the strength to do this'.[221]

This section suggests that judicial inquiries are, to a certain extent, a mechanism through which ministers control both the flow of information and the extent of their own responsibility, particularly in times of crisis. The shortcomings associated with parliamentary accountability are therefore unlikely to be remedied by judicial inquiries (unless Parliament develops the capacity to launch and control such investigations independently).

4.4 The Abdication of Responsibility Through Legal Advice

The role of the law and that of the courts have not only received attention as a means of achieving accountability. It has been suggested that ministers are increasingly using the provision of legal advice as a method for limiting and evading responsibility. As both Lee and Woodhouse have pointed out this has operated through the 'abdication of responsibility through the receipt of legal advice'.[222] Woodhouse provides three case studies: the ruling by the Court of Appeal that Kenneth Baker, then Home Secretary, was in contempt of court (1991); the signing of Public Interest Immunity Certificates (PIIs) in the Matrix Churchill affair; and the debate on Amendment 27 to the European Communities (Amendment) Bill (1993). In each of these examples legal advice was used to justify ministerial action(s). This had the effect of allowing the ministers involved to deflect political responsibility on to their legal advisers and also focus the debate on technicalities rather than on policy or ministerial discretion. While these cases exemplify the point they are not exclusive and Woodhouse detects a trend towards government determined, or justified, by legal advice rather than the traditional exercise of ministerial discretion.[223]

A linked trend involves ministers identifying the Attorney General as the responsible minister.[224] The Attorney General is in a unique position as he or she can employ the veil of legal confidentiality and/or *sub judice*. Additionally the issue or incident in question tends to become depoliticised as the Attorney General portrays it as a matter of legal detail rather than political argument.[225] The trend towards revealing legal advice as a way of limiting or evading responsibility is particularly marked considering that in the Westland affair (1986) Leon Brittan resigned after the leak by his department of the advice by the Attorney General to Michael Heseltine.[226] Lee notes:

> The law officer's advice seemed to have been sacrosanct, shrouded in mystery. In the 1990s, however, Mr Major's government regards it as second nature to pass the buck to lawyers for their advice on all manner of issues.[227]

If a consistent trend can be identified in which legal advice continues to develop as a constitutional tool used by ministers to evade responsibility then a case for reform could be constructed. If blame is to be deflected to department lawyers for provision of inadequate advice then there should be some means of holding those lawyers publicly responsible. Legal advice (like policy advice) is rarely given in definite terms and there is usually an element of choice involved. Ministers should not be able to release only those sections of advice that appear to absolve them of responsibility whilst suppressing the good advice they rejected. (The position of the department lawyer is in many ways analogous to the agency chief executive.)

In strict constitutional theory even the provision of poor or inadequate legal advice should not absolve a minister of responsibility for the actions or decisions they have taken. That evidence suggests ministers are increasingly willing to deflect blame onto their legal advisers demonstrates both changing notions of accountability within central government and the fluidity of the concept. But given the limited number of examples commentators cite in evidence against the huge numbers of decisions taken by ministers daily on legal advice is it really possible to cite a discernible 'trend'? However the assertion alerts us to a possible issue for the future. As society generally becomes more litigious, as judicial review applications continue to increase and the government introduces legislation which empowers the public with legal rights (freedom of information, European Convention on Human Rights, etc.), ministers are likely to become increasingly reliant on legal advice. Because of this it might be suggested that a degree of formality needs to be introduced between a minister and their legal advisers. Questions the case study needs to examine, therefore, include: Can sufficient evidence be collected to substantiate empirically a general trend towards ministers deflecting responsibility onto their legal advisers? How do legal advisers view their relationship with ministers and how has this changed in recent years and especially with the change in government? Would legal advisers like to see any changes to their relationship with ministers?

4.5 Conclusion

This chapter asked: *'To what degree have judicial mechanisms of accountability evolved to remedy the shortcomings commonly identified with ministerial responsibility to Parliament?'* The wider literature and available research suggests that judicial mechanisms have largely failed to remedy Parliament's flaws. Although Lord Justice Brown was correct when he spoke of the dual accountability of the executive to both Parliament and the courts, the constitutional infrastructure ensures that the executive maintains its dominant position and is infrequently troubled by the mechanisms of judicial accountability. [228] If the proceeding chapter supports this view then this would have considerable implications for the rest of this book. It would place an enormous burden on the managerial model of accountability while also emphasising the importance of meaningful parliamentary reform. There is, however, a paradox at the heart of the Labour government's constitutional reform project.[229] It is clear that in certain areas ministers are reluctant to introduce measures that will increase the likelihood of legal challenge, for example moving away from the Carltona doctrine in relation to agencies.[230] Yet at the same time the government is willing to introduce legislation that will ultimately increase judicial oversight and regulation of ministerial action and discretion. Crucially, it is through imposing the reforms within a tenuous framework of ministerial responsibility that the executive legitimates its retention of power and control. Not only does this underline the continuing centrality of the convention, it highlights the inherent tensions and contradictions that will increasingly undermine the credibility of the convention.

Moreover, the degree to which the United Kingdom remains a parliamentary state is also increasingly questionable – the British constitution is rapidly disposing of Dicey.[231] Ministers will find it increasingly difficult to legitimate state action within a credible framework of ministerial responsibility, and intra-governmental relationships within the United Kingdom are likely to become increasingly legalistic.[232] In this context, the role and scope of judicial mechanisms of accountability may well augment within the British constitution.[233] This chapter has, however, raised a number of issues and themes that require empirical analysis. These will form the basis of the next chapter.

Notes

[1] Sedley, J (1994) 'Governments, Constitutions and Judges' in Richardson, G & Genn, H (eds.) *Administrative Law and Government Action: The Courts and Alternative Mechanisms of Review* (Oxford : Clarendon) p.41.

[2] See Mascarenhas, R (1993) 'Building an Enterprise Culture in the Public Sector: Reform of the Public Sector in Australia, Britain and New Zealand' *Public Administration Review* Vol.53 No.4 pp.319-328; Boston, J (1987) 'Transforming New Zealand's Public Sector: Labour's Quest for Improved Efficiency and Accountability' *Public Administration* Vol.65 pp.423-442.

[3] See Le Sueur, A (1996) 'The Judicial Review Debate: From Partnership to Friction' *Government & Opposition* Vol.31 No.1 pp.8-27; Woodhouse, D (1995) 'Politicians and the Judiciary: A Changing Relationship' *Parliamentary Affairs* Vol.48 No.3 pp.401-417. This is not an exclusively British development. See Waltham, J & Holland, K (1988) *The Political Role of Law Courts in Modern Democracies* (London : Macmillan); Holland, K (1990) *Judicial Activism: A Comparative Perspective* (London : Macmillan).

[4] Stone, B (1995) 'Administrative Accountability in the Westminster Democracies: Towards a New Conceptual Framework' *Governance* Vol.8 No.1 p.515.

[5] For a discussion of this, see Brazier, R (1989) 'Government and the Law: Ministerial Responsibility for Legal Affairs' *Public Law* pp.64-94.

[6] Also referred to as legal or quasi-legal accountability. See O'Donnell (1996) 'Legal and Quasi-Legal Accountability' in Pyper, R (ed.) *Aspects of Accountability in the British System of Government* (Eastham : Tudor) pp.82-119; Lawton, A & Rose, A (1991) *Organisation and Management in the Public Sector* (London : Pitman) p.25.

[7] See Harlow, C & Rawlings, R (1992) *Pressure Through Law* (London : Routledge).

[8] 'Justice demands some regular, efficient and non-political system of investigating individual complaints against the powers that be. This is exactly what ministerial responsibility does not provide...Parliament cannot

possibly control the ordinary run of daily government except by taking up occasional cases which have political appeal' Wade, H (1961) *Administrative Law* (Oxford : Clarendon) pp.11-12.

[9] Oliver, D (1989) 'The Judge Over Your Shoulder' *Parliamentary Affairs* Vol.42 p.302.

[10] Drewry, G (1992) 'Judicial Politics in Britain: Patrolling the Boundaries' *West European Politics* Vol.15 p.9.

[11] *International Political Science Review* (1994) Special Edition 'The Judicialization of Politics' Vol.15; *West European Politics* (1992) Special Edition 'Judicial Politics and Policy Making in Western Europe' Vol.17.

[12] For example, Oliver, D & Drewry, G (1996) *Public Service Reforms: Issues of Accountability and Public Law* (London : Pinter).

[13] Richardson, G & Jordan, G (1996) 'Judicial Review: Questions of Impact' *Public Law* pp.79-104.

[14] See *The Times* 16/3/00, *The Telegraph* 29/6/99.

[15] For example Le Sueur, A (1996) 'The Judicial Review Debate: From Partnership to Friction' *Government and Opposition* Vol.31 No.1 pp.8-27; Drewry, G (1990) 'Judicial Review - Quite Enough of a Fairly Good Thing?' *Public Policy and Administration* Vol.5 No.1 pp.20-32.

[16] This statement needs to be qualified in the light of recent events such as the creation of a Crown Office List in the QBD. For a European perspective see Ridley, F (1984) 'The Citizen Against Authority: British Approaches to the Redress of Grievances' *Parliamentary Affairs* Vol.37 pp.1-32; Mancini, G (1980) 'Politics and Judges - The European Perspective' *The Modern Law Review* Vol.43 No.1 pp.1-17.

[17] For a discussion of the development of non-legal and informal structures of controlling behaviour and conduct in the British political system, see Doig, A (1996) 'From Lynskey to Nolan: The Corruption of British Politics and Public Service' *Journal of Law & Society* Vol.23 No.1 pp.36-56; Levi, M & Nelken, D (1996) 'The Corruption of Politics and the Politics of Corruption' *Journal of Law & Society* Vol.23 No.1 pp.1-18.

[18] See Allen, M, Thompson, B & Walsh, B (1990) *Constitutional and Administrative Law* (London : Blackstone) p.131.

[19] Dicey, A V (10th ed. 1959) *Introduction to the Study of the Law of the Constitution* Originally published 1885 p.202-203.

[20] For an in-depth analysis of Dicey's work see *Public Law* (1985) *Dicey and the Constitution* Special Issue; Craig, P (1990) 'Dicey: Unitary, Self - Correcting Democracy and Public Law' *Law Quarterly Journal* Vol.106 pp.105-143.

[21] De Smith, S & Brazier, R (1994) *Constitutional and Administrative Law* (London : Penguin) p.18.

22 See Drewry, G (1995) 'Public Law' *Public Administration* Vol.73 pp.45-46.
23 See Phillips, M 'M'Lud wants to govern? Objection!' *The Observer* 9/6/96 p.5.
24 *The Observer* 9/5/93 p.13.
25 Cmnd 4060 (1932) p.111.
26 Stephens, R (1993) *The Independence of the Judiciary: The View from the Lord Chancellor's Office* (Oxford : Clarendon).
27 Wade, H (5th ed. 1982) *Administrative Law* (Oxford : Clarendon) p.101.
28 See *Carltona v. Commissioner of Works* (1943) *2 All ER 560* and affirmed in *Allingham v. Minister of Agriculture* (1948); *Barnard v. National Dock Labour Board* (1953) 2 QB 18. A more recent affirmation came from *Oladehinde v. Home Secretary* (1990).
29 See Wade & Forsyth (1994) *Administrative Law* (London : Penguin) p.347; Craig, P (1994) *Administrative Law* (London : Butterworths) p.386.
30 Freedland, M (1996) 'The Rule Against Delegation and the *Carltona* doctrine in an Agency Context' *Public Law* pp.19-31.
31 Oliver, D & Drewry, G (1996) *Public Service Reforms: Issues of Accountability and Public Law* (London : Pinter) p.59.
32 Freedland, M (1995) 'Privatising the *Carltona* Doctrine: Part II of the Deregulation and Contracting Out Act' *Public Law* pp.21-26. See also Freedland, M (1995) 'Contracting the Employment of Civil Servants: A Transparent Exercise?' *Public Law* pp.224-234; Freedland, M (1994) 'Government by Contract and Public Law' *Public Law* pp.86-104.
33 Oliver, D & Drewry, G (1996) *Public Service Reforms: Issues of Accountability and Public Law* (London : Pinter) p.61.
34 See HC 313-V *Ministerial Accountability and Responsibility* Second Report of the Public Service Committee, Session 1996/97, HMSO, London. Memorandum of evidence by Mr Derek Lewis pp.93-106.
35 *Town Investments v. Dept. of the Environment (1978)* AC 359, HL.
36 'It is when there is a state of perfect harmony between the judges and executive that citizens need worry' Lord Steyn *The Weakest and the Least Dangerous Department of Government* Administrative Bar Association Annual Lecture 27/11/96.
37 For an excellent discussion and history, see Rozenberg, J (1997) *Trial of Strength: The Battle Between Ministers and Judges Over Who Makes The Law* (London : Richard Cohen).
38 As seen in the *sub judice* rules and parliamentary conventions that forbid judicial criticism by MPs in the House. See Cocks, B (21st ed. 1968) *Erskine May's Parliamentary Practice* (London : Butterworths) p.380.
39 Drewry, G (1992) 'Judicial Politics in Britain: Patrolling the Boundaries' *West European Politics* Vol.17 p.11.

40 'Acting beyond one's powers'.
41 Oliver, D (1994) 'Parliament, Ministers and the Law' *Parliamentary Affairs* Vol.47 No.4 pp.630-646.
42 1942 AC 206.
43 Quoted in Waldron, J *The Law* (London : Routledge) p.127.
44 Hutton, W (1996) *The State We're In* (London : Vintage) p.36.
45 Sir Thomas Bingham *The Courts and the Constitution* lecture delivered at Kings College London, 14/2//96.
46 '...the subject matter of a putative judicial review cannot be consigned outside the court's jurisdiction on the footing that the merits of the decision under challenge are politically controversial... There is certainly no judicial self restraint on the ground that the subject matter is politically controversial' Laws, J (1995) 'Law and Democracy' *Public Law* p.76.
47 Griffiths, J (1991) *The Politics of the Judiciary* 4th ed. (Fontana : London).
48 See, for example Le Sueur, A (1996) 'The Judicial Review Debate: from Partnership to Friction' *Government and Opposition* Vol.31 No.1 pp.8-27; Woodhouse, D (1995) 'Politicians and the Judiciary: A Changing Relationship' *Parliamentary Affairs* Vol.48 No.3 pp.401-417.
49 Woodhouse, D (1996) 'Politicians and Judges: A Conflict of Interest' *Parliamentary Affairs* Vol.49 No.3 pp.424.
50 Laws, J (1995) 'Law and Democracy' *Public Law* pp.72-93; Laws, J (1994) 'Judicial Remedies and the Constitution' *The Modern Law Review* Vol.57 pp.213-227.
51 Jones, G 'Judges warned to keep in line' *The Telegraph* 7.12.95 p.1.
52 Gibb, F '"Dirty Tricks" row on speech that never was" *The Times* 8/12/95 p.6; 'Lest ye be judged' *The Times* 8/12/96 p.19; *Daily Telegraph* 8/12/95 p.1.
53 See Dyer, C 'Top judge hits at mandatory sentences' *The Guardian* 18/7/00 p.10; Gibb, F 'Put fewer offenders in jail' *The Times* 30/01/01; Riddell, M 'Interview – Lord Woolf' *The New Statesman* 16/10/00 pp.18-19.
54 See Marquand, D (1988) *The Unprincipled Society: New Demands and Old Politics* (London : Fontana).
55 Feldman, D (1988) 'Judicial Review: A Way of Controlling Government?' *Public Administration* Vol.66 p.28.
56 See Zellick, G (1985) 'Government Beyond the Law' *Public Law* pp.283-308.
57 Laws, J (1995) 'Law and Democracy' *Public Law* pp.73.
58 Elliott, M (1999) 'The Demise of Parliamentary Sovereignty? The Implications for Justifying Judicial Review' *The Law Quarterly Review* Vol.115 pp.119-137.

[59] For an interesting discussion and defence of the role of the judiciary see Weir, S & Beetham, D (1998) *Political Power and Democratic Control in Britain* (London : Routledge) Ch. 15.

[60] See Forsyth, C (1996) 'Of Fig Leaves and Fairy Tales: The *Ultra Vires* Doctrine, the Sovereignty of Parliament and Judicial Review' *Common Law Journal* Vol.122 pp.88-112.

[61] Laws, J (1995) 'Law and Democracy' *Public Law* pp.79.

[62] Laws, J (1993) 'Is the High Court the Guardian of Fundamental Constitutional Rights?' *Public Law* pp.59-79.

[63] Laws, J (1994) 'Judicial Remedies and the Constitution' *Modern Law Review* Vol.57 pp.224.

[64] Lord Woolf of Barnes (1995) 'Droit Public - English Style' *Public Law* p.69.

[65] Lord Woolf of Barnes (1995) 'Droit Public - English Style' *Public Law* pp.67-71.

[66] Lord Irvine of Lairg (1996) 'Judges and Decision-Makers: The Theory and Practice of *Wednesbury* Review' *Public Law* p.65.

[67] Lord Irvine of Lairg (1996) 'Judges and Decision-Makers: The Theory and Practice of *Wednesbury* Review' *Public Law* pp.59-79.

[68] Lord Irvine of Lairg (1996) 'Response to Sir John Laws' *Public Law* pp.636-638.

[69] 'Interview: Lord Irvine of Lairg' *The New Statesman* 6/12/96 pp.18-21.

[70] For more details see Allen, M, Thompson, B & Walsh, W (1990) *Constitutional and Administrative Law* (London : Blackstone) pp.535-573.

[71] Oliver, D (1994) 'Parliament, Ministers and the Law' *Parliamentary Affairs* Vol.47 No.4 pp.634.

[72] At the time of writing the commissioner is Lord Nolan.

[73] Gibb, F 'Watchdog proposes new law on corruption' *The Times* 17/3/97 p.8.

[74] See Leigh, D & Vulliamy, E (1997) *Sleaze: The Corruption of Parliament* (London : Fourth Estate).

[75] Committee on Standards in Public Life *Misuse of Public Office*.

[76] Home Office (1996) *Clarification of the Law Relating to the Bribery of Members of Parliament*.

[77] Home Office (1997) *The Prevention of Corruption (Consolidation and Amendment of the Prevention of Corruption Acts 1889-1916) - A Government Statement*.

[78] Home Office 'Government Determined to Root Out Dishonest in Public Life' Press Release, No.24/98 20/1/98. See Cm 3908 *Home Office Annual Report 1998* pp.30-31.

[79] See Brown, C 'Bribery overseas will be offence in Britain' *The Independent* 19/3/98 p.13.

80   Cormack, P (1996) 'Restoring Faith in Parliament' *The Journal of Legislative Studies* Vol.2 No.4 pp.277-283.
81   Hansard. HC Debs. 14/12/93 col.873 (Mr Richard Shepherd).
82   The procedure is governed by the Supreme Court Act 1981, section 31.
83   Rozenberg, J (1997) *Trial of Strength* (London : Richard Cohen) pp.79-143.
84   During the Pergau Dam incident the Foreign Secretary, Douglas Hurd, survived a robust appearance in front of the Foreign Affairs Select Committee and harsh criticism from the Public Accounts Committee, but admitted that he only ever considered resigning after the High Court ruled against him and declared the project illegal. Douglas Hurd speaking on the *Today Programme*, BBC Radio 4, 11/11/94. Quoted in James, S (1996) 'The Political and Administrative Consequences of Judicial Review' *Public Administration* Vol.74 p.626.
85   *R. v Secretary of State for Trade ex p. Vardy* (1992) (See *The Times* 30/12/92).
86   Lord Chancellor's Department (2000) *Review of the Crown Office List* (London : HMSO) [The Bowman Report].
87   Bridges, L Meszaros, G & Sunkin, M (2000) 'Regulating the Judicial Review Case Load' *Public Law* p.654.
88   Le Sueur, A (1996) 'The Judicial Review Debate: From Partnership to Friction' *Government & Opposition* Vol.31 No.1 p.11. For a detailed analyses of the growth in judicial review see Bridges, L, Meszaros, G & Sunkin, M (1995) *Judicial Review in Perspective* (London : Cavendish).
89   Lord Irvine of Lairg (1996) 'Judges and Decision-Makers: The Theory and Practice of *Wednesbury* Review' *Public Law* pp.59-79.
90   Informal rules that prevented members of the judiciary writing on or talking to the media about constitutionally sensitive issues.
91   Laws, J (1994) 'Judicial Remedies and the Constitution' *Modern Law Review* Vol.57 p.223. Bridges, Meszaros and Sunkin emphasise how 'Judicial review has been increasingly celebrated, not least by the judiciary itself, as a means by which the citizen can obtain redress against an oppressive government, and as a key vehicle for enabling the judiciary to prevent and check the abuse of executive power'. Bridges, L, Meszaros, G & Sunkin, M (1995) *Judicial Review in Perspective* (London : Cavendish) p.7.
92   Woodhouse, D (1995) 'Politicians and the Judiciary: A Changing Relationship' *Parliamentary Affairs* Vol.48 No.3 p.405. See, for example, the remarks of Sir Thomas Bingham and Lord Woolf in *The Observer* 9/5/93.
93   Justice - All Souls Committee (1988) *Administrative Justice: Some Necessary Reforms* (Oxford : Oxford University Press) pp.1-2.

94 See James, S (1996) 'The political and administrative consequences of judicial review' *Public Administration* Vol.74 pp.614-615; James, S (1996) 'The Judges into Politics; The Rise of Judicial Review Since 1945' in James, S & Preston, V (eds.) *Old Politics, New Politics and Post-War Britain* (London : Macmillan).

95 Smith De, Jowell & Woolf (1995) 5th ed *Judicial Review of Administrative Action* (London : Stevens) p.9.

96 These are the three grounds specified by Lord Diplock in *Council of Civil Service Unions v. Minister for the Civil Service* (1985) AC 374. The irrationality head is known as the '*Wednesbury* rule'. *Associated Provincial Picture Houses Ltd V. Wednesbury Corporation* (1947) 2 AER 680 CA. See Lord Irvine (1996) 'Judges and Decision-Makers: The Theory and Practice of *Wednesbury* Review' *Public Law* pp.59-79.

97 See *R. v. Secretary of State for the Home Department, ex p. Norney and others*. Reported in *The Times* 6/10/95 p.42.

98 Rawlings, H (1986) 'Judicial Review and the Control of Government' *Public Administration* Vol.64 pp.135-145.

99 Feldman, D (1988) 'Judicial Review: A Way of Controlling Government?' *Public Administration* Vol.66 pp.21-34.

100 James, S (1996) 'The Political and Administrative Consequences of Judicial Review' *Public Administration* Vol.74 pp.613-637.

101 For example, the Labour government's entire civil aviation policy was undermined by the decision of the Court of Appeal that ministers had acted illegally and their intentions could only be realised through new legislation (*Laker Airways v. Dept. of Trade* [1977] 2 AER 182. See Griffiths, J (1991 4th ed.) *The Politics of the Judiciary* (London : Fontana) pp.310-316.

102 For example, Norman Tebbit noted that when he became Minister of State for Trade in 1980 he read the Lord Jennnings judgement in the Laker Case with great care before taking decisions. Tebbit, N (1988) *Upwardly Mobile* (London : Wiedenfeld & Nicholson) p.167.

103 For example, Mrs Thatcher backed down from several planned policies with regard to local government due to concerns that she might have lost the ensuing court case. See Thatcher, M (1993) *The Downing Street Years* (London : Harper Collins) p.644.

104 *Council of Civil Service Unions v. Minister for the Civil Service* (1985) A.C. 374. [The GCHQ Case].

105 See *R. v. Secretary of State for the Home Department, ex p. Moon* See: Home Office Press Release 1/1195; 'Judicial Moonshine: Howard was right to refuse Moon entry to Britain' *The Times* 17/10/95 p.18; Phillips, M 'Who watches over the wigocracy? Loss of faith in the democratic process cannot be cured by an inevitably partial judiciary' *The Observer* 12/11/95 p.22.

[106] See Le Sueur, A (1991) 'The Judges and the Intention of Parliament: Is Judicial Review Undemocratic?' *Parliamentary Affairs* Vol.44 pp.283-297.

[107] De Smith, S (1980 4th ed.) *Judicial Review of Administrative Action* (London : Stevens) p.3.

[108] A 'trawling' parliamentary question involves the same question being put to each central government department simultaneously.

[109] See Bridges, L, Meszaros, G & Sunkin, M (1995) *Judicial Review in Perspective* (London : Cavendish) p.42.

[110] Hansard, HC Debs. WA 16/7/97.

[111] Hamsard, HC Debs. WA 23/3/00.

[112] Sunkin, S (1987) 'What is Happening to Applications for Judicial Review?' *Modern Law Review* Vol.50 p.465.

[113] Barker, A (1996) 'The Impact of Judicial Review: Perspectives from Whitehall and the Courts' *Public Law* p.618. See Young, H 'When judges put ministers in the dock' *The Guardian* 17/10/95 p.19.

[114] See for example *R. v. Secretary of State for Defence, ex p. Smith*. Reported in *The Times* 6/11/95.

[115] Lord Nolan *The Judiciary* Third Radcliffe lecture delivered at the University of Warwick 7/12/96. See also the article by Lord Mackay in *The Times* 12/3/97 p.39. On the continuing deference of the courts to the executive, see Weir, S & Beetham, D (1998) *Political Power and Democratic Control in Britain* (London : Routledge) pp.440-473; and Le Sueur, A (1996) 'The Judicial Review Debate: From Partnership to Friction' *Government & Opposition* Vol.31 No.1 p.20.

[116] Le Sueur, A (1996) 'The Judicial Review Debate: From Partnership to Friction' *Government & Opposition* Vol.31 No.1 p.20. Le Seuer provides an extensive list of judicial review cases in which the court has upheld controversial government policy.

[117] Justice - All Souls Committee (1988) *Administrative Justice: Some Necessary Reforms* (Oxford : Oxford University Press); Smith De, A, Lord Woolf & Jowell, J (1995) *Judicial Review of Administrative Action* (London : Sweet & Maxwell).

[118] Bridges, L Meszaros, G & Sunkin, M (2000) 'Regulating the Judicial Review Case Load' *Public Law* pp.651-670.

[119] Norton, P 'The Judiciary' in Jones, B *et al* (eds.) *Politics UK* (London : Longman) p.512.

[120] Bridges, L, Meszaros, G & Sunkin, M (1995) *Judicial Review in Perspective* (London : Cavendish) pp.164-170.

[121] See Le Sueur, A & Sunkin, M (1997) *Public Law* (London : Longman).

[122] Weir, S & Beetham, D (1998) *Political Power and Democratic Control in Britain* (London : Routledge) p.446.

[123] For an in-depth discussion of the costs see: Bridges, L, Meszaros, G & Sunkin, M (1995) *Judicial Review in Perspective* (London : Cavendish) Ch. 7.

[124] See Zellick, G (1985) 'Government beyond the Law' *Public Law* pp.283-308; Rawlings, H (1986) 'Judicial Review and the Control of Government' *Public Administration* Vol.64 pp.135-145.

[125] Prosser, T (1979) 'Politics and Judicial Review: The Atkinson Case and its Aftermath' *Public Law* p.78. See also Prosser, T (1983) *Test Cases for the Poor* (London : Child Poverty Action Group); McAuslan, P & McEldowney, J (1985) 'Legitimacy and the Constitution: The Dissonance Between Theory and Practice' in McAuslan, P & McEldowney, J (eds.) *Law, Legitimacy and the Constitution* (London : Sweet & Maxwell) pp. 1-38.

[126] See Rozenberg, J (1997) *Trial of Strength* (London : Richard Cohen) pp.98-101.

[127] See *The Times* 18/7/00.

[128] Rawlings, H (1986) 'Judicial Review and the "Control of Government"' *Public Administration* Vol.64 p.138.

[129] Most clearly seen in the courts avoidance of cases involving exclusion orders. See *R v. Secretary of State for the Home Department, ex p. Galligher* (1994), reported in *The Times* 4/2/94; *R v. Secretary of State for the Home Department, ex p. Adams* (1994), reported in *The Independent* 7/7/94; *R v. Secretary of State for the Home Department ex p. McQuillan* (1994), reported in *The Independent* 23/3/94.

[130] *Conway v. Rimmer* (1968) reversed what had been settled law since *Duncan v. Cammel Laird* (1942). See Kerry, M (1986) 'Administrative Law and Judicial Review - The Practical Effects of Developments Over The Last 25 years on Administration in Central Government' *Public Administration* Vol.64 p.165.

[131] For a detailed discussion see Dickson, B (1995) 'Judicial Review and National Security' in Hadfield, B (ed.) *Judicial Review - A Thematic Approach* (Dublin : Gill & Macmillan) pp.187-228.

[132] HC 669 *Administrative Law: Judicial Review and Statutory Appeals* The Law Commission, 1994, Law Commission Report No.226, HMSO, London.

[133] Adapting these phrases from Harlow, C & Rawlings, R (1984) *Law and Administration* (London : Weidenfeld) p.44.

[134] Cabinet Office (1987) *The Judge Over Your Shoulder*.

[135] At p.2. See Oliver, D (1989) 'The Judge Over Your Shoulder' *Parliamentary Affairs* Vol.42 p.304.

[136] Cabinet Office (1995) *Judicial Review - Balancing the Scales*. See Oliver, D (1994) 'The Judge Over Your Shoulder - Mark II' *Public Law* pp.514-515.

[137] Cabinet Office (1995) *Judicial Review - Balancing the Scales* p.i.

[138] See *Anisminic Ltd. v. Foreign Compensation Commission* (1969) 2 AC 147, where the House of Lords overruled a decision of the defendant Commission even though the statute that established the agency stated explicitly 'the determination by the commission of any application made to them under this Act shall not be called in question in any court of law'.

[139] Wade noted that the courts disregard for ouster clauses was: '...total disobedience to Parliament...inconsistent with the constitutional position of the judiciary'. Wade, H (1982 5th ed.) *Administrative Law* (Oxford : Clarendon) pp.604-606.

[140] Oliver, D (1989) 'The Judge Over Your Shoulder' *Parliamentary Affairs* Vol.42 p.314.

[141] Le Sueur, A (1996) 'The Judicial Review Debate: From Partnership to Friction' *Government & Opposition* Vol.31 No.1 p.10.

[142] Michael Howard is said to have considered his courts defeats as 'badges of honour' to use as ammunition against the judiciary. Grove, M *The Times* 16/11/96 p.2.

[143] Ward, S & Newman, C 'Judges versus the government' *The Independent* 3/11/95.

[144] Barker, A (1996) 'The Impact of Judicial Review: Perspectives from Whitehall and the Courts' *Public Law* p.613.

[145] Lee, S (1994) 'Law and the Constitution' in Kavanagh, D & Seldon, A (eds.) *The Major Effect* (London : Macmillan) p.138.

[146] See, for example, Oliver, D & Drewry, G (1996) *Public Service Reforms: Issues of Accountability and Public Law* (London : Pinter); Oliver, D (1994) 'Law, Politics and Public Accountability: The Search for a New Equilibrium' *Public Law* pp.238-253; Weir, S & Beetham, D (1998) 'The Rule of Law' in Weir, S & Beetham, D (eds.) *Political Power and Democratic Control in Britain* (London : Routledge) pp.440-473.

[147] For an introduction to the Act and its background, see Greer, S (1999) 'A Guide to the Human Rights Act 1998' *European Legal Review* Vol.24 No.1 pp.3-22.

[148] Griffiths, J (1979) 'The Political Constitution' *Modern Law Review* Vol.42 p.1. See Hansard, HL Debs. 3/11/97 Vol.582 col.1234 (Lord Kingsland).

[149] See Marston, G (1993) 'The United Kingdom's Part in the Preparation of the European Convention on Human Rights, 1950' *International and Comparative Law Quarterly* Vol.42 pp.796-827; Lester, A (1997) 'Acceptance of the Strasbourg Jurisdiction: What Really Went on in Whitehall in 1965?' *Public Law* pp.237-265; Wicks, E (2000) 'The United Kingdom Government's Perceptions of the European Convention on Human Rights at the Time of Entry' *Public Law* pp.438-455.

150   See Ewing, K (1999) 'The Human Rights Act and Parliamentary Democracy' *The Modern Law Review* Vol.62 No.1 pp.79-99.

151   Mandelson and Liddle wrote praising the strength of: '...their strictures [the judges'] against the excesses of the Conservative government in recent years' which were such as '...to have convinced even the most prejudiced class warrior not to question the judges' independence and integrity'. Mandelson, P & Liddle, R (1996) *The Blair Revolution - Can New Labour Deliver?* (London : Faber & Faber) pp.195-196.

152   'Citizens should have statutory rights to enforce their human rights in the UK courts. We will by statute incorporate the European Convention on Human Rights into UK law to bring these rights home and allow our people access to them in their national courts.' Labour Party (1997) *New Labour, Because Britain Deserves Better*. See also, Straw, J & Boateng, P (1996) *Bringing Rights Home* (London : The Labour Party).

153   The European Convention for the Protection of Human Rights and Fundamental Freedoms is published in the appendix of Oliver, D (1991) *Government in the UK: The Search for Accountability, Effectiveness and Citizenship* (Buckingham : Open University Press) pp.217-222. For an in-depth analysis, see Gearty, C (ed.) (1997) *European Civil Liberties and the European Convention on Human Rights* (The Hague : Kluwer). The Human Rights Act 1998 does not incorporate the ECHR into domestic law in the way that the European Communities Act 1972 incorporates the EC Treaty. Although the Act gives effect to certain provisions of the Convention via a defined status in law there is no question of the Convention rights in themselves '...becoming part of our substantive domestic law'. Hansard HL Debs. 18/11/97 vol. 583 col.508.

154   Cm 3782 (1997) *Rights Brought Home: The Human Rights Bill* p.6 paras.1.14-1.17.

155   Although the *Human Rights Act 1998* has Royal Assent it is not yet in force.

156   See Hansard HC Debs. 21/10/98 col.1300.

157   'A declaration of incompatibility does not affect the validity, continuing operation or enforcement of the provisions in respect of which it is given' *Human Rights Act* 1998 Clause 4 (6).

158   Cm 3782 (1997) para. 2.13. For a comparative perspective see Spencer, S & Bynoe, I (1998) *A Human Rights Commission: The Options for Britain and Northern Ireland* (London : IPPR) Ch.3 pp.45-70.

159   The issue of abortion has been raised in Parliament as an example where the 'right to life' section of the ECHR may well lead to declarations of incompatibility with which the executive is unlikely to have sympathy. For example, see Hansard HC Debs. 21/10/98 col.1297 & col.1301.

160   *The Guardian* 21/9/00 p.11.

161 Hansard HC Debs. 21/10/98 col.1305. See Gearty, C 'What Are Judges For?' Inaugural lecture delivered at Kings College, London, 11/12/00.
162 *Human Rights Act* 1998 Clause 10 (2). See Cm 3782 (1997) para. 2.18.
163 Hansard HC Debs. 21/10/98 col.1325.
164 An amendment to the Act to limit and define 'compelling reasons' was comfortably defeated by the government by 362 votes to 110. See Hansard HC Debs. 21/10/98 col. 1334.
165 For a full discussion see: Spencer, S & Bynoe, I (1998) *A Human Rights Commission: The Options for Britain and Northern Ireland* (London : IPPR).
166 See Straw, J (1996) *Bringing Rights Home: A Consultation Paper* (London :The Labour Party); Report of the Joint Consultative Committee on Constitutional Reform (1997). It is interesting how the white paper specifically notes that no commitment to create a Human Rights Commission was contained in the manifesto. See Cm 3782 (1997) para. 3.8 p.14.
167 See Cm 3782 (1997) paras. 3.8-3.12; Hansard HC Debs. 21/10/98 cols.1312-1323; Lord Irvine of Lairg, Radio 4 *Analysis* 6/11/97. The government has not allowed cost, remit or organisational issues to prevent it from creating a plethora of new quangos in several other policy areas. See Flinders, M & Cole, M (1999) 'Opening Pandora's Box: New Labour and the Quango State' *Talking Politics* Vol.12 No.1 pp.234-240; Flinders, M (1999) 'Accounts and Accountability' *Fabian Review* Vol.111 No.1 pp.8-9.
168 Cm 3782 (1997) p.14 paras. 3.6-3.7.
169 The wider literature condemns this move and severely doubts the ability of a parliamentary committee. On this specific issue see: The Constitution Unit (1996) *Human Rights Legislation* (London : The Constitution Unit) pp.78-86; Spencer, S & Bynoe, I (1998) *A Human Rights Commission: The Options for Britain and Northern Ireland* (London : IPPR) pp.39-41.
170 Croft, J (2000) *Whitehall and the Human Rights Act* (London : The Constitution Unit).
171 *The Guardian* 21/7/00, *The Independent* 21/7/00.
172 Department of Health 'Shipman Crimes – Milburn Confirms Public Inquiry' press release 2000/0529 21/9/00.
173 Jowell, J (2000) 'Beyond the Rule of Law: Towards Constitutional Judicial Review' *Public Law* 671-683.
174 Drewry, G (1996) 'Judicial Inquiries and Public Trust' *Public Law* p.373.
175 Two specific types of inquiry are excluded from my research. The first is what might be called the policy-driven inquiry - the kind that in past years would have been referred to as a Royal Commission or Departmental Committee of Inquiry - on broad questions like local government, consumer credit or electoral reform. The second type of inquiry that I shall not consider here are those conducted by either House of Parliament. The kind

of inquiry I am concerned with here is that triggered not by some broad policy question but by a specific event or incident that would be inappropriate for investigation by either House of Parliament.

[176] Donaldson, F (1962) *The Marconi Scandal* (London : Quality Book Club).

[177] Inquiries set up under this act include: Cmnd 2009 (1963) *Tribunal of Inquiry (Evidence) Act 1921 - Report of the Tribunal Appointed to Inquire into the Vassall Case and Related Matters* Chairman: The Rt. Hon. Viscount Radcliffe; HC 133 (HL 80) (1972) *Tribunal of Inquiry (Evidence) Act 1921 - Report of the Tribunal Appointed to Inquire into Certain Issues in Relation to the Circumstances Leading up to the Cessation of Trading by the Vehicle and General Insurance Co. Ltd.* Chairman: Hon. Mr Justice James.

[178] Drewry, G (1975) 'Judges and Political Inquiries: Harnessing a Myth?' *Political Studies* Vol.23 p.58.

[179] Under which the inquiries by Lord Scarman into the Red Lion Square disorders (1974) and the Brixton disorders (1981) were established.

[180] Used, for example, to investigate the Clapham Railway Disaster of 1989.

[181] Used, for example, to investigate the Zeebrugge Disaster of 1987.

[182] See House of Commons Library (1996) *Forms of Investigatory Inquiry & the Scott Inquiry* Research Paper 96/22.

[183] Segal, Z (1984) 'Tribunals of Inquiry: A British Invention Ignored in Britain' *Public Law* pp.206-214.

[184] There had been 21 such tribunals between 1921 and 1982 but none since the Crown Agents Tribunal Report of 1982 (HC 364 [1982] *Tribunal of Inquiry (Evidence) Act 1921 - Report of the Tribunal Appointed to Inquire into Certain Issues Arising out of the Operations of the Crown Agents as Financiers on Own Account in the Years 1967-74*. Chairman: Sir David Powell Croom-Johnson).

[185] See Hencke, D 'Since the Crown Agents Case the use of Tribunals of inquiry has been played out' *The Guardian* 7/10/96.

[186] Although Michael Heseltine stated that the government would constitute the inquiry under the 1921 act should the chairman feel it was necessary: 'Lord Justice Scott knows that if he feels unable to obtain satisfactory attendance or answers, he is free to ask the government to convert the inquiry into a 1921 Act inquiry. If he asks, the government will agree to his request'. Hansard, HC Debs. 23/11/92 Vol.214, col. 651.

[187] Under the chairmanship of Lord Cullen. Inquiry announced in Hansard, HC Debs. 14/3/96 Vol.273 cols. 1107-16.

[188] Under the chairmanship of Sir Ronald Waterhouse. Inquiry announced in Hansard, HC Debs. 17/6/96 Vol.279 cols.521-35.

[189] See Winetrobe, B (1997) 'Inquiries after Scott: The Return of the Tribunal of Inquiry' *Public Law* pp. 61. Under the Labour government neither the Phillips Inquiry into BSE, the Stuart-Smith Inquiry into Hillsborough nor the Macpherson Inquiry into the murder of Stephen Lawrence was established under the 1921 Tribunals of Inquiry (Evidence) Act.

[190] Cmnd 3121 (1966) *Royal Commission on Tribunals of Inquiry* para.72.

[191] See Sedley, S (1989) 'Public Inquiries a Cure or a Disease?' *Modern Law Review* Vol.52 pp.469-479.

[192] Woodhouse, D (1995) 'Matrix Churchill: A Case Study in Judicial Inquiries' *Parliamentary Affairs* Vol.48 No.1 p.25.

[193] Drewry, G (1996) 'Judicial Inquiries and Public Trust' *Public Law* p.368. As Lord Devlin noted in 1979: 'In our country the reputation of the judiciary for independence and impartiality is a national asset of such richness that one government after another tries to plunder it'. Devlin, P (1979) *The Judge* (Oxford : Oxford University Press) p.9.

[194] See Dhavan, R (1985) 'Judges and Accountability' in Dhavan, R, Sudashan, R & Khurshid, S (eds.) *Judges and Judicial Power* (London : Sweet & Maxwell). As Andrew Marr wrote in relation to the Arms to Iraq affair: 'As it became clear that Parliament seemed to have been misled, Mr Major ordered in a judge. He wanted a tough judge for a very good reason. The administration was so lacking in authority that it was protecting itself, for the time being, with the borrowed authority of Lord Justice Scott'. Marr, A 'Behold the backlash, sabres drawn' *The Independent* 8/6/95. (In December 1987 the then Mr Justice Scott had rejected the government's application for a permanent ban on Peter Wright's book *Spycatcher*.)

[195] As Lee noted: 'There could be no better illustration of my thesis, a shift from political to legal models of controlling government, than to contrast the poor performance of the select committee on Trade and Industry's investigation into Matrix Churchill with the brutal demolition of ministerial and civil service reputations by the Scott inquiry'. Lee, S (1994) 'Law and the Constitution' in Kavanagh, D & Seldon, A (eds.) *The Major Effect* (London : Macmillan) p:131.

[196] Major, J (1999) *The Autobiography* (London : Harper Collins) p.561.

[197] See HC 313-III (1996/97) Evidence by Lord Howe pp.50-59. See also Howe, G (1999) 'The Management of Public Inquiries' *Political Quarterly* Vol.70 No.3 pp.294-304.

[198] Though it was later revealed that any 'Scott statements' had to be cleared by the department before the official went to the committee and there were concerns over how evidence might affect the future prospects of the civil servants in question. Private Information.

199   Lord Phillips, Chairman of the Inquiry into BSE launched 27/1/98: 'I have been authorised by the Head of the Civil Service to say that no other evidence or other assistance given by any civil servant will be used as the basis for any disciplinary proceeding against him or her'. *The Times* 28/1/98 p.10.

200   Parker, G 'Labour and Lib Dem leaders demand judicial probe into "cash for questions"' *Financial Times* 9/10/96.

201   Quoted in Hencke, D 'Tribunal idea in Hamilton Case' *The Guardian* 25/3/98.

202   See Foreign and Commonwealth Office Daily Bulletin 18/5/98. Newton, P 'Arms Inquiry will raise fear of a whitewash' *The Times* 19/5/98 p.10; *The Times* 'Lines in the sand' 19/5/98 p.25.

203   Hansard, HC Debs. 18/5/98 col. 607.

204   For example, the inquiry into Barlow Clowes, chaired by Sir Geoffrey Le Quesne (1988), was precluded by its terms of reference from allocating blame. (Against this, both Nolan and Scott extended their original terms of reference.)

205   The *sub judice* rule was used by John Major to prevent the establishment of the Scott inquiry under the 1921 Act. It was argued that use of the Act would have rendered the topic *sub judice* which would have damaged parliamentary accountability by preventing debate on the topic. See HC 115 *Report of the Inquiry into the Export of Defence Equipment and Dual-Use Goods to Iraq and Related Prosecutions* Session 1995/96, HMSO, London. [The Scott Report] para A2.11, for Lord Scott's comments and support on this. The *sub judice* rule was a particular issue in relation to the Child abuse allegations in North Wales. See Hansard HC Debs. 17/6/96 Vol.279 cols. .521-35. Hansard HC Debs. 19/6/96 Vol.279 cols. 880.

206   Woodhouse, D (1995) 'Matrix Churchill: A Case Study in Judicial Inquiries' *Parliamentary Affairs* Vol.48 No.1 p.25.

207   Hadfield, B (2000) '*R v. Lord Saville of Newdigate, ex p. anonymous soldiers:* What is the Purpose of a Tribunal of Inquiry?' *Public Law* pp.663-681.

208   For example, the Warnock inquiry (estb. 1982) which examined the issue of infertility treatment. The creation of the inquiry reassured the public and the media that the issue was receiving attention while distancing it from the minister. The final report was published in 1984.

209   Hansard WA 25/1/01 Q147183 col.709W.

210   Woodhouse, D (1993) 'Ministerial Responsibility: The Abdication of Responsibility Through the Receipt of Legal Advice' *Public Law* pp.412.

211   This has been particularly prevalent in the sphere of the Home Office and prison escapes and the resultant inquiries. See Barker, A (1996) *Political Responsibility for the UK Prison Service* Essex Papers in Politics and Government No.104.

212 Drewry, G (1975) 'Judges and Political Inquiries: Harnessing a Myth?' *Political Studies* Vol.23 p.57.
213 See Tomkins, A (1996) 'Government Information and Parliament: Misleading by Design or by Default?' *Public Law* pp.472-489.
214 For example, the Scott report was published at 3.30 on a Thursday, a time when most MPs have left the House to return to their constituencies, when the Prime Minister has stopped answering questions for the week and when it is too late for the report to make that day's papers or news bulletins.
215 For example, the published Bingham Report (1978) into oil sanctions against Rhodesia had all references to cabinet documents removed. The more recent inquiry report by Lord Justice Bingham, into the BCCI incident (1993), was published without several appendices which were believed to relate to the roles played by ministers and the security services.
216 See Barker, A (1997) 'Practising to Deceive: Whitehall, Arms Exports and the Scott Inquiry' *Political Quarterly* Vol.68 No.1 pp.46-47.
217 Woodhouse, D (1996) 'Politicians and Judges: A Conflict of Interest' *Parliamentary Affairs* Vol.49 No.3 pp.483.
218 HC 87 *Export Licensing and BMARC* Third Report of the Trade & Industry Select Committee, Session 1995/96, HMSO, London. Ch. 4 para.s 172-3.
219 HC 313 (1996/97) para.133.
220 HC 323 *The Work of Select Committees* First Report of the Liaison Committee, Session 1996/97, HMSO, London.
221 Thompson, B (1997) 'Judges as Troubleshooters' *Parliamentary Affairs* Vol.50 No.1 pp.188.
222 Woodhouse, D (1993) 'Ministerial Responsibility: The abdication of responsibility through the receipt of legal advice' *Public Law* pp.412-419. Lee, S (1994) 'Law and the Constitution' in Kavanagh, D & Seldon, A (eds) *The Major Effect* (London : Macmillan) pp.134-136. (A similar argument could be put forward in relation to the abdication of ministerial responsibility through the receipt of scientific advice given the deflection of blame by ministers onto their scientific advisers during the BSE and Gulf War Syndrome affairs.)
223 Woodhouse, D (1997) *In Pursuit of Good Administration: Ministers, Civil Servants and Judges* (Oxford : Oxford University Press).
224 Woodhouse, D (1997) 'The Attorney General' *Parliamentary Affairs* Vol.50 No.1 pp.97-109.
225 As in the argument between the Attorney General and Sir Richard Scott over the use of PIIs.
226 HC 519 *Westland Plc: Government Decision-Making* Fourth Report of the Defence Committee, Session 1985/86, HMSO, London. See Hennessy, P (1990) *Whitehall* (Glasgow : Fontana) pp.302-307.

227   Lee, S (1994) 'Law and the Constitution' in Kavanagh, D & Seldon, A (eds.) *The Major Effect* (London Macmillan) p.134.

228   'Many in government are accountable to Parliament and yet also answerable to the supervisory jurisdiction of this court.' *R. v. PCA ex parte Dyer* (1994) 1 AER 375.

229   There are a number of inconsistencies and gaps in the Labour government's constitutional reform project. Many have acute implications for the accountability and responsibility of ministers and their officials. These will be explored in Chapter Nine. See: Marquand, D 'The Blair Paradox' *Prospect* May 1998 pp.19-24; Wood, S (1999) 'Constitutional Reform - Living with the Consequences' *Renewal* Vol.7 No.3 pp.1-10.

230   As Oliver & Drewry noted: 'In the absence of such reforms the accountability gap which existed, so thinly camouflaged by outmoded constitutional rhetoric, even before the new public management revolution will continue to grow wider as that revolution continues.' Oliver, D & Drewry, G (1996) *Public Service Reforms: Issues of Accountability and Public Law* (London : Pinter) p.146.

231   Harlow, C (2000) 'Disposing of Dicey?' *Political Studies* Vol.48 No.2 pp.356-369.

232   Craig, P & Walters, M (1999) 'The Courts, Devolution and Judicial Review' *Public Law* pp.274-304 ; McEldowney, J (1998) 'Legal Aspects of relations between the UK and the Scottish Parliament' in Oliver, D & Drewry, G (eds.) *The Law and Parliament* (London : Butterworths).

233   Oliver, D (2000) 'Democracy, Parliament and Constitutional Watchdogs' *Public Law* pp.553-555.

5 Judicial Accountability in the Home Office

> The modern public law has carried forward a culture of judicial assertiveness to compensate for and in places repair the dysfunctions in the democratic process.[1]

5.1 Introduction

The aim of this chapter is to examine whether judicial forms of accountability exert a degree of scrutiny over the Home Office which offsets the deficiencies Chapter Three identified with Parliamentary oversight of the department. In addition to the research questions outlined in the conclusion of the previous chapter this chapter has three particular objectives. First, it seeks to uncover and emphasise issues and influences which the wider literature has neglected, especially if these challenge the negative conclusions of the preceding chapter by suggesting that judicial forms of accountability have a greater impact than is widely thought. Secondly, this chapter aims to address the insularity of the wider literature by comparing and contrasting the views of the academic commentators with those of the Home Office ministers, officials and government lawyers who operate within the context of judicial scrutiny. Thirdly, through examining both the evolution of judicial forms of accountability within the Home Office and current legislative plans the chapter attempts to consider tentatively which mechanisms of judicial accountability might increase in significance in the future.

Semi-structured elite interviews were conducted with Home Office ministers, government lawyers (from the Home Office and Treasury Solicitor's Department), senior civil servants (notably within the Prison Service and the Immigration and Nationality Directorate) and members of the judiciary sitting in the High Court or above. Several interviewees followed up our meeting with anecdotal or statistical evidence to substantiate issues they had raised. Written comments were provided by a small number of judges who declined my request for an interview. Parliamentary questions were tabled on my behalf and requests were made under the Code of Access to Government Information to secure statistical information and specialist documents. A number of interviews were also conducted with representatives of other departments (specifically the Department of Trade and Industry, Department for Education and Employment and the Department for Social Security). The aim was to allow a degree of comparison between departments whilst also highlighting the degree to which the Home Office is an atypical department within Whitehall with regard to judicial oversight. Therefore the findings of this chapter are likely to be mirrored, to a lesser extent, in other departments. While this warrants further research, it is plausible to suggest that judicial oversight of Whitehall is felt most strongly within the Home Office. This fact is arguably best demonstrated with reference to judicial review.

5.2 Judicial Review as a Mechanism of Accountable Government in the Home Office

As Chapter Four highlighted, quantitative data regarding judicial review in central government is difficult to obtain. Many departments have failed to record the numbers or nature of judicial review challenges. Certain parts of some departments have maintained records, but overall the statistical data is incomplete. Labour ministers have attempted to rectify this issue and several departments are now maintaining databases for the first time.[2] Although data could be obtained retrospectively this would involve substantial archival work and my requests for this information, indirectly through PQs and directly through the Code of Access to Government Information, were rejected due to 'disproportionate costs'.[3] There is also a procedural problem in relation to quantifying review challenges in that applications are considered 'on the papers'. In this process a High Court judge considers the application for leave and communicates his or her decision in writing, usually by inscribing a laconic comment in the appropriate place on the form. It may be, therefore, that a department never receives notice of the application against them if the case is dismissed at this first stage. Such an application is strictly *ex parte*.[4] As Table 4.2

illustrated the Home Office is a department which does not keep central records of review applications. The research of the Public Law Project found that it was by far the biggest recipient of review applications (see Table 5.1).[5]

Table 5.1 Number of Applications for Leave to Seek Judicial Review Against Selected Central Government Departments 1987-1991

Department	1987	1988	1989	1991(Jan.-Mar.)	Total
Home Office	563	254	335	89	1241
Environment	21	32	55	13	121
Inland Revenue	22	6	39	3	70
Social Security	11	10	11	-	32
Transport	4	14	5	3	26
Agriculture	5	7	5	-	17
Customs and Excise	6	3	5	-	14
Health	8	-	6	-	14
Welsh Office	11	2	-	1	13
Foreign Office	-	2	6	2	10
Trade and Industry	4	-	4	-	8
Defence	5	2	-	-	7

Source: Bridges, L Meszaros, G & Sunkin, M (1995) *Judicial Review in Perspective* (London : Cavendish) p.43

Table 5.2 Judicial Review Applications Granted Leave in Selected Departments 1994-1997

Department	1994	1995	1996	1997
Home Office*	162	258	301	338
Transport	n/a	9	8	5
Scottish Office	10	10	4	n/a
Education and Employment	12	22	22	7
M.O.D.	n/a	4	4	n/a

Source: Hansard, HC Debs. WA 16/7/98 Q7841; 22/12/97 Q21321; 18/7/97 Q7834; 17/7/97 Q7845; 11/12/97 Q21321. Correspondence with the author from the DfEE 12/11/97.

* Home Office figures relate only to the Immigration and Nationality Directorate

Table 5.2 updates the work of Bridges, Meszaros and Sunkin to underline the disparity between the Home Office and other departments.

The vast majority of these challenges, which now number several thousand a year, are against specific areas of the Home Office, notably the Immigration and Nationality Directorate (IND) and the Prison Service.[6] Only the IND has maintained a record of review challenges which is illustrated in Table 5.3 below.

Table 5.3 Judicial Review Challenges Against the Immigration and Nationality Directorate of the Home Office 1991-1999

Year	Total number of judicial review applications lodged	Total number of judicial applications where leave granted	Outcome of cases where leave granted		
			Applications withdrawn	Applications dismissed	Applications upheld
1991	506	93	33	40	33
1992	544	104	58	27	14
1993	668	111	61	18	15
1994	935	162	110	32	68
1995	1,220	258	71	39	99
1996	1,748	301	105	42	131
1997	1,572	338	120	33	146
1998	1,874	308	n/a	n/a	n/a
1999	2,170	436	n/a	n/a	n/a

Note: The figures relate to the number of applications dealt with at each stage during the year concerned. For any given year, the total number of cases decided will not necessarily tally with the number of applications in which leave was granted, since applications may not be dealt with in the year in which they are lodged.

Figures for 1997 refer to 1 January to 31 October 1997 only.

Source: Hansard HC Debs. WA 16/7/98 Q7841; Hansard HC Debs. WA 22/12/97 Q21321; Hansard HC Debs. WA 23/3/00 Q115971.

Table 5.3 highlights some key issues which validate some important arguments that were made in Chapter Four. Although the growth in judicial review applications was enormous between 1991 and 1999, increasing by over 400%, the vast majority of applications (approximately 80%) are rejected at the leave stage. Of those granted leave only a tiny proportion are upheld by the courts, the majority being either withdrawn or dismissed.[7]

The statistics invite a number of questions with regard to the ability of judicial review to enforce the accountability of the core executive. What does the large number of individuals who wish to challenge the Home Office but are unable to obtain leave to appeal suggest about judicial review as a mechanism of accountability? Without substantial empirical research into a large number of individual cases it is impossible to know if the courts are simply rejecting a large number of cases that lack legal foundation and are designed purely as delaying tactics. Alternatively are they rejecting a large number of strong cases and, if so, for what reasons? The latter question links in with concerns over the highly discretionary leave process and widely varying approaches to leave between individual judges. A second further research question addresses why so many cases granted leave are then withdrawn. (It has been suggested that departments frequently remedy the grievances of those granted leave to avoid an adverse ruling which may have wider implications.)[8]

The statistics do allow a number of conclusions to be drawn. Given the massive numbers of decisions taken within the Home Office daily only a tiny proportion are ever challenged by judicial review. Of those that are challenged only a small number are successful. It illustrates the falsity of the perception of judicial activism created by selective media reporting on infrequent cases. The statistics also underline the fact that within the Home Office judicial review is not a comprehensive mechanism of accountability. While the IND and Prison Service attract a comparatively large number of cases large sections of the Home Office receive very few challenges - the Police Directorate and Organised and International Crime Directorate for example - due to the courts' continued deference to issues of national security and defence.

> Judicial review is really only specific to immigration and prison issues. Although police and security issues often generate cases the courts are

extremely reluctant to grant leave in areas of national security and this reluctance shows no sign of easing.[9]

Therefore judicial review is not a mechanism of accountability which is applied consistently across the Home Office. Despite the statistical evidence and the fact that only certain areas of the Home Office receive the vast majority of challenges it is clear that there is a widespread awareness of judicial review which many interviewees felt had markedly changed both the procedures and culture of the department. This is most clearly illustrated in relation to the role of the legal advisers.

Traditionally there has been little interaction between administrators and lawyers within British central government[10] (reflecting both the lack of a legal basis for the machinery of state and also '...the domination of political rather than legal accountability in the British system of government').[11] Within the Home Office this has changed. The growth of judicial review has altered the relationship and position of the legal advisers within the department in relation to both fellow officials and ministers.[12] The duty of a legal adviser is to '...prevent their Secretary of State from acting unlawfully or from acting in a way which unnecessarily exposes them to the risk of legal challenge'.[13] This, in the words of one legal adviser, involves:

> ...advising on legislation from a legal perspective; drafting secondary legislation, policy preparation; writing legal guidelines for staff; and reviewing and briefing on European issues (March, 1998).

Judicial review cases against the Home Office are handled by a specific team within the Treasury Solicitor's Department's litigation division.[14] The litigation division employs over 200 solicitors and 50 paralegals. The Home Office's legal branch has grown rapidly in recent years - in February 2000 it employed 33 lawyers compared with only 18 in 1997.[15] The role of the legal adviser within the Home Office has changed dramatically. One indicator of this is ministerial contact. Each of the advisers interviewed stated that they met the Home Secretary weekly and would meet junior ministers almost daily. This was in marked contrast to the past:

> When I first came to the Home Office in the late 1970s ministerial contact was rare but with the increase in judicial review, Europe and a greater

public awareness of legal recourse ministers have realised we should be amongst the first to be consulted, not the last (Legal adviser, March 1998).

Not only has the position of legal advisers altered in relation to ministers but also in relation to the wider department. Legal advisers are now involved in the policy making process from the earliest planning stages. An adviser (February 1998) noted:

> I think judicial review has enhanced the position of the lawyer and made people realise that lawyers are not tiresome individuals who come along and tell them that they cannot do what they wanted to do but are important members of a team who should be brought on board at the earliest opportunity rather than being a bolt - on extra when that policy is hauled up in front of the courts.

Although specific concerns existed, the general view of civil servants within the Home Office, with very few exceptions, was that judicial review was a positive force within the department and was an important, although restricted, form of accountability. Typical comments included:

> I think judicial review in Whitehall is at one with open government, transparency, accountability and in general making sure that ministers and civil servants act within their powers and treat the public in a fair and reasonable way (Legal adviser, March 1998).

> In recent years ministers have had a clear agenda and known what they have wanted. During this time I can't help but feel that the restraining influence of the courts was a positive feature of the policy - making process (Senior official, April 1998).

> Things are thought through much better and in more depth. It ensures that ministers act carefully and must take into account: procedure, rationality, fairness and reasonableness. Ministers might not like this but as a result the final decisions are much better (Legal adviser, May 1998).

Officials did not perceive their role as 'judge proofing' ministerial actions nor did they adopt an adversarial attitude towards judicial review. On the contrary, there was general agreement that judicial review is a facilitator of good government which provides a protection against arbitrary behaviour and an appeal against the state.[16] As one senior official noted:

> I think officials in the Home Office understand what judicial review is all about. They know it is not a bogeyman and they know if they do their job properly they will have nothing to worry about. This is all about people having the right to know why you have taken a decision and ensuring that the decision has been taken in the proper way. Of course it should! No civil servant would argue that a decision should be taken unreasonably or without all the facts being in front of you or in a biased way.

(This positive perspective amongst officials is supported by related literature.)[17]

Officials are, however, under no illusions as to the impact of judicial review as a form of accountability and highlighted a range of issues in order to place its influence in perspective. The first revolves around the fact that extremely few judicial review cases in the Home Office involve ministers. The great majority of cases rest on administrative/operational disputes involving the exercise of discretionary powers by junior officials. As one official noted:

> Judicial review in reality is nothing to do with what the papers or academics like to talk about...it is nothing to do with ministers. It is about - 'Was the immigration officer at Bombay entitled to regard the marriage certificate as being bogus?' It is low level operational stuff (March, 1998).

This fact is pertinent for several reasons. First, it suggests that the impact of judicial review on ministers is minimal. The process is not being employed to hold ministers responsible for decisions they have actually taken. Home Office ministers are rarely made aware of any of the judicial review cases against the department. Secondly, officials were concerned about the attention given by the media to atypical cases which had vastly overinflated the effect of judicial review. As one official noted: 'The implication you get from the press is that every decision in Whitehall is preceded by the question - Will we lose a judicial review? It is not!'. Ann Widdecombe noted:

Judicial review is a form of accountability but you really need to look at the actual facts and statistics rather than the media coverage it receives. As Minister for Prisons I was well aware of judicial review but it is a very weak form of accountability, it rarely involves ministers and is rarely more than an irritation (March, 1998).

Judicial review's emphasis on operational issues suggests that judicial review may fulfil an important role within the context of managerial reform. Several senior officials suggested a link between new public management and the rise of judicial review. They were of the opinion that since the mid - 1980s some areas of Home Office work had been delegated too far down the administrative hierarchy. Whereas the senior officials who had previously handled the work had developed a high degree of knowledge about the policy areas and the legal procedures to follow, those to whom new public management had delegated the task lacked the expertise and were unaware of the principles of administrative law. Judicial review, in their opinion, was '...clearing up the consequences of wave upon wave of managerial reforms which have swept through the [Home] Office'. Officials also stressed the increasingly litigious nature of British society. A legal adviser in the Department for Education and Employment noted:

> The British public used to be deferential but in the last decade it has become aware of its rights. I think this reflects both an 'Americanisation' of the public in that they are much more willing to use the courts and also the European influence which has made people aware of their rights.

The growth in judicial review was the manifestation of the increasingly legalistic society and was not related to either the personalities of ministers or the party in government. It was, and is, an inevitable growth.

Research within the Home Office also illustrated the uncertainty of judicial review as a mechanism of accountability. Judicial creativity and a capricious body of case law made predictions problematic; an issue for officials and litigants. A lack of clear guidelines and a highly discretionary system prevented officials from being able to advise ministers or plan policy with any legal certainty. As a legal adviser in the Treasury Solicitor's Department noted: 'Most of all ministers want one-handed legal advisers so they cannot say, as they do at the moment, on the one hand it might go this way but on the other hand it might not'. Officials felt that the unpredictability of judicial review was central to the debate as to whether Conservative Home Office ministers, particularly Michael Howard, had adopted a 'firefighting' strategy in the 1990s.[18] Officials were adamant that the wider literature was erroneous on this point. Although Mr Howard would often seek a second or third opinion on a matter of law it had never been known for him to go against clear legal advice:

> I do not believe he was a minister who would ride rough shod over legal advice. We often had meetings where he would start with an opposing view but we managed to persuade him that the course of action he was proposing would not be sensible and he listened to us and changed his mind (Legal adviser, Home Office, March 1998).

The issue revolved around the lack of clear advice and the unpredictability of judicial review. As a consequence officials stress that often Mr Howard had little option but to make a decision and see if he was challenged in court: '...but that was due to our confused system of public law rather than a desire to take on the judges as the media and some commentators prefer to portray it'.[19] In addition, the Home Secretary will often have to make decisions personally in their quasi-judicial capacity. In these cases it is increasingly common for the losing side to appeal to the courts. 'The Home Secretary is between a rock and a hard place when making many decisions. One party will lose and the likelihood is that they will seek to have his decision reviewed.'[20] The 'firewatching' capacity of the Home Office was also strengthened in the late - 1980s via improvements in administrative decision-making procedures,[21] improvement in statutory provision in direct response to review cases[22] and the provision of improved training and guidance for Home Office officials.[23]

This study has emphasised how the impact of multiple forms of accountability upon an organisation can exert a negative, even pathological influence.[24] This arose as an issue during interviews with officials who stressed the impact of judicial review on specific parts of the Home Office, most notably the Prison Service.[25] While officials were content for the courts to act as an appeal process for aggrieved individuals, there is a general concern that the courts often fail to take into account either the unique environments in which their decisions will have effect or the administrative consequences of their decisions. This may be viewed as a clash of judicial and administrative values. Judicial review has brought about major changes within the Prison Service, particularly in the areas of improving conditions, formalising discretionary powers and empowering prisoners.[26] Livingstone went as far as to state that the values which judicial review seeks to inculcate (openness, transparency and accountability) have now become the values by which the Prison Service operates.[27] For example, in the case of *ex parte Duggan* the public right was established that all Category A prisoners should be given a 'gist' of the documents that a review board will use to review their categorisation.[28] This created a right to informatory accountability that did not previously exist. Prison Service officials highlighted that the *Duggan* case had placed a substantial administrative burden on an already overstretched service.[29] As a consequence, officials felt that if the courts were going to scrutinise their decisions the judiciary had to take into account the needs of the officials and the demands of the work being undertaken:[30] A senior Prison Service official noted, 'I'm not sure that the courts understand the very specific pressures and circumstances within which the Prison Service operates'.

This point raises a number of issues. It illustrates that any accountability mechanism must explore the issue or action under challenge while also taking into account the particular pressures and demands upon the organisation or individual(s) involved and the future ramifications of the court's judgement. However, it might be suggested that the strict divide that has always existed between politics and law in relation to the machinery of state hinders the courts' appreciation of the administrative consequences of their decisions. Boyle suggests the problem stems from the fact that the judges who exercise authority over Whitehall '...are by training lawyers; they do not enjoy the mixture of legal and administrative training that members of the French Conseil d'Etat possess'.[31]

Examining the impact of review challenges also raises the question of costs. All mechanisms of accountability have to be paid for either directly or indirectly.[32] Judicial review, as a form of holding civil servants and ministers to account for the decisions they make, is expensive. The direct costs of the courts, the legal aid and the government solicitors are substantial. So are the less tangible costs in terms of the delay, extra administrative hours it takes to ensure a decision is reached in line with the principles of administrative law and the costs imposed by the courts' decisions in terms of introducing new administrative procedures or taking into account new factors (compliance costs) in a decision-making process even if the end result is the same. For example, the Prison Service has complained that the *Duggan* case has placed severe administrative and therefore financial burdens on the Service.[33]

Chapter Four highlighted that a department could adopt a number of strategies to evade or nullify judicial review as a form of accountability. The first tactic was the inclusion of ouster clauses within legislation to theoretically remove the courts' right to review the decision of the minister in that policy area. Home Office legal advisers were doubtful of the capacity of any ouster clause to insulate a decision from the courts. Within the Treasury Solicitor's Department the view was less sanguine. An adviser noted:

> I've never drafted an ouster clause nor recommended their inclusion...I don't think anybody has really expected them to have any serious effect since as far back as the 1940s (April, 1998).

This sentiment is supported by Home Office case law. For example, in 1997 the Al Fayed brothers challenged the Home Secretary's refusal to grant them British citizenship.[34] The statutory power contained a very explicit ouster clause.[35] Despite this the Court of Appeal overturned the Home Secretary's decision.[36] Any judicial decision can be invalidated through the passing of new legislation which theoretically gives ministers the power to nullify judicial decisions. Margaret Hodge tabled a PQ that asked on how many occasions had the Home Office introduced legislation to remove the effects of judicial review decisions? The Home Office response stated that an answer could not be given due to the 'disproportionate costs of collecting the data'.[37] Nevertheless during conversation no Home Office official or legal adviser could recall an example of legislative nullification.[38] On the contrary, they were confident that legislation was more often introduced to enforce judicial review decisions, most clearly in the Criminal Justice Act of 1991.[39]

In contrast to officials, ministers largely viewed judicial review negatively. How a minister views judicial review will depend on a range of factors. These include: their specific ministerial responsibilities; length of tenure; when they held office; specific policy issues; their personal political views; and, to a large degree, chance. During the course of interviews with a range of individuals who had held ministerial office within the Home Office a number of common themes and arguments emerged. Taken together, these represent the ministerial perspective. The perspective changes markedly depending on when the individual held office. For Douglas Hurd and David Waddington judicial review was less of an issue due to the relatively low number of review challenges in the 1980s.[40] As Douglas Hurd noted: 'It was coming up as an issue, and was a puzzle to me conceptually, but it did not weigh on my mind'.[41] Despite holding office during a period in which the number of review challenges escalated both Michael Howard and Ann Widdecombe were keen to place the impact of those challenges in perspective.[42]

Ministers, like officials, were particularly critical of the acute uncertainty surrounding any review challenge. Michael Howard used the case concerning his reforms to the criminal injuries compensation scheme as an example of several issues and inconsistencies.[43] The original scheme was established in 1964 under Royal Prerogative. Provision was made within the Criminal Justice Act of 1988 to place the scheme on a statutory footing but a commencement order had never been granted. The Home Secretary therefore sought to reform the scheme under Royal Prerogative rather than statute. The courts employed a novel technicality to strike down the policy. This case highlights a number of issues. First, on the basis of legal history the Home Secretary was within his powers to reform policies established under prerogative without legislation. The court had in effect created a new rule to legitimate a decision that the courts had made on the basis of the judges' belief that Parliament should be consulted over such a fundamental reform. As the Treasury Solicitor noted in relation to this case: '...the court did not shrink from marking with its disapproval what it saw as constitutional impropriety'.[44] Secondly, ministers were not only concerned about the degree of uncertainty over the final decision but also the fact that often as a case progressed up the judicial hierarchy the majority of the judges would rule in the minister's favour but they would still lose the case. As Michael Howard noted:

> There was one case against me, the Criminal Injuries Compensation Case, where the House of Lords decided against me three to two but if you look at how the judges in the High Court and the Court of Appeal went and totted up the judges' rulings then you'll find there was an equal split or in fact one more judge found in favour of me than against me but obviously as it was 3/2 against in the Lords I lost.

The antipathy of ministers towards judicial review arose not just from the uncertainty surrounding the final decision but also due to the fact that there was rarely any agreement between judges on why they had come down against the minister, thereby increasing ministerial suspicions that the judges were inventing reasons for their decisions rather than applying coherent rules. For example, in the case of *ex parte Pierson* the House of Lords struck down the Home Secretary's decision to increase the tariff in respect of a prisoner serving a mandatory life sentence.[45] But Lords Hope, Steyn and Goff each reached their verdict for different reasons.

The uncertainty connected with judicial review was particularly problematic for a Home Secretary with a very clear agenda. It mitigated against being able to design policies that satisfied legal requirements as there was no certainty as to what those requirements were. Mr Howard rejected notions of firefighting stating that such was the degree of uncertainty that where the case law was unclear he had no option but to take a decision and wait for any legal challenge. Ann Widdecombe defended Mr Howard against the literature that suggests he adopted an aggressive attitude towards the courts:[46]

> I think he is in some ways a much maligned Home Secretary and that is one of the areas. Everybody portrays Michael as somebody who is very impulsive and did things without regard to the consequences. This is simply not true. If we had very clear advice that we could not do something then we would not do it. The problem was that often the advice was equivocal, as it often is from lawyers, so we would decide to go ahead (March, 1998).

The ministerial perspective also challenges the right of the judiciary to enforce the accountability of the core executive from a constitutional perspective. While no minister challenged the right of the courts to enforce the rule of law they were under no illusions about the degree to which judicial creativity had, on occasions, gone far beyond constitutional theory. This, ministers believed, had negative constitutional implications for a number of reasons.

First, Ann Widdecombe questioned the legitimacy of judges challenging the duty of elected ministers to introduce policies, the vast majority of which will have been in the party's manifesto. 'You have to ask yourself whether it can really be good for an unelected and largely unaccountable elite to be fulfilling this role.' This statement illuminates a number of oversimplifications which are often made in relation to the Westminster model. No minister is elected. Ministers are appointed by the Prime Minister. Several ministers are drawn from the House of Lords and therefore enjoy no electoral mandate. There is also reason to question the mandate of the executive given the infrequency of elections and anomalies created by the electoral system. As a senior Court of Appeal judge noted noted: 'I do not believe that the judiciary is unaccountable any more than Parliament is unaccountable'.[47] He noted how he must provide a public explanation for every decision and can be overruled through the appeal system.

A second constitutional issue was raised by David Waddington who felt that far from remedying the shortcomings associated with ministerial responsibility there was a risk that judicial review may well undermine ministerial responsibility to Parliament. Using the case of *ex parte Pierson* as an example, the former Home Secretary suggested that if judicial creativity and the scope of review challenges continued to expand, bolstered by the European Convention of Human Rights, a situation might develop in which Parliament increasingly held ministers responsible for judicially dictated action or non-action. In such circumstances ministers would seek to deflect responsibility onto the courts with the inevitable conclusion that ministerial responsibility to Parliament would become even more confused and elusive. Using, as a case study, the House of Lords' judgement to overturn Michael Howard's decision to increase the sentence of a convicted murderer Lord Waddington noted:

> ...those people have got a life sentence because of the abolition of capital punishment and Parliament being told: "Don't worry capital punishment has been removed but from this time onwards nobody will be released into the community who has been convicted of murder save on the say so of the Home Secretary and he is directly responsible to Parliament if anything goes wrong". Well it's stretching judicial review a bloody long way when the judges step in and say "Oh no the Home Secretary has no right to increase the tariff and no right to say that no one has to stay in prison longer than the Chief Justice thought necessary" they are undermining the responsibility of the Home Secretary to Parliament and if a prisoner was released because of the judgement and committed a serious crime the Home Secretary would be responsible for a decision an unaccountable judge made (November, 1997).

The final constitutional argument made by ministers revolved around the dangers of rectifying 'dysfunctions in the democratic process' through transferring legitimacy from elected to unelected individuals.[48] Ministers asserted that if there were problems in the relationship between the executive and Parliament and this was causing public cynicism in the democratic process then it was up to Parliament, and the public through elections, to repair the constitution. Norman Tebbit noted succinctly:

> There is no point the British public taking less and less interest in politics and thinking their sloppiness can be corrected by judges because if we go down that road we are going to be governed by wise men of good intent - why not the generals? I am beginning to feel some sympathy for that famous phrase of Michael Foot when he said 'How long will it be before the cry goes up lets hang the judges? (January, 1998).

Lord Tebbit's point generates a number of questions and refocuses attention on the primacy of ministerial responsibility to Parliament. Yet it overlooks the fact that there have always been severe problems with the constitution's capacity to ensure the accountability of the core executive. The dysfunctions in the democratic process have not been repaired because they operate in the interest of an executive that dominates Parliament. The public's attempts to remedy the constitution's ailments by electing governments committed to constitutional reform have been dismantled by the decisions of those governments to renege upon commitments that might fetter their capacity for strong government. Freedom of Information legislation is a clear example (see Chapter Eight). A Court of Appeal judge noted that:

> Accountability is essentially what modern judicial review is about. It is not about judges trying to run the country which journalists try and say it is. It is about judges making sure that the people who run the country run it according to principles of legality and fairness. And for that they are required to account from time to time to the courts just as they are required to account to Parliament (March, 1998).

And yet research within the Home Office reveals that the judicial review suffers from serious flaws in relation to depth, scope, access and certainty. These stem from the fact that in the British constitution judicial accountability is secondary to the primacy of Parliamentary accountability.

It would be wrong to conclude that judicial review is inconsequential. It forms an important boundary within which the core executive must operate.[49] But it does not, and for constitutional reasons cannot, remedy the deficiencies associated with parliamentary accountability. Judicial scrutiny of the Home Office via judicial review is: comparatively infrequent; not comprehensive in terms of scrutinising the whole department; lacking in certainty in terms of values applied and decisions reached. (What is striking is that the rapid proliferation of case law seems to be doing little to foster certainty.) Examining the impact of review within one department is useful not just to test wider theories (for example, I found no evidence that Conservative ministers adopted a firefighting strategy nor instances of legislative nullification) but also to alert us to secondary issues, for example *quis custodiet ipsos custodes*? There are also many examples of cases that challenge the assertion that the time has come to transfer the constitutional functions of scrutinising the executive from Parliament to the courts.[50]

These conclusions are vital to the overall book for a number of reasons. First, as the statistical data demonstrates the Home Office is by far the major recipient of review challenges. The degree of scrutiny offered by judicial review of the other Whitehall departments is therefore likely to be markedly less than in the Home Office. Secondly, the inconsistencies associated with judicial review take on added importance given the failure of Parliamentary mechanisms of scrutiny. This (thirdly) places greater significance on the utility of the other mechanisms of judicial accountability outlined within the model - not least judicial inquiries.

5.3 Judicial Inquiries in the Home Office

Section 4.3.3 examined the literature on judicial inquiries to assess the role they play in ensuring the accountability of the core executive. Judicial inquiries are important as the demand for their creation in light of specific events involving ministers and civil servants is both a reflection of and response to the shortcomings commonly identified with ministerial responsibility to Parliament. This section employs empirical research to test the rather negative conclusions reached about this mechanism of accountability in the previous chapter. It also aims to introduce new issues and perspectives to the wider debate. An inquiry is defined as any ad hoc inquiry set up by a minister or ministers bringing in expert or lay opinion and chaired by someone from outside government to investigate either a specific event or a more general issue. (I have not included inquiries set up routinely in pursuance of responsibilities under a statutory requirement, for example public inquires held under planning legislation).[51]

Although there is no constitutional or legal reason why the chairperson should be a judge the list illustrates that this is most commonly the case, especially where the inquiry is examining a specific incident which involves ministers. The media and academic attention surrounding certain inquiries chaired by senior judges (I have in mind particularly Scott, Taylor, Woolf, Bingham, Macpherson, Nolan, Neill and Phillips) might create the false impression that the judiciary has taken on a new and more active role. This would be inaccurate as ministers have regularly called upon the good name of the judiciary to examine salient issues and/or incidents. The sensitive and volatile policy areas for which the Home Office is responsible make it a fertile arena for the creation of judicial inquiries. Between April 1989 and May 1998 the department established 12 inquiries, the majority headed by a judge. These include Lord Justice Stuart-Smith's inquiry into the Hillsborough disaster, Sir William Macpherson's inquiry into the murder of Stephen Lawrence and Lord Lloyd's inquiry into terrorism. It is important to tease out the factors that determine whether an inquiry is judicial or non-judicial. The Home Office offers a comparative perspective as on occasion ministers have launched non-judicial inquiries - for example, the Woodcock and Learmont Inquiries into prison escapes.

The Home Office regulations and guidance on inquiries are contained in a document entitled *Managing Inquiries*.[52] An interviewee alerted me to the existence of this document but obtaining a copy proved extremely difficult. Eventually, after prolonged contact with the permanent secretary's office and an official request under the Code of Access to Government Information the document was released into the public domain. The document was drafted in the wake of the Scott Inquiry and its overall approach to the topic explains the Home Office's initial reluctance to release the document.[53] It provides a checklist for those charged with considering the creation of a departmental inquiry into an incident. Topics include: scope, powers, remit, length, cost, publication of the final report and selection of the chair. The general thrust of the document is very

Judicial Accountability in the Home Office   205

negative. Inquiries are to be avoided if possible. Officials are encouraged to support a range of alternative options. For example, under the title 'Political Dimensions' the document asks:

> What is the *real* level of Parliamentary concern? Will the Secretary of State have to make a statement in Parliament? Does the Prime Minister need to be involved if he is not involved already? Does there really have to be an inquiry? - Continue to ask this question and consider the alternatives.[54]

The alternatives outlined are:

- Special investigation and report by Inspectorate (report to be published?).
- Departmental/Whitehall policy review leading to consultation document as prelude to change in law/primary legislation.
- Instruct local review (for example by local authority/particular local service(s)) on basis that product to be reported by a specified date and monitored thereafter. (Feasible particularly where question is not adequacy of law/HO guidance but its application. An intelligent and well thought out research project can play a useful role.)
- Encourage/welcome review by Home Affairs Committee where subject seems suitable, for example, where issues not party political, controversial or, though of national importance, especially urgent. (Very dependent on current business management strategies.)
- Respond to crisis speedily with special briefings to Parliamentarians, media and other opinion formers to help steer immediate pressures.
- Secure space by whatever available means to distance incident and any knee-jerk reaction but *never* complacently or smugly. (Easier to contemplate during Parliamentary recess, and very dependent on what ever news supervenes.)[55]

This list of alternatives to launching an inquiry is illuminating for a number of reasons. First, it is clear from the document (and subsequent interviews with senior Home Office officials reinforced this view) that the creation of a inquiry is an accountability mechanism of the last resort. This reluctance to establish an independent inquiry, possibly chaired by a judge, might suggest that the Home Office views an inquiry as a powerful and uncontrollable procedure. Secondly, it is interesting how the Home Office views a parliamentary inquiry by the Home Affairs Select Committee as preferable to an inquiry. This might arguably be interpreted as an insightful glimpse of the Home Office's true opinion of the capacity of parliamentary accountability. It is also interesting that a Parliamentary committee is thought unsuitable when the subject is controversial. That the term 'dependent on current business management strategies' is also used in relation to the possible relationship between the Home Office and Parliament is critical. It suggests that the Home Office believes it can control the relationship rather than vice versa. While this might not be a revelation in itself it is unusual to uncover a civil service manual that discusses key constitutional relationships so crudely (for example 'Secure space by whatever available means to distance incident...but never complacently or smugly').[56] Finally, the tone of the document is extremely defensive. The thrust of the document clearly emphasises the need to defend both the Home Office and its ministerial team. The constitutional relationships enshrined in the Westminster model create this defensive stance but it clearly conflicts with the demands of accountable government.

Judicial inquiries are conditioned by the context in which they are established and function. A key issue raised by Home Office officials was that judicial inquiries into incidents involving the behaviour and actions of ministers and their officials are restricted by a lack of agreed criteria. As previous chapters have discussed, there is no agreement as to what constitutes accountable government, nowhere does an accepted universal definition of ministerial responsibility exist and the codes of accountability between ministers and officials and between the core executive and Parliament are based largely on tacit understandings. In this context not only is it difficult for inquiries to deliver informatory or explanatory accountability for an incident, but also their final conclusions are undermined by the truism that they can only be opinions rather than fact.

Interviewees placed great importance on the need for an inquiry to be chaired by a member of the judiciary. Not only were they of the opinion that public confidence would only be restored with a judicial inquiry, but also that judges were staunchly independent and would not yield to any ministerial or media pressure. Ministers, officials and members of the judiciary were adamant that a 'safe' judge could not be appointed, whereas doubts were raised with regard to non-judicial intra-departmental appointments where the individual was appointed by the minister on the advice of the permanent secretary.⁵⁷ One Court of Appeal judge had no doubts:

> The selection of personnel for some inquiries, where it has happened intra-departmentally, has been geared towards getting the result that the department wanted (March, 1998).

Although this sentiment was echoed by several interviewees, obtaining unequivocal evidence was difficult. One inquiry in which statements have been made on the record which support this view was the 1994 inquiry into prison security by Sir John Learmont.⁵⁸ In the House Ann Widdecombe claimed that the inquiry was far from independent and that the original findings of the final report were reversed after the Home Secretary, Michael Howard, wrote to Sir John.⁵⁹ Although, during our interview, Ms Widdedombe refused to comment on this issue one senior Home Office official was less reserved:

> The Learmont inquiry was nothing to do with finding out what went wrong it was set up to provide the Home Secretary with an excuse to remove Derek Lewis...it's obvious why a general, rather than a judge, was given the job.

The appointment of Sir Anthony Hammond QC to chair the inquiry into the Home Office Hinduja Passport affair has been criticised. Several commentators have questioned whether someone who worked in the Home Office for 24 years can be truly regarded as 'independent'. Peter Mandelson has stated his concerns that he is the subject of 'a Home Office stitch up'.⁶⁰

The fact that judicial inquiries are a departmental rather than Parliamentary mechanism is crucial. Correlations can be made linking the degree of ministerial involvement and the type of inquiry established. The fact that David Waddington established the judicial inquiry, led by Lord Woolf, into the riots at Manchester Prison may well have reflected his acceptance of a very strict interpretation of ministerial responsibility: 'I knew the game was well and truly over...in my heart of hearts I knew I had to take responsibility and that was that'.⁶¹ Michael Howard, however, viewed his responsibilities for prison incidents quite differently: 'If there is anything for which I am personally at fault I will accept responsibility but if it was not something to do with me then I won't'.⁶² This might explain his preference for non-judicial inquiries to investigate prison incidents especially in light of the comments made above regarding the Learmont Report. It will be interesting to see how Jack Straw deals with the major incidents which inevitably occur in the Home Office. He has been highly praised for his decision to launch judicial inquiries into the Stephen Lawrence murder and the Hillsborough disaster. Neither has been unproblematic.[63] Yet whether he will be as willing to establish judicial inquiries into incidents which may have a direct impact upon the central administration or occurred under his tenure in office remains to be seen.[64]

Home Office officials advanced a number of administrative, financial and political issues to explain their generally negative perspective on inquiries. The key issue for officials revolved around the complexity of central government and the pressures on ministers and senior officials to make decisions.

> We do not have a perfect administrative structure and occasionally things will go wrong, communications will fail, but the idea that you can send in a judge to pinpoint what went wrong and prevent it happening again is ridiculous. As the Scott Inquiry found and Lord Phillips is finding out now specific incidents in Whitehall are the product of deeper problems (Home Office Official, April 1998).

Officials identified the key problem for inquiries as being 'information overload' which forces the chairperson to take a decision about how they will approach the inquiry:

> ...you can take the view that you will never get to the precise truth and you will take a view based on a reasonable cross - section of the evidence; or you will go for a comprehensive nit - picking history of the world approach and you will never get to it.

One official linked this problem to the current BSE inquiry:

> Some inquiries have no choice but to go for the 'history of the world approach' - the BSE inquiry, for example. It has already received over half a million papers from Whitehall and has been extended to June 1999. They must be drowning in paper but I doubt they're any closer to the truth.[65]

A factor which officials felt was under-appreciated centred on the impact of an inquiry on the department(s) involved. The attention of whole directorates, and to a lesser extent departments, can be distracted by a high-profile inquiry:

> When an inquiry is under way it's as if the department is holding its breath and when the report comes out we can deal with it, take a great sigh of relief and get on with our day to day business again (Home Office Official, April 1998).

One official noted how the Police Directorate had been '...largely ticking over since the creation of the Lawrence Inquiry'. This issue links in with the rather invidious position senior civil servants have been placed in under current constitutional relationships. Senior Home Office officials were wary of judicial inquiries due to a fear that they would identify culpable officials onto which ministers may deflect responsibility. Interviewees felt this concern had increased since Michael Howard's dismissal of Derek Lewis. As a consequence the senior departmental officials were likely to over-concentrate their attention on an inquiry to the detriment of the working efficiency of the wider department. In addition officials questioned the cost of inquiries. The recent Home Office inquiry into the Hillsborough disaster was relatively inexpensive at £38,000 whereas the inquiry into Whitemoor cost £349,760, the inquiry into prison security cost £653,000, the Lawrence Inquiry cost £2.3 million and the North Wales Child Abuse Inquiry has a budget of £10 million. The Phillips Inquiry into BSE cost £27 million (£16 million spent buy the inquiry and £11 million by government departments including legal fees). As of 31 December 2000 the cost of the Saville Inquiry into the Bloody Sunday disaster amounted to £34 million.

Chapter Four noted how the traditional limits on officials giving evidence to select committees are frequently lifted for judicial inquiries. However it was suggested that it would be naive to give credence to the view that officials would risk endangering their minister or line manager, and therefore their career, simply because the Head of the Civil Service had stated the Osmotherly rules would not apply in relation to the inquiry: 'No official is going to appear before an inquiry and drop their guard'.[66] This suggests that lifting of constitutional limitations might be an empty advantage. Officials agreed that it was doubtful that either a minister or official could refuse to give evidence to an inquiry but that was no guarantee they would be as helpful as they might be. (A Home Office legal adviser also highlighted that during the Scott Inquiry the DTI had blocked the attendance of two officials called by the inquiry.)[67]

Ministers too added a number of dimensions to the debate. Ann Widdecombe strongly opposed the creation of judicial inquiries viewing them as little more than a knee-jerk reaction to assuage public concern or, more commonly, media attention. She noted,

> The route we tend to go down in my view is a farce which is: we always have an independent inquiry, the inquiry comes up with a massive number of highly expensive recommendations which ministers then feel obliged to put into being. You show me a minister who has rejected an independent inquiry's report and said 'No...I reject this report!' You more or less have to accept them even if you think they are a load of nonsense (March, 1998).

Ministers admitted that establishing an inquiry often created a useful buffer zone between them and the incident but insisted the degree of attention and scrutiny of the final report ensured a far greater degree of public accountability overall. They also disputed whether it was possible to delay the publication of the final report until a politically opportune moment. As Widdecombe noted:

> ...delaying the publication of a report often heightens media interest as they feel there must be something to hide...you cannot sneak them out in the way people have suggested.

Sir Richard Scott challenged this view stating that the establishment of an inquiry was a procedure which was advantageous to ministers rather than Parliament or the public: 'I think they are used by ministers as a tool to evade accountability very regularly'. Members of the judiciary were also well aware particular impediments an inquiry would encounter when examining a politically salient incident in Whitehall involving ministers as opposed to wider non-specific inquiries or inquiries focusing on incidents in local government. Where ministers were implicated the capacity of the inquiry would be affected and '...the search for the truth would, by the nature of Whitehall, be almost impossible to arrive at' – as a Court of Appeal judge lamented. Members of the judiciary did, however, suggest that their efforts had a less tangible but important consequence for the accountability of the core executive. Sir Richard Scott suggested: '...the use of inquiries headed by judges sends out a signal that sooner or later dark deeds may be dragged out into the light and inspected'. A Court of Appeal judge echoed this sentiment:

> I think that since Scott we have seen a willingness for departments to come clean and admit that they misled Parliament if they did so by accident and I think that they are now more willing to come out with their hands up rather than wait for somebody to find out (March, 1998).

Whether the senior judiciary actually believe this or are developing an unrefutable theory to embellish the work of judicial inquiries is unknown. Within the Home Office there was certainly no mention among officials of this benign impact. Conversely, given the dominance of the traditional loyalties within the department coupled with the defensive attitude towards inquiries it could be suggested that their creation might encourage a reduction in openess, an unwillingness to place advice or meetings on the record and a reluctance on behalf of ministers to establish judicial inquiries.

Empirical research has largely supported the negative conclusions of section 4.3.3. Indeed, the value of several of Table 4.3's positive factors have been severely challenged. Ironically it is the primacy of ministerial responsibility within the core executive which creates many of the mechanism's limitations. Any judicial inquiry examining British central government is operating within an environment which is permeated by the norms and values of ministerial responsibility. The defensiveness of Home Office officials therefore has its roots in the tradition and structure of the Westminster model which promotes departmental and ministerial loyalty above all else. During conversation several senior members of the judiciary advocated that judicial inquiries should be parliamentary rather than departmental mechanisms of accountability, thus creating a degree of independence between the inquiry and the executive. While this mirrors the views of several select committee reports it underestimates the executive's influence in the House and the reality of parliamentary politics.[68] Judicial inquiries cannot remedy the shortcomings commonly identified with ministerial responsibility because: they are a creation of that executive; no external body has the capacity to impose a judicial inquiry without the executive's support; the constitutional structure cements a culture in which officials are loyal to their department and minister above Parliament and the public interest;[69] and, finally, no matter what the final report concludes only Parliament can enforce the responsibility of ministers. The latter point brings the discussion back to the rather circuitous argument that as we have a parliamentary constitution in which the executive dominates Parliament many of the mechanisms of accountability are flawed. There is, however, one mechanism of judicial oversight that challenges both the sovereignty of Parliament and the dominance of the executive and is likely to have a dramatic impact on the Home Office.

5.4 The Home Office and the European Convention on Human Rights

Section 4.3.2 suggested that the incorporation of the ECHR could have a significant impact upon the core executive as litigants seek to enforce their human rights under the convention.[70] Given the nature of the Home Office's functions (policing, prisons, criminal policy, security, etc.) it is likely to attract more ECHR challenges than any other department. Indeed, this has been the case in the past and the Home Office's record is poor (having lost 21 of the 33 cases it has been involved in).[71] In light of this, coupled with the fact that the Home Office is the lead department on incorporation, the perspective of the officials and ministers within the department provides a critical case study on this mechanism of scrutiny. While incorporation of the ECHR has provoked much academic and media interest the most crucial issue has been largely overlooked. It is to do with power. Jack Straw is the first Home Secretary to voluntarily relinquish significant powers to the judiciary. This has ramifications for ministerial responsibility and the role of Parliament while also theoretically challenging the position of the executive at the pinnacle of the constitutional order. Jack Straw has stated:

> I think it is very proper that the very substantial powers of Home Office ministers should be under judicial supervision... It is a constraint on the arbitrary powers of ministers.[72]

There are, however, a number of uncertain factors which will each have a profound impact on this form of accountability. An exception to this is timescale. Judicial oversight of ministerial action against the ECHR will become much quicker. Cases will be considered in the High Court within weeks rather than having to wait five to six years to be heard in Strasbourg. This may well encourage more challenges as litigants will not be put off by the long delay and costs involved in a Strasbourg hearing. It will also have an important impact on ministers. Home Office officials highlighted that the threat of an adverse ECHR ruling carried little weight in the past as ministers knew that the long waiting list would make it extremely unlikely that the minister would still be in the department when a decision was eventually announced. Court rulings within weeks were therefore likely to exert a greater influence on ministers.[73]

The main problem with examining the incorporation of the ECHR is the degree of uncertainty surrounding how the judiciary will interpret the wide non-specific protections in the convention. There are no agreed criteria that will allow judges to determine whether ministerial action has fettered the ECHR. Cases will be decided according to the balancing and nuancing of arguments based on subjective beliefs. What happens when the judges' definition of the public interest differs from that of the executive?[74] It is not clear how such a situation will be resolved. The Human Rights Act 1998 attempts to reconcile parliamentary sovereignty with a clear transfer of power to the judiciary. It does not give the courts the power to strike down legislation but only issue an order of incompatibility. It would then be up to the executive to introduce measures to remedy the perceived incompatibility. But what happens when the executive disagrees with the courts and refuses to amend the legislation or retract a decision? Home Office officials were concerned that the process for dealing with this scenario had not been clarified.

> The articles of the convention are simply too broad and imprecise. It is likely that ministers may well simply disagree with the courts that the legislation is incompatible or the exemption not justified. In that situation there would be a constitutional stalemate.[75]

This concern was underpinned by the fact that in several cases involving the Home Office where the United Kingdom had lost cases at the European Court of Human Rights the government had refused to give effect to the decisions of the court and had taken steps to avoid doing so.[76] The white paper on human rights ('Bringing Rights Home') and debates in the House had clearly indicated that a declaration of incompatibility would not necessarily be accepted.[77] This unresolved tension highlights a paradox that can be found throughout the Labour government's constitutional reform agenda. There is a clear conflict between the government's commitment in *principle* and the reality of reform in *practice* (see Chapter Nine).[78]

The uncertainty surrounding how the courts will interpret the act has created major differences of opinion within the Home Office with regard to the impact of incorporation. Ministers were adamant that the 'momentous implications' of incorporation, raised by a wide range of observers, had been vastly overstated.[79] As Mike O'Brien, parliamentary under-secretary of state at the Home Office noted: 'I, too, do not anticipate a massive landslide which will overwhelm the courts'.[80] But officials within the Home Office were less sanguine. One legal adviser stated:

> This is going to have a major impact on the whole British constitution...it will be the most significant change since we joined the EC but I'm not sure ministers really understand this (April, 1998).

Officials stressed the importance of judicial discretion. Because the convention lacked intricate detail it would be up to the courts to develop a case law. Consequently it would be impossible for ministers to guarantee their policies were compatible with the convention until challenged. As a result officials expected a great number of legal challenges in the short term until the convention bedded down, and reports indicate that a large number of test cases are already in preparation.[81] A legal adviser noted:

> I think that the impact will be enormous and it will be fascinating to see what happens... I think you will see magistrates' courts up and down the country grinding to a halt as defendants start taking ECHR cases.

Although the Home Secretary stated in the House 'We are ensuring that government departments are properly prepared for the obligations that the Bill places on them', officials also stressed that ministers may have underestimated not just the political consequences of the incorporation but also the administrative, operational and financial impact on the department.⁸² No officials had received any training on the likely implications of the act nor how it may affect their work. The Home Secretary established a Human Rights Task Force in October 1998 to assist with the training and preparation of Whitehall.⁸³ But in its first six months the task force had met only twice and had produced no guidance.⁸⁴ The Cabinet Office are in the process of redrafting 'The Judge Over Your Shoulder' to include a section on the ECHR but officials suggested the issue was not receiving either the urgency or the seriousness it deserved:⁸⁵ 'Those sections of the [Home] Office which have traditionally borne the brunt of judicial review challenges are concerned that too little is being done, too late'.⁸⁶

Former Home Office ministers were unequivocal that incorporation would have dramatic consequences for both the department and wider constitutional relationships. For example, Ann Widdecombe noted:

> I think that the impact will be very considerable indeed. I think that if you give an extra raft of rights to people and an extra legal base on which to mount a challenge then you will see it let loose in quite a big way (March, 1998).

What factors might explain the apparently relaxed attitude of current Home Office ministers towards the impact of incorporation? Interview evidence suggests the main factor appears to be a ministerial belief that the convention has (*de facto*) already been incorporated into English law and therefore incorporation is simply bringing the law into line with reality. As Beloff and Mountfield argued in 1996: '...the judiciary is effectively engaged in the infusion of the substance of the Convention into English law, if not the "backdoor incorporation" of its text'.⁸⁷ Hunt noted that the 1991 *Brind*⁸⁸ case, in which the courts had famously refused to give credence to the ECHR, had by the late 1990s '...become intellectually indefensible in light of recent judicial practice'.⁸⁹

The convention has undoubtedly had a 'warming effect' on the British courts, particularly in the last five years, but there is reason to doubt whether this will mellow the impact of incorporation.⁹⁰ A rigorous analysis of the LEXIS database⁹¹ by Klug and Starmer suggested that in reality the courts have been far less willing to infer judgements against the ECHR than selective media reporting might suggest.⁹² Where the courts have resorted to the convention this has largely been dictated by legislation or the executive taking it upon itself to conform to the convention.[93] Evidence is scant that the ECHR is already operating through British common law leading Klug and Starmer to conclude: '..."backdoor incorporation" has not yet taken place'.[94] This challenges the view of Home Office ministers that incorporation through the front door (legislation) will have little impact. Officials were convinced that the legitimisation through the political process would increase both the number of cases and the degree of judicial assertiveness over the core executive. Incorporation of the ECHR may also have important ramifications for parliamentary accountability. As Michael Howard noted:

> The [Human Rights] Act will transfer power from elected representatives in Parliament to unelected judges. It increases the power of the judges at the expense of the power of ministers who are accountable to Parliament.[95]

At present ministers are the final decision making body in our political structure. It is for making decisions, or failing to take a decision, that they are responsible to Parliament. When incorporation of the ECHR takes effect this may change. The decisions of ministers will no longer be final as, increasingly, their decisions will be confirmed or overturned in the courts. This clearly fetters parliamentary accountability as ministers will be able to deflect responsibility for the decision, which may well have wider ramifications than the specific case, on to the judiciary. The judicial abdication of ministerial responsibility may well become an issue as ministers consciously cede issues into the judicial arena to distance themselves from responsibility. As the former Home Secretary Roy Jenkins noted:

> In the Home Office I often had to take some very hard decisions. I knew I was the final arbiter and it was up to me. I would have much preferred to delegate responsibility for those decisions to the courts.[96]

The fundamental problem posed by the Human Rights Act is about the authority of judges in a democratic society to take decisions that have hitherto been perceived to be the exclusive prerogative of elected politicians.[97] Incorporation, therefore, creates a real danger of further obfuscating ministerial responsibility to Parliament. This raises further questions about the role and accountability of those to whom responsibility might be deflected. Forecasting the impact of incorporation is difficult largely due to the uncertainty surrounding how the judiciary will interpret the convention. Although ministers set aside £60 million to help the courts cope with the expected initial surge in Human Rights cases, between 2 October 2000 and 8 January 2001 only 60 cases were brought under the Human Rights Act.[98] Of these cases just 11 were upheld by the courts and one declaration of incompatibility was issued. On January 26 2001, Jack Straw triumphantly declared that "the courts are coping well, prisons are not over-flowing and the Higher courts' judgements show that the ECHR should not be seen as a 'get out of jail free card'".[99] Despite the fact that the much vaunted 'flood' of human rights cases is currently little more than a trickle, it is clear that Home Office ministers will increasingly rely on their legal advisers for guidance which may, in turn, lead to the abdication of ministerial responsibility on legal advice.

5.5 The Abdication of Ministerial Responsibility Through Legal Advice

Section 4.4 discussed how several commentators had highlighted a trend whereby ministers increasingly deflected responsibility onto legal advisers or the Attorney General.[100] Woodhouse detected a tendency whereby legal advice was used to justify ministerial actions thereby allowing ministers to deflect political responsibility onto their legal advisers and also focus the debate on legal technicalities rather than policy or ministerial discretion.[101] This theory was used as the justification for proposing reforms that would open up legal advice to public inspection so that ministers could not release only those sections that appear to absolve them while suppressing the good advice that they rejected. Within the Home Office and the Treasury Solicitor's Department legal advisers were well aware of these issues and the proposals for reform. They neither agreed with the thesis nor the need for reform: 'This is one area where academics have misunderstood the relationship between legal advisors and ministers and made sweeping statements from atypical examples'.[102] None of the advisers interviewed was concerned that ministers might abuse the advice they had given: 'I have no fear that my legal advice will be misused or misrepresented by ministers. It is simply not the way ministers act'.

Home Office legal advisers were relaxed about the use of their advice and explained how their ministerial advice was often copied to outside groups and politicians as a way of explaining the legal position of a decision. Advisers would often brief opposition politicians personally to outline and answer questions on specific legal areas. The advisers were happy with this system although there was a convention that ministers would always ask permission before copying legal advice outside the department. While legal advisers were content that ministers followed the convention research suggests that ministers have been less than loyal on occasion.[103] This was illustrated during the incident involving the Prison Service and the early release of prisoners in 1996. The release programme was based on a reinterpretation of the Criminal Justice Act 1967. The Prison Service followed the advice of a Home Office legal adviser and released a large number of prisoners without notifying ministers. Public outcry followed and the convention of the confidentiality of legal advice was wounded. Michael Howard publicly blamed inadequate legal advice for the incident and even named the individual official concerned.

The position of the Attorney General was also portrayed as unproblematic. There is a convention that the Attorney General's advice is never disclosed and nor is the fact that a minister has requested advice. Woodhouse has used the Arms to Iraq Affair as an example of ministers breaking with this convention to allow them to deflect responsibility for signing Public Immunity Certificates (PIIs) onto the advice of the Attorney General. This, the legal advisers claimed, was, in fact, in line with the convention as the Attorney General is free to waive his or her anonymity in appropriate cases. The legal advisers were unanimous in their opposition to proposals to publish their advice and are no doubt glad that the proposed freedom of information act provides a blanket exemption for all legal advice.[104] It was not thought that this would change the advice given but it might stop administrators seeking advice in the first place in the fear that it may show that they sought legal advice but did not follow it.

5.6 Conclusion

'Aside from Parliament and its associated mechanisms, the most important form of accountability of the government comes from the judiciary.'[105] This statement might be true but it is clear that within the Home Office judicial mechanisms of accountability do not remedy the deficiencies commonly associated with parliamentary accountability. They are an important adjunct, but in a parliamentary democracy judicial mechanisms of accountability cannot be a substitute for Parliament. This is critical for a number of reasons. First, this highlights an issue that resonates throughout the course of this study: the problems associated with parliamentary accountability may well create support for alternative models of ensuring responsible government but those alternatives in themselves create a range of equally difficult, if not worse, constitutional dilemmas. How would the transfer of powers to an unelected judiciary be reconciled within a representative democracy? Dysfunctions in a parliamentary system cannot be repaired by creating new external power centres. Such a move would completely break the democratic loop, which works less then well at the moment. The emphasis returns to Parliament.

This argument leads us back to the paradox to be found within the government's constitutional reform agenda. Many parts of that agenda will empower the courts over the executive and in light of this the government has ensured that none of the plans directly undermine parliamentary sovereignty. While this has created clear tensions it retains the responsibility of ministers for the final decision. For example, if the Home Secretary decides not to amend a piece of legislation which the courts have declared incompatible with the ECHR then the minister is responsible for that decision. If sovereignty did not lie in Parliament and the courts were empowered to strike down legislation directly that would be inimical to accountable government. It is arguably better for that decision to be taken by an individual who is held responsible through a problematic mechanism of accountability than no mechanism at all. Yet this chapter has demonstrated a clear judicial trend that challenges the sovereignty of Parliament. This is likely to be exacerbated with further European integration and the incorporation of the ECHR.[106] The dilution of parliamentary sovereignty weakens the validity of ministerial responsibility both in theory and practice. (In the light of this trend it might be argued that ministerial responsibility is a fated convention.) Finally, the inability of a judicial model of accountability to rectify the flaws in the parliamentary model places an extra burden on the final model of accountability to be examined in this book. This will be topic of Chapter Six.

Notes

1. Sedley, S (1995) 'Human Rights - a Twenty First Century Agenda' *Public Law* pp.386-400. See also: Sedley, S (1990) 'Law and State Power - A Time for Reconstruction' *Journal of Law and Society* Vol. 17 No.2 pp.234-241; Sedley, S (1997) 'The Constitution in the Twenty First Century' in Lord Nolan & Sedley, S *The Making and Remaking of the British Constitution* (London : Blackstone); Sedley, S (1997) 'The Common Law and the Constitution' in Lord Nolan & Sedley, S *The Making and Remaking of the British Constitution* (London : Blackstone); Sedley, S (1994) 'The Sound of Silence: Constitutional Law Without a Constitution' *Law Quarterly Review* Vol.110 pp.270-291.
2. Hansard, HC Debs. WA 18/7/97 Q7834.
3. Hansard, HC Debs. WA 22/12/97 Q21321.
4. Made on the application of one party without the other being entitled to be involved.
5. Bridges, L, Meszaros, G & Sunkin, M (1995) *Judicial Review in Perspective* (London : Cavendish) p.43.
6. See Blake, C & Sunkin, M (1998) 'Immigration: Appeals and Judicial review' *Public Law* pp.583-591.
7. Supporting the statements of both the previous and current Home Secretaries that the Home Office wins over 90% of all its cases. See Hansard, HC Debs. WA 11/2/97 Q14375 (Mr Howard) and Hansard, HC Debs. WA 16/7/98 Q7841 (Mr Straw).
8. Daintith, T (1997) *Constitutional Implications of Executive Self Regulation: The New Administrative Law* (London : Institute of Advanced Legal Studies, University of London).
9. Legal Adviser, Home Office, interview with the author March 1998.
10. See MacKenzie, W & Grove, J (1957) *Central Administration in Britain* (London : Longmans); Daintith, T (1997) *Constitutional Implications of Executive Self Regulation: The New Administrative Law* (London : Institute of Advanced Legal Studies, University of London).
11. Woodhouse, D (1997) *In Pursuit of Good Administration: Ministers, Civil Servants and Judges* (Oxford : Oxford University Press) p.93.
12. All departments now have their own legal advisers and/or some solicitors from the Treasury Solicitor's Department on secondment.
13. Legal Adviser, Department for Education and Employment, interview with the author February 1998.
14. The Treasury Solicitor's Department deals with all litigation against every department apart from MAFF, Health, Social Security, Inland Revenue and Customs and Excise.

15 Chief Legal Adviser, Home Office, correspondence with the author 1/2/2000.
16 Cabinet Office (1995) *Judicial Review - Balancing the Scales*. This states that judicial review is '...part of the whole process of good administration'. At para. 3.
17 'We in the Treasury Solicitor's Department do not see our relations with our opponents, much less the judiciary, in terms of conflict. It is true that the adversarial system encourages the polarisation of positions. My department's perception is that the delay in decision-making or implementation which judicial review can bring about is an advantage which has not escaped the notice of some applicants.' Hammond, A (1998) The Continuing Interplay Between Law and Policy' *Public Law* p.39.
18 See: Woodhouse, D (1997) *In Pursuit of Good Administration: Ministers, Civil Servants and Judges* (Oxford : Oxford University Press) pp.131-135; Sedley, S (1997) 'The Common Law and the Constitution' in Lord Nolan & Sedley, S *The Making and Remaking of the British Constitution* (London : Blackstone) p.24; Le Sueur, A (1996) 'The Judicial Review Debate: From Partnership to Friction' *Government and Opposition* Vol.31 No.1 pp.8-27; Barker, A (1996) 'The Impact of Judicial Review: Perspectives From Whitehall and the Courts' *Public Law* pp.612-621.
19 Legal Adviser, Home Office, interview with the author, March 1998.
20 Legal Adviser, Home Office, interview with the author, March 1998.
21 For example, the 'gisting' procedure adopted after *ex parte Duggan* with regard to the release of information to prisoners regarding their security categorisation.
22 For example, the creation of the Immigration Appeals Tribunal (IAT) with the Asylum and Immigration Appeals Act 1993 occurred as a response to concerns expressed by the courts in a high number of judicial review cases.
23 Manuals of guidance, for example 'The Judge Over Your Shoulder', departmental training courses and attendance of advanced public law courses for senior officials at the Civil Service College.
24 Hogwood, B & McVicar, M (1997) 'The "Pondlife" of Executive Agencies: Parliament and "Informatory" Accountability' *Public Policy & Administration* Vol.12 No.2 pp.95-115; Hogwood, B 'The Quantitative Analysis of Agency Accountability: What Can It Tell Us and What Does It Miss Out?' Paper presented at the Conference of the Structure and Organisation Group (SOG) of IPSA on Taking the Measure of Government, Pittsburgh, USA, 30/10/97; Hogwood, B, Judge, D & McVicar, M 'Too Much of a Good Thing? The Pathology of Accountability' paper presented to the Political Studies Association Annual Conference, University of Keele, 7-9/4/98.

[25] It is also a critical issue in relation to the Immigration and Nationality Directorate. This is demonstrated by the government's plans to reform the system of immigration appeals to lessen recourse to judicial review. See Cm 4018 (1998) *Fairer, Faster, Firmer: A Modern Approach to Immigration and Asylum*; Blake, C & Sunkin, M (1998) 'Immigration: Appeals and Judicial Review' *Public Law* pp.583-591; Ford, R 'Straw acts to curb appeals' *The Times* 18/2/99 p.12.

[26] See Livingstone, S & Owen, T (1993) *Prison Law: Text and Materials* (Oxford : Oxford University Press).

[27] Livingstone, S (1995) 'The Impact of Judicial Review on Prisons' in Hadfield, B (ed.) *The Impact of Judicial Review on Prisons* (Dublin : Gill & Macmillan) p.167.

[28] *R. v. Secretary of State for the Home Department, ex p. Duggan* (1994) 3 All E.R. 277.

[29] The *Duggan* case also exemplifies the 'snowball effect' of judicial review. Since the case a large number of cases have sought to increase the amount of information contained in the 'gist' and it has been contended that nothing less than full disclosure of all relevant material will do. See, for example, *R v. Secretary of State for the Home Department, ex parte McAvoy*. Reported in *The Times* 12/12/97.

[30] For example, a common criticism was the courts attempts to regulate and control previously discretionary powers. Prison governors, it was argued needed discretionary powers to enable them to react to emergency situations or sudden issues.

[31] Boyle, A (1994) 'Sovereignty, Accountability and the Reform of Administrative Law' in Richardson, G & Genn, H (eds) *Administrative Law and Government Action: The Courts and Alternative Mechanisms of Review* (Oxford : Clarendon) p.101. For a case study on this issue see: Loveland, I (1988) 'Housing Benefit: Administrative Law and Adminstrative Practice' *Public Administration* Vol.66 No.1 pp.42-57.

[32] For example the select committee system in Parliament cost £3,758,286 for the session 1994/95 and £3,975,545 for the session 1995/96 (excluding directly employed staff). See HC 323 *The Work of Select Committees* First Report of the Liaison Committee, Session 1996/97, HMSO, London. p.xx.

[33] 'It's got to the point when we can't do anything without a judicial review case and I'm not sure the courts understand the very specific pressures and circumstances within which the Prison Service operates' Senior Official, Prison Service, interview with the author April 1998. This issue raises a number of important theoretical issues. Firstly, how could the true costs of different mechanisms of accountability be measured? Could such measurement facilitate agreement about inefficient/effective forms of

accountability? Might this lead to the decision to abolish some forms of accountability and if so who would take that decision?

34 *R v. Secretary of State for the Home Department, ex p. Fayed and Another* (1997) All E.R. 228.

35 '...the decision of the Secretary of State on any such application shall not be subject to appeal to, or review in, any court.' British Nationality Act 1981 section 44 (2).

36 '[The applicants] have not had the fairness to which they are entitled and the rule of law must be upheld.'

37 Hansard, HC Debs. WA 16/7/97 Q7842.

38 Research suggests that this is true for the majority of departments. For example see: Hansard, HC Debs. WA 15/7/97 Q7844; Hansard, HC Debs. WA 11/2/97 Q7835; Hansard, HC Debs. WA 15/7/97 Q7846; Hansard, HC Debs. WA 17/7/97 Q7840.

39 In *R v. Secretary of State for the Home Office ex parte Handscomb* the Court of Appeal considered the Home Secretary's practice of waiting for up to four years after the end of a prisoner's tariff period before referring the case to the parole board. The court concluded this was irrational and that the Home Secretary should consult with the judiciary at the time the tariff is set and the first referral should be shortly before the end of the tariff period. This judicial review decision was enshrined in the Criminal Justice Act 1991, after which the Home Secretary has to refer cases to the parole board as soon as the tariff period has expired.

40 Douglas Hurd was Home Secretary from September 1985 to October 1989, David Waddington from October 1989 to November 1990.

41 Interview with the author, April 1998. David Waddington noted of his time: 'It was just beginning to be a bit of a worry to the government'. Interview with the author, November 1997.

42 Michael Howard was Home Secretary May 1993 to May 1997. Ann Widdecombe was Minister for Prisons October 1992 to May 1997.

43 *R v. S. of State for the Home Department, ex p. Fire Brigades Union & Others* (1995) 2 A.C. 513.

44 Hammond, A (1998) 'Judicial Review: The Continuing Interplay Between Law and Policy' *Public Law* p.37.

45 *R v. Secretary of State for the Home Department ex parte Pierson.* Reported in *The Times* July 28/7/97.

46 Sedley, S (1997) 'The Common Law and the Constitution' in Lord Nolan & Sedley, S *The Making and Remaking of the British Constitution* (London : Blackstone) p.24; Le Sueur, A (1996) 'The Judicial Review Debate: From Partnership to Friction' *Government and Opposition* Vol.31 No.1 pp.8-27;

47. Barker, A (1996) 'The Impact of Judicial Review: Perspectives From Whitehall and the Courts' *Public Law* pp.612-621.
48. Interview with the author, March 1998.
49. Sedley, S (1995) 'Human Rights - a Twenty First Century Agenda' *Public Law* pp.386-400.
50. See: Hammond, A (1988) 'Judicial Review - The Continuing Interplay Between Law and Policy' *Public Law* pp.34-43.
51. I have in mind that it was the judicial (not statutory or Royal prerogative) doctrine on which the Thatcher government relied in the *Spycatcher* cases (*Attorney General v. Guardian Newspapers* [No.1] [1987]); it was the jury which acquitted Clive Ponting despite rather than because of the judge's summing up (*R v. Ponting* 1985), and it has been the courts that have upheld both the candour argument and class claims in the law on Public Interest Immunity Certificates (see *Taylor v. Anderton* 1995).
52. See Hansard, HC Debs. WA, 25/5/95 Q23145.
53. Home Office (1997) *Managing Inquiries*.
54. The Scott Report prompted the production of a wealth of literature on the role, procedure and powers of inquiries. See Lord Chancellor's Department (1994) *Disasters and the Law: Deciding the Form of Inquiry*; Council on Tribunals (1996) *Advice to the Lord Chancellor on the Procedural Issues Arising in the Conduct of Public Inquiries Set Up by Ministers*.
55. Home Office (1997) *Managing Inquiries* p.8.
56. Home Office (1997) *Managing Inquiries* pp.8-9.
57. Home Office (1997) *Managing Inquiries* p.9.
58. This is inevitably tied to the scope for selection. Due to the relatively small size of the senior judiciary and the pressures on the court system when the Lord Chancellor's Department is approached regarding the availability of a judge to chair an inquiry it will usually only produce one candidate. If the Secretary of State decides on a non-judicial appointment the permanent secretary will draw up a list of candidates after consulting the Public Appointments Unit. The scope for selection is therefore much wider for non-judicial appointments.
59. Cm 3020 (1995) *Review of Prison Security in England and Wales and The escape from Parkhurst Prison on Tuesday 3rd January 1995* , HMSO, London. [The Learmont Report].
60. Hansard, HC Debs. 19/5/97 col. 403.
61. *The Sunday Times* 11/2/01 p.14.
62. Interview with the author 4/11/97. David Waddington did not resign from the government but was re-shuffled to become Leader of the House.
63. Interview with the author 4/11/97. Mr Howard called this '...the Prior approach'.

63 Concerns were raised regarding the suitability of Sir William Macpherson to lead to the Lawrence Inquiry. See Dodd, V & Mills, H 'Father may ask Lawrence judge to stand down' *The Times* 15/3/98 p.3; Pallister, P 'Drama as Lawrence inquiry adjourned' *The Guardian* 17/3/98 p.3. The final report of Lord Stuart-Smith's inquiry into Hillsborough was critically received and calls were made for what would be the fourth judicial inquiry into the incident. See Grice, A & Rufford, N 'Straw to veto new disaster inquiry' *The Sunday Times* 15/2/98 p.1; *The Independent* 'Hillsborough ruling sparks families fury' 19/2/98 p.1.

64 Evidence from other departments is not encouraging. For example, the Foreign Secretary's decision to establish a non-judicial inquiry into the Sierra Leone affair and Lord Justice Phillips' inquiry into BSE is strictly limited to examining the incident under the previous administration.

65 Home Office Official, interview with the author, March 1998. This is a sentiment expressed to the BSE Inquiry by the former Health Secretary, Kenneth Clarke: 'You are wandering through a maze of documents but, with the greatest respect, you don't know the picture at all. I am convinced that you do not have the faintest understanding of how decisions are taken'. See Elliott, V 'Clarke's BSE Fury' *The Times* 22/10/99 p.2.

66 Home Office Official, interview with the author, April 1998. Several interviewees implied that they felt their future careers might be endangered if their evidence was viewed as critical of either the department or their ministers. They also doubted that the Public Interest Disclosure Act 1999 would offer adequate protection. On the act see Dehn, G (1999) 'Whistleblowing - Special Briefing on the New Public Interest Disclosure Act' *The Stakeholder* Vol.2 No.6 pp.14-18.

67 Roger Harding and Robert Primrose. See HC 115 *Report of the Inquiry into the Export of Defence Equipment and Dual-Use Goods to Iraq and Related Prosecutions* Session 1995/96, HMSO, London. [The Scott Report] B1.22, F4.54 & F4.57-66.

68 It also overlooks the fact that the Tribunal of Inquiry (Evidence) of Act 1921 was a response to the failure of Parliamentary mechanisms of accountability.

69 See Barker, A & Wilson, G (1997) 'Whitehall's Disobedient Servants? Senior Officials' Potential Resistance to Ministers in British Government Departments' *British Journal of Political Science* Vol. 27 pp.223-46.

70 For a discussion, see Ewing, K (1999) 'The Human Rights Act and Parliamentary Democracy' *The Modern Law Review* Vol.62 No.1 pp.79-99; Jacobs, F (1999) 'Public Law: The Importance of Europe' *Public Law* pp.232-246; Klug, F (1999) 'The Human Rights Act 1998: *Pepper versus Hart* and all that' *Public Law* pp.246-274; Lord Beloff (1998) 'Amery on

[71] the Constitution: Britain and the European Union' *Government & Opposition* Vol.33 No.2 pp.167-183.

[72] Chief Legal Adviser, Home Office. Correspondence with the author 1/2/2000.

[73] BBC Radio 4 *Matrix of Power* 14/10/99.

Jack Straw noted: 'It is already having an educative impact and the ECHR is mentioned in all submissions to me'. BBC Radio 4 *Matrix of Power* 14/10/99.

[74] McHarg, A (1999) 'Reconciling Human Rights and the Public Interest: Conceptual Problems and Doctrinal Uncertainty in the Jurisprudence of the European Court of Human Rights' *The Modern Law Review* Vol.62 No.5 pp.671-696.

[75] Legal Adviser, interview with the author 25/3/98. For a discussion of the consequences of the broad terms of the convention, see Pannick, D (1998) 'Principles of Interpretation of Convention Rights under the Human Rights Act and the Discretionary Areas of Judgement' *Public Law* pp.545-552; Oliver, D (1991) *Government in the United Kingdom: The Search for Accountability, Effectiveness and Citizenship* (Buckingham : Open University Press) pp.155-158.

[76] See *Abdulaziz v United Kingdom* (1985) 7 EHRR 471 (immigration rules); *Brogan v United Kingdom* (1988) 11 EHRR 117 (prevention of terrorism); and *Tyrer v United Kingdom* (1978) 2 EHRR 617 (corporal punishment within prisons).

[77] The white paper states that a declaration will '...*almost* certainly prompt the government and Parliament to change the law'. Cm 3782 (1997) *Rights Brought Home* p.9 para.2.10. See also Hansard, HC Debs. 21/10/98 col.1301.

[78] Other examples include while the government devolved power to a Scottish Parliament new candidate selection procedures were introduced to increase the centre's capacity for selection and control. The paradox is most crudely displayed in the sphere of Freedom of Information.

[79] See Hansard HC Debs. 21/10/98 col.1312 (Dr Tony Wright).

[80] Hansard HC Debs. 21/10/98 col.1322.

[81] See Gibb, F 'Courts prepare for Act that will change lives' *The Times* 26/10/98 p.4; 'Flood of legal challenges will put new law to the test' *The Times* 17/2/98 p.4.

[82] Hansard HC Debs. 21/10/98 col.1359. Although the Human Rights Act received Royal Assent in December 1998 it has not yet come into force, the interim period being designed to allow public authorities to prepare for the act.

[83] See Hansard HC Debs. 21/10/98 col.1360.

[84] The Constitution Unit (1999) *The Monitor* Vol.6 March p.3.

85   See Watson, R 'Civil service learn about human rights' *The Times* 26/10/98 p.1.
86   Senior Civil Servant, interview with the author 8/4/98. The majority of cases in which the United Kingdom has been taken to the European Court of Human Rights have involved policy responsibilities of the Home Office. For example, prisoners rights (*Golder v United Kingdom* [1975] 1 EHRR 524.); degrading treatment and punishment (*Republic of Ireland v United Kingdom* [1978] 2 EHRR 25.); extradition of suspected terrorists (*Soering v United Kingdom* [1978] 2 EHRR 1.); prevention of terrorism (*Brogan v United Kingdom* [1988] 11 EHRR 117.); telephone tapping (*Malone v United Kingdom* [1984] 7 EHRR14.); and contempt of court laws (*Sunday Times v United Kingdom* [1979] 2 EHRR 245.) for example. For a complete list of all UK cases heard by the European Court of Human Rights, see The Constitution Unit (1996) *Human Rights Legislation* (London : The Constitution Unit).
87   Beloff, M & Mountfield, H (1996) 'Unconventional Behaviour? Judicial Uses of the European Convention in England and Wales' *European Human Rights Law Review* Vol.5 pp.122-144. See also Lord Browne-Wilkinson (1992) 'The Infiltration of a Bill of Rights' *Public Law* pp.397-410; Kinley, D (1993) *The European Convention on Human Rights: Compliance Without Incorporation* (Aldershot : Dartmouth).
88   *Brind v Secretary of State for the Home Department* (1991) 1 All E.R. 735.
89   Hunt, M (1997) *Using Human Rights Law in English Courts* (Oxford : Hart) p.163.
90   See Hammond, A (1988) 'Judicial Review - The Continuing Interplay Between Law and Policy' *Public Law* p.36.
91   A database containing over 91,000 court reports including all reported cases since 1945 and all cases heard in the High Court, Court of Appeal and House of Lords since 1980.
92   As Lord Browne-Wilkinson openly acknowledged: 'I have on occasion had to reach conclusions in cases which I knew to be contrary to the convention because I was not able to do otherwise'. Hansard HL Debs. 25/1/95 col.1150.
93   For example in 1993 the Home Secretary issued a policy statement indicating that, in future, deportation cases involving marriage and the existence of children would be dealt with in light of Article 8 of the ECHR. See *R v Secretary of State for the Home Department, ex p. Eugeye-Gbemre*, CA 19/10/95 unreported; *Hing Fai Tong v Secretary of State for the Home Department*, CA 7/5/96 unreported.
94   Klug, F & Starmer, K (1997) 'Incorporation Through the Back Door?' *Public Law* pp.223-233. See also Klug, F Starmer, K & Weir, S (1996)

The Three Pillars of Liberty: Political Rights and Freedoms in the United Kingdom (London : Routledge) pp.105-109.

95 BBC Radio 4 *Matrix of Power* 14/10/99.

96 BBC Radio 4 *Matrix of Power* 14/10/99.

97 See Lord Kingsland in *The Times* (Law) 26/9/2000 p.5.

98 Statistics based on information supplied to the Home Office by the Human Rights Act Research Unit, Kings College, London.

99 Straw, J 'Rights Brought Home' speech to the Conference for Public Authorities, Blackburn Rovers FC, 26/1/01.

100 See Woodhouse, D (1997) *In Pursuit of Good Administration: Ministers, Civil Servants and Judges* (Oxford : Oxford University Press) p.106; Lee, S (1994) 'Law and the Constitution' in Kavanagh, D & Seldon, A (eds.) *The Major Effect* (London : Macmillan) pp. 134-136.

101 Woodhouse, D (1993) 'Ministerial Responsibility: The Abdication of Responsibility Through Receipt of Legal Advice' *Public Law* pp.412-419.

102 Head of Litigation, Treasury Solicitor's Department, April 1998.

103 Travis, A 'Lawyer in jail release row named' *The Guardian* 31/3/96; Daintith, T (1997) *Constitutional Implications of Executive Self Regulation: The New Administrative Law* (London : Institute of Advanced Legal Studies, University of London) pp.10-12.

104 CM 3818 (1997)*Your Right To Know - The Government's Proposals for a Freedom of Information Act* para. 2.22 p.10. The Public Administration Committee recommended that legal advice should not be given a blanket exclusion - see HC 398 *Your Right to Know: The Government's Proposals for a Freedom of Information Act* Third Report of the Select Committee for Public Administration, Session 1997/98, HMSO, London. para.s.31-32 p.XXVI.

105 HC 27-II *The Role of the Civil Service* Fifth Report by the Treasury and Civil Service Committee, Session 1993/94, HMSO, London. p.190 (Sir Robin Butler).

106 See *Political Studies* (Special Issue) 'Sovereignty at the Millennium' Vol.47 No.3.

6 Managerial Accountability and the Contract State

6.1 Introduction

This chapter examines to what extent the managerial model of accountability has mitigated the deficiencies commonly associated with ministerial responsibility to Parliament. It argues that although the managerial model was designed as a direct response to the challenges of reconciling ministerial responsibility with an increasingly fragmented state its implementation may generate as many problems as it solves. This is principally because the model is constructed within, and limited by, a framework of ministerial responsibility.

This chapter is central to the wider study for a range of reasons, not least because the conclusions of earlier chapters have been critical of the parliamentary and judicial models of accountability - which, in turn, heightens the significance of the managerial model. The voluminous literature on managerialism and 'new public management' (NPM) has largely ignored the very specific and novel approach to accountability encapsulated within this model. Not only does this model seek to remedy many of the flaws frequently linked to traditional forms of accountability but it also promotes a discussion of many of the theoretical dimensions of the maintenance of responsible government that were highlighted in Chapter One. For example, managerialism challenges the common orthodoxy on the direction of accountability flows by attempting to emphasise downward accountability to the public, arguably at the expense of the upward accountability of ministers to Parliament. In the light of this, distinctions emerge between high and low level accountability and internal and external accountability. The managerial model also illuminates the role of codes of accountability within the state and how these have evolved. A trend is particularly discernible within the associated discourse as relationships become contracts, citizens become consumers and accountability becomes audit.

Appreciating the evolution of an innovative managerial model of accountability is useful as it might provide an opportunity to understand the debate as to whether NPM has clarified or further obscured responsibility within the core executive. In essence the two sides of the argument are discussing two different models of accountability. The detractors are maintaining the sanctity of ministerial responsibility (political accountability) while the supporters are championing the benefits of contractual relationships and consumer responsiveness (managerial accountability). Therefore it is problematic to pronounce how the overall level of responsibility has been affected as it depends on the relative values attached to each model of accountability. For example, Next Steps agencies might be seen as attenuating the responsibility of ministers, but from the managerialist perspective they may be considered more accountable as agencies are arguably more efficient and responsive to consumers.

The managerial model of accountability has been applied to a constitutional infrastructure designed to facilitate the responsibility of ministers to Parliament. It is therefore 'path dependant' and the arrangements create the potential for considerable friction. Examining how managerial relationships have been moulded and affected by the wider political context could expose a number of tensions that have implications for the utility of both managerial and parliamentary accountability. Finally, it is vital to examine whether the managerial model delivers the results in terms of greater clarity, information and responsibility as promised by the theoretical model. Following on from this, a range of unintended consequences may accrue which undermine the benefits of this model; especially the further blurring of the convention of ministerial responsibility. To appreciate both the logic of managerialism and the vigour with which it was embraced it is worthwhile examining the political and economic background.

6.2 The Background to Managerialism

The Keynesian post - war bureaucracy has been the subject of a prolonged reform agenda. Whether one views this as 're-inventing' government,[1] a new global paradigm[2] or even the abandoning of government[3] is disputable. However, the structure of the state has changed dramatically in recent decades.⁴ As a consequence there has been a fundamental questioning of the role of the state and a concomitant blurring of the lines between the public and the private sectors.⁵ The post-war Keynesian welfare state is central to the recent reforms due to both its background as the context in which New Right ideas emerged and because of its contribution to the economic and political difficulties of the late 1970s. The welfare state and the mixed economy, in conjunction with the use of Keynesian economic techniques to maintain full employment, constitute the basis of the post-war consensus in Britain. Criticisms of this model focused on: the functioning of the nationalised industries; the supposed expenses of the welfare state; the alleged inefficiency of state provision and control of industries; the perceived ineffectiveness of Keynesian economics; and the inexorable propensity for voters to demand more services, politicians to accommodate these demands and bureaucrats to share in these expansionary interests. These attacks formed the context within which New Right ideas were formulated, promoting alternative economic, political and social policies and evaluative criteria.

The economic background to managerialism is reasonably straightforward - a long post war economic boom until the global economic crisis, brought about by the oil crisis of 1973, and then slow and partial recovery in the early 1980s. The emergence of 'stagflation' in the 1970s combined with the sharp squeeze on take-home pay caused by lower economic growth and rising public spending had already led to government steps towards retrenchment and breaks with Keynesian policies.⁶ Assumptions about the persistence of economic growth began to change and, according to Heald, the consensus became 'tarnished'.⁷ From a political viewpoint the main criticism was that government had become 'overloaded'. There was a widespread perception that Edward Heath's government had been a failure, that Britain was becoming ungovernable and that the state was suffering from political overload.⁸ Governments were viewed as having assumed too many roles and lacking the resources to fulfil these responsibilities adequately. Rose and Peters termed this 'political bankruptcy'.⁹ Several commentators suggested that political bankruptcy raised serious difficulties for the governability of advanced liberal democracies. Political confidence declines and a state unable to meet its commitments, or to expand public services, necessarily loses support and legitimacy. The simple logic of the New Right, with its intrinsic belief in the superiority of the market, offered a powerful and attractive solution to these concerns.[10]

By the late 1970s the New Right had plenty of apparent failures to cite in support of their proposed solutions.[11] Its main theoretical sources were monetarism, public choice theory[12] and Austrian School economics[13] - notably the work of Menger, Schumpeter and Hayek. Of particular importance was the management and organisational literature which became popular in the early 1980s.[14] This focused on a critique of bureaucracy and formed an important point of legitimation for the development of contract relations within the state. The influence of public choice theory fostered the belief that the lack of market forces had led to the growth of government due to the self-interested actions of both politicians and bureaucrats.[15] Public choice theory fused with market theory to produce a powerful new ideology which challenged the Keynesian welfare state. Whereas Keynesianism had emphasised the limitations and failures of market economics and stressed the benefits of state planning in both economics and social policy, the New Right ideology reversed these beliefs and stressed the benefits of the market and focused on the failures and limitations of the state.[16] Public choice theory played a vital part in this new synthesis as it claimed to expose the intrinsic defects in the political process, especially when compared with the benefits of the market. Central to this belief was the work of Niskanen who pointed out the problems of the dysfunctional bureaucracy and advocated a move towards a competitive bureaucracy based on principal/agent theory.[17]

Nigel Lawson defined Thatcherism as '...free markets, financial discipline, firm control over public expenditure, tax cuts, nationalism, Victorian values, privatisation and a dash of populism'.[18] This highlights how Mrs Thatcher selected strands of English liberalism and conservatism and combined these socially conservative values with the liberal economics of the New Right.[19] Yet certain strands appear contradictory.[20] Stuart Hall noted:

> Thatcherite populism is a particularly rich mix. It combines the resonant themes of organic Toryism - nation, family, duty, authority, standards, traditionalism - with the aggressive themes of a revived neo-liberalism - self interest, competitive individualism and anti-statism.[21]

The contradiction between neo-liberalism and neo-conservatism concerning the role of the state is striking. Where liberalism implies a limited government, conservatism requires a strong state to maintain social order.[22] Despite these contradictions these strands can also be seen as mutually supportive. Liberalism is the source of the New Right economic and political theories, conservatism provides a set of residual claims to cover the consequences of pursuing liberal policies. Liberalism required fundamental structural change in the state and therefore necessitated the strong state which traditional conservatism supports.

Thatcher, like President Reagan in America, offered solutions to her country's problems by reference to liberal arguments.[23] Liberal economic arguments for the free market were joined with political arguments about individualism and a reduced public sector. The solution to the United Kingdom's problems was deregulation and market forces, not government. Not only would this address the inefficiency and ineffectiveness of the state bureaucracy but it would also increase accountability directly to the individual at the point of delivery.[24] Many public servants found commitments to increased freedom, pay and grading and autonomy to manage attractive. What they failed to realise was that managerialism '...frequently sugared the pill of New Right public service reductions'.[25] Pollitt describes managerialism as the '...acceptable face of New Right thinking with regard to the state'.[26] Yet as a prescriptive model of the state managerialism appears apolitical. 'Better government' and 'increased efficiency' are the goals of all political parties. To this end managerialism is described as a transferable system of bureaucracy.[27] This, however, obscures the fact that restructuring the state will have important political and constitutional implications. Not least with regard to the responsibility of ministers for that reformed state. The result has been the implementation of a more managerial approach to the public sector which has at its core a new perspective on accountability.[28] To understand this it is necessary to explore the concept of managerialism.

6.3 Managerialism

In recent decades the structure of the state has been reconfigured via the imposition of a range of private sector derived processes and practices, most notably privatisation, contracting-out and agencification.[29] Public administration has, it is argued, been supplanted by 'new public management'.[30] However neutral the permutation from administration to management might appear, the reforms have created and exacerbated a number of concerns regarding the responsibility of ministers. As Massey noted:

> The shift from administration to management has an impact greater than that of providing work for etymologists it reflects a reappraisal of the structures and processes of accountability.[31]

Managerialism has been a major component of public sector reform in the 1980s and 1990s and has generated a wealth of literature.[32] Managerialism, like most political labels, is a loose expression but it is useful as an umbrella term drawing together a set of similar administrative reforms which have dominated the bureaucratic reform agenda in many countries.[33] As Sir Robin Butler noted:

> I think that the label - whilst exotic - is quite helpful in drawing attention to both the evolutionary and revolutionary changes in public management that we have experienced in the last two decades.[34]

Managerialism is a spectrum of reform which has broken down the traditional Weberian hierarchically based bureaucracy. Where possible the reforms have placed public functions on a spectrum that ranges from maintaining services within a department to hiving them off into a quasi-contractual agency to contracting them out into the private sector to privatising the service completely.[35] Indeed, the Prior Options Scheme examines the most suitable location along this spectrum of autonomy for every central government function.[36] Departments are increasingly fluid organisational umbrellas under which a range of quasi-autonomous units and bodies operate and interrelate. There is a discernible tendency for these units to drift further along the arm's length axis (as long as the body enjoys public confidence and there are no major incidents) while new candidates for hiving-off are continuously coveted.[37] Managerialism cannot be easily defined, though Massey captures its main elements succinctly:

- reducing bureaucratic rules and hierarchies;
- ensuring budgetary transparency and identifying the costs of inputs and outputs;
- the use of a network of contracts, rather than fiduciary relationships;

- disaggregating organisations and their functions, introducing purchaser/provider distinctions;
- increasing provider competition; and
- increasing consumer power through enhanced scope for exit and redress.[38]

Therefore managerialism is reflected in: a preference for disaggregated rather than unified structures; the growth of internal markets; greater flexibility in personnel and budgetary systems; the precedence given to service users rather than service providers; devolution of responsibilities to service delivery units; the predominantly operational focus of public management reform; and a tendency to use business analogues and to adopt the private sector as a role model. The organisational structure that is emerging is less reliant on rigid rules and regulations and favours contracts, targets, performance indicators and customer choice. Painter notes:

> ...we have witnessed the increased dominance of the 'business-consumerist' model as opposed to a 'government-citizenship' model seen in a preoccupation with customer not political rights and with managerialism rather than constitutionalism.[39]

Following on from this observation, Gray stresses the implications for traditional notions of accountability:

> The underlying theme of this revolutionary process contained a shift in emphasis from democratic accountability to economic accountability: a concern with the public as economic actors rather than citizens.[40]

There has, though, been some confusion in the understanding of certain terms, most notably 'privatisation' and 'contractualisation'. In the latter although private contractors may be used to provide services they remain within the public sector and the government continues to accept political and financial responsibility. This point was clarified by William Waldegrave:

> The attack on market testing and contracting out is surely based on a fundamental misunderstanding of the underlying policy. Contracting out is somehow thought to be the same thing as privatisation. But where a

service is contracted out, the government recognises the need to retain control at a strategic level, and hence accepts the accountability for that service as if it were provided in house.[41]

However, it is argued that some aspects of accountability are inevitably reduced under contracting out and that contracting out, at best, involves a trade off between efficiency and accountability. Indeed, a reduction in accountability requirements may be one of the reasons for the greater efficiency of the private sector.[42] There is an important difference in the degree of control exercised by ministers over their departments and contracted out functions which, in turn, affects the degree of accountability. The scope of ministerial intervention is limited by the contract. This creates a definite break in the chain of general oversight and accountability. Accountability is therefore limited to the terms of the contract.[43] The practical impact of this difference depends on the degree of specificity within the contract. But where the service is provided by a contractor, the minister may be powerless. Contracting out therefore fetters the minister's capacity to discharge amendatory responsibility (see Chapter One) as immediate remedies may not be available. Nevertheless, it has always been doubtful whether the traditional forms of political accountability provided a sufficient basis for public accountability. A more complex society and a more questioning public give added point to these doubts.[44] Set against this context the potential of managerial accountability becomes vital.

6.4 Accountability and Tensions in the Managerial Model

Managerial accountability involves harnessing the benefits of moving from bureaucratic to contractual relationships in central government. As the 1991 *Competing for Quality* white paper noted: '...public services will increasingly move to a culture where relationships are contractual rather than bureaucratic'.[45] Viewed against the reality of ministerial responsibility several observers have stressed the potential which the contractual approach offers the core executive. Harden noted:

> Although contract is not a panacea for the problems of discretion, it does offer the opportunity to make real progress towards greater accountability by clearly identifying who is responsible for policy, what it is, whether it is

being carried out in practice and if not why not... The contractual framework inevitably leaves some unstructured, unchecked discretion, but the appropriate basis for comparison is with the realities, not the theory, of ministerial responsibility. 'Customer satisfaction' is a simplistic notion which, if pushed too far, risks being a cloak for arbitrariness. However, to a large extent ministerial responsibility itself operates as precisely such a cloak.[46]

The enthusiasm for contractual relationships was founded on concerns regarding the 'overloaded' nature of the state, a desire to move towards a system of 'governance' rather than 'government' and a commitment to market forces.[47] These considerations accelerated the fragmentation of the state as reforms fostered: the separation of purchasers from providers; the growth of contractualism in service delivery; increased accountability for performance; the establishment of market or quasi-market relationships; and the separation of political processes from managerial processes.[48]

In theory contracts reflect a desire to increase control, efficiency, openness and accountability by making government more transparent. Hood has highlighted how contracts allow the active, visible, discretionary control of organisations by named individuals 'free to manage'.[49] This is justified by the belief that accountability requires clear assignment of responsibility for actions and not the diffusion of power found in traditional bureaucracies. A contract also necessitates the definition of goals and indicators of success for services and therefore a criterion against which the agent can be held to account. Such a move also theoretically increases accountability by requiring organisations to reappraise their objectives and strive to achieve them in the most efficient manner possible while taking into account the demands of users.

Contractualism immediately creates three sets of actors: the body purchasing the service on behalf of the public - the principal (department/local government); the body actually providing the service - the agent (contractor/quango/executive agency); and the public or 'consumers'. The purchaser becomes responsible for drawing up and monitoring the contract but operates at a strategic level.[50] The contract is crucial for clarifying the relationships between these constitutional actors, like ministers and agency chief executives. The contractual approach has the benefit of creating a structural distinction between purchaser and provider. This is seen as a valuable development as it reduces unnecessary administrative discretion and delegates decision-making authority to theoretically accountable and effective units.[51] Contracts therefore offer the possibility of resolving the dilemma of 'independence versus control' and in so doing the inherent contradiction found within the New Right between neo-liberalism and neo-conservatism as it theoretically allows the freedom necessary to maximise efficiency and the control demanded by politicians.[52] It is important to stress how contractual relationships have been established throughout the core executive. Not only are interorganisational (department-agency-contractor) relationships bound by contracts but interpersonal relationships within Whitehall have been placed on a quasi-contractual basis.[53] For example, all senior civil servants now operate according to personal contracts that clarify roles and responsibilities and form the basis for future career progression.[54]

In addition, charters represent a contract between service providers and service users. The trend towards managerialism, with its shift to contractual relations, was a direct response to the New Right belief that the traditional mechanisms of political accountability were failing. As William Waldegrave, then Minister for Public Services, noted:

> It has more importantly, made more transparent the links in the accountability chain which were pretty obscure before...contracts also make explicit the performance and standards that are expected. In the same way, the management of contracts within the public service sharpens and clarifies the responsibility of ministers, and hence to Parliament, for meeting those targets and standards. Thus the accountability links are not only unbroken; they are made clearer.[55]

> We want to make a reality of the all-too-often theoretical concepts of accountability in the public service... The old myth of personal responsibility for every action was not only a myth but a dangerous myth...far from impairing accountability I believe the purchaser/provider separation and management by contract have helped make a reality of it.[56]

This creates a paradox. Critics of managerialism claim that the move towards a contractual approach has weakened traditional notions of political accountability while supporters maintain that the traditional structures of government were palpably failing to deliver accountable government. Hence, managerialism is seen as a remedy to the deficiencies commonly associated with ministerial responsibility. For example, Mather believes managerialism solves the efficiency and accountability problems of contemporary government. He rebuts attacks that such reforms have made accountability elusive believing that before the reforms central government lacked '...the four virtues of accountability, contestability, precision and transparency' and that:

> The irony [of these attacks on the reforms] is that executive agencies and framework agreements for fixed periods governing specified tasks and open to inspection have fostered exactly those four elements. Agency chief executives are accountable, have functions which are contestable, define those functions precisely and are obliged to make them transparent and public.[57]

Therefore, beneath the innocent guise of management reform lies a radical and innovative response to the concerns surrounding the responsibility of ministers. To determine whether managerial accountability has repaired or exacerbated the deficiencies associated with ministerial responsibility, it is necessary to understand the importance and implications of seven inter-related themes.

- Theme 1 - The emphasis on downward accountability within the managerial model.
- Theme 2 - The difference between 'high' and 'low' level accountability.
- Theme 3 - The distinction between 'internal' and 'external' accountability.
- Theme 4 - How managerial accountability has been affected and legitimated by ministerial responsibility to Parliament.
- Theme 5 - Problems concerning the maintenance of the minister/agency distinction.
- Theme 6 - The dangers of information asymmetries between agency and department.
- Theme 7 - The role of audit mechanisms in devolved management accountability relationships.

The managerialist model of accountability encapsulates a distinctive approach to accountability by instituting mechanisms through which the users of public services can hold service providers directly to account. This reflects the intrinsic belief in the superiority of market mechanisms as the facilitator of optimum levels of accountability.[58] The imposition of this economic model arguably increases the significance of notions of efficiency above notions of accountability and responsibility.[59] As William Waldegrave noted:

> It is the output, the end product, not the internal 'whys' and 'wherefores', that are of crucial concern. It is the steady improvement in the day-to-day quality of service to the individual citizen that is the reality of public service accountability today.[60]

This approach to accountability obviously stands against traditional political forms of accountability in that it is not embodied in particular institutional arrangements but it involves organising the public sector with the aim of maximising the direct incentives providers have to take their customers into account and satisfy their customers' expectations. Managerial accountability emphasises the responsiveness of service providers to a body of 'sovereign' customers.[61] As a result structural reforms have attempted to increase the public's 'voice' mechanisms while privatisation, deregulation and the creation of quasi-markets have created 'exit' mechanisms.[62] These ambitions are encapsulated within the Citizen's Charter programme.[63] This specifies service standards and highlights grievance procedures where those standards have not been achieved.[64] The introduction of charters represents a more substantial political development for accountability than is commonly appreciated. Charters create a direct accountability relationship between the public and officials.[65] As Falconer noted:

> In placing the responsibility for service delivery squarely in the hands of the public sector managers it establishes a direct relationship between the providers and the customers, with the balance of power deemed primarily to lie with the customer. As such, though not stated explicitly, the Charter embodies an approach to accountability quite different in form and application to the more traditional forms of political accountability which bind governments to the public they serve, namely a managerial accountability which renders the providers of public services directly accountable to their customers through the mechanisms of quality assurance and redress enshrined in the Charter.[66]

It might therefore be suggested that charters break the circuit of accountable government whilst resurrecting a neo-Athenian model of direct democracy.[67] If that is so, the concept of accountability has come full circle.[68] The growing complexity of the state has generated a demand and the creation of a more direct form of accountability.

This change of directional emphasis is linked to the New Right desire to alleviate ministerial overload as Citizen's Charters act as 'buffers' between the government and the public. It might be argued that this, far from reducing accountability, has increased accountability due to the fact that most grievances are operational in nature and it is therefore better that these matters are dealt with quickly and efficiently by those in charge of operational affairs, rather than the issue consuming the valuable time of ministers who, in reality, have little knowledge of the grievances and problems they are asked to examine. This new form of managerial accountability could be seen therefore as an improvement on the traditional system as it has not displaced traditional channels of political accountability. If an aggrieved individual is not satisfied by the appropriate complaint mechanism they can still follow the traditional accountability channels by contacting either the minister or their MP.

> The critics fail to see that the underlying accountability has been strengthened ...we have strengthened these formal lines of accountability by making our public services directly accountable to their customers.[69]

According to the Conservative government, therefore, consumer responsiveness is a new mode of accountability. But charters, and contracts more generally, do affect ministerial responsibility to Parliament by establishing a political buffer for ministers. As earlier chapters have emphasised, the policy/operational dichotomy coupled with the rules and conventions underpinning ministerial responsibility permit ministers to restrict and define their spheres of responsibility. In this environment the relationship between citizens and the state becomes more complex. It is claimed by proponents of managerialism that contracts and charters have empowered the public. In so doing they have instituted a direct link between service providers and service users that enhances direct accountability and reduces the need for traditional channels of political accountability.

> The Citizen's Charter empowers through greater openness and the ending of anonymity and it empowers through public accountability with the publication of standards and results.[70]

However, a distinction can be made between 'high' and 'low' level accountability. High level accountability revolves around the responsibility of ministers for broad policy and resources decisions. Low level accountability covers the responsibility of civil servants to implement and administer those policies.[71] Therefore, no matter how responsive or efficient a service provider becomes managerial accountability can never replace parliamentary accountability as the service provider will always work within the parameters set by the minister. Stewart sums up this argument:

> The real fallacy is, however, to assume that providing responsive services can meet the requirements of public accountability. Accountability to the customer can never replace the need for public accountability, because the nature of the service is not determined by the customer alone. The issue of public accountability is where accountability lies for that policy framework.[72]

Harden highlights that: '...charters do not "empower" individuals in relation to decisions about the kind or level of public services that should be provided'.[73] Nor are service providers obliged to act on the views of their users.[74] Therefore while managerial accountability may offer an increased standard of 'low level' accountability it is crucial that the cost for this is not the further diminution of ministerial responsibility.[75] Managerialism therefore increases, rather than reduces, the need for Parliament to be effective - as the scrutineer of the public impact of ministerial policy and resource decisions. This would prevent managerial accountability becoming a veil for the consequences of 'high level' policy decisions and in so doing preclude the deflection of blame by ministers onto officials.

Within the context of the managerial model a distinction can also be made between 'internal' and 'external' accountability.[76] The hierarchical flow of information within a department is 'internal' accountability, while the flow of information from the department to Parliament and other bodies is 'external' accountability. It might be suggested that managerialism has increased the capacity of ministers to control and direct their departments.[77] Directorates, sections and individual officials now operate according to carefully costed quasi-contractual agreements. This situation is in marked contrast to when Lord Rayner joined Mrs Thatcher's Efficiency Unit in 1979 and found no capacity for discovering civil service spending levels.[78] The question arises of whether internal accountability has been increased to the detriment of external accountability to Parliament. Research by Deakin and Walsh suggested that officials believed that accountability within organisations was improved by contracts but external accountability was diminished.[79] The Conservative government did not feel that external accountability was affected: 'The further delegation of authority to managers inherent in the Next Steps concept concerns internal accountability within departments and does not conflict with the external accountability of ministers to Parliament'.[80]

It could also be suggested that managerialism has actually increased governmental overload rather than reduced it. The Conservative governments of the 1980s imposed the managerial model on local government through compulsory competitive tendering. There has also been a clear trend whereby services that were once the responsibility of local government or regional health authorities have been transferred to non-departmental public bodies (NDPBs).[81] Accountability has therefore, in recent years, been framed in terms of the predilections of the centre - a centre which has favoured the primacy of a managerial and narrowly economic strain of accountability. NDPBs are accountable through the tenuous line of ministerial responsibility via their parent department. Therefore, in many areas of the state, parliamentary accountability has replaced local political accountability. Such reforms increase the responsibilities of central government and add further tension to the realistic scope of ministerial responsibility. While the reforms may deliver economic benefits this might be to the detriment of accountability.[82] As Stewart notes:

> Most of the reforms mean that what accountability there is within the system will increasingly rest on central government. A burden is being put on the accountability of ministers that is probably beyond their capacity to bear. It is difficult enough to expect ministers to accept responsibility for the acts of civil servants who are directly under their control, without expecting them to extend their responsibilities as is required by the erosion of accountability at the local level. It is likely that the increasing burden of

accountability on ministers will not be matched by an acceptance of responsibilities.[83]

This highlights the conscious selection of forms of accountability by the executive to legitimate public sector reform. The 'hollowing out' of the state, and particularly the substitution of elected by appointed government, has been justified by the theory of ministerial responsibility, thus demonstrating the importance of the convention for British government and its usefulness as a tool for the executive. Yet the flexibility of the state is not infinite, the convention's malleability arguably has been exhausted and the tensions within the governance model of the state are acute.

The underlying model for managerial accountability is that of 'principal' and 'agent'; yet, in addition to the political and constitutional concerns regarding managerialism, the validity of the widespread application of simple contractual logic has been questioned.[84] The principal/agent (PA) model was developed in the context of new institutional economics and is of pivotal relevance to the current accountability arrangements in central government.[85] PA theory advances a specific form of organisational structure which prioritises a contractual relationship over traditional hierarchical Weberian top-down relationships. The principal engages the agent to undertake a particular task. The specific elements of the task are laid out in a contract and the agent is held accountable for the completion of the task through predetermined performance criteria and measurement. This model theoretically limits the discretion of the agent, provides transparency of roles and facilitates accountability by clarifying exactly who is responsible for what; whilst at the same time allowing the agent the maximum managerial flexibility to complete the task in the most efficient manner (see Figure 6.1).[86]

While the theoretical framework is powerful, in that it suggests general results that are attainable in many circumstances, the level of abstraction of the theory is arguably a drawback to its more specific and detailed application. Many have argued that the theoretical model does not fit the empirical evidence arguing that it '...creates a theoretical model of bureaucratic behaviour in an institutional vacuum'.[87]

The model is derived from the private sector but has been applied to complex areas of the public sector in which it is not always possible to create a clear and lasting distinction between principal and agent. Without the clear separation of roles and responsibilities the increased transparency and accountability promised by the model is lost. Mather captured the problem succinctly when he noted:

> The purity of the model is often obscured by the messiness of actual practice. Strategic objectives for public organisations are almost always political. The language of politics is rhetorical, ambiguous and persuasive...it does not lend itself easily to the clarity of specification required in the devolved management model.[88]

Figure 6.1 Accountability Relationships: A Summarised Picture of Theoretical Insights[89]

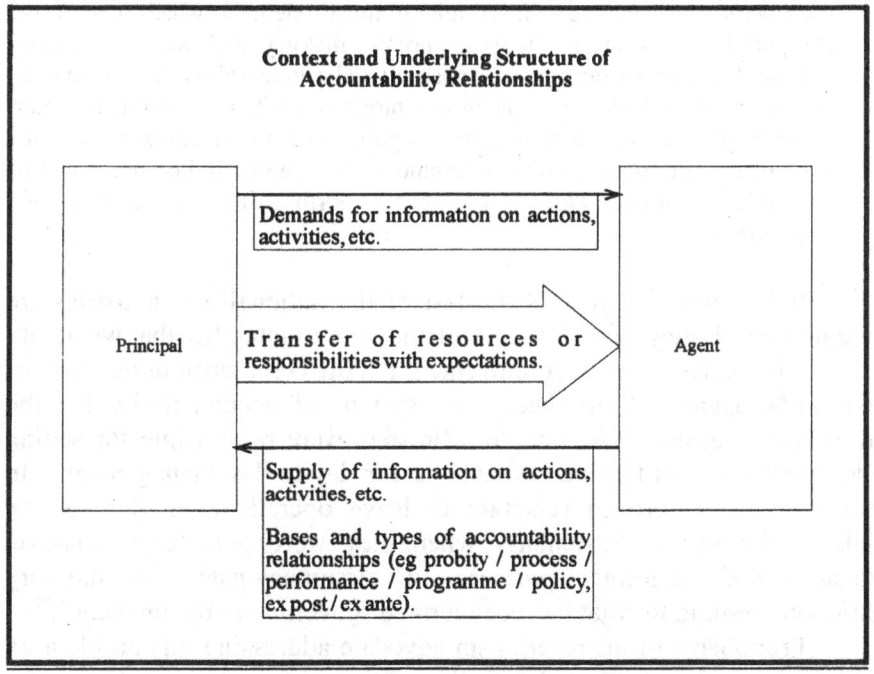

This problem is particularly acute in politically salient areas of government.[90] In those areas the complexity of the task demands a greater degree of devolved discretion than the contract model would ideally accommodate. The drafting of contracts that clearly designate responsibilities without being vacuous and impeding flexibility for politically salient tasks is a key challenge for the managerial model.[91] In light of this the Public Service Committee's recommendation, below, seems naive: 'We recommend that framework documents should specify more precisely the respective roles of ministers and chief executives'.[92] At the same time the temptation for ministers to intervene is greater due to the political sensitivity surrounding the function. There is no guarantee that the principal (minister) will abide by the contract and resist interfering in the responsibilities of the agent (agency). In this situation the contract becomes a convenient mechanism which ministers may use to distance themselves from the consequences of their actions.[93] Bogdanor noted:

> The fundamental premise is that public services can be made both more efficient and more accountable if the two functions of policy and service delivery are separated. It is this political element which makes the separation of powers between policy making and service delivery unworkable under our present constitutional arrangements. It will never be clear whether the failure to achieve a target is due to an operational factor, the inefficiency of the agency, or to a policy factor - the interference of the minister. The 'revolution in government', then, will fail, because it will be found to offend against our basic norms of accountability and democracy.[94]

It is ironic that just as the last of the nationalised industries are being privatised, they, and all the problems of accountability that went with them, are in many ways being reinvented in a different guise in the form of Next Steps agencies.[95] In theory the system of accountability for the nationalised industries was simple. Ministers were responsible for setting policy with the board being responsible for day-to-day management.[96] In practice ministers proved reluctant to leave operational matters in the hands of the board, particularly when they were politically sensitive. Ministers used informal pressure to circumnavigate the statutory restrictions leading to what has been termed 'government by luncheon'.[97]

Proponents of managerialism advocate addressing this problem by pushing the contractual model further rather than returning to a neo-Weberian model of bureaucracy.[98] This would involve adopting the Swedish model in which agencies exist on a statutory basis making it illegal for ministers to intervene in areas clearly designated as operational under the contract. As Mather notes:

Establishing the link between strategic purpose and operational management by means of a contract creates a need for specificity that can otherwise be avoided. It is at that point, where ministers intervene and the clarity provided by the contract is fudged, that agency proponents may regret that framework agreements are not enforceable in law. British agencies follow the Swedish model, but lack the underpinning provided by the Swedish system of public law.[99]

Although the Public Service Committee advocated a statutory framework for agencies, such a reform would fundamentally challenge the British constitution.[100] Placing agencies on a statutory basis would further undermine the responsibility of ministers for those units, whilst also demanding the direct accountability of the civil servants responsible for the agency, which would remove their traditional anonymity. The proposal also overlooks the fact that although the nationalised industries were established on a statutory basis this failed to prevent informal ministerial interference, which led to responsibility becoming blurred. Finally, the maintenance of the Carltona doctrine, discussed in Chapter Four, protects the power of ministers. Ministers are unlikely to approve reforms that limit their scope for flexibility and intervention in times of public concern.

Maintaining the principal/agent distinction is not the only challenge for the application of PA theory to central government. Asymmetrical information flows create the problem of 'principal ignorance'.[101] PA theory will only deliver optimum benefits where there is a relationship of 'perfect information'. Where this situation exists the principal is able to monitor the performance of the agent and any failures will be instantly and accurately observable.[102] Without 'perfect information' there may be monitoring and incentive difficulties.[103] The problem revolves around the maintenance of the principal as an 'intelligent customer'.[104]

The separation which is seen as a benefit of the contractual approach can also be a weakness if it means that the learning and information that come from the direct provision of the service is lost.[105] Contracts necessitate the construction of pre-established objectives against which the adequacy of an agency's discharge of its responsibilities can be assessed. These objectives are the result of a process of negotiation between the principal and agent, but if the principal lacks the necessary esoteric information then in many ways the agent, or contractor, is in the dominant position to the point where the agent will gradually develop a monopoly and '...use their authority to structure the behaviour of the principal, who is not free to leave'.[106] The 1994 Trosa Report examined the relationship between agencies and departments on behalf of the Cabinet Office. It noted how PA theory would dictate that the principal would set the targets for the agent to achieve but in reality the departments lacked the knowledge to set targets and the agencies design their own:

> The theory is that targets are set by ministers then by a department and then implemented by agencies. Nevertheless, the practical expertise about targets is in the agencies and often targets are proposed by agencies.[107]

A 1995 report into this issue (the Massey Report) highlighted the inefficient duplication of agency functions by departments in an attempt to retain the minister as an 'intelligent customer'.[108] Sir Peter Kemp believes this issue is more important than the controversy surrounding accountability:

> I don't think accountability is in such a bad state. Much more important than accountability is the relationship between purchaser and provider - they [departments] need to be intelligent customers but there is still a backlog of thinking to be done within departments.[109]

Braun argues that agencies clearly have greater access to more detailed information about their services than do ministers.[110] Where the agency has information that could affect the contract it is in their interest to misrepresent their information to the principal.[111] Williamson termed this 'information impactedness', which combines with opportunism to weaken the power and control of the principal.[112] Information impactedness is a particular problem if the agent knows that the principal will use the 'ratchet effect' to increase performance targets.[113] In order to reduce the problem of asymmetrical information principals are forced to expand their contract teams, creating 'counterpart bureaucracies', in order to police the purchaser/provider relationship and ensure the contractor remains an intelligent customer.[114] But the problem with developing large teams of 'agency shadowers' is that the cost of such bodies negates the efficiency savings that accrued from moving to the contractual approach.[115] Massey notes:

> There is a danger here that in order to retain the ability to make informed decisions about contracts with agencies, privatised agencies and the private sector, the government will squander such savings as the process might have made by employing large numbers of contract or procurement staff. Moving to a system of contract based accountability is not a cheap option...it may prove more expensive than the system being dismantled.[116]

The ability of the principal to secure unadulterated information from the agent is vital to the effectiveness of managerial accountability. Lovell has highlighted how the role of the public sector audit is fundamental to this model of accountability.[117] Despite criticisms of the current predominance of the rationalist perspective of accountability (and the increasingly prominent role of auditing within this perspective), just as contracts are the foundations on which the PA relationship is built, audit is the mechanism used to police this relationship.[118]

The 'audit explosion' is a direct result of the increase in use of contractual relationships, reflecting the need to make organisations and individuals accountable when there has been a conscious and explicit attempt to dismantle the public/private divide.[119] It represents an attempt to reconcile the contradictory forces of the recent reinvention of government. Namely the centrifugal pressures for decentralisation and devolution with the centripetal desire to retain control over functions that have been devolved.[120] It is a means of checking and verifying the account that has been given by the agent. It can add to that account information not contained in the original account. Audit is therefore a risk reduction exercise that seeks to control the agent's behaviour while attempting to reduce some of the information asymmetries mentioned earlier. Accounting is seen as a way of both making visible and disciplining performance so that accountability can be demanded, policed and enforced.[121] Hirst and Kilhani noted how increasingly '...public accountability is expressed in managerial terms. In this redefinition of accountability accountancy has become the key profession'.[122]

Such is the role of audit mechanisms within the managerial model of accountability that it has been suggested that audit has assumed a constitutional significance.[123] This has, however, coincided with an increasing questioning of the capacity of audit mechanisms - indeed, an 'auditing crisis'.[124] It is therefore necessary to recognise that audit mechanisms are not a panacea for the problems of responsible government. As Miller notes:

> To do so is not to dismiss the potential. It is simply to raise the possibility that accounting information may be more suited to some tasks rather than others...and that there may be some important issues that it neglects.[125]

The fact that an audit takes place does not equal accountability itself. Audit mechanisms produce information which will be used by those to whom an account is owed. Therefore audit is a means of improving or increasing the effectiveness of the accountability relationship. It supports rather than supplants other forms of accountability.[126] To conduct an audit it is necessary to construct objective quantifiable performance criteria against which the agent can be held to account. Designing such criteria in the public sector can be difficult.[127] The clear measurement of outputs may not always be possible when the tasks in question are indeterminate.[128] Where outputs do not lend themselves easily to quantification there is a risk that those outputs may be neglected because of their lack of auditability.[129] As a consequence tacit processes may lead to imprecise outcomes and the problems of defining and controlling the agent's actions may be complex.[130] It is in the interpretation of complex goals into measurable criteria where audit is at its most innovative and unsafe. The dangers of spurious surrogate measures are recognised in the wider literature, and set, in the context of the accountability relationship between agencies and departments, the role of these criteria, spurious or otherwise, becomes significant.[131] It may be suggested that certain areas of the public sector are not amenable to the imposition of measurable criteria against which the body can be held accountable. The design of such measures may be worthless, while the costs incurred in the design, implementation and audit of those criteria may negate the efficiency savings accrued by the contractual approach. Hood and James note:

> Such potential costs have so far attracted little official recognition or debate. Indeed, what is perhaps the major insight of social science analysis - that policy interventions, especially in administrative reform, commonly produce unexpected side effects and sometimes unintentionally produce reverse effects, bringing about consequences the opposite of which was originally intended, has been little applied to new public management up until now.[132]

In addition there is a danger that over-auditing may have dysfunctional side effects and there is a need for a greater empirical understanding of the consequences of audit on both organisations and individuals. Taken together these issues suggest that audit should not be viewed as an '...easy solution to the more messy problems of democratic accountability'.[133]

6.5 Conclusion

Recent changes in the management of the core executive have had an impact, in many ways, on the extent and form of its responsibility to the public and Parliament. The development of managerialism has strained the traditional machinery of responsible government. For example, inherent in the nature of the private sector is the notion of 'commercial confidentiality'. Such confidentiality is antagonistic to public accountability for the provision of public services. However, in the pre- 'new public management' state the responsibility of ministers was, admittedly, flawed. The Conservative government believed its explicit philosophy of market mechanisms would increase managerial accountability, operationalised in greater consumer responsiveness and efficiency. This belief was to become all the more important when allied with the government's view that it was intending to become more of an enabler or commissioner of public services rather than provider. Yet the transition from 'government' to 'governance' has exacerbated tensions which have always existed. It is suggested that managerialism further obfuscates the responsibility of ministers, while the promotion of a managerial model of accountability that advances the direct accountability of service providers to the public challenges both the role and sovereignty of Parliament.

More broadly, the greatest change is in the complex web of new organisations and inter - agency relationships that have developed under the guise of managerialism.[134] This is a subtle yet critical point. A change in accountability models between organisations changes relationships and expectations. Managerialism not only promises better accountability, but a substantially different set of accountability relationships from those that previously applied to the core executive. Consequently, managerialism does not deny the need for government to operate fairly and accountably, rather, it redefines what is meant by these terms. And yet contextually the fragmented structure does not sit well with traditional relationships between the public and the state. As Bruce and McConnell noted:

> The hiving off of functions to private contractors and unelected bodies not only confuses responsibility, but it also creates a vacuum because there is no single agency with overall responsibility.[135]

Despite the executive's insistence that this tension is appeased by the continuing validity of ministerial responsibility the malleability of the convention has arguably been exhausted. Bureaucratic flexibility and organisational hybridity imposes a duty on Parliament and the public to keep abreast of this change. What was once the responsibility of a department is now the responsibility of an agency, non-departmental public body, quango, contractor or is part of the private sector. Parliament was designed to oversee a reasonably stable structure and is ill - equipped for dealing with change. And yet the continuing centrality of the convention within the Whitehall-Westminster model has shaped the introduction of the managerial model. If the model had been free of this encumbrance and implemented to its logical conclusion, with ministers being directly responsible for policy and officials directly responsible for operations, with Parliament being the mediator, the whole constitutional configuration would have demanded reconstruction. Ministerial responsibility provided a useful veil for maintaining the dominant position of the executive. As a result a structural reformation has been awkwardly established while maintaining a constitutional orthodoxy that increasingly lacks credibility. Nevertheless, it is important to remember that a central rationale for the implementation of managerialism was a belief that traditional political mechanisms of accountability were inadequate. Managerial accountability was designed to reconcile an increasingly fragmented and complex state within a continuing framework of ministerial responsibility to Parliament. The next chapter examines whether in the case of the Home Office managerial accountability has successfully remedied the problems associated with ministerial responsibility. It also explores to what extent the various challenges which this chapter has highlighted with the managerial model have been encountered and overcome in practice.

Notes

1. Osborne, D & Gaebler, T (1992) *Re-Inventing Government* (London : London); Ridley, F (1995) 'Re-Inventing British Government' *Parliamentary Affairs* Vol.48 No.3 pp.375-401.
2. Hood, C (1995) 'Contemporary Public Management: A New Global Paradigm' *Public Policy and Administration* Vol.10 No.2 pp.104-117.
3. Painter, C (1994) 'Public Service Reform: Re-Inventing or Abandoning Government' *Political Quarterly* Vol.65 No.3 pp.242-263.
4. For a comparative perspective on new public management, see Ridley, F (1996) 'The New Public Management in Europe: Comparative Perspectives' *Public Policy and Administration* (special edition) Vol.11 No.1 pp.16-29.
5. See Flinders, M & Smith M J (1998) *Quangos, Accountability and Reform: the Politics of Quasi-Government* (London : Macmillan); Flinders, M, Thiel, S van & Greve, C (1998) 'Quangos - What's in a Name? - Defining Quangos From a Comparative Perspective' *Governance* Vol.12 No.2 pp.129-147; Flinders, M & Greve, C (1997) 'Opening up the Grey Zone - EGOs, NGOs and Quangos in Denmark and Scandinavia' *The Stakeholder* Vol.2 No.5.
6. Hood, C & Wright, M (1981) *Big Government in Hard Times* (Oxford : Martin Robertson).
7. Heald, D (1983) *Public Expenditure* (Oxford : Martin Robertson) p.3.
8. Birch, A (1984) 'Overload, Ungovernability and Delegitimation: The Theories of the British Case' *British Journal of Political Science* Vol.14 pp.135-160; King, A (1976) *Why Is Britain Becoming Harder To Govern?* (London : BBC); King, A (1975) 'Overload: Problems of Governing in the 1970s' *Political Studies* Vol.23 pp.289-96; Rhodes, R (1995) *The New Governance: Governing Without Government* (Swindon : ESRC/RSA); Rhodes, R (1996) 'The New Governance: Governing without Government' *Political Studies* Vol.44 No.4 pp.652-667.
9. Rose, R & Peters, G (1977) *Can Government go Bankrupt?* (New York : Basic Books).
10. The core of the New Right liberal political and economic tenet is the superiority of market mechanisms as the promoter of economic prosperity, accountability and maximising individual freedom. There is an ideological preference for increased reliance upon market forces and *laissez faire* policies consistent with the traditional liberal beliefs. This leads to a belief in competitive individualism, a reduced role for the state and a maximisation of the market. The key principle is to allow market forces to operate freely, to as great an extent as possible, coupled with the belief that social order

will be largely self regulating, in a way similar to the classical liberalism of Adam Smith.

11 It supported its attacks on the public sector with extensive academic work from right wing think tanks. These included: The Institute of Economic Affairs; Centre for Policy Studies; and the Adam Smith Institute.

12 See Mueller, D (1989) *Public Choice* (Cambridge : Cambridge University Press); Nozick, R (1975) *Anarchy, State and Utopia* (Oxford : Blackwell).

13 See Hayek, F (1944) *The Road to Serfdom* (London : Ark); Seldon, A (1984) *Hayek's Serfdom Revisited* (London : Institute of Economic Affairs).

14 For example Peters, T & Waterman, R (1982) *In Search of Excellence* (London : Harper & Row). See also: Rhodes, R (1994) 'Reinventing Excellence: Or How Best Sellers Thwart the Search for Lessons to Transform the Pubic Sector' *Public Administration* Vol.72 No.2 pp.281-288.

15 Minford, P (1987) 'The Role of the Social Services: A View From the Right' in Loney, M (ed.) *The State of the Market: Politics and Welfare in Contemporary Britain* (London : Sage).

16 See Ashford, N (1985) 'The Bankruptcy of Collectivism' in Seldon, A (ed.) *The 'New Right' Enlightenment* (London : Economic and Literary Books) p.45.

17 Niskanen, W (1971) *Bureaucracy and Representative Government* (New York : Aldine & Atherton); Niskanen, W (1973) *Bureaucracy: Servant or Master? Lessons from America* (London : IEA).

18 Lawson, N (1992) *The View From No.11* (London : Bantam) p.64.

19 See Jenkins, S (1995) *Accountable to None: The Tory Nationalisation of Britain* (London : Hamilton).

20 This contradiction is well documented. See Gamble, A (1988) *The Free Economy and the Strong State: The Politics of Thatcherism* (London : Macmillan); Gamble, A (1996) *Hayek : The Iron Cage of Liberty* (Oxford : Polity Press); Gamble, A (1986) 'The Political Economy of Freedom' in Levitas, R (ed.) *The Ideology of the New Right* (Oxford : Polity Press).

21 Hall, S (1983) 'The Great Moving Right Show' in Hall, S & Jacques, M (eds.) *The Politics of Thatcherism* (London : Lawrence & Wishart) p.29.

22 King, D (1987) *The New Right: Politics, Markets and Citizenship* (Basingstoke : Macmillan).

23 Savoie, D (1994) *Thatcher, Reagan, Mulroney: In Search of a New Bureaucracy* (Toronto : University of Toronto Press).

24 There is a wealth of literature offering an in-depth analysis of the New Right. See Levitas, R (1986) *The Ideology of the New Right* (Oxford : Polity Press); King, D (1987) *The New Right: Politics, Markets and Citizenship* (Basingstoke : Macmillan); Joseph, K & Sumption, A (1979) *Equality* (London : Murray); Friedman, M & Friedman, R (1980) *Free to*

Choose (Harmondsworth : Penguin). For the New Right perspective on the public sector, see Pollitt, C (1993) *Managerialism and the Public Services* (Oxford : Blackwell).

25   Pollitt, C (1993) *Managerialism and the Public Services* 2nd ed. (Oxford : Blackwell). p.48. This assertion has been disputed. See Kemp, P (1996) 'Beyond Next Steps: Obstacles to Fulfilment' in Barberis, P (ed.) *The Whitehall Reader* (Buckingham : Open University Press) p.213.

26   Pollitt, C (1993) *Managerialism and the Public Services* (Oxford : Blackwell) p.49.

27   Hood, C (1991) 'A Public Management for all Seasons?' *Public Administration* Vol.69 No.2 pp.3-19.

28   Massey, A (1995) 'Civil Service Reform and Accountability' *Public Policy and Administration* Vol.10 No.1 p.24.

29   Rasmussen, K & Yeates, N 'Performance Management and the Divided Worlds of Accountability' Paper to the International Institute of Administrative Sciences Conference, Civil Service College, Sunningdale, 12-15/5/99.

30   Gray, A & Jenkins, B (1995) 'From Public Administration to Public Management' *Public Administration* Vol.73 pp.92-99; Dunleavy, P & Hood, C (1994) 'From Old Public Administration to New Public Management' *Public Money and Management* Vol.14 No.3 pp.9-17.

31   Massey, A (1995) 'Civil Service Reform and Accountability' *Public Policy and Administration* Vol.10 No.1 p.22.

32   See Pollitt, C (1993) *Managerialism and the Public Services: Cuts or Cultural Change in the 1990s?* (Oxford : Blackwell); Zifcak, S (1994) *New Managerialism: Administrative Reform in Whitehall and Canberra* (Buckingham : Open University Press); Ransom, S & Stewart, J (1994) *Management for the Public Domain* (Basingstoke : Macmillan); Farnham, S & Horton, S (1993) *Managing the New Public Services* (Basingstoke : Macmillan).

33   '...a convenient but inherently vague label for a family of linked institutional reforms adopted in the attempt to impose new disciplines on public bureaucracies.' Hood, C & James, O *Reconfiguring the UK Executive: From Public Bureaucracy State to Re-Regulated Public Service* Paper presented to ESRC conference 'Understanding Central Government: Theory into Practice' University of Birmingham 16-18/9/96.

34   Butler, R (1992) 'The New Public Management: The Contribution of Whitehall and Academia' *Public Policy and Administration* Vol.7 No.3. pp.77-95.

35   For a more detailed discussion of this spectrum and an elaborate diagram of the evolving nature of the state, see Flinders, M & McConnel, H (1997)

[35] 'Maybe Minister: Quangos and Accountability' in Flinders, M, Harden, I & Marquand, D (eds.) *How To Make Quangos Democratic* (London : Charter 88) pp.42-50.

[36] See Lewis, N (1994) 'Reviewing Change in Government: New Public Management and Next Steps' *Public Law* pp.105-113.

[37] Flinders, M (1998) 'Setting the Scene: Quangos in Context' in Flinders, M & Smith, M (eds.) *Quangos. Accountability and Reform: The Politics of Quasi-Government* (London : Macmillan) pp.3-17. See: Cm 4273 (1999) *Next Steps Report 1998* Annex B 'Activities announced by ministers as candidates for agency status as of 31 December 1998' pp.327-329.

[38] Massey, A (1995) 'Civil Service Reform and Accountability' *Public Policy and Administration* Vol.10 No.1 p.18.

[39] Painter, C (1995) 'The Next Steps Reforms and Current Orthodoxies' in O'Toole, B & Jordan, G (eds.) *The Next Steps: Improving Management in Government?'* (Aldershot : Dartmouth) p.19.

[40] Gray, C (1994) *Government Beyond the Centre: Sub-National Politics in Britain* (Basingstoke : Macmillan) p.65.

[41] Waldegrave, W 'The Reality of Reform and Accountability in Today's Public Service' Lecture to the Public Finance Foundation 5/7/93; See also Kemp, P (1993) *Beyond Next Steps: A Civil Service for the 21st Century* (London : Social Market Foundation).

[42] Roth, D (1996) 'Finding the Balance: Achieving a Synthesis Between Improved Performance and Enhanced Accountability' in *Performance Auditing and the Modernisation of Government* (Paris : OECD) pp.249-259.

[43] Mulgan, R (1997) 'Contracting Out and Accountability' *Australian Journal of Public Administration* Vol.56 No.4 pp.106-116.

[44] Stewart, J (1994) 'The Rebuilding of Public Accountability' in Flynn, N (ed.) *A Reader: Change in the Civil Service* (London : Public Finance Foundation) p.75.

[45] Cm 1730 (1991) *Competing for Quality* HMSO, London. p.199.

[46] Harden, I (1992) *The Contracting State* (Buckingham : Open University Press) p.71.

[47] See Osborne, D & Gaebler, T (1992) *Reinventing Government* (London : Plume) pp.25-49.

[48] Stewart, J & Walsh, K (1992) 'Change in the Management of Public Services' *Public Administration* Vol.70 No.4 pp.499-518.

[49] Hood, C (1991) 'A Public Management for All Seasons' *Public Administration* Vol.69 No.2 p.4.

[50] Stone, B (1995) 'Administrative Accountability in the Westminster Democracies: Towards a New Conceptual Framework' *Governance* Vol.8 No.1 p.513.

51 Harden, I (1992) *The Contracting State* (Buckingham : Open University Press) p.29.
52 Smith, B & Hague, D (1971) *The Dilemma of Accountability in Modern Government: Independence versus Control* (London : Macmillan).
53 This arose from the 1993 Efficiency Unit report *Career Management and Succession Planning Study* [The Oughton Report] and was established in the 1994 white paper *The Civil Service: Continuity and Change* (Cm 2627) pp.3-4, 36-37, 43-4.
54 Hood, C (1998) 'Individualized Contracts for Top Public Servants: Copying Business, Path Dependent Political Re-Engineering - or Trobriand Cricket?' *Governance* Vol.11 No.4 pp.443-462.
55 Waldegrave, W (1993) *The Reality of Reform and Accountability in Today's Public Service* (London : Public Finance Foundation) p.10.
56 Waldegrave, W (1993) *Public Service and the Future: Reforming Britain's Bureaucracies* (London : Conservative Political Centre) p.17.
57 Mather, G (1994) 'The Market, Accountability and the Civil Service' *Public Policy and Administration* Vol.9 No.3 p.9.
58 Glynn, J (1996) 'Public Management: Failing Accountabilities and Failing Performance Review' *International Journal of Public Sector Management* Vol.9 No.5/6 pp.125-137.
59 Bruce, A & McConnell, A (1996) 'Accountability in Local Government and the NHS' in Pyper, R (ed.) *Aspects of Accountability in the British System of Government* (Eastham : Tudor) p.126; Mayston, D (1993) 'Principals, Agents and the Economics of Accountability in the New Public Sector' *Accounting, Auditing and Accountability* Vol.6 No.3 p.69.
60 Waldegrave, W (1993) *The Reality of Reform and Accountability in Today's Public Service* (London : Public Finance Foundation) p.3.
61 Stone, B (1995) 'Administrative Accountability in the Westminster Democracies: Towards a New Conceptual Framework' *Governance* Vol.8 No.1 p.521.
62 Hirschman, A (1970) *Exit, Voice and Loyalty* (Harvard : Harvard University Press); Andrews, C & Kouzmin, A (1999) 'Re-legitimating "Voice" and "Loyalty" with Economic Theories of Democracy and Accountability' *International Review of Administrative Sciences* Vol.65 No.3 pp.395-409; Paul, S (1992) 'Accountability in Public Services: Exit, Voice and Control' *World Development*, Vol.20 No.7 pp.1047-1060.
63 Cm 1599 (1991) *The Citizen's Charter. Raising the Standard* HMSO, London.
64 Pollitt, C (1994) 'The Citizens Charter: A Preliminary Analysis' *Public Money and Management* April/June p.13; Connolly, M (1994) 'Making The Public Sector More User Friendly? A Critical Examination of the Citizen's

[65] Charter' *Parliamentary Affairs* Vol.47 No.1 pp.23-36; Tritter, J (1994) 'The Citizen's Charter: Opportunities for User Perspectives' *Political Quarterly* Vol.65 No.4 pp.397-414.

[66] Lovell, R (1992) 'The Citizen's Charter: The Cultural Challenge' *Public Administration* Vol.70 pp.395-404; Lewis, N (1993) 'The Citizen's Charter: A New Way of Governing?' *Political Quarterly* Vol.64 No.3 pp.316-326.

[67] Falconer, P (1996) 'Charterism and Consumerism' in Pyper, R (ed.) *Aspects of Accountability in the British System of Government* (Eastham : Tudor) p.213.

[68] Roberts, J (1982) *Accountability in Athenian Government* (Madison, Wisc : UOW Press).

[69] Day, P & Klein, R (1987) *Accountabilities : Five Public Services* (London : Tavistock) pp.20-21.

[70] Waldegrave, W (1993) *The Reality of Reform and Accountability in Today's Public Service* (London : Public Finance Foundation) p.13.

[71] Waldegrave, W 'Speech given to the Institute of Directors' Press Release (Office of Public Service and Science) No.18 1992.

[72] This distinction mirrors Bulpitt's division between 'high' and 'low' politics. See Bulpitt, J (1983) *Territory and Power in the United Kingdom* (Manchester : Manchester University Press).

[73] Stewart, J (1994) 'Reply to Waldegrave' in Flynn, N (ed.) *A Reader: Change in the Civil Service* (London : Public Finance Foundation) p.89.

[74] Harden, I (1992) *The Contracting State* (Buckingham : Open University Press) p.7.

[75] For a local authority case study on this point, see Bayliss, R (1996) *Conflicting Modes of Accountability: A User Perspective* Newcastle Discussion Papers in Politics No.20, University of Newcastle.

[76] Evidence suggests that the public have made little use of Citizen's Charters. See Pollitt, C (1994) 'The Citizens Charter: A Preliminary Analysis' *Public Money and Management* April/June p.13.

[77] Flinders, M, Smith, M & Richards, D (1999) 'The Accountability of Public Bodies' memorandum of evidence to the Public Administration Committee at: HC 209-II *Quangos* Sixth Report by the Public Administration Committee, Session 1998/99, HMSO, London. pp.196-205.

[78] Indeed this was a central aim of the Next Steps initiative. See, Foster, C & Plowden, F (1996) *The State Under Stress* (Buckingham : Open University Press), Campbell, C & Wilson, G (1995) *The End of Whitehall* (Oxford : Blackwell).

See: Massey, A (1993) *Managing the Public Sector: A Comparative Analysis of the United Kingdom and the United States* (Aldershot : Edward Elgar) pp.40-51; Hennessy, P (1989) *Whitehall* (London : Secker & Warburg) pp.592-605.

79 Deakin, N & Walsh, K (1996) 'The Enabling State: The Role of Markets and Contracts' *Public Administration* Vol.74 pp.33-48.
80 Cm 524 (1989) *Civil Service Management Reform: the Next Steps: Government Reply to the Eighth Report from the Treasury and Civil Service Committee (1987-88)* HMSO, London. para. 9.
81 See Flinders, M & Smith, M (1998) *Quangos, Accountability and Reform: The Politics of Quasi-Government* (London : Macmillan); Skelcher, C (1998) *The Appointed State: Quasi-Governmental Organizations and Democracy* (Buckingham : Open University Press).
82 This was noted by Bruce and McConnell: '...if the hollowed out state in local government and the NHS increases efficiency and so leads to less pressure on taxation, maintains service levels, provides the public with more information through Charters and performance indicators and puts more pressure on public authorities to meet public expectations, then we must be prepared to concede that there are some positive benefits accruing from this regime. If, even in some degree, people want cheap, high quality services, then the new system of accountability will act on their behalf in an attempt to ensure that they obtain this'. Bruce, A & McConnell, A (1996) 'Accountability in Local Government and the NHS' in Pyper, R (ed.) *Aspects of Accountability in the British System of Government* (Eastham : Tudor) p.147.
83 Stewart, J (1994) 'The Rebuilding of Public Accountability' in Flynn, N (ed.) *A Reader: Change in the Civil Service* (London : Public Finance Foundation) p.77. Elsewhere John Stewart noted: 'Where choices are made on behalf of local people accountability to Parliament is inappropriate - accountability should be to those on whose behalf those choices are made. The burden [of ministerial responsibility] has now been increased to the point where it is almost bound to be ineffective, not merely through the creation of appointed boards, whose only accountability is to ministers, but also by the assumption by ministers of control over decisions previously made by local authorities'. Stewart, J (1994) 'Reply to William Waldegrave' in Flynn, N (ed.) *A Reader: Change in the Civil Service* (London : Public Finance Foundation) p.89.
84 Quirk, B (1997) 'Accountable to Everyone: Post-modern Pressures on Public Managers' *Public Administration* Vol.75 p.583.
85 Campbell, C & Wilson, G (1995) *The End of Whitehall: Death of a Paradigm* (Oxford : Blackwell) p.304. For a discussion of principal/agent theory, see Pratt, J & Zeckhauser, R (1985) 'Principals and Agents: An Overview' in Pratt, J & Zeckhauser, R (eds) *Principals and Agents: The Structure of Business* (Boston : Harvard Business School); Miller, G (1992)

[86] *Managerial Dilemma: The Political Economy of Hierarchy* (Cambridge : Cambridge University Press).

[87] Rees, R (1985) 'The Theory of Principal and Agent' *Bulletin of Economic Research* part 1: pp.3-26, part 2: pp.77-95.

Chan, H & Rosenbloom, D (1994) 'Legal Control of Public Administration: A Principal - Agent Perspective' *International Review of Administrative Sciences* Vol.78 p.563.

[88] Mather, G (1990) 'Management by Contract - Viewpoints' *Public Money and Management* Vol.10 No.3 p.1.

[89] Adapted from Laughlin, R (1993) *Rethinking Models of Accountability: The Influence of Professionalism and 'Higher' Principals on Actions and Reactions of Agents* Discussion Paper 10 (Sheffield : SUMS) p.27.

[90] See Dudley, G (1994) 'The Next Steps Agencies, Political Salience and the Arms-Length Principle' *Public Administration* Vol.72 pp.219-240.

[91] If the discretion is minimised to achieve clear responsibilities between purchaser and provider: '...the timespan of the contract can introduce a rigidity into the workings of government, limiting its capacity to respond to the unanticipated, except through the burdensome process of re-negotiation'. Stewart, J (1993) 'The Limitations of Government by Contract' *Public Money and Management* Vol.13 No.3 p.12.

[92] HC 313 *Ministerial Accountability and Responsibility* Second Report of the Public Service Committee, Session 1996/97, HMSO, London. p.ixxxii para.21.

[93] Stewart, J (1994) 'The Rebuilding of Public Accountability' in Flynn, N (ed.) *A Reader: Change in the Civil Service* (London : Public Finance Foundation) p.78.

[94] Bogdanor, V 'Markets must not sell democracy short' *The Times* 7/6/93 p.7.

[95] The link between the nationalised industries and Next Steps agencies has been noted by many authors. See, for example Harden, I (1992) *The Contracting State* (Buckingham : Open University Press).

[96] Coombes, D (1966) *The Member of Parliament and the Administration: The Case of the Select Committee on Nationalised Industries* (London : George Allen & Unwin).

[97] See Prosser, T (1986) *Nationalised Industries and Public Control* (Oxford: Blackwell) Chs. 2-4.

[98] See HC 313-V (1996/97) Evidence by Mr Derek Lewis, para.600.

[99] Mather, G (1990) 'Management by Contract - Viewpoints' *Public Money and Management* Vol.10 No.3 p.1. Elsewhere Graham Mather noted: 'The boundaries between the state and the market, public and private, are increasingly fuzzy. This is desirable as it facilitates transition. Yet it has left a crisis of accountability in British public life. If civil servants could only

100 overcome their reluctance to replace administrative discretion with market style contracts many of the problems on the border could disappear'. Mather, G (1994) 'The Market, Accountability and the Civil Service' *Public Policy and Management* Vol.9 No.3 p.9.

101 'We recommend that at each agency review, the government consider whether the agency in question should be converted into a statutory body.' HC 313 (1996/97) p.ixxxii para.22.

102 The existence of this problem is not new to systems of decentralised government. See Stanyer, J (1974) 'Divided Responsibilities: Accountabilities in Decentralised Government' *Public Administration Bulletin* No.17 December pp.14-30.

103 The simplest example of the problem of asymmetrical information in PA theory is the example of a traveller in an unknown city who takes a taxi to a destination but cannot be sure, due to a lack of knowledge, whether the driver is taking the shortest or most efficient route. See Broadbent, J, Dietrich, M & Laughlin, R (1996) 'The Development of Principal-Agent, Contracting and Accountability Relationships in the Public Sector: Conceptual and Cultural Problems' *Critical Perspectives on Accounting* Vol.7 p.266.

104 See Walsh, K (1995) *Public Services and Market Mechanisms* (Basingstoke : Macmillan) pp.36-38.

105 See Hogwood, B (1994) 'A Reform Beyond Compare? The Next Steps Restructuring of British Central Government' *Journal of European Public Policy* Vol.1 No.1 p.71-94.

106 Mayston, D (1993) 'Principals, Agents and the Economics of Accountability in the New Public Sector' *Accounting, Auditing and Accountability* Vol.6 No.3 pp.73-76.

107 Lipsky, M (1993) *Street Level Bureaucracy: Dilemmas of the Individual in Public Service* (New York : Russell Sage Foundation).

108 Trosa, S (1994) *Next Steps: Moving On* (London : OPSS) p.9-10 para.2.25.

109 Massey, A (1995) *After Next Steps* (London : OPSS) para 2.17 p.9.

110 Kemp, P (1996) *Delivering Public Services* Annual Lecture to the Centre for Socio-Legal Studies, Sheffield University, 12/11/96.

111 Braun, D (1993) 'Who Governs Intermediary Agencies? Principal-Agent Relations in Research Policy-Making' *Journal of Public Policy* Vol.13 No.2 pp.135-162.

Rees, R (1985) 'The Theory of Principal and Agent: Part Two' *Bulletin of Economic Research* Vol.37 No.2 pp.75-95. See also Behn, R (1998) 'The New Public Management Paradigm and the Search for Democratic Accountability' *International Public Management Journal* Vol.1 No.2 pp.131-164.

[112] Williamson, O (1975) *Markets and Hierarchies* (New York : Free Press).

[113] Sappington, D (1991) 'Incentives in Principal-Agent Relationships' *Journal of Economic Perspectives* Vol.5 No.2 pp.45-66.

[114] A phrase adapted from Yin, R (1980) 'Creeping Federalism: The Federal Impact on the Structure and Function of Local Government' in Glickman, N (ed.) *The Urban Impacts of Federal Policies* (Baltimore : Johns Hopkins University Press).

[115] For example, Osborne and Gaebler noted how American cities often spend 20% of the costs of services on contract management. Osborne, D & Gaebler, T (1993) *Reinventing Government* (London : Plume) p.87.

[116] Massey, A (1995) 'Civil Service Reform and Accountability' *Public Policy and Administration* Vol.10 No.1 p.28; see also Power, M (1993) 'The Politics of Financial Auditing' *The Political Quarterly* Vol.64 No.3 pp.272-283; Pollitt, C (1995) 'Justification by works or by faith? Evaluating the new public management' *Evaluation* Vol.1 No. 2 pp.133-154.

[117] Lovell, A (1996) 'Notions of Accountability and State Audit: A UK Perspective' *Financial Accountability & Management* Vol.12 No.4 pp.261-280. See also Glynn, J (1996) 'Public Management: Failing Accountabilities and Failing Performance Review' *International Journal of Public Sector Management* Vol.9 No.5/6 pp.125-137.

[118] Harmon, M (1995) *Responsibility as a Paradox: A Critique of Rational Discourse of Government* (London : Sage). Power, M (1994) *The Audit Explosion* (London : Demos); Power, M (1996) 'Making Things Auditable' *Accounting, Organizations and Society* Vol.21 No.2/3 pp.289-315; Power, M (1997) *The Audit Society* (Oxford : Oxford University Press).

[119] Power, M (1997) *The Audit Society* (Oxford : Oxford University Press); Glynn, J (1996) 'Performance Auditing and Performance Improvement in Government: Public Sector Management Reform, Changing Accountabilities and the Role of Performance Audit' in *Performance Auditing and the Modernisation of Government* (Paris : OECD) pp.125-136.

[120] Rose, N & Miller, P (1992) 'Political Power Beyond the State: Problematics of Government' *British Journal of Sociology* Vol. 43 pp.173-205.

[121] Rist, R (1989) 'Management Accountability: The Signals Sent by Auditing and Evaluation' *Journal of Public Policy* Vol.9 No.3 pp.355-369.

[122] Hirst, P & Kilhani, S (eds.) (1996) *Reinventing Democracy* (Oxford : Blackwell) p.3.

[123] White, F, Harden, I & Donnelly, K (1994) *The Changing Constitutional Role of the Public Sector Audit: A Framework for Comparative Analysis* (Sheffield : PERC/Department of Law).

[124] Power, M (1994) *The Audit Explosion* (London : Demos) p.7.

[125] Miller, P (1996) 'Dilemmas of Accountability: The Limits of Accounting' in Hirst, P & Khilnani, S (eds.) *Reinventing Democracy* p.61.

[126] Stewart, J (1987) 'The Role of Information in Public Accountability' in Hopwood, A & Tomkins, C (eds.) *Issues in Public Sector Auditing* (Oxford : Philip Allan) pp.14-344.

[127] See Gorz, A (1989) *A Critique of Economic Reason* (London : Verso). This would seem particularly true where the agents see themselves as professionals and where accountabilities have been characterised by the 'clan' model. See Ouchi, W (1987) 'Markets, Bureaucracies and Clans' *Administrative Science Quarterly* Vol.25 No.1 pp.129-141.

[128] Stewart, J (1994) 'Performance Management When Performance Can Never Be Finally Defined' *Public Money and Management* Vol.14 No.2 pp.45-50.

[129] Lovell, A (1996) 'Notions of Accountability and State Audit: A UK Perspective' *Financial Accountability and Management* Vol.12 No.4 p.267.

[130] Broadbent, J Dietrich, M & Laughlin, R (1996) 'The Development of Principal-Agent, Contracting and Accountability Relationships in the Public Sector: Conceptual and Cultural Problems' *Critical Perspectives on Accounting* Vol.7 p.272.

[131] Power, M (1996) 'Making Things Auditable' *Accounting, Organizations and Society* Vol.21 No.2/3 pp.289-315.

[132] Hood, C & James, O 'Reconfiguring the UK Executive: From Public Bureaucracy State to Re-Regulated Public Service' Paper presented to ESRC conference 'Understanding Central Government: Theory into Practice' University of Birmingham 16-18/9/96.

[133] Miller, P (1996) 'Dilemmas of Accountability: The Limits of Accounting' in Hirst, P & Khilnani, S (eds.) *Reinventing Democracy* (Oxford : Blackwell) p.66.

[134] Massey, A (1995) 'Civil Service Reform and Accountability' *Public Policy and Administration* Vol.10 No.1 p.29.

[135] Bruce, A & McConnell, A (1996) 'Accountability in Local Government and the NHS' in Pyper, R (ed.) *Aspects of Accountability in the British System of Government* (Eastham : Tudor) p.145.

7 Managerial Accountability and the Home Office

7.1 Introduction

This Chapter applies the issues identified in Chapter Six to a case study of the Home Office to examine to what degree managerial accountability has remedied the shortcomings which have been identified with ministerial responsibility. Its findings are central to the wider study. If managerial accountability is found to be inadequate whilst also further obscuring the convention of ministerial responsibility then this may have important ramifications for the current state and future of responsible government in the United Kingdom. This argument is based on the clear trend away from the departmental structure of government towards a nexus of inter - and intra - organisational contracts which will increasingly threaten the continuing validity of ministerial responsibility. In order to examine the strengths and weaknesses of managerial accountability this chapter is structured around five interrelated themes.

> Theme 1. The problems of clarifying and maintaining the minister/agency distinction.
> Theme 2. Internal versus external accountability within the Home Office.
> Theme 3. How information asymmetries are avoided, the role of audit mechanisms in the accountability relationship and the degree to which Home Office ministers remain 'intelligent customers'.
> Theme 4. The impact of contracting out on accountability, efficiency and ministerial control.
> Theme 5. The effect of managerial accountability on ministerial responsibility to Parliament.

The Home Office is an apt case study for several reasons. A number of incidents, not least with the Prison Service and Passport Agency, have focused attention on the implications of managerial reforms for ministerial responsibility. The Home Office also offers a clear hierarchy and framework of contractual relationships in which named individuals, ministers and officials, are held responsible for the achievement of specified targets. Indeed, a clear hierarchy of contractual relationships can be identified from the Treasury's allocation of funding to the Home Office down to the operation of individual prisons. This hierarchy flows as follows: in July 1998 the Government announced the outcome of the Comprehensive Spending Review.[1] In turn, the Home Office Public Service Agreement (PSA) was published in December 1998.[2] The PSA provides details of the resources allocated to the Home Office, and sets out what the department will deliver with those resources. It contains specific, measurable and time-limited targets for each of the Home Office's aims (see Figure 7.1).[3] Following the establishment of the Home Office's seven aims a new senior management structure was introduced. Under this, responsibility for achieving each aim is assigned to an 'Aim Owner' who is a senior official and member of the department's management board. The Director, Sentencing and Correctional Policy, is therefore responsible for achieving the targets specified in the PSA for the Home Office's Fourth aim.[4]

The transfer of resources and responsibilities between the Home Office and the Prison Service are contained in the framework document which also includes a list of targets (Key Performance Indicators) and timescales. Below this, contracts exist between the Prison Service and contracted out prisons and state prisons operate under quasi-contractual Service Delivery Arrangements (SDAs), again specifying resource allocation and targets.[5]

Figure 7.1 Home Office Departmental Aims 1999-2000

> 1) Reduction in crime, particularly youth crime, and in the fear of crime; and the maintenance of public safety and good order.
> 2) Delivery of justice through effective and efficient investigation, prosecution, trial and sentencing, and through support for victims.
> 3) Prevention of terrorism, reduction in other organised and international crime, and protection against threats to national security.
> 4) Effective execution of the sentences of the courts so as to reduce reoffending and protect the public.
> 5) Helping to build, under a modernised constitution, a fair and prosperous society, in which everyone has a stake, and in which the rights and responsibilities of individuals, families and communities are properly balanced.
> 6) Regulation of entry to and settlement in the UK in the interests of social stability and economic growth and facilitation of travel by UK citizens.
> 7) Reduction in the incidence in fire and related death, injury and damage, and ensuring the safety of the public through civil protection.

7.2 The Problems of Clarifying and Maintaining the Minister/Agency Distinction

Managerial accountability revolves around the belief that a move to a (quasi-) contractual relationship clarifies roles, increases transparency and thereby increases accountability. The relationship between the Home Office and the Prison Service is contained within the agency's framework document.[6] This attempts to clarify the respective responsibilities of the Home Secretary, permanent secretary and the Agency Chief Executive (ACE).[7] The framework document is supported by secondary documents including an Annual Report and Business Plan.[8] This attempt to specify the responsibilities of the key stakeholders is in line with the contractual logic that advances the delineation of roles to secure, clarify and increase accountability. However, the degree to which the framework document has successfully clarified roles and responsibilities is questionable (see Figure

7.2).⁹ This underlines the challenges faced by business style contracts in politically sensitive and volatile areas of government. It is difficult to reconcile the conflicting demands of specificity and flexibility.¹⁰

Figure 7.2 The Michael Howard/Derek Lewis Affair

> HM Prison Service became an executive agency of the Home Office on 1 April 1993. Against criticism from the Civil Service Commissioners and the First Division Association, the Home Secretary Kenneth Clarke appointed an external candidate, Derek Lewis, as its first chief executive.¹¹ The Prison Service was launched during a period in which the prison population was rising dramatically. The average population for 1997-1998 was 62,500, an increase of 40% over the average population or 44,600 for 1992/1993.¹² Initially Derek Lewis appeared to be doing well. In 1994 he received a substantial bonus after the agency met 15 out of 16 targets. Far from ending, however, the problems came to a head at the end of that year. In November, six Category A prisoners escaped from Whitemoor prison, followed by the escape of three more high-risk prisoners from Parkhurst Prison only weeks later. The escapes were acutely embarrassing for the government, and the Home Secretary, now Michael Howard, came under heavy parliamentary criticism.
>
> Mr Howard refused to resign claiming the escapes were operational failures and ordered an inquiry into the Parkhurst breakout. The Inquiry's report, published in October 1995, was highly critical of Prison Service management and the Home Secretary announced Lewis' dismissal on the same day he published the report. This aroused intense controversy which did not abate when Lewis sued for wrongful dismissal. He claimed that as chief executive, he had been subject to a great deal of ministerial interference notwithstanding the supposed operational latitude of agencies. The Home Office chose to settle out of court: Lewis received a total of £280,000 in damages.¹³

Since the Howard/Lewis affair, the policy/operational dichotomy has been widely lamented.¹⁴ The Home Affairs Committee inquiry failed to do more than state the problem:

> We accept that it is not possible to lay down a rigid dividing line between the roles of ministers and of the Director General of the agency. If the arrangements for running the agency are to work properly there has to be a good relationship between the Home Secretary and the Director General. The Home Secretary must leave proper freedom to the Director General to do his or her job. At the same time there is no point in ministers, the Director General, or Parliament, harbouring unrealistic expectations of the extent to which ministers can be excluded from the operational process; the needs of accountability and responsibility to Parliament will require some measure of ministerial involvement.[15]

Having made much political capital out of the problems with the Prison Service, the Labour Party in its 1997 election manifesto, committed the party to 'reassert proper ministerial responsibility' over the agency.[16] Shortly after assuming office the Home Secretary, Jack Straw, announced that in future all parliamentary questions would be answered by a minister.[17] In July 1998 the Home Secretary announced the quinquennial review of the Prison Service which would consider both the agency's relationship with the department and its future organisational form.[18] The Prior Options Report recommended that the Prison Service remain an agency.[19] The Home Secretary accepted this recommendation and agency status was reconfirmed in February 1999.[20] However, while agency status remains, the Prison Service's relationship with the Home Office has changed markedly; the reimposition of ministerial responsibility has led to a recentralisation of the agency. This drift is encapsulated in the agency's revised framework document which was published, without academic or media comment, in March 1999. As the Home Secretary stated:

> The document reflects the government's commitment to take proper ministerial responsibility for the service and the role of the Prison Service as a major component of the wider criminal justice system.[21]

The revised framework document contains some important alterations to the previous relationship. A new Prison Service Strategy Board will be chaired by the Minister for Prisons and will usurp many of the strategic and planning functions previously decided by the Prisons Board. The Director General of the agency will in future hold formal quarterly meetings with the Home Secretary to ensure ministers are kept abreast of all matters likely to generate public or parliamentary concern.[22]

The Director General's role as the Home Secretary's principal policy adviser has also been weakened by the strengthened role of both the permanent secretary and the Director, Sentencing and Correctional Policy. The revised framework document emphasises the role of the permanent secretary as the Home Secretary's main adviser on all matters relating to the Home Office and specifically states their responsibility '...for advising the Home Secretary on Home Office plans, targets and performance, including those of the Prison Service'.[23] Moreover, the revised document suggests that with the introduction of resource accounting and budgeting from 2000 to 2001 the Director General will lose his additional Accounting Officer status with the permanent secretary becoming the Accounting Officer for the agency as part of his responsibilities for the whole department.[24] The Director, Sentencing and Correctional Policy also takes on an innovative role as the Home Secretary's main adviser on correctional policy as a whole.[25] He or she is the designated aim owner for the Home Office's fourth aim (see Figure 7.1 above) and is responsible for the overall co-ordination of programmes which contribute to this aim. The quinquennial review also highlighted that Home Office ministers required advice on handling the media in support of their responsibility as ministers for the work of the Prison Service. The Prison Service Media Relations Unit (PSMRU) had provided such a service to the Director General but it was felt that this made the delivery of a coherent message by the Home Office problematic. (It might be suggested that ministers felt the Unit defended the agency too well and, in so doing, deflected responsibility onto ministers.) In January 1998 the Home Office assumed 'professional supervision' of the PSMRU to '...underscore the responsibilities of the Unit towards ministers'.[26]

Through the creation of quantifiable targets managerial accountability emphasises performance and efficiency. The revised framework document attempts to balance this downward accountability with the upward responsibilities of the Prison Service to ministers, particularly in supporting them in their accountability to Parliament and in helping them to set the service's strategic direction in the context of the government's plans for the criminal justice system as a whole.[27] The revised framework document represents a clear strengthening of the links between the Prison Service and the Home Office in order to realise the government's commitments to ministerial responsibility and 'joined-up' government. (There was a feeling among interviewees in both the Prison

Service and the Home Office that a process of centralisation had been occurring since the dismissal of Derek Lewis.)[28] As the Home Office notes:

> These measures are strengthening the links between the Home Office and its largest agency and suggest that ministerial accountability and better integration of the Prison Service into the wider criminal justice system can be achieved satisfactorily by adapting agency status in light of the experience thus far.[29]

Experience suggests that the framework document has not been able to clarify or maintain the minister/agency distinction in the case of the Prison Service.[30] Interviewees suggested that the process of interpretation of the document was more important than its specific detail. But interpretation immediately undermines clarity and obscures the responsibility that moving to the contractual approach was intended to deliver. For example, Ann Widdecombe believed that the framework document was always a '...pretty loose document and at the end of the day responsibilities merged'.[31] She saw the framework document as the basis of a relationship rather than a fixed agreement. But problems occur when the main stakeholders interpret their responsibilities differently. It has been suggested that Derek Lewis interpreted the original framework document as giving the agency far more independence than the Home Office ever planned. One senior official within the Home Office described Lewis as 'politically naive' in that he did not understand the politics of the Home Office. This fact was reflected in Lewis' approach to the framework document, which he interpreted as a hard and fast private sector contract. He believed as long as the targets were achieved he would enjoy autonomy. Landers outlined Lewis' approach:

> I think that Derek Lewis had ideas about the way agencies ought to operate that clearly were not shared by ministers or the Home Office and in particular he thought that if he was hitting his targets that was what it was all about. In that sense he believed in the printed word rather than the subtext.[32]

Lewis' interpretation might expose a tension in the appointment of external candidates to senior positions. Several interviewees suggested that Lewis never understood the 'rules of the game' that govern the relationship between ministers and their senior civil servants. Recounting how he was far more willing to argue with ministers Lewis had sympathy with this intimation: 'Technically I was a member of the civil service but culturally I did not feel that way'.[33] Differences in interpretation are also more likely to occur where the appointing minister is replaced by a minister who holds conflicting views, as happened when Michael Howard replaced Kenneth Clarke. In this situation the personal relationship is unlikely to support a devolved management model and the policy/operations dichotomy may be used by the minister to replace the agency chief executive with a more compliant official. Ann Widdecombe noted how Michael Howard damaged the agency concept when he used the distinction to dismiss Derek Lewis:

> I think we did a massive disservice to the whole concept of agencies by trying to make that rigid distinction when we defended the sacking. We could only do it if we made that rigid distinction. In my view we should never have made it. It was not practical nor sustainable (March, 1998).

To date the challenges of clarifying and maintaining the minister/agency distinction have not been resolved. Although the revised framework document illustrates the flexibility within the agency concept it does not constitute a clear statement of responsibilities while the potential for ministerial interference and blame shift remains. This failure of managerial accountability reinforces rather than reduces the need for effective mechanisms of political accountability to prevent the unfair deflection of ministerial responsibility. With regard to the Prison Service the contractual logic of managerial accountability cannot guarantee the increased clarity and responsibility promised by the theoretical model whilst the reforms undermine the constitutional conventions that underpin ministerial responsibility (tenure, anonymity, uniformity, etc.). Nevertheless it might be suggested that managerial accountability facilitates a greater degree of internal and external accountability, which lessens the need for demarcation.

7.3 Internal versus External Accountability within the Home Office

The term 'internal accountability' mirrors what Hogwood, Judge and McVicar describe as 'accountability to departments'.[34] This relates to the internal accountability pressures placed on an agency by its sponsor department or by the general requirements of Whitehall and government. External accountability involves the relationship between an agency and the public and Parliament. It is suggested that whereas the reformed structure of government facilitates greater internal accountability this case study indicates that too much internal accountability may be as problematic as too little. Moreover, while managerial accountability may well have increased the amount of available information this does not necessarily equate to being an increase in external accountability.

The structure of the Home Office is designed to increase the internal accountability of officials to ministers. Ministers oversee a clear hierarchy in which managerialism has promoted the visible association of responsibilities with named officials. This is particularly apparent in the creation of 'Aim Owners'. The Home Office's permanent secretary, David Omand, stressed how the new senior management structure clarified responsibility within the department and plugged the gaps that had existed previously.[35] In particular, he highlighted how the structure allowed ministers to take the appropriate official to Cabinet sub-committees to account for progress. In addition, the introduction of agencies and contracts for the senior civil service has made the topography of the department clearer while also creating new information flows (both vertically within the department and horizontally across government).[36]

Yet it was in the area of internal accountability that my research encountered complaints about accountability overload and related pathological effects. While this rarely involves ministers directly, it relates to a constant and substantial informatory demand. Senior Prison Service officials remonstrated about continual requests for information from the Home Office. In particular emphasising that responding to such demands often affected the performance of their primary duties. Not only had the frequency of requests for information increased, notably since Derek Lewis' departure, but interviewees stressed that requests now emanated from a range of departments, particularly the Cabinet Office, Number 10 and the Treasury. The thrust towards cross-departmental working arrangements had also exacerbated the demands for information, from the

Lord Chancellor's Department and the Probation Service in particular. These demands challenge the traditional unilinear relationship between officials and their minister(s) as civil servants are increasingly accounting directly to a range of government power centres. Such multiple accountabilities may well have implications for ministerial responsibility.[37] A tension may develop when the interests of a particular department are not served by the demands of joined up government. In such a situation the officials' constitutional duty to serve their minister may be challenged by the wider duty of the civil service to serve the government as a whole. Indeed, in a presentation to the Prime Minister the Performance and Innovation Unit, as part of their 'Accountability and Incentives for Joined Up Government' project, stressed the need for officials to be '...willing to give priority to "corporate" over departmental objectives'.[38]

Within the Prison Service interviewees were annoyed that information they passed to the Home Office was frequently challenged and would inevitably lead to more questions. There was a perception that the Home Office lacked a collective or long - term memory as it was common for the Home Office to request information that had recently been provided to another section or been provided in the last six months. The following remark was typical:

> It is right that we are monitored and that the information flows work but I think things have gone too far. The amount of form filling and paperwork I have to do is ridiculous and often stops me from getting on with what I am here to do (Senior Prison Service official, April 1998).

The pressure caused by these internal informatory demands is typical of the tensions to be found in any principal/agent relationship. Kettl has highlighted how it is difficult for a principal to acquire the necessary information about an agent's performance without inundating the agent with information requests.[39] My research suggests this is currently an acute problem for the Home Office. To accommodate the Home Office's information requests the Prison Service has established an elaborate internal audit structure to ensure the department's requests can be answered promptly. This involves substantial costs to the agency in terms of staffing, finances and information technology.

Officials stressed how the informatory accountability demands of the Home Office on the Prison Service were augmented by the constant flow of fundamental reviews of the agency. One interviewee noted the agency was '...reform and review weary'. The Prison Service has undoubtedly been the subject of extensive review. The 1997 Prison Service Review identified 14 major reviews of its management and organisation in the last 30 years.[40] More recently, the agency was reviewed during the Comprehensive Spending Review,[41] the Prison/Probation Review[42] and the Cross-Departmental Review of the Criminal Justice System.[43] In addition, exhaustive public reviews followed the prison breakouts in 1994 and 1995,[44] the Home Affairs Committee published a far-reaching review in March 1997[45] and the government, fulfilling a pledge in their manifesto, conducted two major reviews, also in 1997.[46] In 1998/1999 the agency was fundamentally inspected by the quinquennial review and the Prior Options Programme.[47] This constant flow of reviews, interviewees suggested, had a pathological impact on the agency in terms of staff morale, the resource implications of the reviews and the distraction of senior staff away from day-to-day duties. Interviewees felt the organisational impact was substantial. One senior official noted: '...for the last six months most of our attention was on the review and the Prison Service was left just ticking over'.[48]

My research findings within the Home Office are supported and complemented by the related work of Brian Hogwood. For example, an interviewee in his research, from a regulatory non-departmental public body, mirrored the views detected within the Home Office:

> I think we have had pathological management initiative accountability. We were getting a new initiative a week (on efficiency, effectiveness, value for money, output performance measures). I think we went through something like fifteen reviews - that I think was pathological over-management and accountability from the centre...we've just been quinquennial reviewed....[the process] wasn't painless and it took an enormous amount of time confirming what we already knew.[49]

The capacity to identify and hold responsible specific sections of departments is perceived as a benefit of managerial accountability. Yet my research has generated a number of questions and issues. First, an appreciation of internal accountability adds a new dimension to debates on accountability within the core executive. Agencies that may display quantitatively low levels of parliamentary interest do not necessarily enjoy low levels of internal accountability. This, in turn, raises theoretical issues regarding the extent to which the parliamentary dimension is the key to understanding accountability in practice. Appreciating the channels and impact of internal accountability also highlights the interaction between different models of accountability. The increased capacity for internal accountability which managerialism generates has, in the case of the Prison Service, been used to bolster the minister's capacity to answer to Parliament. Consequently, a vicious circle can be identified in which devolved management is established to maximise managerial accountability which generates public and political unrest leading to the *de facto* partial reintegration of the agency to ensure the minister can adequately account to the House. The distraction away from operational duties, due to the demands of internal accountability, identified during interviews with Prison Service officials, creates the potential for a paradoxical situation in which civil servants may not be able to achieve their minister's targets due to these multiple accountabilities.[50] In the United Kingdom more research is needed on the tradeoff between establishing reliable structures of internal accountability involving multiple reporting relationships that avoid pathological impacts while also allowing officials to respond to their minister's directions expeditiously and efficiently.

External accountability, the accountability of departments and their agencies to Parliament and the public, has clearly been affected by managerialism. While the impact on ministerial responsibility to Parliament will be discussed later, the increase in publicly available documents specifying responsibilities, targets and performance might suggest an increase in external accountability. The Public Service Committee were of this opinion: 'We welcome the increase in the amount of published information about agencies and their performance, which, we believe, has lead to an increase in accountability'.[51] Clearly there has been an increase in the amount of published information regarding both the Prison Service and the Home Office. This includes the framework document, annual reports, business plans and various reviews. Taken together these documents contain a wealth of information which supports parliamentary accountability (for example by allowing MPs to ask ministers more perceptive questions) and wider notions of public accountability.

However, a less sanguine observer might raise a number of issues. First, neither Parliament nor the public has a legal right to these documents. They are released at the discretion of the executive and could theoretically be restricted under the Open Government Code or the forthcoming Freedom of Information Act (see Chapter Eight). Second, many of these documents were published long before the creation of agencies, for example Prison Service Annual Reports, and therefore the relationship between managerial accountability and increased information is not as direct as is often suggested.[52] Third, the value of documents, such as the framework documents, that may propound a policy/operations distinction that does not exist in reality might be doubted. Fourth, the content of the documents, while not being untrue, may not present the whole picture. For example, the 1996/97 Prison Service Annual Report accounts for the agency's failure to achieve five out of its nine targets on the rapidly growing prison population and the effect this had on manpower and resources.[53] Although the burgeoning population was a key factor, of equal or greater significance was the dismissal of Derek Lewis by the Home Secretary, which led to a period of crisis management in which targets were jettisoned. Therefore the increased publication of information, as a central component of managerial accountability, should not become a mechanism through which ministers can veil the consequences of their actions as 'managerial' and therefore operational issues. Fifth, despite the importance of these documents within the managerial model bureaucratic resistance to disclosure has been encountered. It took several months, including many letters and phone calls, before the documents relating to the Prison Service were released to me. This problem has been noted elsewhere and is particularly problematic and time consuming where multiple agency research is being conducted. For example, Hyndman and Anderson faced a 60% non-disclosure rate.[54] (Ironically, Sir Robin Butler has highlighted how agencies often produce material that is never requested.)[55] Finally, members of the Home Affairs Committee suggested that too much information could be as pernicious as too little.[56] MPs suggested that the documentation tended to be technical and statistical and not, therefore, easily accessible. One might intimate that a problem with managerial accountability may be that it has replaced too little information with an abundance of information which can obfuscate rather than clarify issues. In so doing the increased amount of published information, far from contributing to accountability and transparency, may in fact be undermining it.[57]

This case study suggests that managerialism has affected both internal and external accountability. The structural reforms have provided ministers with increased clarity and control while the drive towards joined up government has exacerbated horizontal internal accountability. Research in the Prison Service indicates that the overuse of this increased capacity may have pathological consequences in extreme cases. The increase in published information has supported external accountability, both to Parliament and to the public generally. However, the documents need to be approached with a degree of caution. Not least because they are published at the discretion of ministers and are unlikely to include politically damaging explanations. The role of Parliament in challenging the accounts given and compelling the executive to release additional information therefore is increased as a counterbalance to managerial accountability. But the challenges of obtaining unadulterated information are not reserved to Parliament. The preceding chapter outlined the difficulties in establishing information flows between departments and agencies. This is the topic of the next section.

7.4 How Information Asymmetries are Avoided, The Role of Audit Mechanisms in the Accountability Relationship and the Degree to Which Home Office Ministers Remain 'Intelligent Customers'

As Chapter Six stressed, in a principal/agent relationship it is vital that the principal has the capacity to validate the information provided by the agent and, in so doing, remain an intelligent customer. This section examines how the Home Office designs and measures targets for the Prison Service and the degree to which the issues raised in the previous chapter exist in practice. When the Prison Service was given agency status, like much of Whitehall, the Home Office had little experience of the use of targets or knowledge of how to measure them. Contrary to principal/agent theory it was the agent, the Prison Service, that proposed its own targets for the first year.

> Despite their long standing disdain for figures, my colleagues in the Prison Service embraced the concept jealously, wanting to create performance indicators for virtually everything and set targets for things that we could not measure. Eventually, we honed the list down to eight

Managerial Accountability and the Home Office 279

points, Clarke endorsed our recommendations, and the brief for the year was agreed.[58]

The targets, officially Key Performance Indicators (KPIs), are set out in the agency's corporate plan (see Figure 7.3). Ministers set targets for each KPI and the Director General accounts for the agency's past performance in the annual report. The Prison Service's performance against its KPIs has been good. Of the nine original KPIs, two (the provision of 24 - hour access to sanitation and the minimum visiting entitlement) were discontinued in 1996/1997 when the targets were fully achieved and it was not possible to further improve upon them.

Figure 7.3 Prison Service Key Performance Indicators 1998-1999[59]

- Number of Category A prisoner escapes.
- All escapes as a proportion of the population (excludes prisoners recaptured within 15 minutes, where no further criminal offence has been committed).
- Assaults on prisoners, staff and others resulting in a positive disciplinary adjudication, as a proportion of the average population.
- Drugs: positive results from random drugs tests, as a proportion of the total number of random tests carried out.
- Overcrowding: proportion of the prison population above the uncrowded capacity of the estate.
- Regimes: numbers of hours prisoners spend on average per week engaged in purposeful activity.
- Time unlocked: proportion of prisoners held in establishments which normally unlock all prisoners on the standard or enhanced regime for at least ten hours per weekday.
- Programmes: completions by prisoners of offender behaviour programmes accredited as being effective in reducing reoffending.
- Efficiency: current expenditure per uncrowded prison place.
- Training: average number of days staff spent on training.

Additional KPIs were introduced for 1995/96 (Category A escapes) and for 1996/97 (the amount of drugs misuse, provision of reoffending programmes and staff training). Since their introduction the Prison Service has met its targets for these three indicators in all but three instances. Of the six KPIs that have remained in place since 1992/93, there has been a tremendous improvement in the rate of escapes (down 78%) and a substantial reduction in the rate of assaults (down 7.8%). Performance against the KPI for overcrowding has also been impressive in light of the rising prison population. Police cells have not been used since June 1995 and trebling in cells was eliminated in 1994. The targets for the number of hours prisoners are unlocked and the cost per prisoner place have been consistently achieved, the latter having been reduced by over 7% by 1997/98.[60] The setting and measurement of targets within a contractual relationship is the basis of managerial accountability. Ann Widdecombe noted:

> Accountability in the Prison Service was best performed against its targets. Those were the real accountabilities. There are targets which are both performance and financially related. They were the real mechanisms of accountability and by regularly monitoring them you could see how the organisation was progressing and where the problems were and that is real accountability (March 1998).

However, research suggests that ministers are aware that managerial accountability cannot and does not replace political accountability. The most telling indicator of this might be the revised framework document which creates a tighter infrastructure to keep the Home Secretary fully informed. Interviewees also stressed how during the period surrounding the dismissal of Derek Lewis the then Home Secretary knew that parliamentary criticism was not going to be appeased by telling the House how successful the Prison Service had been in achieving its targets. Landers noted:

> I remember her [Ann Widdecombe] grilling us on one occasion about our deteriorating performance after Derek Lewis was fired (as shown by our failure to achieve our KPIs) she had just got Lewis' successor to admit that he had stopped bothering with KPIs (without telling ministers) when she was cut short by Michael Howard who airily dismissed the relevance of KPIs at all.[61]

Derek Lewis received the support of Ann Widdecombe and the former Prisons Minister Sir Peter Lloyd.[62] But as Polidano noted: 'It seems that managerial accountability clashed head-on with crude political accountability - and lost'.[63] It is, however, quite clear that ministerial responsibility is frequently discharged via ministers declaring, to the House or the media, that a body under their jurisdiction has successfully achieved the (vast) majority of its targets, thereby undermining adverse comment. Nevertheless, the achievements of the Prison Service have led to suggestions that the targets are insufficiently rigorous. One member of the Home Affairs Committee, John Hutton, compared the agency's KPIs with the performance indicators used for British Rail: '...even though we always knew that trains arrived late they all mysteriously managed to arrive on time according to the indicators for the railways'.[64]

Neither the Prison Service nor ministers want to be responsible for the agency failing to achieve its targets. This creates a pressure to set 'soft' targets, the Prison Officers Association has accused the Home Office of setting targets low in order to foster support for the agency concept.[65] However, Chapter Six highlighted the dangers of information asymmetries which may invert principal/agent theory thereby allowing the agent to dictate their own targets. As the Trosa Report noted, the agency will in reality be able to set the targets for which it will be held to account and, as pay bonuses are linked to targets, ensure the targets are easily attainable.[66] (There is evidence that the Home Office also follows this line of thinking.)[67]

Research implies that in the past the relationship between the Home Office and the Prison Service could be termed one of 'principal capture'. Targets have been set through a process of negotiation and compromise in which the Prison Service has dominated the process. Annually a review team consisting of the permanent secretary, members of the Home Office Efficiency and Consultation Unit and external advisers is formed. They examine Prison Service performance against current targets, consider the agency's explanation for non-achievement and examine future prison population forecasts and the possible impact of forthcoming government policy on the agency. A briefing with recommendations is then presented to the Home Secretary and copied to the Prison Service. The Prison Service will then submit an official response. Any changes to the agency's targets have to be approved by the Treasury and Cabinet Office.

Senior Home Office officials admitted that in reality the Prison Service, through its official response and subsequent meetings, holds the dominant position for operational and political reasons. It was felt that the Home Office lacked an awareness of the operational implications of any target. Therefore, if the agency stated that as a result of trying to achieve a certain target the danger of major disruptions would increase greatly, the department lacked the capacity to validate this response. This, in turn, had a political dimension as Home Office ministers are acutely aware of the possible consequences of a major riot or breakout for political careers. One official noted: 'It would take a very brave minister to enforce a change in targets which the Prison Service said was unrealistic and could have dangerous consequences'. Officials felt that this imbalance was waning as the Home Office developed its own expertise in prison policy, which empowered it to verify or challenge the agency's information. But the Home Office's lack of a capacity to challenge the veracity of the views of the agency has, research suggests, been a source of serious tension.

In 1994 Michael Howard established the Prison Service Monitoring Unit (PSMU) as a direct attempt to rectify the information asymmetries identified above.[68] The PSMU's formation encapsulated the deteriorating relationship between the Home Office and the agency and was an attempt to resolve some of the pressures created by the introduction of devolved management in a system built on the responsibility of ministers. Its role was to bolster the ability of ministers to supervise performance of the Prison Service in accordance with the framework document, authenticate the information given to the department by the agency and provide ministers with alternative policy advice and information.[69] If the Prison Service was to be truly accountable it could not provide the only information on which it was held to account. Ministers needed an independent source of information with which to test and gauge the information emanating from the agency. There were, however, other tensions behind the creation of the PSMU. One former Home Office minister noted:

> The PSMU was set up as an anti-Derek Lewis device by the then Home Secretary and its job was ludicrous. Its job was to second guess and question every single submission that we had up from the Prison Service. It served no other purpose at all than to undermine Derek Lewis and was disbanded the minute the Tories left office (April, 1998).

The PSMU was also an attempt to diminish other tensions that existed due to the confused lines of accountability outlined within the framework document. The permanent secretary is the 'Fraser figure', the link between the department and the agency.[70] This role is central to the permanent secretary's wider responsibilities. The permanent secretary is the Accounting Officer for the whole department including the Prison Service, and is also the Home Secretary's principal adviser on matters affecting the department as a whole (this includes specific obligations to advise on the plans, targets and performance of all the department's agencies).

When Richard Wilson moved from the Department of the Environment to replace Clive Whitmore as the Home Office's permanent secretary the potential stresses in the agency arrangement took on added impetus. Not only was Wilson less supportive of the agency concept than his predecessor but he also took his responsibilities as the Fraser figure seriously. Wilson supported Howard in the establishment of the PSMU as a source of independent information and a mechanism to hold the agency to account for its performance. This, Lewis suggested, had a pernicious impact on the agency as without the support of Wilson the relationship with the Home Office stagnated.[71] Prison Service officials recounted how delays and protracted arguments ensued which damaged organisational trust between the department and agency. A senior Prison Service official remarked:

> It was an extremely irritating piece of machinery from our point of view because everything we put to the department the PSMU would express its own opinion on it which was usually an opposite one. None of them had ever worked near a prison and the people in this building just got heartily sick of it and relations were very bad. Everything you did there would be a two or three week delay whilst the PSMU asked what were often plain stupid questions and it slowed the whole process down.

Jack Straw disbanded the PSMU in June 1997 and since then the Efficiency and Consultancy Unit (ECU) has undertaken many of the agency shadowing duties. However, Labour ministers have also been anxious about the relationship between the agency and the department. In March 1998 Norman Warner, Jack Straw's political adviser, outlined how ministers felt a need to counterbalance the position of the agency with alternative sources of policy advice and information.

> The Chief Executive's responsibility as the Home Secretary's principal policy adviser on Prison Service issues not only makes a mockery of the policy/operations divide but, without other sources of policy advice, it also gives the agency a commanding position (interview with the author).

Perceptively, Warner indicated that the appropriate opportunity to address this concern would be the quinquennial review of the agency and the framework document review.

The previous chapter emphasised the role of audit mechanisms as a way to reconcile the centrifugal pressures of devolved management with the centripetal pressures of political control. Audit mechanisms police the principal/agent relationship to validate the information provided by the agent. In so doing they are central to reducing information asymmetries and facilitating both internal and external accountability. Research suggests that the Prison Service operates among a dense web of audit mechanisms that may have wider implications. The Home Office has an internal audit department that scrutinises the Prison Service. The Prison Service has its own internal audit department that covers the agency and its contracted out establishments. The companies operating the contracted out prisons also have their own internal audit systems. This complex hierarchical structure of audit mechanisms operates within the jurisdiction of the National Audit Office, which has a dedicated Prison Service team. This is where new public management meets the audit explosion.[72] One agency official noted:

> Ten years ago financial monitoring systems were largely non-existent. Money just trickled down through the department like water down a waterfall but now the financial system is strictly regulated. It's gone from the sublime to the ridiculous!

Exposing the complex network of audit mechanisms which cover the Prison Service is useful for a number of reasons. Audit is an important tool of internal accountability and yet it is responsible for many of the pathological impacts that were discussed earlier, particularly form filling instead of concentrating on primary duties. The costs of maintaining this substantial auditing framework are high. The Prison Service spends in excess of £600,000 per year on internal audit while the Home Office spends over £1,000,000 on internal audit.[73] Not only must these costs be offset against the economic benefits of moving to the agency model but interviewees suggested that the increased managerial flexibility that managerialism was intended to occasion has been reduced or even nullified by the increase in explicit and intrusive financial control mechanisms. This research is supported by Christopher Hood's wider work. By revealing the growth in internal regulation within central government, Hood has proposed that a mirror image development has taken place in which traditional state bureaucracies have been replaced by regulatory state bureaucracies.[74] The existence of substantial and overlapping audit frameworks might also circumscribe moves to make the civil service less risk averse - which in itself may have important ramifications for ministerial responsibility.[75]

The previous chapter highlighted the pitfalls of imposing on the public sector audit mechanisms of accountability, derived from the private sector.[76] These were particularly problematic when the task did not lend itself to quantification. In these environments audit mechanisms tended to concentrate on the quantifiable, possibly to the detriment of more important qualitative indicators. Research suggests that the Home Office is well aware of these issues and safeguards are in place to ensure a qualitative dimension to targets: for example, that 'purposeful activity' involves prisoners receiving education or training rather than simply being unlocked or watching television. Safeguards are in place, particularly in the contracted out prisons, to ensure that efficiency savings are not generated from a reduction in the quality of the regimes. Financial safeguards are supported by a range of qualitative safeguards including HM Inspector of Prisons, the Prisons Ombudsman, Prison Service inspection teams, Boards of Visitors, Prison Controllers and the National Audit Office.

Nevertheless, the relationship between the Prison Service and the Home Office does demonstrate an important tension between managerial accountability's focus on target achievement and the government's intention to tackle society's 'wicked issues' which can only be resolved through cross-departmental interagency working.[77] The fragmentation of the state, which is in part a consequence of NPM, makes 'joined up' government harder and managerial accountability reinforces those difficulties. Senior civil servants are being asked to concentrate on how their role affects wider social issues and realign their work within networks to approach those problems, while also, at the same time, being required to fulfil performance targets that emphasise and strengthen organisational boundaries. This tension is likely to increase with the introduction of Resource Accounting and Resource Budgeting (RAB) in central government.[78] RAB offers the Home Office the potential for increased scrutiny of its agencies. For the Prison Service, and individual prisons, the pressure to ensure the achievement of targets within resource parameters is likely to intensify, reinforcing insularity rather than risky networking. Lovell and Hand provide the example of recidivism and therapeutic care in the Prison Service.[79] The provision of intensive therapeutic care for violent offenders has significantly reduced recidivism rates. However, the provision of such care is expensive while the financial benefits of the policy are not felt by the Prison Service, but by the Police, Courts and Probation Service who no longer have to provide a service to the individual. In this case managerial accountability acts as a disincentive to joined up working as the agency would best achieve its targets by not providing the service but by implementing the cheaper standard regime. (This problem is being addressed by the Home Office who plan to set a target for recidivism for the Prison Service in 2000-2001.)[80] The tension between broad policies and tunnel-vision managerial accountability has also proved an obstacle to closer working between the Prison Service and the Probation Service. The 1997 Prison/Probation Review stressed the challenge presented by '...different aims, objectives and systems of accountability'.[81]

It appears that several of the problems with the principal/agent model have been encountered within the Home Office/Prison Service relationship. 'Principal capture' appears to have been a particular issue. Although the revised framework document seeks to bolster the department's position in relation to the agency it is not clear whether the confused lines of accountability between the minister, permanent secretary and agency chief executive have been clarified. The creation of a powerful new actor in the relationship (Director, Sentencing and Correctional Policy) may exacerbate rather than clarify the intricate matrix of responsibilities. The Prison Service operates within a substantial framework of audit mechanisms. These ensure the Prison Service is held to account for both the quantitative and qualitative aspects of its work thus dispelling concerns that audit mechanisms police only quantifiable tasks. But the demands of this tight audit framework constitute a heavy accountability burden which, in addition to other forms of accountability, can have negative consequences for the agency. Given these tensions exist between department and agency it might be suggested that they would be even greater when functions are devolved further down the spectrum of autonomy.

7.5 The Impact of Contracting Out on Accountability, Efficiency and Ministerial Control

As the previous chapter stressed, contracting out is not the same as privatisation. Nevertheless, contracting out does represent a further step along the spectrum of autonomy. As a result the degree of direct ministerial control is diminished, prompting concerns that ministers will seek to minimise their responsibility. Contracting out therefore stretches the realistic scope of ministerial responsibility to its maximum. In this context managerial accountability is crucial as a surrogate form of accountability both to repair the exposed tensions in the political model and provide the information through which ministers can remain accountable. Examining the accountability framework and performance for contracted out prisons might also allow propositions to be made as to whether accountability and efficiency are incompatible goals. Moreover, the financial pressures on the public sector are likely to increase. The Prison Service, for example, has been obliged consistently to reduce the average annual cost per place of each prisoner. In this environment the temptation to devolve responsibilities via contracting out is likely to increase while public concerns about fragmentation and accountability are also likely to greaten. For example, in opposition Jack Straw referred to privately managed prisons as 'morally repugnant' but fiscal restraints and increasing prisoner numbers have forced the Labour government to explore private sector involvement. As the Home Secretary noted:

> In principle, incarceration should be a direct function of the state. However we live in an imperfect world and if the alternative to overcrowded prisons is to go ahead with this type of contract we will go ahead with it.[82]

The Home Secretary overlooks the fact that the British government has contracted out the incarceration of individuals for several decades. It was a Labour government which in the 1960s contracted out the detention of illegal immigrants, which continues today. However, twenty years ago the suggestion that prisons might one day be privately managed would have seemed absurd; indeed the prison sector in England and Wales was nationalised at a stroke in 1877.[83] However, there is a wealth of contemporary literature on private sector involvement,[84] the accountability of that sector[85] and international comparisons.[86] It was the Home Affairs Select Committee, after visiting the USA, that recommended that the Home Office experiment with privately managed prisons.[87] To a government in favour of reducing big government, strong on law and order and committed to the market, the idea of private prisons had a strong ideological appeal. An attraction nurtured by influential think tanks.[88] In 1987 Douglas Hurd ruled out private prisons[89] only to change his mind two years later following the publication of a green paper on the topic.[90] Despite criticism that the Home Affairs Committee's 1987 report was highly misleading the committee chairman, Sir Edward Gardner, lobbied junior ministers in support of introducing the private sector.[91] Mrs Thatcher pressurised the Cabinet[92] and on 1 March 1989 the government announced to the House its intention to introduce the private sector to the prison system.[93]

April 1992 saw the opening of the first privately managed prison, the Wolds remand centre operated by Group 4. This was quickly followed by Blakenhurst Prison in May 1993 (UK Detention Services) and Doncaster Prison in September 1993 (Premier Prisons Limited). In September 1993, the government announced a policy of moving towards a situation in which 10% of prisons (12) would be run by the private sector.[94] Market testing was introduced alongside the launch of new privately managed prisons. This involved open bidding to run existing prisons that were due to reopen after refurbishment. An in-service bid won the competition to run Strangeways, which reopened in March 1994, but the private company Group 4 won the competition to run Buckley Hall which reopened in December 1994. The introduction of the private sector into the prison sector is advancing at pace, by February 2001 there were eight privately managed prisons in the United Kingdom. As well as these new prisons it is expected that some existing ones may be transferred in some way to private management. It is vital to keep the extent of private provision in perspective. As in America, privately managed prisons account for less than 8% of the total prison estate (135 prisons). It also remains an anglophone enthusiasm, there are no privately managed prisons anywhere in mainland Europe.

The arguments surrounding the accountability of privately managed prisons are both pragmatic and moral. There is a perception among some observers that the introduction of the private sector will lead to an *a priori* reduction in the accountability of prisons. For example, the Howard League referred to prisons as a '...responsibility which the state should not abdicate'.[95] However, the Prison Reform Trust took the view that the '...core custodial function should remain the unfettered responsibility of the state'.[96] Most pertinently Lord Scarman noted: 'Contracting out, while not necessarily ending legal responsibility, does endanger the directness of the state's responsibility. The risk of unelected abuse is a real one'.[97] However, empirical research fails to substantiate these concerns. As Ryan noted:

> It is certainly easier for those who argue in favour of private rather than communal responsibility to make their case: and conversely, why do opponents of privatisation find the accountability argument so difficult to advance with real conviction when they debate the issue in empirical rather than principled terms?[98]

During the course of my research requests for interviews and information were replied to positively and swiftly by the companies managing contracted out prisons. The chief executives were happy to be interviewed and discuss sensitive issues. One even provided extensive comments while working in New Zealand. Members of the Home Affairs Committee also remarked on the difference between the contracted out prisons and state managed prisons. Several indicated that the responses they received to their letters tended to be far more comprehensive from privately managed prisons. For example, Robin Corbett stressed how he was satisfied with the 'pyramid of accountability' from the prison to the Prison Service to the Home Secretary but in relation to contracted out prisons he had never needed to refer his query elsewhere.[99] This general finding may well reflect the fact that contracted out prisons operate within a far greater and more open accountability framework.

They are part of the wider prison estate and are therefore subject to all the accountability requirements of public prisons. These include HM Inspector of Prisons, the Prisons Ombudsman, Boards of Visitors and the audit mechanisms outlined above. They must also adhere to the Prison

Rules and Prison Service directives. Parliamentary oversight applies to the contracted out prisons as if they were state run. It might also be suggested that they are subject to a greater degree of public accountability, via the media and interest groups, in direct response to concerns about their lack of accountability. In fact the formal accountability controls applied to contracted out prisons are far more comprehensive than those applied to public prisons. In particular, they must deliver a more exacting degree of informatory accountability about their regimes. For example, in contracted out prisons all minor assaults must be recorded and reported to the Prison Service while no such requirement exists for public prisons. The contracts necessitate the collection, dissemination and publication of information which is simply not available for public prisons. The Chief Executive of a company running a contracted-out prison noted:

> The information we are required to collect and publish makes complaints about a lack of accountability ridiculous...especially when you compare our information and output to a public prison (April 1998).

Not only are the information requirements higher but the expected regime standards are also greater. Another accountability mechanism unique to private prisons is the controller.[100] These are senior Prison Service officials who are responsible for monitoring contract compliance and adjudicating on disciplinary proceedings.[101] The post of controller is a rare example of permanent on-site regulation charged with enforcing and overseeing both the qualitative and quantitative aspects of the contract.[102] The controller ensures an ongoing day-to-day accountability that is absent in public prisons, leading one survey to conclude that the controller was '...a vital safeguard not only for public and political accountability, but also for safeguarding the rights and interests of prisoners'.[103]

Due to these increased safeguards and controls many commentators have suggested that contracting out represents an opportunity to deliver a degree of real accountability that the state system had hitherto failed to provide.[104] Yet Chapter Six suggested that contracts may reduce accountability by mitigating against direct ministerial intervention in times of crisis. Moreover, it was suggested that contracts, far from increasing managerial freedom, actually impose rigidity. Neither of these concerns seems to have developed in relation to contracted out prisons. Although they are reserve powers, the contracts make clear that the Home Secretary enjoys the right to intervene in the running of any prison, or even take over full control, at any time. This prevents the abdication of ministerial responsibility in times of public concern. Contractual rigidity is avoided by the inclusion of procedures for alterations. The contractual negotiations were described as a constant two-way process in which both sides regularly asked for modifications and changes. Often these changes might involve added costs which either side would accept without going through time consuming financial costings. Private sector representatives felt that, if anything, the contract was loaded in favour of the minister as they were free not to renew a contract or even use their reserve powers and take over a prison.[105] Contracted out prisons are also subject to a specific type of financial accountability (in the form of penalties) that does not exist in the wider prison estate. For example, Group 4's contract to run The Wolds Prison includes a set penalty of £50,000 per prisoner escape. As MacGowan noted: 'That is clearly a level of accountability that is not present anywhere else'.[106] These penalties are based on the failure to achieve specified targets and may lead, in the worst scenario, to the non-renewal or withdrawal of a contract.[107] To date, two private firms have lost their contracts to run contracted out prisons due to poor performance.[108]

Several interviewees suggested that the public debate surrounding contracted out prisons needed to be inverted. For them it was not contracted out prisons that lacked accountability but state run prisons. Consequently the answer was to transfer accountability mechanisms from the contracted out to the public prisons. One senior Prison Service official advocated the creation of controller posts within all prisons. Ann Widdecombe suggested that the financial accountability applied to privately managed prisons should apply across all prisons:

> The slightest breach of their contract means that there is a financial penalty imposed on them. That is a level of accountability which is absent in the public sector but should be imposed (March 1998).

This sentiment was echoed by private sector representatives. One noted:

> In the private sector we can be penalised financially if we do not achieve targets. At worst we can lose our contract. What happens when a public sector prison fails to perform?[109]

One area where research found a tension that has been noted in the previous chapter involved balancing commercial confidentiality with contradictory obligations. There is a concern that information that is politically or managerially embarrassing will be hidden under the veil of commercial confidentiality. As the Home Affairs Committee noted: '...commercial confidentiality should be interpreted very narrowly and must not be used as an excuse not to publish information.'[110] However, the failure of a contracted out prison to release information may be due more to the inherent conflict within establishing markets in the public sector than a praetorian desire to suppress information. In a market situation no company is going to volunteer information that may undermine its position. One chief executive noted:

> As far as detailed, facility specific commercial information is concerned, how much comparable detail is available from individual public sector prisons? Our detractors are annoyed that we will not reveal more information than we need to and they therefore cannot understand how we can be so cost-effective and efficient. That is our competitive edge and we see no reason to part with it, other than to those who have a legitimate and unbiased reason for having it.[111]

This tension may impede the government's stated objectives in relation to modernising government. The 1999 white paper aims, as one if its central commitments, to '...identify and spread best practice'.[112] But those companies, in a market situation, who are perceived as having 'best practice' are also likely to be winning contracts, making it improbable that they would release the information that preserves them in that position. Despite this, research suggests that, overall, contracted out prisons are more accountable than state prisons. As the Home Affairs Committee concluded:

> ... the fears hitherto expressed over the principle of contracting out - that it would mean the abdication of state responsibility for public safety and the deprivation of freedom - have not proved justified, and the idea of privately managed prisons is undoubtedly more generally accepted, and should be allowed to develop further.[113]

This opinion is supported by the Prisons Ombudsman who has praised the privately managed prisons in his reports and noted: 'In general

I think there is more openness and accountability within the private prisons'.[114] Contracted out prisons have also received favourable reports from HM Inspectorate of Prisons.[115] In addition the Inspectorate has indicated which positive aspects could be transferred to the public estate.[116] There is, however, within the wider literature a general perception that to be both accountable and efficient inevitably involves a tradeoff.[117] They are presented as a zero-sum equation in which an increase in efficiency is offset by a reduction in accountability and vice versa. However, contracted out prisons appear to challenge this common assumption. While observers have highlighted the difficulties in comparing public with contracted out prisons,[118] independent auditors concluded that contracted out prisons generated cost per prisoner savings of 13% in 1994/95.[119] The Home Office calculated savings of 11% per prisoner in 1995/96[120] and 15% in 1996/97.[121] Although the Prison Governors' Association disputes these figures,[122] the Prison Service accepts them as a realistic statement of increased efficiency[123] as did the Home Affairs Committee.[124]

The case of contracted out prisons is particularly important as it suggests that accountability and efficiency are not opposing goals. Yet, as noted above, contracting out does push the realistic scope of ministerial responsibility to its maximum. This has a number of implications, not least because a future Home Secretary may not adopt such a rigorous approach to their responsibility for contracted out prisons. The current Home Secretary, Jack Straw, does not see his responsibility for contracted out prisons as any different to his responsibility for state prisons. As his political adviser noted:

> I don't think that he [Jack Straw] would see a contracted prison as in any way letting the Director General or himself off the hook in terms of his accountability. If the DG does not police the contract with the private contractor he is as much in dereliction of his duty as if he fails to manage properly a public institution. There is no accountability difference. The method of management is different but the accountability remains the same (March, 1998).

Senior Prison Service officials saw no difference between their responsibility for privately or state managed prisons, a view supported by the Prison Service's response to incidents.[125] There is, however, a danger that increasing financial pressures may well encourage a greater private sector involvement in the prison sector. In this situation a future Home Secretary may be less willing to accept responsibility for such a large contracted out prison estate. If an incident occurred an incumbent Home Secretary might deflect responsibility onto their predecessor. The state would have evolved even further away from the departmental model, making ministerial responsibility increasingly tenuous. However, increasing the number of contracted out prisons would not sit comfortably with Jack Straw's commitments to ensure proper ministerial responsibility. Yet the scenario is not absurd which illustrates the increasing pressures between governance and ministerial responsibility. It was exactly this pressure, the tension between an increasingly fragmented state and ministerial responsibility, that managerialism was intended to control.

7.6 Conclusion: The Effect of Managerial Accountability on Ministerial Responsibility to Parliament

It is clear that managerial accountability does not remedy the deficiencies associated with ministerial responsibility. If anything it reinforces the importance of the convention and the need for effective mechanisms of parliamentary scrutiny. Although managerialism was designed to reconcile an increasingly complex state with the traditional responsibility of ministers it creates as many tensions as it solves. Managerialism is a secondary form of accountability which relies on the executive behaving decently. Where ministers publish misleading information, abuse their discretionary powers or deny the consequences of their actions it is only Parliament that can enforce their responsibility. Critically, managerial accountability does not improve 'high level' accountability for ministerial resource and policy decisions. If anything, it diverts attention away from ministerial action and facilitates a greater degree of scrutiny on 'low level' operational aspects of departmental functions. Therefore managerialism cannot replace the primacy of political accountability in a representative democracy. Parliament's role assumes a greater, rather than lesser, significance in ensuring the implications of 'high level' ministerial decisions are understood and acknowledged, thereby mitigating against blame shift.

This case study has been useful in illuminating many of these tensions while also demonstrating a number of issues which are of wider importance to this study. The first issue focuses on compatibility. Is managerial accountability compatible with political accountability? From one perspective managerial accountability can be interpreted as entirely compatible with political accountability. The central tenets of managerial accountability, such as clarifying responsibilities, specifying goals, holding the public sector responsible for performance, and increasing citizen input are entirely consistent with enhancing political accountability. Indeed, the promise of managerial accountability was that it should provide a means of combining managerial autonomy and democratic accountability. What is problematic is the superimposition of managerial accountability on an already strained and confusing structure of political accountability.[126] As a consequence managerial accountability can be viewed as obfuscating political accountability by increasing the opportunity for ministers to deflect responsibility while also publishing a flow of carefully scripted documents. The fact that managerial accountability has been imposed on a system built around the demands of political accountability is critical. Discretion, Royal prerogative and political codes ensure ministers remain in a dominant position. The danger of blame transfer for ministerial decisions underlines the need for effective parliamentary scrutiny.

However, this case study suggests that it is not clear that contractualisation has always facilitated political blame shift in the simple manner many observers have suggested.[127] As the Derek Lewis incident demonstrated, instead of making blame shift easier contractualisation may in fact make ministers more likely to be exposed to acrimonious public arguments about who has residual responsibility when errors occur, particularly in a parliamentary system where blame shift is constitutionally problematic.[128] Far from clarifying responsibility contracts may expose how complex and indeterminate relationships within the core executive are. As a result the residual responsibility of ministers may become more rather than less contestable.[129] In addition, the recruitment of agency chief executives on fixed - term contracts makes dismissal by ministers more cumbersome and politically awkward than the traditional form of civil service employment. It puts great pressure on ministers to provide a convincing account of why they dismissed the official. Managerial accountability is therefore potentially a double-edged sword for ministers as the extra rigidity of contractualisation may make it harder both to deflect responsibility and remove officials.

Managerialism represents a way of re-engineering the state that intentionally discontinues a number of conventions which underpin ministerial responsibility. Anonymity is replaced by civil servants being made conspicuously responsible for tasks, security of tenure is supplanted by time-limited contracts. The case study also suggests that managerial accountability, with its emphasis on targets and performance, may be incompatible with a number of the government's broader ambitions - particularly 'joined up' government, making the civil service less risk averse and spreading 'best practice'. The Home Office demonstrates the multiplicity of lines of accountability which managerialism creates. Certain organisations, the Prison Service in particular, are subject to a dense web of internal and external accountability mechanisms. Paradoxically a great number of these lines of accountability exist both to counteract the risks involved in moving to a devolved management model and also to support the convention of ministerial responsibility. Importantly, this case study has illustrated how successive Home Secretaries have adopted their own interpretations of what is necessary to fulfil the demands of ministerial responsibility. It is unlikely that Michael Howard would have felt the need to implement the reforms that Jack Straw felt were necessary to discharge his view of ministerial responsibility. This raises questions of why other ministers have not felt compelled to introduce similar measures for equally problematic agencies for which they are constitutionally responsible. That the Prison Service is unique in receiving special attention demonstrates the *ad hoc* nature of accountability arrangements in the British constitution.

Several commentators have observed that the agency model has not proved problematic in the vast majority of cases.[130] They insist the Prison Service therefore represents the exception, not the rule. Indeed, this case study has highlighted that managerial accountability has generated a number of positive developments in terms of attempted clarification and increased internal and external accountability, while also generating efficiency gains. Nevertheless, problems have been experienced in other agencies. Taken together these demonstrate the inbuilt potential for responsibility transfer within the agency model. The Prison Service, as a case study, also illustrates the existence of some of the problems with, and negative consequences of, managerial accountability - particularly the tensions surrounding internal accountability and the risk of creating counterpart agency shadowing bureaucracies. These findings are critical to

Managerial Accountability and the Home Office 297

the overall thesis of this book. Managerial accountability does not remedy the failings associated with ministerial responsibility. If anything, it makes ministerial responsibility to Parliament even more important. Moreover, managerialism has demonstrated the increasing complexity of the evolving state which, along with other factors, confounds attempts to construct a credible framework of ministerial responsibility. It has also illustrated how the evolution of managerial accountability has been moulded within a structure of ministerial responsibility despite the fact that it is increasingly hard to legitimate state action with a credible elucidation of how the convention operates in practice. It is possible to identify this tension and the restrictive imposition of ministerial responsibility in a number of areas, although perhaps it is most visible in relation to freedom of information. This will be the topic of the next and penultimate chapter.

Notes

1. Cm 4011 (1998) *Modern Public Service for Britain: Investing in Reform.*
2. Cm 4181 (1998) *Public Services for the Future: Modernisation, Reform, Accountability.*
3. Cm 4205 (1999) *The Government's Expenditure Plans 1999-2000 to 2001-2002 for the Home Office and the Charity Commission.*
4. These are specified at Cm 4205 (1999) Ch. 6 p.34.
5. Home Office (1999) *Quinquennial Review of the Home Office: Prior Options Report* pp.15-16.
6. HM Prison Service (1999) *Framework Document.*
7. See HM Prison Service (1999) *Framework Document* pp.7-10 para.s 3.1-3.24.
8. HC 748 (1999) *Prison Service Annual Reports and Accounts 1998/9* HC 748; HM Prison Service (1996) *Corporate Plan 1996-99*; Cm 3908 (1999) *Home Office. Annual Report 1998;* Cm 3908 (1998) *The Government's Expenditure Plans 1998/99 for the Home Office and Charity Commission.*
9. Talbot, C (1995) 'The Prison Service - A Framework of Irresponsibility' *Public Finance Foundation Review* No.8 pp.16-19.
10. Kate Jenkins admits that government ministers were aware of this dilemma well before the launch of the Next Steps programme but reluctantly accepted that no successful solution could be found. HC 313 *Ministerial Accountability and Responsibility* Second Report of the Public Service Committee, Session 1996/97, HMSO, London. p.115 Q703. See also Goldsworthy, D (1991) *Setting up Next Steps: A Short Account of the*

Origins, Launch and Implementation of the Next Steps Project in the British Civil Service (London : HMSO).

11 Hood, C (1998) 'Individualized Contracts for Top Public Servants: Copying Business Path Dependent Political Re-Engineering - or Trobriand Cricket?' *Governance* Vol.11 No.4 p.545.

12 Home Office (1999) *Quinquennial Review of the Home Office: Evaluation of Performance 1992-93 to 1997-98* p.2.

13 See Polidano, C (1997) 'The Bureaucrat Who Fell Under a Bus: Ministerial responsibility, Executive Agencies and the Derek Lewis Affair' *Governance* Vol.12 No.2 pp.201-231; Barker, A (1996) *Political Responsibility for UK Prison Security: Ministers Escape Again* Essex Papers in Politics and Government No.106, Colchester, Essex; Barker, A (1996) *Myth Versus Management: Individual Ministerial Responsibility in the New Whitehall* Essex Papers in Politics and Government No.105; Lewis, D (1997) *Hidden Agenda: Politics, Law and Order* (London : Hamish Hamilton).

14 See in particular the evidence presented to the Public Service Committee: HC 313-I/II/III (1996/97).

15 HC 57 *The Management of the Prison Service (Public and Private)* Second Report of the Home Affairs Committee, Session 1996/97, HMSO, London. p.xliv para.111.

16 The Labour Party (1997) *New Labour: Because Britain Deserves Better* (London : Labour Party) p.23.

17 Hansard, HC Debs. 19/5/97 col.396.

18 Hansard, HC Debs. WA 30/7/98 col.404 Q54883.

19 Home Office (1999) *Quinquennial Review of the Home Office: Prior Options Report*.

20 Hansard, HC Debs. WA 1/2/99 col.431 Q69049.

21 Hansard, HC Debs. WA 31/3/99 col.700 Q80077.

22 See HM Prison Service (1999) *Framework Document* Annex D 'Circumstances in which reports will be required by Ministers on Prison matters'. The quinquennial review of the Prison Service suggested that since it had become an agency its capacity to identify issues which may have political implications had deteriorated. It noted: 'The capacity of Prison Service staff to assess and take account of the potential implications of an incident, or policy or caseworking recommendation, is therefore important. Our discussions with key stakeholders suggests that agency status - in improving standards of outward looking service delivery - may have rendered the service somewhat less well placed to detect and advise on the small number of highly sensitive issues and cases'. p.28 para.5.7.

23 HM Prison Service (1999) *Framework Document* p.7 para.3.6.

24 HM Prison Service (1999) *Framework Document* p.9 para.3.15-3.17.

25 HM Prison Service (1999) *Framework Document* p.8 para.3.13.
26 Home Office (1999) *Quinquennial Review of the Home Office: Evaluation of Performance 1992-93 to 1997-98* pp.28-29 para.s 5.10-5.11.
27 See Home Office (1999) *Quinquennial Review of the Home Office: Evaluation of Performance 1992-93 to 1997-98* pp.27-29 para.s 5.1-5.19.
28 Derek Lewis discusses the increased centralisation of the agency on BBC Newsnight 16/10/95.
29 Home Office (1999) *Quinquennial Review of the Home Office: Prior Options Report* p.8 para.18.
30 The former Director of Finance, Brian Landers, has written that the framework document was '...a sham right from the start'. Landers, B (1998) 'Of Ministers, Mandarins and Managers' in Flinders, M & Smith M (eds.) *Quangos, Accountability and Reform: The Politics of Quasi-Government* (London : Macmillan) p.121.
31 Interview with the author, March 1998.
32 Interview with the author, July 1996.
33 Interview with the author, June 1996.
34 Hogwood, B, Judge, D & McVicar, M 'Too Much of a Good Thing? The Pathology of Accountability' paper presented to the Political Studies Association Annual Conference, University of Keele, 7-9/4/98.
35 Interview with the author, June 1999.
36 See Home Office (1999) *Quinquennial Review of the Home Office: Evaluation of Performance 1992-93 to 1997-98* Section 6 'Working with the Home Office and the Wider Criminal Justice System' pp.31-35 para.s 6.1-6.24.
37 Polidano, C (1998) 'Why Bureaucrats Can't Always do what Ministers Want: Multiple Accountabilities in Westminster democracies' *Public Policy and Administration* Vol.13 No.1 pp. 35-50.
38 See Cabinet Office (2000) *Wiring It Up: Whitehall's Management of Cross-Cutting Policies and Services*, Performance & Innovation Unit, London.
39 Kettl, D (1993) *Sharing Power: Public Governance and Private Markets* (Washington DC : The Brookings Institution).
40 HM Prison Service (1997) *Prison Service Review*.
41 Cm 4011 (1998) *Modern Public Service for Britain: Investing in Reform*.
42 Home Office (1998) *Prisons-Probation Review: Final Report*.
43 See Cm 4205 (1999) *The Government's Expenditure Plans 1999-2000 to 2001-2002 for the Home Office and the Charity Commission* Ch. 2 'Modernising the way the Home Office works' pp.10-13.
44 Cm 3020 (1995) *Review of Prison Security in England and Wales and The escape from Parkhurst Prison on Tuesday 3rd January 1995*.

45 HC 57 *The Management of the Prison Service (Public and Private)* Second Report of the Home Affairs Committee, Session 1996/97, HMSO, London.

46 HM Prison Service (1997) *Prison Service Review*; HM Prison Service (1997) *Audit of Resources*.

47 Home Office (1999) *Quinquennial Review of the Home Office: Prior Options Report*; Home Office (1999) *Quinquennial Review of the Home Office: Evaluation of Performance 1992-93 to 1997-98*.

48 Senior Official, Prison Service, interview with the author April 1998. These problems were noted by the Learmont Report (1995) as it noted that the Prison Service had been subject to a constant stream of initiatives emanating from the Home Office. It listed 38 initiatives that the Prison Service had been forced to implement irrespective of its own priorities or needs (Cm 3020 [1995] Annex L).

49 Hogwood, B 'The Quantitative Analysis of Agency Accountability: What Can It Tell Us and What Does It Miss Out?' Paper presented at the Conference of the Structure and Organisation Group (SOG) of IPSA on Taking the Measure of Government, Pittsburgh, USA, 30/10/97.

50 See Langford, J (1984) 'Responsibility in the Senior Public Service: Marching to Several Drummers' *Canadian Public Administration* Vol.27 No.4 pp.513-21.

51 HC 313-I (1996/97) p.li para. 108.

52 For example Cm 6877 (1977) *HM Prison Service 1976*; Cm 7290 (1978) *HM Prison Service 1977*; Cm 7619 (1979) *HM Prison Service 1978*.

53 HM Prison Service *Annual Report 1996/97* p.4.

54 Hyndman, N & Anderson, R (1997) 'A Study of the Use of Targets in the Planning Documents of Executive Agencies' *Financial Accountability and Management* Vol.13 No.2 pp.139-164. See also HC 313-II (1995-96) p.50 (Prof. Colin Talbot).

55 HC 313-III (1996/97) p.145 Q817.

56 The Public Service Select Committee also highlighted this as a key issue. See: HC 313-I (1996/97) p. Ii para.s 105-108.

57 See Power, M (1997) *The Audit Society* (Oxford : Oxford University Press).

58 Lewis, D (1997) *Hidden Agendas* (London : Hamish Hamilton) pp.70-71.

59 HM Prison Service (1999) *Framework Document* Annex A 'Prison Service Key Performance Indicators 1998-99'.

60 Home Office (1999) *Quinquennial Review of the Home Office: Evaluation of Performance 1992-93 to 1997-98*.

61 Landers, B (1997) 'Of Ministers, Mandarins and Managers' in Flinders, M & Smith, M (eds.) *Quangos, Accountability and Reform: The Politics of Quasi-Government* (London : Macmillan) p.122.

62 'Howard should have congratulated Mr Lewis on the job he was doing, instead of sacking him. What he did was totally unjust.' *The Independent* 16/5/97.
63 Polidano, C (1997) 'The Bureaucrat Who Fell Under a Bus: Ministerial Responsibility, Executive Agencies and the Derek Lewis Affair' *Governance* Vol.12 No.2 p.213.
64 HC 57-II (1996/97) p. 149 Q1336.
65 HC 57-II (1996/97) Appendix 16.
66 'The theory is that targets are set by ministers, then by a department and then implemented by agencies. Nevertheless, the practical expertise about targets is in the agencies and often targets are proposed by agencies.' Trosa, S (1994) *Next Steps: Moving On* (London : OPSS) pp.9-10 para.2.25 See also Kemp, P (1996) 'Delivering Public Services' Centre for Socio-Legal Studies, The University of Sheffield, annual lecture, 12/11/96.
67 'We had a deal, though no one had even discussed the targets or performance on which the bonus would be paid. Whitmore was quick to reassure me. I need not worry, he said "...the Home Office believes that bonuses, although demanding, should be very much available". With a nod and a wink he told me I could expect to earn most of it.' Lewis, D (1997) *Hidden Agendas* (London : Hamilton) p.13.
68 Hansard, HC Debs. 19/12/94 col.1400; See also HC57-I (1996/7) p.148 Q1324.
69 HC 57-II (1996/97) p.161 Appendix 1.
70 Efficiency Unit (1991) *Making the Most of Next Steps: The Management of Ministers' Departments and their Executive Agencies* HMSO, London. paras 2.11 & 2.12 [The Fraser Report].
71 Interview with the author, June 1996. For a discussion of the importance of this fact see Landers, B (1998) 'Of Ministers, Mandarins and Managers' in Flinders, M & Smith M (eds.) *Quangos, Accountability and Reform: The Politics of Quasi-Government* (London : Macmillan).
72 Hood, C et al. (1998) 'Regulation Inside Government: Where New Public Management Meets the Audit Explosion' *Public Money and Management* April/June pp.61-68.
73 Home Office, correspondence with the author 3/7/98 & 10/7/98.
74 Hood, C et al. (1996) *Regulation Inside British Government: The Inner Face of the Regulatory State* Project Discussion Paper No.1 (London : LSE); Hood, C et al. (1996) *Bureaucratic regulation and New Public Management in the UK: Mirror Image Developments* Project Discussion Paper No.2 (London : LSE); Hood, C & James, O 'Reconfiguring the UK Executive: From Public Bureaucracy State to Re-Regulated Public Service' Paper presented to ESRC conference 'Understanding Central Government:

75   Theory into Practice' University of Birmingham 16-18/9/96; Hood, C *et al.* (1997) *Waste Watchers, Quality Checkers and Sleazebusters* (London : LSE).
76   Wilson, R 'The Civil Service in the New Millennium' speech given at City University, London, 5/5/99.
77   In 2000 the Chief Secretary to the Treasury announced the establishment of a Review of Audit and Accountability for Central Government. It is chaired by Lord Sharman and aims to report towards the end of 2001.
78   Clarke, M & Stewart, J (1997) *Handling the Wicked Issues* (Birmingham : INLOGOV).
79   Resource Accounting and Resource Budgeting brings to the management of central government departments and agencies charges for the use of resources which have previously not been accounted for. The cost of using assets such as equipment, vehicles, computers, fixtures and fittings, will all now be charged against 'business units'. For example, each of England and Wales's 135 prisons will become a separate accounting unit and the governor will have to account for all resources used including wear and tear of the prison's assets and the level of capital tied up in the prison.
80   Lovell, A & Hand, L (1999) 'Expanding the Notion of Organisational Performance Measurement to Support Joined Up Government' *Public Policy and Administration* Vol.14 No.2 pp.17-29.
81   HM Prison Service (1999) *Framework Document* Annex A.
82   Home Office (1999) *Quinquennial Review of the Home Office: Evaluation of Performance 1992-93 to 1997-98* p.32 para.6.8.
83   Richards, S 'Interview: Jack Straw' *The New Statesman* 23/5/97 pp.16-17.
84   Home Office (1982) *Prisons Over Two Centuries* (London : Home Office).
85   Donahue, J (1989) *The Privatization Decision: Public Ends, Private Means* (London : Basic Books); Matthews, R (1989) *Privatising Criminal Justice* (London : Sage); Shichor, D (1995) *Punishment for Profit* (London : Sage); Moyle, P (ed.) (1994) *Private Prisons and Police: Recent Australian Trends* (Australia : NSW); James, A *et al.* (1997) *Privatising Prisons: Rhetoric and Reality* (London : Sage).
86   Vagg, J Morgan, R & Maquire, M (eds.) (1985) *Accountability and Prisons* (London : Tavistock); Christie, N (1993) *Crime Control as Industry* (London : Routledge); Harding, R (1997) *Private Prisons and Public Accountability* (Buckingham : Open University Press).
    Ryan, M & Ward, T (1989) 'Privatization and the Penal System: Britain Misinterprets the American Experience' *Criminal Justice Review* Vol.14 No.1 pp.1-12; Vagg, J (1994) *Prison Systems - A Comparative Study of Accountability in England, France, Germany and The Netherlands* (Oxford : Clarendon).

[87] HC 291 *Contract Provision of Prisons* Fourth Report of the Home Affairs Committee, Session 1986/87, HMSO, London. See also HC 35 *State and Use of Prisons* Third Report of the Home Affairs Committee, Session 1986/87, HMSO, London.

[88] Adam Smith Institute (1987) *The Prison Cell* (London : Adam Smith Institute).

[89] Hansard HC Debs. 16/7/87 col.1303.

[90] Home Office (1989) *Report on the Practicality of Private Sector Involvement in the Remand System.*

[91] See Ryan, M (1994) 'Private prisons in the UK: radical change and opposition' in Moyle, P (ed.) *Private Prisons and Police: Recent Australian Trends* (Australia : NSW) pp.235-239.

[92] Ryan, M & Ward, T (1989) *Privatization and the Penal System: the American Experience and the Debate in England* (Milton Keynes : Open University Press) p.47.

[93] Hansard, HC Debs. 1/3/89, col. 278.

[94] Cm 2508 (1995) *Home Office Annual Report 1994* para. 6.24.

[95] HC 35 (1986/87) Appendix 10 para 4.1.

[96] HC 35-II (1986/87) Q184.

[97] Report of the General Synod of the Church of England Board for Social Responsibility (1997) *Private Sector Involvement in Prisons.*

[98] Ryan, M (1994) 'Private Prisons in the UK: Radical Change and Opposition' in Moyle, P (ed.) *Private Prisons and Police: Recent Australian trends* (Australia : NSW) p.248.

[99] Interview with the author, March 1998.

[100] Controllers are governor grade officials who will usually move back to governor appointments on completion of their term.

[101] Empowered by the *Criminal Justice Act 1991* section 85. See Creighton, S & King, V (1996) *Prisoners and the Law* (London : Butterworths).

[102] The only other equivalent in the public sector would be the Food Hygiene Inspectors stationed in each abattoir by the Ministry of Agriculture, Fisheries and Food.

[103] Home Office (1997) *Monitoring and Evaluation of the Wolds Remand Prison* p.58.

[104] Morgan, R (1993) 'Prisons Accountability Revisited' *Public Law* pp.320.

[105] There have been calls for Jack Straw to do this at the new privately managed HMP Parc, in South Wales. See BBC 2 Newsnight 2/6/98.

[106] HC 57-II (1996/97) Q499 p.54 (Mr Walter MacGowan, Director HMP Buckley Hall, Group 4).

[107] See, for example, Ford, R 'Securicor fined £105,000 as jail runs into trouble' *The Times* 29/7/98 p.9. The maximum total for penalties is 5% of

the annual contract value. See Hansard, HC Debs. WA 10/11/99 col.585 Q97733.
[108] Blakenhurst prison, which was managed by United Kingdom Detention Services, and Buckley Hall prison, which was managed by Group 4, have been transferred back to the Prison Service.
[109] Correspondence with the author 8/6/98.
[110] HC 57-I (1996/97) p.LXIIIxiii para.170.
[111] Correspondence with the author 8/6/98.
[112] Cm 4310 (1999) *Modernising Government* HMSO, London.
[113] HC 57-I (1996/97) para.162.
[114] Sir Peter Woodhead, interview with the author, March 1998.
[115] See, for example, *The Times* 'Siege prison wins praise' 7/4/98.
[116] See, for example, HM Inspectorate of Prisons (1996) *HMP Doncaster*.
[117] For example, see Roth, D (1996) 'Finding the Balance: Achieving a Synthesis Between Improved Performance and Enhanced Accountability' in *Performance Auditing and the Modernisation of Government* (Paris : OECD) pp.249-259.
[118] See HC 57-I (1996/97) pp.lxiv-lxix paras. 175-190.
[119] Coopers & Lybrand (1996) *Review of Comparative Costs and Performance of Privately and Publicly Operated Prisons* (London : HM Prison Service).
[120] HC 57-I (1996/97) p.lxiii para.169 (Home Office).
[121] Home Office (1999) *Quinquennial Review of the Home Office: Evaluation of Performance 1992-93 to 1997-98* p.23 para.3.20.
[122] HC 57-II (1996/97) Q 309.
[123] HC 57-II (1996/97) Q 970.
[124] HC 57-I (1996/97) pp. lxviii-lxix para.187.
[125] For example, during the controversy surrounding the death of Alton Manning in HMP Blakenhurst, run by United Kingdom Detention Services Ltd. See Hall, J 'Jail officers suspended over death' *The Guardian* 26/3/98 p.4.
[126] See Rasmussen, K & Yeates, N 'Performance Management and the Divided Worlds of Accountability' Paper to the International Institute of Administrative Sciences Conference, Civil Service College, Sunningdale, 12-15/5/99.
[127] See, Boston, J, Martin, J, Pallot, J & Walsh, P (1996) *Public Management: The New Zealand Model* (Oxford : Oxford University Press) p.320.
[128] Hood, C (1998) 'Individualized Contracts for Top Public Servants: Copying Business. Path Dependent Political Re-engineering - or Trobriand Cricket?' *Governance* Vol.11 No.4 pp.443-462 p.455; Horn, M (1995) *The Political Economy of Public Administration* (Cambridge : Cambridge University Press) p.45.

[129] The leading example of this occurred in New Zealand and involved the collapse of a viewing platform which led to the death of the 14 students. See Gregory, R (1998) 'A New Zealand Tragedy: problems of political responsibility' *Governance* Vol.11 No.2 pp.231-40.

[130] Polidano, C (1997) 'The Bureaucrat Who Fell Under a Bus: Ministerial Responsibility, Executive Agencies and the Derek Lewis Affair' *Governance* Vol.12 No.2 pp.201-231.

PART THREE
FREEDOM OF INFORMATION AND CONCLUSION

PART THREE
FREEDOM OF
INFORMATION AND
CONCLUSION

8 The Executive Morality and Inverted Conventions: Ministerial Responsibility and Freedom of Information

8.1 Introduction

The government's intention to introduce Freedom of Information (FOI) legislation is fundamental to this book. Not least because FOI reflects the nature and balance of power within the state. Examining the evolution from the non-statutory Code of Practice on Access to Official Information[1] to the white paper on FOI[2] and finally to the draft FOI Bill[3] reveals a number of tensions and issues that resonate throughout this book: in particular, how the rationale behind the fundamental u-turn between the white paper and draft Bill was legitimated through recourse to upholding both collective and individual ministerial responsibility. Beyond this, FOI is critical as it bolsters alternative mechanisms of accountability and creates a new context in which information flows operate. It creates a potentially vital base for any system of checks and balances. The introduction of cogent FOI legislation could also have tremendous implications for the convention of ministerial responsibility and a range of constitutional relationships. For example, the release of policy advice would undermine the anonymity of officials while possibly limiting ministerial capacity for blame shift. However, this chapter demonstrates how the planned FOI legislation has been enfeebled due to its construction within a framework of ministerial responsibility. This is, in itself, a critical reflection of the executive morality and an example of the inversion of ministerial responsibility to block and limit a reform designed to increase transparency and accountability.

FOI legislation is also pertinent as the many statutes which have gradually increased the public's rights of access to information, in areas such as local government and health records, have largely neglected central government.[4] Instead, demands for a statutory right of access to information in central government were to some extent appeased by the Conservative government's commitment to 'open government'.[5] This illuminates the fundamental difference between FOI and open government, the former being a positive right to receive information, while the latter is a negative right to receive the information the executive decides to release. Given the substantial variance between the original white paper *Your Right to Know* and the Freedom of Information Bill it might be argued that the draft Bill is actually a commitment to greater open government rather than FOI. (This links into wider concerns with regard to the differences between the *principles* and *practice* of the government's commitment to constitutional reform.) The variance between the white paper and the draft Bill might also be interpreted as an example of the different yet mutually compatible Whig and Peelite views of ministerial responsibility, as discussed in Chapter One.[6]

   FOI legislation is also related to wider concerns about the workings of our parliamentary system. It may offer the opportunity to reduce these anxieties.[7] Yet there are dangers with the introduction of FOI if ministers no longer take the final decision on the release of information. This brings the argument back to the enduring centrality of ministerial responsibility and, as a result, making the parliamentary constitution effective rather than transferring power to unelected and unaccountable mechanisms. This chapter does not examine a number of secondary topics, for example: the possible impact of FOI on departments;[8] the cost of FOI;[9] or the effect FOI might have on parliamentary procedures.[10] Instead it focuses on the extent to which the planned FOI regime is constructed and confined within a framework of ministerial responsibility, and the degree to which it will improve the means by which ministerial responsibility can be enforced. To examine these issues it is necessary briefly to outline the progression from the Code to the white paper and then the draft Bill.[11]

8.2 The Code of Practice on Access to Official Information

The Code of Practice on Access to Government Information came into force on the 4 April 1994.[12] It is enforced by the Parliamentary Ombudsman.[13] Under the non-statutory Code there is no right to documents but to 'information' which is sifted by civil servants before being disclosed. However, the Ombudsman has indicated that most Code requests can only be satisfied by the release of documents if that is what is requested.[14] Although decisions of the Ombudsman have generally been complied with, critics have argued that an independent judicial body should have the power to enforce decisions against the executive. The Ombudsman does have the power to balance the public interests involved in deciding whether the public interest is better served by disclosure or non-disclosure. Only bodies covered by the Parliamentary Commissioner Act 1967 come within the Code. This has left a number of bodies, particularly the Cabinet, beyond its jurisdiction. There are 15 categories, or classes, of information that are exempt under the Code.[15] These are broadly in line with overseas legislation.[16] Requests for information under the Code have been limited.[17] There were 3772 Code applications made in 1997 and 3803 in 1998, a rise of just 0.8%.[18] A lack of publicity, public apathy at using a Code without legal power and the failure of the monitoring scheme have all been advanced to explain the lack of public interest. In his 1997/98 report the Ombudsman complained of a complete lack of awareness of the existence of the Code in some departments.[19]

Refusals to Code requests are rare. For example, the Home Office received thirty-four official requests for information in 1996, forty-four in 1997 and fifty-three in 1998 but refused only three requests in 1996, two in 1997 and seven in 1998. What is noticeable is an annual reduction in the refusal rates for Code requests by departments, down from 9.1% in 1996 to 7.3% in 1998 (in 1997 the figure was 4.2%). These statistics are frequently quoted as evidence both of an increasingly liberal approach by officials to discretionary elements of the Code and a reflection of a more open culture within Whitehall.[20] Of those requests that are refused by departments, only a small fraction are appealed to the Ombudsman (thirty appeals in 1997 and thirty-nine in 1998).

The Code occupies a central position within the plethora of non-statutory codes that govern the accountability of ministers to Parliament.[21] References to the Code are to be found in *Questions of Procedure for Ministers*, the Osmotherly rules (*Departmental Evidence and Response to Select Committees*), the *Guidance on Answering Parliamentary Questions: Basic Dos and Don'ts*, the *Civil Service Code*, and the *Parliamentary Resolution on Ministerial Accountability to Parliament*. However, the Code's breadth of coverage in central government was limited. The

Democratic Audit revealed that only one in seven executive non-departmental bodies (NDPBs) came under the jurisdiction of the Code.[22] In response to this criticism, and in light of their FOI commitments, the Labour government extended the jurisdiction of the parliamentary Ombudsman to cover all executive and some advisory NDPBs.[23] While this commitment still has not been realised (by July 1999 73% of executive NDPBs and 15.5% of advisory NDPBs had been brought under the Ombudsman's jurisdiction), this move was seen as a powerful indicator of the government's commitment to FOI.[24] Nevertheless, the radical and far-reaching proposals contained in the government's white paper on FOI were unexpected.

8.3 The White Paper *Your Right to Know*

The Labour party and FOI have a long history.[25] Their election manifesto of 1974 contained a commitment to FOI; but when James Callaghan's government lost the confidence vote in March 1979, not only did the government fall but so did Clement Freud's private member's bill on FOI which the government had supported.[26] The fact that five years had passed since the government won office reflects the lack of commitment by the Labour party to FOI throughout the 1970s.[27] Constitutionally, the key issue was how to reconcile ministerial responsibility with a statutory right to information. As Mrs Thatcher stated:

> Under our constitution, ministers are accountable to Parliament for the work of their departments, and that includes the provision of information...Ministers' accountability to Parliament would be reduced, and Parliament itself diminished... In our view the right place for ministers to answer for their decisions in the essentially 'political' area of information is in Parliament.[28]

Yet while FOI was regarded as incompatible with ministerial responsibility within the United Kingdom, plans were being prepared to introduce FOI within a framework of ministerial responsibility in a range of Westminster democracies (Australia,[29] Canada[30] and New Zealand[31] all legislated in 1982).[32]

In the run up to the 1997 general election both the Liberal Democrat and the Labour parties were committed to the introduction of an act and it featured in the Joint Consultative Committee Report issued by both parties on 5 March 1997.[33] There was some initial concern from FOI supporters when it was announced that a Bill would not feature in the first session of the new Parliament.[34] On 14 May 1998 David Clark, Chancellor of the Duchy of Lancaster, issued a press notice adding that he hoped to publish a white paper by the summer recess.[35] On 22 May Ann Taylor announced that an FOI Bill would be one of the draft Bills to be issued to allow more time for scrutiny.[36] In the event the white paper did not appear until December 1998 and even then its contents were leaked on 9 December.[37] Dr Clark apologised to the House and on 11 December the white paper *Your Right to Know* was published.[38]

The white paper was widely welcomed. The Public Administration Committee declared it '...a radical advance in open and accountable government'.[39] The Canadian Information Commissioner noted that the white paper had left Canada's highly regarded provisions '...trailing in the dust'.[40] The main differences between the Code and the white paper's proposals are:

- The Code of Practice has no legal force; the proposed act would give the citizen a statutory and legally enforceable right of access to information;
- The Code of Practice covers only those bodies subject to the jurisdiction of the Parliamentary Commissioner for Administration - principally government departments, executive agencies and some non-departmental public bodies; the proposed act would cover the entire public sector and some private bodies;
- The Code of Practice gave access only to 'information'; the proposed act would give a right of access to documents, records and information;
- The Code had fifteen exemptions; the white paper only seven;
- Under the Code public bodies could prevent disclosure by pleading that it would cause 'harm'; under the proposed act they would have to be able to prove in the majority of cases that disclosure would cause 'substantial harm', which is a more exacting level of proof;
- Under the Code complaints regarding the non-disclosure of information had to be made through an MP; under the proposed act there would be no MP filter to the Information Commissioner;

- Under the Code the parliamentary Commissioner had no formal power to order the release of information; under the act the Information Commissioner would be able to order departments to disclose information;
- Cabinet committees are not excluded from the scope of the proposed act and there is no right of ministerial or cabinet veto to prevent disclosure.

The white paper went further than even the most fervent supporters of FOI could have hoped for. The scope, depth and coverage of the proposed act were extensive. The clearest example of the white paper's radicalism and the challenges it presented to the constitutional order lay in the area of enforcement. In most of the FOI legislation around the world the final decision on the release of information lies with the executive. The argument for retaining a ministerial veto is that it is a way of preserving ministerial responsibility. In Australia, Canada and New Zealand ministers have the final decision and they are responsible to Parliament for their decision through the requirement to table a report setting out the reasons for the veto (ministerial override). Tabling a statement in Parliament has proved in practice to be an insufficient safeguard as the statements have usually passed without comment. This fact has led New Zealand to introduce an Order in Council procedure which requires individual ministers to obtain the approval of the Cabinet before using the veto. This is an interesting comment on the utility of ministerial responsibility to Parliament: '...collective responsibility is hoped to provide a more effective sanction than an individual minister's responsibility to Parliament'.[41]

The white paper proposed that the Information Commissioner (IC), and not ministers, would have the final decision. Unlike the 1993 Fisher Bill, the white paper did not include a tribunal to hear appeals from the IC[42] and, unlike the current situation with the PCA, ministers would have no powers to stop the IC disclosing information.[43] A failure to comply with the IC's demands to release information would be ruled by the courts to be a contempt of court. The deliberate destruction of records required for an investigation by the IC would be made an offence.[44] Officials who exposed the destruction or alteration of information would be protected by the Public Interest Disclosure Act 1999.[45]

Despite the fact that the provisions outlined in the white paper could have gone further (it was not the 'All singin' all dancin' affair' that

David Clark portrayed it to be), the proposals were simply too radical. It challenged the *ancien regime* and particularly the prerogative powers of ministers. Few commentators noticed *Your Right to Know* was a white paper 'with green edges'.[46] Even fewer predicted that the drift from the white paper to the draft Bill would be significant. The Constitution Unit was an exception:

> The white paper offers a very generous FOI regime. It is almost too good to be true. That is a central concern; that this is an unreal white paper which has been brought out without full understanding or wholehearted commitment on behalf of departments or their ministers or proper consultation with the other bodies which will be affected. FOI risks becoming a hollow shell.[47]

This observation proved pertinent. David Clark was discharged from the Government and authoritative media reports indicated a degree of unrest over the white paper within the Cabinet, led by the Home Secretary.[48] Following a review of the Cabinet Office by Sir Richard Wilson the Prime Minister announced on 31 July 1998 that responsibility for FOI would be taken forward by the Home Office.[49] Justification for this transfer was based on the Home Office already being responsible for data protection, official secrets and human rights legislation. Many commentators viewed the transfer as a Cabinet victory for the Home Office with worrying implications for FOI - a view David Clark concurred with: 'I was disappointed when I saw that the Home Office had claimed it and the dedicated office I had set up was split asunder'.[50] In April 2000, Lord McNally remarked in the Lords that 'putting the present Home Secretary in charge of freedom of information was like asking Count Dracula to look after the blood bank'. On 24 May 1999 the draft Bill was finally published.[51]

8.4 The Draft Freedom of Information Bill

Whereas the white paper had received near universal praise the draft Bill received near universal hostility.[52] On the day it was published the Campaign for Freedom of Information issued a press release entitled 'Deeply disappointing information bill, weaker than the Conservative's openness code'.[53] They noted:

It achieves a remarkable feat of making the Code, introduced by a government opposed in principle to FOI, appear a more positive measure than legislation drawn up by a government committed to the issue for 25 years.

The draft Bill represents a significant retreat from the Government's own white paper published only 17 months previously with a preface from the Prime Minister and the backing of the Cabinet. The draft Bill does contain some positive attributes. For example: there is a presumptive right of access to information in legislation; it places a substantial degree of emphasis on the publication of statutory publication schemes; the extensive coverage of private bodies makes it unique; it covers all forms of recorded information; there is a direct right of access to the IC; public interest must be considered for most exemptions; and the IC can investigate services that have been contracted out. There is also access to personal information about others, subject to Data Protection Act safeguards. Despite this, the proposals fail to satisfy the commitment made in the white paper to bring in FOI legislation that goes beyond the existing Code of Practice on Access to Official Information. Not only does it fail to do this, but in many ways it is weaker than the Code. It would allow government departments to withhold some kinds of information that at present they are expected to disclose under the Code (see Table 8.1). In numerous areas the white paper's commitments have been weakened. The 'substantial harm' test has been replaced by the lower test of 'prejudice'. The 'simple harm' test for policy advice has been replaced by an absolute exemption. The binding public interest test has been replaced by one that is unenforceable, and also it permits authorities to insist on knowing why the applicant wants the information and to apply restrictions to the use of released information. The proposed right of access to unrecorded information has been dropped, whereas new catch-all exemptions, unlike any found in other FOI legislation, have been devised.[54] While the rights of public bodies to withhold information have been systematically strengthened, modest rights that would help the public have been weakened. Three valuable provisions which appear on the face of many FOI laws have been relegated into unenforceable codes of practice or 'publication schemes': authorities will not be legally obliged to help applicants; they will not have to give reasons for their decisions; and they will not be required to publish their internal manuals and guidance. Under the draft Bill authorities will only be encouraged, not required to comply with these provisions.

Table 8.1 Differences Between the Draft Bill on FOI and the Non-Statutory Openness Code

Draft Bill	Openness Code
Exempts all information relating to the 'formulation or development of government policy'.	Information about policy formulation is available so long as disclosure does not 'harm the frankness and candour of internal discussion'.
Exempts the analysis underlying new government decisions or policy proposals.	'the facts and analysis of the facts' leading to decisions or proposals must be published once the decision or proposal in announced.
Prohibits the Commissioner from ordering disclosure of exempt information on the grounds of public interest.	The parliamentary Ombudsman can recommend that exempt information should be disclosed in the public interest.
No duty to publish internal guidance used by an authority in its dealings with the public.	Requires authorities to publish such internal guidance.
No duty to give reasons for administrative decisions.	Requires authorities to give reasons for administrative decisions.
Information must be supplied within 40 days.	Information must be supplied within 20 working days.

Examination of the documentary and oral evidence provided to the Public Administration Committee indicates that the main concerns are as follows:

- A class exemption applies to all information relating to the development of policy, including factual information, regardless of whether disclosure would harm decision-making. This represents a retreat from the existing standards of disclosure under the Code.

- Class exemptions apply to information obtained during investigations by the police and all the regulatory bodies, including those dealing with safety. Information whose disclosure could not harm law enforcement or regulatory functions is exempt.
- Authorities will be able to refuse to confirm whether they hold information in the above categories, even where to do so would not cause harm.
- Authorities will be able to withhold information indicating that they are guilty of an offence.
- It replaces the white paper's enforceable public interest tests with one that is discretionary and unenforceable and will allow authorities to withhold evidence of their own misconduct.
- In many cases authorities will be able to insist on knowing the applicant's motives for seeking information and to release the information only subject to a 'gagging order'.
- The white paper's 'substantial harm' test has been replaced by the weaker test of 'prejudice'.
- A 'catch-all' exemption allows authorities to withhold harmless information if, together with any other information including confidential information which authorities have no intention of disclosing, the combined information could cause harm.
- New exemptions could be created by parliamentary order at short notice to deal with requests already received that cannot otherwise be refused.
- The white paper's plans for enforcement by an independent Commissioner are replaced by the introduction of a ministerial veto.

The variance between the government's white paper and the draft Bill goes far beyond actual content. There is a fundamental difference between the general tone of the documents, the perspectives from which they approach the issue of FOI and the degree to which they are willing to challenge or alter the current constitutional equilibrium. The rationale and justifications for this volte-face explain and underpin the continuing centrality and enduring qualities of ministerial responsibility to Parliament. A valuable tool in understanding this point lies in the difference between Open Government and Freedom of Information.

8.5 The Difference between 'Open Government' and 'Freedom of Information'

Pressure for greater freedom of information in the United Kingdom grew in the 1960s and 1970s, fuelled by the adoption of FOI regimes abroad. In 1977 the Croham Directive, issued by the then Head of the Civil Service Sir Douglas Allen, was intended to secure the release of more of the background detail and information behind ministerial decisions.[55] In recent years, successive governments have made significant advances in providing information about the processes of government and in exposing the core executive to public scrutiny. Some argue that the Code of Practice has already had an effect on the culture of government. The Home Office's consultation document accompanying the draft Bill provides many examples of the voluntary disclosure of information as the context against which FOI legislation is proposed.[56] This sort of voluntary openness has sometimes been called 'open government'. Indeed, this was the title of the 1979 green paper and the white paper of 1993.[57] But there is a profound difference between a non-statutory Code, which exists at the grace and favour of ministers, and a statutory framework which is there whether ministers like it or not, has been passed by Parliament and has the force of law. This is a crucial distinction. The central question is whether the draft Bill would deliver FOI or more 'open government'?

The Bill does create a statutory right to information. But, as the majority of witnesses to the Public Administration Committee stressed, that right is fettered by so many exemptions, qualifications and discretionary clauses that it will not cover a lot of the information that the public might want. Nor does it guarantee that the information covered by the act would be released. As Robert Hazell noted:

> The Government still does not fully understand the difference between open government and freedom of information. Open government means the Government publishing information largely for its own purposes: information that the Government thinks we need to know or would like to know. Freedom of information requires the government to disclose information which we decide for ourselves we want to know.[58]

The draft Bill perpetuates a paternalistic model of open government, as opposed to FOI, with the government deciding what is released. Open government is selective, with the government largely engaging in public consultation before formulating policy or coming to a decision, and publishing green and white papers accordingly. This is arguably in the government's interest rather than the public's. It wants to tests its proposals and refine them, thus sharpening up the policies and softening up public opinion. However, open government rarely involves the government releasing information once a decision has been reached. Open government therefore means publishing what the government wants the public to know rather than entitling people to ask for what they want to know. It is understandable that the government has tried to quell demands for FOI by demonstrating how much more open the government is; but the information published in the name of open government is unlikely to be the sort of information people would demand under FOI. No government is likely to volunteer information that is likely to undermine its case.

In many areas the draft Bill has more in common with non-statutory open government regimes than with statutory FOI ones. For example, many matters which are laid down as duties in other FOI regimes are left to be included in a non-statutory Code of Practice. The government presents a number of arguments to legitimate the stark retreat from the white paper; among these are the need to maintain ministerial responsibility, and that parliamentary accountability works. Clearly this logic is far from uncontested. The inconsistencies and flaws in the government's position form the basis of the next section.

8.6 The Rationale Underpinning the Draft Bill on Freedom of Information

At its crudest, the rationale underpinning the draft Bill is a commitment to cultural change, a belief in the morality of ministers and the contention that parliamentary control of the executive works. There are three problems with this position. First, in several areas the draft Bill goes against the stated aims of this government. Second, the importance of FOI is that it relieves the public of their need to rely on the morality of ministers. Finally, it is widely held that parliamentary oversight is not effective. To unravel these points it is helpful to focus on four interlinked areas: international experience, cultural change, the disclosure of policy advice, and the need to protect ministerial responsibility to Parliament.

FOI legislation has been operating in a number of countries for some time. British policy need not, therefore, be drawn up in isolation; there is a wealth of international expertise and experience on which to draw. Indeed, international benchmarking is one of the government's maxims in the 1999 *Modernising Government* white paper, as is a more systematic use of evidence-based policy.[59] Yet the draft Bill is, in many ways, unique. As the Public Administration Committee noted:

> Many of the features which we criticise in this report are home-grown. We are puzzled that the Government have not benefited more from the experience of these tried and tested models in countries with political and legal systems very similar to our own.[60]

The government has failed to adequately respond to this criticism, instead stressing the unique political context and culture in which FOI will operate in Britain.[61] Yet there are clear inconsistencies within the government's evidence in support of the draft Bill. For example, the Home Secretary, Jack Straw, repeatedly stressed the importance of cultural change as the real catalyst behind FOI. The government insists that the exemptions, lack of clarity, ministerial override, and so on do not matter as officials and ministers could be trusted to interpret the act in a liberal manner.[62]

> ...we are proposing in this Bill to change the culture of openness and the culture of government. That is being changed not only by the specific terms of the legislation but also by the practice of government and that is what we are doing and have already started to do.[63]

Hence the emphasis in the consultation paper accompanying the publication of the Bill on the government's achievements on voluntary disclosure. And yet the essential value of FOI, as opposed to 'open government', is that it removes, or at least reduces, the discretionary powers of ministers and officials.

The Home Secretary also seemed unable to sustain his faith in the cultural dexterity of senior officials. On the topic of the release of policy advice, he suggested that if it were released under British FOI legislation, senior officials would simply undermine the provision by failing to record their advice in a retrievable form:

> ...you get cynical evasion of what the Bill is trying to achieve. I am not in favour of setting up a system which goes too far and which people cynically evade and that is not consistent with our British cultural tradition.[64]

The draft Bill reimposes ministerial discretion over vast swathes of information which would have been disclosed as of right under the white paper. The government's defence is that ministers will interpret this discretion in a liberal manner. Such a position negates the certainty that FOI is designed to ensure. It also provides no protection for the future. Governments change and it may well be that in the future ministers will exercise their discretion in a less liberal manner.[65] It also provides no reassurance that previous incidents will not be repeated. For example, the 'arms to Iraq' affair confirmed the need for FOI legislation in the United Kingdom to many - not least Tony Blair who in 1996 argued that the Scott Report '...has made the case for a Freedom of Information act absolutely unanswerable'. Yet under the draft Bill none of the information that came before Sir Richard Scott's inquiry would be released as of right. It would be covered by the exemptions of policy advice to ministers, commercial confidentiality and national security. The Bill also allows authorities to withhold, without IC scrutiny, information that would expose illegal action.[66] In doing so it denies the very purpose of holding to account governments or departments of state.

The justification relies on the need to maintain the conventions of collective and ministerial responsibility - for example, the exemption for decisionmaking and policy formulation has been heavily criticised. The issue has always been to what extent open advice is compatible with the collective responsibility of ministers and a neutral civil service. Proponents of openness have argued that with the gradual opening up of government over the last two decades and the increased fragmentation of the state the validity of a blanket exemption on policy advice is no longer tenable.[67] As the First Division Association recognised:

> We are in a different position politically and organisationally in the civil service from where we were 15 or 20 years ago and the notion of collective responsibility itself is an evolving concept. It is an important one for the integrity of government but it is not something that we now see in quite as cast iron form as we might have seen if we look back in earlier editions of political textbooks and the like.[68]

All FOI laws contain some protection for policy advice. This is generally defined as material relating to the development of government policy which consists of opinion, recommendation, the exchange of views or similar material. However none of the main overseas laws exempts material in the comprehensive and absolute terms of the draft Bill.[69] The government will not even have to acknowledge whether information within this substantial class exists at all.[70] There are no exceptions to this all-embracing exemption and no attempt is made to discriminate between disclosures that are likely to be harmful and those that are innocuous or perhaps beneficial. All material which has been considered during the development of policy would be exempt. This will absolve the government of the need to account for even the simplest questions about the basis for its decisions. Research suggests that the Home Office has failed to comprehend the nature of these exemptions.[71] They also clash with the stated aims of the government in other white papers; particularly the *Modernising Government* white paper which contains a commitment to greater openness, debate and inclusion in the policy - making process.[72]

The government insists the exemption is necessary to enforce and protect the collective responsibility of ministers:

> One of the good things about British government is that people are collectively responsible for what goes on and it actually makes holding government ministers to account easier than other administrations where ministers quite often act on their own and pursue their own agendas openly and it is much more difficult to hold the government as a whole to account.[73]

The Home Secretary noted elsewhere:

> ...if what officials were saying to ministers was going to be immediately available, then it would very seriously constrain what they could actually say and actually undermine the responsibility of ministers for their decisions. It would place officials in a political arena and make for much less efficient government.[74]

Under the draft Bill there is no right of appeal to the IC for a 'public interest' test, no right of access to factual as opposed to policy advice, and the policy information will be subject to the 30 - year rule. This is particularly worrying given recent ministerial pronouncements narrowing their sphere of responsibility to 'policy'.[75] Some internal discussions clearly demand confidentiality but once decisions have been taken the case for access is greater. This allows the public and Parliament to judge whether the implications of the policy have been properly considered, whether ministers have decided against the advice of their officials (therefore isolating responsibility on ministers and mitigating against blame shift) and whether potential objections have been addressed. The anticipation of such scrutiny would itself improve the quality of policy analysis and encourage greater rigour. Exposing the true complexity of an issue may also lead to a greater public understanding of the difficulties faced by government and the constraints within which ministers operate. There is evidence to support these arguments from the United States and New Zealand, where the post-decisional disclosure of information has become common.[76]

Following on from this, the draft Bill also provides no requirement for public authorities to account for their refusals to release information, nor does it provide the IC with the power to review the reasons adduced for the refusal.[77] This stands in stark contrast to the previous government's acceptance of the Public Service Committee's recommendation that a refusal to answer a parliamentary question should be accompanied by a statement of the grounds for the refusal.[78] As Sir Richard Scott noted:

> If no reasons are given there can be no worthwhile review and there will be no confidence that refusals are based on legitimate reasons, no confidence that refusals are not based on a desire for a quiet life and the avoidance of embarrassment.[79]

Once again the government's response to this criticism revolves around the need to uphold ministerial responsibility and the vaunted belief that parliamentary accountability is an effective mechanism of scrutiny. This sentiment is most clearly displayed in the area of enforcement.

The Bill establishes an IC to enforce the obligations placed on authorities under the Bill.[80] There will be two ways in which the Commissioner enforces the Bill's provisions. First, the IC can issue a practice recommendation to any public authority that is failing to follow one of the Codes of Practice issued by the Secretary of State or to conform to its own publication scheme made under clause 7 of the Bill. But the IC will have no direct coercive force. Second, if the IC believes a public authority has improperly withheld information, they may issue a decision notice. This requires the authority to reconsider its decision. In some circumstances the IC can order the disclosure of information, but such a decision could be subject to a ministerial veto or 'override'. Therefore, the final decision on the release of information lies with ministers and is bolstered by the power to create new exemptions to cover requests already received. The government insists that this is a trivial point, stressing that although the Commissioner cannot enforce disclosure they will have a very real influence and it is unlikely that a department would refuse to comply with an order.[81] Once again the government emphasises trust and precedent:

> The Commissioner will have a great deal of influence over what should and should not be released, particularly under the discretionary provisions. Plainly if a department like mine has already been in the business of releasing case worker instructions in the immigration and nationality department and we then (not that we would) seek to refuse to release similar documents in other fields, we are on the back foot to explain that, and quite rightly.[82]

Observers, however are not so sanguine. The government is stressing custom and practice rather than statutory obligation, a theme which runs throughout the draft Bill. But there is nothing to guarantee compliance. Even Elizabeth France, the current Data Protection Registrar who will become the first IC, has stated that without plenipotentiary powers her influence '...could prove more illusory than real'.[83] Yet the government's reasoning for maintaining the ministerial override is both perplexing and coherent. They argue that in a parliamentary democracy it was for ministers to be accountable to Parliament for identifying what was, or was not in the public interest in any particular instance; it was not something which could, or should, be delegated to an independent, and therefore effectively unaccountable official.[84]

> There are some suggestions that final arbiter of the public interest should be officials or should be a Commissioner. My view is that the public interest is quintessentially in a parliamentary democracy a matter for ministers to propose and then to explain themselves to the House of Commons.[85]

As Kim Howells MP, Minister of State at the DTI, noted: 'It is the minister who is paid to take those kinds of decisions about whether a department should release information or not'.[86] Not only does the government insist on the need for ministers to make the final decision as they are responsible to Parliament for that decision but Parliament is praised for its ability to enforce the responsibility of those ministers. For example, Jack Straw defended the draft Bill against international comparisons by stating:

> What is true here is that ministers are much more accountable than in most other administrations. People abroad are often amazed, for example, at the degree to which Prime Ministers and ministers are put on the spot. People may write risible things about Question Time, and sometimes those are deserved, but Americans who have this great freedom of information regime are astonished, absolutely astonished, that senior members of the executive routinely - not just to select committees - have to go before Parliament and explain themselves.[87]

The convention of ministerial responsibility, therefore, forms the foundation of a circular argument. The perception that ministers and Parliament have failed to deliver/enforce accountable government has fostered support for proposals that involve transferring decisions regarding deciding the 'public interest' away from ministers. This, however, would involve the transfer of power away from an individual bound by a problematic form of accountability to an individual who is not accountable at all. *Ergo* we return to the enduring quality of ministerial responsibility both in theory and practice. However, the argument that the maintenance of discretion is necessary to protect ministerial responsibility would be more persuasive if Chapter Three had found parliamentary accountability to be effective.

One interpretation of the drift from the white paper to the draft Bill might suggest a repositioning of the Labour government in relation to the competing interpretations of ministerial responsibility (as discussed in Chapter One). In essence, a transfer of allegiances from the Whig view of ministerial responsibility (stressing representation, openness, participation, etc.) to the Peelite view (emphasising stability, strong government, distance, etc.). The white paper approached the issue from a Whig perspective whereas the draft Bill embodied the Peelite view. There is an obvious link with the move from opposition to government and many commentators had feared that the longer the delay in introducing legislation the more cautious the government would become as it experienced the usual leaks and information disclosures.[88] Perhaps the most telling admission came from Kim Howells in evidence to the Public Administration Committee:

> I think it is fair to say - and since you are asking a brutal question I will give you a brutal answer - that I suspect that what very often looks very good in opposition and in the first flush of government, when it is tested hard against the practice of a government department like the DTI, one finds there are some difficult areas and some grey areas.[89]

The Labour government's approach to FOI, therefore, provides a neat illustration of a number of key issues and tensions that underpin this book's central thesis.

8.7 Conclusion

The decision to introduce FOI legislation in place of non-statutory codes of access involves a conscious decision regarding the balance and redistribution of power within a society.[90] The Labour government is committed to FOI in *principle* and yet it is increasingly aware of the political realities of introducing FOI in *practice*. The result of this tension is a hybrid act which seeks, in essence, to create a discretionary scheme of official control of public information in statutory form. In his evidence to the Public Administration Committee the Home Secretary repeatedly sought to recreate the idea of 'honourable secrecy'. Implicit in the government's rationale is the principle that decisions on disclosure rightly belong in the hands of ministers (and their officials) who could be trusted to use their discretion in the public interest. Yet incidents have undermined public trust in the propriety of ministers. Hence the support for FOI legislation that guarantees minimum standards, reduces the scope for ministerial discretion and introduces independent validation that the public interest has been served.

There is a clear trend running throughout the Bill that tends towards encouraging authorities to exercise their discretion liberally, rather than creating rights that can be used effectively by members of the public. The majority of commentators reject the view, tacit in the government's evidence, that because the United Kingdom has effective systems of political accountability (a view which is open to challenge) a different kind of FOI regime than elsewhere is somehow acceptable.[91] Some amendments to the draft Bill have been made in response to the Public Administration Committee's recommendations[92] and the need to bring the proposals in line with European law.[93] While these have dealt with some minor issues the most important areas (particularly enforcement and policy related information) have not been rebalanced away from the discretionary power of ministers.[94]

The Freedom of Information Bill faced five backbench revolts during its Commons report stage (4 and 5 April 2000). An all-party group of MPs tabled a number of amendments to strengthen the bill in favour of disclosure. None of the amendments was successful, but the Home Secretary did, under intense pressure, offer some concessions to the bill's critics. He undertook to amend the bill to make it clear that only a Cabinet minister or the Attorney-General (but not junior ministers) could exercise the veto; to require some form of collective consultation within the Cabinet before a veto was issued (possibly writing this requirement into the Ministerial Code); to amend the bill to prevent quangos from being able to veto disclosure requirements in their own right but having to acquire ministerial approval; and to reconsider whether a veto should be available to local authorities. Although these changes would make the veto slightly more difficult to exercise, critics are still unhappy with its existence and scope. Moreover, while the Home Secretary is willing to consider curbing the powers of quangos and local authorities, he is unwilling to fetter the dominant position of ministers. Throughout the process ministers have conceded minor amendments, but these have dealt with some relatively nugatory issues, while the most important areas (particularly enforcement and policy-related information) have not been rebalanced away from the discretionary power of ministers.

When the Freedom of Information Bill had its second reading in the Lords on 20 April 2000 the debate suggested that the bill's passage through the second chamber would not be smooth. Indeed, a large number of significant amendments had been tabled. The government was facing the prospect of being defeated in the Lords by an all-party alliance, including the Conservatives, which were ready to force through substantial improvements or lose the bill altogether. However, the Liberal Democrats were accused of ruining cross-party efforts to improve the Bill when they unexpectedly agreed to support the government in return for four minor amendments.[95] Maurice Frankel, Director of the Campaign for Freedom of Information stated:

> We find it incomprehensible that, in return for these modest concessions, the Liberal Democrats are proposing to abandon their support for essential amendments which would have given the public greater rights...This means the weak Freedom of Information Bill will become law with all its serious defects intact.[96]

The agreement with the Liberal Democrats meant the government was safe from defeat and the Freedom of Information Act received Royal Assent on 30 November 2000, although it is not expected to come into force for central government until April 2002.

This chapter examined the evolution of the Freedom of Information Act and the extent to which its contents will improve the means by which the full discharge by the executive of their accountability obligations can be obtained and, if necessary, enforced. It concludes that the Act, as it stands, represents little more than a statement of good intentions rather than freedom of information. This conclusion has a number of ramifications for this book. It demonstrates that the position of Parliament and the responsibility of ministers to Parliament remain central aspects of the British constitution. The fact that it is the executive which champions ministerial responsibility to Parliament as an effective mechanism of scrutiny is critical. It reveals the executive morality and reflects the balance of power in the Whitehall-Westminster model. A far-reaching FOI regime would have radical implications for a constitutional convention which serves the executive well. Accordingly, the act has been designed within a framework which theoretically fulfils the party's manifesto commitment whilst maintaining the executive's dominant position.

And yet there is merit in the argument that transferring power from ministers to other constitutional actors might further diffuse responsibility and undermine Parliament. In a parliamentary state power resides in Parliament; that is why Parliament matters. The answer to concerns regarding the (ir)responsibility of ministers can only be solved, therefore, by making parliamentary accountability more effective. This goal is often seen as being frustrated by the executive's majority in Parliament; but this study has identified clear trends, anomalies and issues which may well produce a new agenda for the responsibility of the core executive in the United Kingdom. For example, the introduction of separate FOI legislation in Scotland, which is likely to be far stronger than the Westminster regime, may expose and undermine the rationale and arguments outlined above. These emerging agendas will be the topic of the next and concluding chapter.

Notes

[1] Cabinet Office (1998 2nd ed.) *Code of Practice on Access to Government Information*. See also Cabinet Office (1997 2nd ed.) *Code of Practice on Access to Government Information Guidance on Interpretation*.

[2] Cm 3818 (1997) *Your Right To Know - The Government's Proposals for a Freedom of Information Act* HMSO, London.

[3] Cm 4355 (1999) *Freedom of Information: Consultation on Draft Legislation*, HMSO, London.

[4] I have in mind the government supported Private Member's Bills including: Chris Smith's *Environment and Safety Information Act 1988;* Archie Kirkwood's *Access to Personal Files Act 1987* and *Access to Medical Records Act 1987;* Robin Squire's *Local Government Access to Information Act 1985;* and Doug Henderson's *Access to Health Records Act 1990*.

[5] See Tant, A (1990) 'The Campaign for Freedom of Information: A Participatory Challenge to Elitist British Government' *Public Administration* Vol.68 pp.477-491.

[6] HC 398 *Your Right to Know: The Government's Proposals for a Freedom of Information Act* Third Report of the Select Committee for Public Administration, Session 1997/98, HMSO, London; HC 1020 *Government Response to the Third Report from the Select Committee on Public Administration (Session 1997-98) on Your Right to Know: The Government's Proposals for a Freedom of Information Act* Fourth Special Report by the Public Administration Committee, Session 1997/98, HMSO, London; HC 570 *Freedom of Information Draft Bill* Third Report by the Public Administration Committee, Session 1998/99, HMSO, London.

[7] As Sir Richard Scott noted: 'If the public could be brought to accept that information held by government could not and would not be withheld simply because disclosure would be embarrassing, I believe that public mistrust of government and cynicism about government explanations might begin to ebb. An effective Freedom of Information Act would, I think, play an important part in that process'. HC 570-I (1998/99) p.xxiii.

8   For example, see HC 398-I (1997/98) Memorandum of Evidence submitted by the Home Office p.120 part. 2 paras. 4-8.
9   The forecasted costs of introducing an FOI regime in the United Kingdom are outlined in Annex L. See also, Guida, R (1989) 'The Cost of Free Information' *The Public Interest* No.97 pp.87-95; Cabinet Office (1998) *Your Right to Know - Background Material* pp.57-58 para. 172.
10 An issue which has been highlighted in relation to parliamentary questions. See HC 820 *Ministerial Accountability and Parliamentary Questions* Fourth Report by the Public Administration Committee, Session 1997/98, HMSO, London. paras. 14-15; House of Commons Library (1997) *The Code of Practice on Access to Official Information* Research Paper 97/69 Chapter IV 'The Code of Practice and Accountability to Parliament' pp.33-38; Woodhouse, D (1997) 'Ministerial Responsibility: Something Old, Something New' *Public Law* pp.262-282; Oliver, D (1998) 'Freedom of Information and Ministerial Accountability' *Public Law* pp.171-176.
11 See Annex J for a comparative analysis.
12 Cm 2290 (1993) *Open Government* HMSO, London. Cabinet Office (1994) *Code of Practice on Access to Official Information.*
13 For a full discussion of the background to the Code, see House of Commons Library (1997) *The Code of Practice on Access to Official Information* Research Paper 97/69.
14 HC 84 *Open Government* Second Report by the Select Committee on the Parliamentary Commissioner for Administration, Session 1995/96, HMSO, London. para.78.
15 Cabinet Office (1994 revised Nov. 1998) *Code of Practice on Access to Government Information* Annex 8.1.
16 Cabinet Office (1994 revised Nov. 1998) *Code of Practice on Access to Government Information* Annex 8.2.
17 Although there have been problems with the Open Government monitoring system. See Cabinet Office (1997) *Open Government - Code on Access to Government Information 1996 Report* paras. 15-21 pp.3-4. The Home Office Openness Officer disclosed that sometimes requests for information which did not specifically mention the Code were registered under the monitoring system whilst on other occasions they were not. Interview with the author February 1998. Officially all requests for information, whether they mention the Code or not, are supposed to be treated as Code requests (see HC 398-I [1997/98] Q5). Home Office officials admitted this was not the case and those mentioning the Code were 'fast-tracked' and given more attention.

18. Home Office (1999) *Code of Practice on Access to Official Information - 1998 Report* p.4. These figures do not include the 20,056 applications made to the Planning Inspectorate.
19. HC 845 *Annual Report for 1997-98* Parliamentary Commissioner for Administration, HMSO, London. paras. 6.4 - 6.5.
20. Cabinet Office (1998) *Open Government - Code on Access to Government Information 1997 Report* para. 21 p.5. See also Foster, C (1998) 'Interview with David Clark' *Parliamentary Brief* March pp.18-19.
21. See House of Commons Library (1997) *The Accountability Debate: Codes of Guidance and Questions of Procedure for Ministers* Research Paper 97/5.
22. Weir, S & Hall, W (1994) *Extra-Governmental Organisations in the United Kingdom and their Accountability* Democratic Audit Paper No.2 (London : Charter 88). See also: House of Commons Library (1994) *Quangos and Non-Departmental Bodies* Research Paper 94/67.
23. See, Cabinet Office (1997) 'Opening Up Quangos'; Cabinet Office (1998) 'Quangos: Opening the Doors' p.12 paras. 30-31.
24. HC 570 *Freedom of Information Draft Bill* Third Report by the Public Administration Committee, Session 1998/99, HMSO, London. p.146-147 paras. 57-63.
25. This history of Labour's commitment to Freedom of Information is well documented at web page - www.cfoi.org.uk/labcmits.htmc.
26. Liberal MP Clement Freud won a place on the Private Members' Ballot and decided to introduce a Bill to reform section 2 of the Official Secrets Act and introduce Freedom of Information legislation. The proposals had been designed by the Outer Circle Policy Unit and had all party support. Throughout the 1980s and 1990s the Labour party supported a number of Private Members Bill's on FOI. For example, those of Archy Kirkwood in 1991 (Bill 22 of 1991/92) and Mark Fisher's 'Right To Know' Bill in 1993 (Bill 18 of 1992/93).
27. For a short account of the politics of Freedom of Information throughout the 1970s see Ponting, C (1985) *The Right to Know: The Inside Story of the Belgrano Affair* (London : Sphere) pp.43-70. For a more extensive history see Birkinshaw, P (1988) *Freedom of Information: The Law, the Practice and the Ideal* (London : Weidenfeld & Nicolson). Merlyn Rees, whilst Home Secretary, told back bench protesters that: '...only one, two or three of your constituents would be interested'. Quoted in Robertson, G 'A Triumph for Sir Humphrey' *The New Statesman* 6/3/98 p.24.
28. Quoted in Ponting, C (1985) *The Right to Know: The Inside Story of the Belgrano Affair* (London : Sphere) p.66.

[29] See Law Reform Commission (1995) *Open Government: A Review of the Federal Freedom of Information Act 1982* (Canberra : Australian Law Reform Commission).
[30] See Article 19 (1990) *Freedom of Information and Expression in Canada* (London : Article 19).
[31] See Eagles, I, Taggart, M & Liddell, G (1992) *Freedom of Information in New Zealand* (Aukland : Oxford University Press); McDonald, A & Terrill, G (1998) 'Open Government in New Zealand' in McDonald, A & Terrill, G (eds.) *Open Government: Freedom of Information and Privacy* (Basingstoke : Macmillan).
[32] Australia in March, Canada in June and New Zealand in December.
[33] *Report of the Joint Consultative Committee on Constitutional Reform* (1997) para. 27. See Birkinshaw, P & Parkin, A (1999) 'Freedom of Information' in Blackburn, R & Plant, R (eds.) *Constitutional Reform: The Labour Government's Constitutional Reform Agenda* (London : Longman) p.173.
[34] Wilson, D 'Whatever happened to Freedom of Information legislation?' *New Statesman & Society* Vol.126 25/7/97 p.27; Hazell, R (1998) 'Freedom of information takes time' *Review* No.1 May pp.13-14. David Clark resisted pressure to take the 'short cut option' and simply enact the Code of Practice on Access to Government Information into legislation. See HC 398-I (1997/98) p.15 Q80.
[35] Cabinet Office 'Commitment to Freedom of Information and More Open Government Reaffirmed' Press Notice 14/5/98.
[36] Cabinet Office 'Record Number of Draft Bills to be Published - Ann Taylor' Press Notice 22/5/98.
[37] 'Act to lift veil of secrecy' *The Guardian* 10/12/97.
[38] Cm 3818 (1997). See also, Cabinet Office (1998) *Your Right to Know - Background Material*.
[39] HC 398 (1997/98) para.1.
[40] 'The Canadian statute has rightly been seen as being in the forefront of enlightened Right to Know laws. Canada's once brave state-of-the-art Access to Information Act is being left behind by Britain, of all countries, the mother not only of Parliaments but the culture of bureaucratic secrecy. To be bypassed by some recent provincial access regimes in Canada is one thing. But by the nation that raised secrecy to an art form, that produced Yes Minister and Sir Humphrey's Law? That is the cruellest cut of all. It is flattering that the Cabinet minister responsible for the Labour Government's blueprint for a freedom of information law made Canada and the Information Commissioner's Office his first port of call. But he has left Canada trailing in the dust.' Information Commissioner of Canada, (1998) *Annual Report 1997/98*.

41   Hazell, R (1989) 'Freedom of Information in Australia, Canada and New Zealand' *Public Administration* Vol.67 p.196.
42   HC 18-IV *Right to Know Bill* House of Commons, Session 1992/93, HMSO, London. See Hansard, HC Debs. 19/2/93 cols. 583-654.
43   Under section 11(3) of the *Parliamentary Commissioner Act 1967* ministers have the power to prevent the disclosure of information by the PCA. See Woodhouse, D (1997) *In Pursuit of Good Administration: Ministers, Civil Servants and Judges* (Oxford : Oxford University Press) pp.80-85.
44   Para. 5.14. The Canadian Information Commissioner has encountered several cases of deliberate destruction of records by administrators and has called for penalties for those who deliberately frustrate applications. See Information Commissioner of Canada *Annual Report 1996-97*.
45   Richard Shepherd's private members' Bill. On whistleblowing see Cabinet Office (1998) *Your Right to Know - Background Material* p.19 paras. 46-48.
46   Cm 3818 (1997) para. 1.9 p.3.
47   Constitution Unit (1998) *Commentary on the White Paper on Freedom of Information* (London : Constitution Unit).
48   Elliott, V 'Lord Chancellor heads off secrecy critics' *The Times* 3/7/98 p.2; 'Straw to weaken code on freedom' *The Times* 12/1/99.
49   Home Office (1999) *Code of Practice on Access to Official Information - 1998 Report* p.1 para.4. See also, Home Office 'Government Sets Out Plans for Draft Bill on Freedom of Information' Press Notice 29/9/98.
50   Interview with the author, July 1999.
51   Cm 4355 (1999). See Hansard, HC Debs. 24/5/99 col. 21.
52   See HC 570-I (1998/99) p.3 Q4. See also: 'Sorry, limited information is available' *The Guardian* 28/5/98; 'Salute to Secrecy' *Financial Times* 28/5/98; 'The Right to say nothing' *The Times* 1/6/98; 'The final triumph of all the butchers and the whisperers' *The Guardian* 25/5/98.
53   Campaign Press Release, 24/5/99.
54   See Annex K 'A Comparative Perspective on Exemptions under Freedom of Information Acts'.
55   The Directive added: '...that when policy studies were being undertaken in future the background material should as far as possible be written in a form which would permit it to be published separately, in the minimum of alteration, once a ministerial decision to do so had been taken'. The text of the Directive is given at Hansard, HC Debs. WA 26/1/78 cols. 691-4 26/1/78. The Croham Directive was judged to be 'ineffective' by the Select Committee on the Parliamentary Commissioner for Administration. See HC 84 (1995/96).
56   Cm 4355 (1999) pp.1-3.
57   Cmnd 7520 (1979) *Open Government*; Cm 2290 (1993) *Open Government*.

58 HC 570-I (1998/99) p.xxv.
59 Cm 4310 (1999) *Modernising Government* HMSO, London. Ch. 2 'Policy Making' particularly para.6.
60 HC 570 (1998/99) p.xx para.15.
61 See HC 831 *Government Response to the Third Report from the Select Committee on Public Administration (Session 1998/99) on the Freedom of Information Draft Bill* Fifth Special Report by the Public Administration Committee, Session 1998/99, HMSO, London. p.2. See also, HC 925 *Freedom of Information Draft Bill: The Committee's Response to the Home Office Reply* Session 1998/99, HMSO, London.
62 'He [Jack Straw] is saying "Never mind what appear to be flaws in the enforceability of this draft legislation such is our commitment to its principles that ministers will always seek the high ground"...should we not legislate for scoundrels and rogues? There are no scoundrels and rogues in this government, but if, by some mischance, another government took our place then it would, no doubt, be packed with them and this legislation provides them with a charter to withhold information. Are you saying that this legislation should not be a lot tougher than it is in order to ensure that scoundrels and rogues are obliged to perform to the same high standards.' HC 570-VII (1998/99) pp.140-141 (Mr Peter Bradley).
63 HC 570-I (1998/99) p.6 Q23.
64 HC 570-I (1998/99) p.194 Q1012.
65 If a future government believed the current FOI regime to be too liberal they could theoretically amend the legislation accordingly. However, it is likely that this would prove deeply unpopular with the public; therefore highlighting the importance of a less discretionary based FOI Bill to prevent substantial executive reinterpretation without recourse to Parliament.
66 Section 44(7) states: 'A public authority shall not be required by virtue of this section to furnish the Commissioner with any information if the furnishing of that information would, by revealing the evidence to the Commissioner of any offence other than an offence under this Act, expose the authority to proceedings for that offence'.
67 See, Scott, R, Barbuk, I & Ecclestone, A (1996) *Is Public Access to Civil Service Policy Advice Possible?* (London : Campaign for Freedom of Information); Legg, B (1994) *Civil Service Reform: The Case For More Radicalism* (London : European Policy Forum). One former Permanent Secretary, Lord Burns, noted the changing context to the Public Administration Committee: 'I think you have to be prepared to recognise nowadays that whatever it is that you may be doing, whatever advice you give, whatever papers you write, there is a significant chance that it will find

its way into the open and you behave accordingly'. HC 570-I (1998/99) p.liii para.83.
68   HC 570-II (1998/99) Evidence by Mr Jonathan Baume, General Secretary of the First Division Association, p.39 Q174.
69   Clause 28(1)(a) states: 'Information held by a government department is exempt information if it relates to...the formulation or development of government policy'.
70   Clause 28(4)(a).
71   The Home Office consultation paper accompanying the draft Bill cites examples of information that the government has released voluntarily, including: the economic analysis behind the policies set out in the [DTI's] white paper 'Our Competitive Future'; the government response to consultation on the green paper 'A Fair Deal for Consumers' [which] contained analysis of the policy decisions; and papers relating to the work of the Advisory Group on Openness in the Public Sector. The consultation paper comments:'The Bill, if enacted, will give the public the *right* to this kind of information. No longer will information be provided only at the discretion of the public authority'. (Cm 4355 paras.5-6). This is highly misleading. All these examples fall squarely within the policy formulation exemption. There will be no *right* of access to any of them under the Bill.
72   Cm 4310 (1999), Ch. 2.
73   HC 570-XII (1998/99) Evidence by Mr Jack Straw MP, p.194 Q1010.
74   Interview with the Home Secretary in *The Stakeholder*, Vol.2 No.6 January-February 1999.
75   Flinders, M (1996) *Enforcing Ministerial 'Policy' Responsibility - The Missing Link in the Chain?* (Sheffield : PERC).
76   The New Zealand Law Commission has reported that: 'Since 1982 [when FOI was introduced] there has been a fundamental change in attitudes to the availability of official information. Ministers and officials have learned to live with much greater openness. The assumption that policy advice will eventually be released under the Act has in our view improved the quality and transparency of that advice'. Law Commission (1997) *Review of the Official Information Act 1982* (Law Commission : New Zealand) p.5. In the United States it is common to develop 'policy records' which are released into the public domain once a final decision is taken. See Lewis, N (1995) 'Responsibility in Government: The Strange Case of the UK' *European Public Law* Vol.1 No.3 pp.371-93.
77   The Code of Practice on Access to Government Information explicitly requires authorities (at part 1, para.3 (iii)) to: 'give reasons for administrative decisions to those affected'. The white paper Your Right to Know stated the FOI Act would establish a similar duty (at para. 2.18).

78   See HC 313 *Ministerial Accountability and Responsibility* Second Report of the Public Service Committee, Session 1996/97, HMSO. London; HC 67 *Government Response to the 2nd Report from the Committee (Session 1995-96) on Ministerial Responsibility and Accountability* First Special Report by the Public Service Select Committee, Session 1996/97, HMSO, London.
79   HC 570-I (1998/99) p.xxxi para.42.
80   This role will be combined with that of the Data Protection Commissioner under the Data Protection Act 1998.
81   Kim Howells MP, Minister of State at the DTI, noted: 'The arrangements are the right ones at the moment, I think. It is going to be very difficult, I think, for any minister to turn down a very firm recommendation from the Commissioner that information should be released, and it will become more difficult, not easier, as a body of experience and case law builds up'. HC 570-VII (1998/99) p.143 Q765.
82   HC 570-I (1998/99) p.4 Q7.
83   HC 570-II (1998/99) p.21 para.6.5.
84   There is however an important precedent which involves the final decision on the disclosure of information being transferred from ministers. I have in mind the examination of Public Interest Immunity Certificates (PIIs) by the courts. The courts can overturn the certificate should they feel disclosure is in the public interest.
85   Jack Straw MP HC 570-XII (1998/99) p.192 Q1007, Q1022.
86   HC 570-VII (1998/99) p.144 Q773.
87   Jack Straw MP HC 570-XII (1998/99) p.193 Q1009. See also HC 570-I (1998/99) p.12 Q45.
88   In light of these concerns Lord Lucas introduced a Private Member's Bill into the House of Lords, the 'Freedom of Information Bill', based largely on the white paper. The Bill received a second reading on 10 February 1999 but made no further progress. See Campaign for Freedom of Information (1999) *Notes on the Freedom of Information Bill Introduced by Lord Lucas* (London : Campaign for Freedom of Information).
89   HC 570-VII (1998/99) p.135 Q721.
90   'It is important to recognise that the issue of Open Government is about power, political power, a shift in power, its redistribution. Open government entails increasing publication of official information to the press and to the public who, with the power given by the greater knowledge of the activities of government, are better able to assess, criticise and bring pressure to bear on the government's performance'. Lord Franks (1979) 'Disclosure and the Law' Civil Service College Working Paper No.5 quoted in Cornford, J (1988) 'Official Secrecy and Freedom of Information' in Holmes, R &

Elliot, M (eds.) *1688-1988 Time For a New Constitution* (Basingstoke : Macmillan) p.165.
[91] HC 570-I (1998/99) p.xxxv para.3.
[92] HC 831 (1998/99). See Evans, R 'Climbdown on secrecy: Straw to offer concessions over FOI in wake of fierce criticism' *The Guardian* 11/10/99 p.1.
[93] Hencke, D 'Straw forced into new openness on environment' *The Guardian* 2/11/99 p.2.
[94] Sherman, J 'Straw fails to placate critics' *The Times* 28/10/99 p.19.
[95] See, Kite, M "Lib-Dems 'caved in on secrecy'" *The Times* 15/11/00 p.14.
[96] The Campaign for Freedom of Information 'Anger at Liberal Democrat decision to back flawed information Bill' press release 13/11/00.

9 Understanding the Politics of Accountability

9.1 Introduction

This book has examined the enduring centrality of ministerial responsibility within the British constitution. It addresses the question of whether alternative models of accountability have evolved in the central state to remedy the shortcomings commonly identified with ministerial responsibility to Parliament. Much of the existing literature focuses on the relationship between ministers and Parliament and overlooks the degree to which alternative models of accountability have evolved. However, this study concludes that the alternative models **do not** fill the vacuum of responsible government created by the deficiencies of ministerial responsibility. The convention of ministerial responsibility to Parliament remains fundamental to the British constitution; not least because through their *de facto* control of the convention the executive can control the degree to which these alternative models develop. Consequently Parliament matters.

Section 9.2 of this chapter outlines the main findings and implications of this study for each of the models examined. Assumptions are then presented that consider the degree to which it is possible to extrapolate the findings of this research beyond the Home Office. The issue of methodological transferability is then discussed in relation to future research agendas. This study has demonstrated how the responsibility of the core executive is a complex and dynamic process. In the light of this the second part of this chapter outlines a number of emerging agendas which may have a significant impact on ministerial responsibility. These include the notion of risk, the challenges of holistic government, technological developments, innovations in political machinery, the constitutional reform agenda and the evolving state. The chapter concludes by pulling all these issues together by discussing the omnipotent link between the convention of ministerial responsibility and power in the modern state. As Chapter One demonstrated, although concerns regarding its practical adequacy are longstanding the convention of ministerial responsibility has continued to occupy a central position in the British constitution. Through legitimating parliamentary sovereignty the convention has reinforced the boundaries of power and action within the state. However, it is suggested that the malleability of the convention has been exhausted and a critical historical and political juncture has been reached.

The structures of the state have changed from standardised hierarchies to a heterogeneity of public, private and voluntary bodies working in flexible and not very transparent networks at supranational, national and sub-national levels. Therefore the concept of accountability highlights the challenge of creating linkages between democratic controls and new practices of management which transcend governmental, institutional and national borders.[1] As a result the position of ministerial responsibility is likely to be radically reconstituted.

9.2 Research Findings and Future Research Agendas

9.2.1 Political Accountability

This research suggests that the wider concerns regarding the utility of parliamentary accountability via the convention of individual ministerial responsibility are valid. This conclusion, in itself, is unlikely to surprise observers, yet this research has captured the contemporary situation while also highlighting a number of key issues, tensions and themes which have been overlooked by the wider literature - each of which merits further research. First, although the variance between the theory and practice of Parliament's capacity to scrutinise the executive is acute it is clear that the core executive does not approach Parliament with impudence. The processes and mechanisms of parliamentary oversight still condition the beliefs, attitudes and behaviour of ministers and officials.[2] However, the executive morality, which is conditioned by the adversarial configuration of the House, emphasises defensiveness. Hence the propensity of interviewees to describe parliamentary accountabity as 'a game'. A game which, due to the executive's majority party support, is rarely played on a level playing field.

This brings us to a second issue - the significance attached to 'subtle' and 'informal' accountability processes during my research is intriguing. The suggestion that these processes deliver a greater degree of information and explanation is based on the presupposition that these mechanisms are somehow removed from the vulgarities of party warfare within the House. Indeed, it was suggested that their use is bound by a parliamentary convention regarding the information divulged. I concluded that these processes undermined parliamentary accountability as the information was not placed on the record; nor should we be grateful that ministers decide to answer questions later that they failed to answer during a select committee session. Nevertheless, there are a number of issues arising from this topic that deserve further examination. These issues include an analysis of the replies to MPs' written correspondence compared with replies to the same questions being tabled in the House. It has also become apparent that the constitutional dichotomy between government and opposition is too simplistic. The relationship between the executive and its parliamentary party is crucial if ministers are to retain the support of the House. It might therefore be suggested that 'party accountability' forms a central component of ministerial responsibility to the House. Norton noted 'A government sometimes encounters more critical scrutiny from its own members than from other members of the House'.[3] And yet the mechanisms and procedures on which this relationship is founded have not been the subject of extensive research.[4] Consequently, a research project which examined the links between the executive and the various thematic Labour backbench committees would provide a valuable and innovative contribution to the wider literature. An awareness of 'formal' and 'informal' procedures of parliamentary accountability also occasions a consideration that their combined impact may in some circumstances be problematic.

The third issue for consideration and further research therefore revolves around the pathological impact of accountability demands on certain government bodies. My research suggests that the formal volume of parliamentary interest, measured in parliamentary questions or select committee coverage, may not reflect the true scale of attention. The impact of unofficial parliamentary contact, via correspondence, may exert a considerably greater demand. Moreover, agencies that receive a relatively low level of formal parliamentary interest may, in fact, be subject to significant attention. The impact of these pressures, in addition to a consideration of the demands of the other models of accountability, underlines the fact that certain government bodies operate within a dense network of accountability processes.

With regard to the formal processes of parliamentary accountability my research indicates that the balance of power within the House usually acts to negate their utility. Consequently they are at their most virulent when the minister has lost the support of their party rather than the House. An issue which has escaped empirical research to date revolves around the role of the select committee chairperson. Evidence from the Home Affairs Select Committee suggests that the chairperson's position allows them to dominate proceedings and therefore the degree to which they can impose parliamentary oversight on their departmental portfolio. Research questions might examine the values and perspectives of the committee chairperson, the degree to which the chairperson have moulded the work of their respective committees, the views of committee members concerning the chairmen and, critically, the processes through which committee chairs are selected, appointed and removed. The final and probably most worrying aspect to emerge from this research was the parliamentary apathy concerning ministerial responsibility. Although backbench MPs preferred to use the term 'realism' few thought that internal parliamentary reform could ever adjust the balance of power within the House.

9.2.2 Judicial Accountability

The discussion of the judicial model of accountability in Chapter Four stressed that it was important exactly because it was external to Parliament and free from party political pressures. However, research within the Home Office, as outlined in Chapter Five, placed the extent and capacity of judicial accountability in perspective. Although the Home Office is by far the biggest recipient of judicial review challenges they remain sporadic and peripheral. As Ann Widdecombe noted: '...it is a very weak form of accountability, it rarely involves ministers and is rarely more than an irritation'.[5] The courts continue to be deferential to Parliament in key areas while the media has overemphasised atypical cases and the pronouncements of a small minority of the senior judiciary. Uncertainty is the main problem with judicial review, both for plaintiffs and defendants. As a result ministers and officials have little choice but to develop policies while waiting to see if a challenge will be mounted in the courts. However to define this as 'firefighting', as some commentators have suggested, underestimates the complex and ambiguous legal environment in which public policy is currently formulated. Judicial inquiries suffer from the fact that they are not completely independent from the political processes that create them. They are created by and report to the executive and not Parliament. While they may identify responsible ministers it is only Parliament that can enforce ministerial responsibility.

Research within the Home Office indicates that it is in the sphere of Europe that the relationship between judicial oversight and ministerial responsibility is likely to become increasingly significant. The incorporation of the European Convention of Human Rights (ECHR) marks a radical transfer of power from the executive to the judiciary. It is symptomatic of the *ad hoc* and atheoretical nature of the British constitution that this potentially radical shift in power has been instituted within an increasingly problematic framework of ministerial responsibility. Ministerial capacity to exercise personal control over swathes of their portfolios will continue to diminish as a consequence of European integration. This will not only alter the role of ministers but also focus attention on the accountability of supranational bodies. The case of the European Union may demonstrate that supranational institution building based on a national formula risks reproducing many of the accountability problems that exist at the national level, but with an extra dimension - finding the right balance between national and supranational democracy. At the same time it will be interesting to monitor the number of cases being decided against the government in the domestic courts and the executive's response to declarations on incompatibility in light of incorporation of the ECHR.

9.2.3 Managerial Accountability

The link between new public management and processes of accountability has not received the attention it deserves. This study and particularly the case study of the relationship between the Home Office and the Prison Service has been useful in demonstrating the tensions and challenges involved in instituting new channels of accountability within an environment permeated by the norms and processes of political accountability. Critically it has demonstrated that accountability processes within the core executive are ad hoc in spite of the fact that new public management implies a systematic and comprehensive approach to government which is quite unrealistic. The framework document has not been able to clarify responsibilities satisfactorily, and there is no guarantee that ministers will abide by even the clearest boundaries. Managerial accountability does not and cannot replace ministerial responsibility. Conversely, it makes effective parliamentary scrutiny more important to monitor devolved management, prevent ministerial blame shift and compel the executive to release information. It is, however, possible to suggest that managerial accountability actually makes blame shift harder, while the controversy surrounding certain agencies makes it harder for ministers to disclaim residual responsibility. The research has also demonstrated how the imposition of managerial accountability may frustrate the government's wider objectives, particularly cross-departmental interagency work and reducing risk aversion.

The Prison Service suffers from a surfeit of accountability mechanisms. Research suggests that managerialism has increased the Home Office's capacity for internal accountability. This, again, adds a new dimension to debates regarding the degree to which organisations are accountable and to whom. Internal accountability also illustrates many of the challenges and unintended consequences which Chapter Six stressed. In particular, the growth and impact of audit processes may well nullify the managerial flexibility that devolution was intended to deliver - while also creating a considerable regulatory bureaucracy that negates the efficiency savings of new public management. Contracting out clearly stretches the realistic scope of ministerial responsibility, but the case study did not generate evidence of a restriction or lessening of the Home Secretary's scope for intervention. The contracted out prisons seem to offer both increased accountability and efficiency which forces a reconsideration of the mutuality of the concepts. However, the contracted out prison estate does present an obstacle to the government's modernisation agenda, particularly in relation to commercial confidentiality and the spread of best practice. It also reflects the latent challenges which are presented by the evolving state. A future Home Secretary may well adopt a narrower interpretation of ministerial responsibility which may not include the contracted out sector. Contracted out prisons, a sector that may enlarge considerably, simply by their existence create the potentiality for ministers to question the extent of their responsibility and the actions necessary to satisfy the obligations of ministerial responsibility.

9.2.4 Future Research

This research has highlighted the fluidity of accountability as a concept within the British state. It has designed and applied a methodological framework based around three models of accountability and this permits a pluralistic analysis. The enhancement of such understanding has driven the analysis in this book. The scope of the models is broad. However, the framework is a useful analytical tool that allows for cross-comparative research within and between departments. The terminology of 'models' of accountability is not one that is employed in the existing literature. Furthermore, the efficacy of these models has not previously been examined via case study analysis. The framework does, moreover, highlight the range and options for accountability processes. Each of the models is constructed on varying theoretical foundations which, in turn, make different assumptions about the right to call to account, the mechanisms by which accountability is to be delivered and the standards of performance to be achieved. The models are not, however, mutually exclusive categories. Rather they perform complementary functions (at least in theory) and may well coexist within the same accountability relationships.

The analysis of various models and processes of accountability has been particularly useful in highlighting that the concept of accountability has a range of objectives. Aucoin and Heintzman posit three such goals: the control of abuse and corruption of power; assurance that public resources are being used in accordance with publicly stated intentions; and the improvement of efficiency and effectiveness.[6] Pollitt adds a fourth - the enhancement of the legitimacy of government.[7] Whatever the contextual priorities, there is, potentially at least, the possibility of some tension between these different goals. Chapter One suggested that increasing weight had been placed on the achievement of the second and third objectives in the 1980s and 1990s leading to a repositioning of emphasis on the first and fourth objectives in recent years. The benefit of this pluralistic analysis is the demonstration that different accountability models and systems can be applied depending on which objective(s) are given priority. It has illustrated that there are many difficult tradeoffs and balances to be struck in the design and implementation of structures of accountability, not least because accountability models structure relationships. Accountability, therefore, is not simply about limiting power in any absolute sense, it may also be a means of channelling power and making its exercise more effective and legitimate.

Despite interviews being conducted in a range of departments, without extensive research it is difficult to extrapolate my findings in the Home Office in anything more than the most general terms. Nevertheless, it is clear from the wider literature that the problems of parliamentary accountability are neither new nor applicable only to the Home Office. It is only in identifying new tensions and challenges that originality can be delivered. The Home Office is by far the most common recipient of judicial challenge. Therefore it can be assumed that the impact of judicial accountability will only be found to a lesser extent in other departments. Due to the nature of the responsibilities of the Home Office it is also possible to forecast that the ramifications of the ECHR will be felt most heavily within this department. It is also conceivable that some of the issues in relation to the managerial model, and particularly the relationship between the department and the agency, exist between other departments and their agencies - the relationship between the Child Support Agency or the Benefits Agency and the Department for Social Security, for example.[8]

Therefore a future research programme might involve applying the same methodological framework to other departments to create a comparative perspective. Alternatively, each model could be applied in isolation to various departments. The evolving nature of the different models, and subtle changes of emphasis, could be observed through a longitudinal study that reapplied the models to case study departments over time. However, it is likely that the framework would need refinement, not least due to a number of emerging agendas which may have fundamental ramifications for the responsibility of the core executive.

9.3 Emerging Agendas for the Responsibility of the Core Executive

In line with the British constitution the convention of ministerial responsibility evolves in light of changing circumstances. This study has examined how the tensions and strains within the convention have been augmented as it has been applied to an institutional structure which increasingly deviates away from the model around which the convention was established. Moreover, the study has concluded that alternative models of accountability have not evolved to remedy the ailments of political accountability. Thus ministerial responsibility remains central to the British constitution as the guarantor of responsible government while trembling under the pressures imposed by the differentiated state.[9] This section argues that these pressures are likely to increase significantly in the short term. There are a number of emerging agendas for the responsibility of the core executive that will further undermine and weaken ministerial responsibility. These agendas are interlinked and mutually reinforcing, involving: the concept of risk; the pressures of 'joined up' government; technological developments; innovations in political machinery; the paradoxes of constitutional reform; and the evolving state.

9.3.1 Risk

More often than not the convention of ministerial responsibility facilitates the distribution of blame rather than credit in the British political system. This has important ramifications for the outlook of ministers and officials. Credit is rare while minor mistakes may well create major parliamentary and public disquiet.[10] As Sir Richard Wilson noted, "We live in an age when the media and Parliament are not very tolerant of people who make mistakes, when the cry 'who was to blame' goes up in seconds when something goes wrong".[11] Hence, officials place more emphasis on avoiding mistakes and protecting their minister than adopting innovative and potentially efficient practices. This defensive disposition is preserved through civil service training, formalised in codes of conduct and reinforced by the adversarial nature of the House. As the 1999 *Modernising Government* white paper states:

> Risk Aversion: the cultures of Parliament, ministers and civil servants create a situation in which the rewards for success are limited and penalties for failure can be severe. The system is too often risk averse. As a result, ministers and civil servants can be too slow to take advantage of new opportunities.[12]

It has been argued that one of the reasons for the comparative inefficiency of service provision by public servants compared with contractors is that public servants are subject to additional pressures of accountability which make them less risk-averse.[13] In order to maximise the efficiency of the public sector the Labour government has indicated that it intends to address this issue. The Head of the Civil Service has stated his intention to

> ...look at our concepts of accountability and make sure that they do not reward too highly the 'safe' way of doing things, at the expense of improving our services...we need to introduce a more professional approach to risk management.[14]

Yet creating a less risk averse civil service would not seem to sit comfortably within the contemporary framework of ministerial responsibility. It assumes a degree of political maturity which is, as yet, absent from the Whitehall-Westminster model. The procedures and mechanisms through which Parliament enforces ministerial responsibility are seen to discourage sensible risk taking. Consequently the goal of increasing reasonable risk taking is obstructed by the constitution's heavy reliance on ministerial responsibility.

9.3.2 'Joined Up' Government

The links and tensions between the concept of risk within the core executive and ministerial responsibility take on added emphasis in light of the government's drive towards 'joined up' government.[15] As the Performance and Innovation Unit (PIU) stressed to the Prime Minister: 'Joined up policy making is innovative and complex. It is therefore relatively risky'.[16] It also challenges the very basis of ministerial responsibility as the relationship between ministers, departments and policies are obscured. Teams of ministers are now responsible for cross-departmental objectives. The danger is that within this coalition of ministerial effort responsibility can become even more opaque. Strategic cross-departmental government also creates a need to reconsider the methods through which ministers and officials are held to account. Parliamentary accountability complicates holistic government by reflecting and reinforcing Whitehall's 'silo' structure. In light of this tension the Prime Minister established a unit within the Cabinet Office to examine the accountability and incentives for joined up government. The unit's report ('Wiring It Up') notes that although governments may set over-arching objectives and budgets which cross departmental boundaries, if they fail to alter the main levers of behaviour - budgetary and accountability systems, relations with Parliament and so on - cross-cutting objectives will remain notional. Thus emphasising that joined-up policy making is a far more complex reform agenda than is readily appreciated. It cannot be contained purely within Whitehall but necessitates a complete reappraisal of the relationship between the executive and Parliament, in addition to relationships within the core executive. The PIU project concluded that 'radical change' is needed in '...the way civil servants and ministers are held to account' and suggested a restructuring of the departmentally related select committees to a thematically organised committee structure.[17]

To some degree this has already happened. Select committees have launched joint inquiries to examine cross-departmental polices. For example the quadripartite committee of Defence, Foreign Affairs, Trade and Industry and International Development conducted a joint inquiry into arms exports.[18] But joint working between committees has proved problematic.[19] A role of the Select Committee Panel, proposed by the Liaison Committee, would have been to address these problems by approving the creation of ad hoc committees to scrutinise inter-departmental policies. The government rejected this proposal; suggesting that the Liaison committee should highlight the need for ad hoc committees and make the case to the government. 'The Government would have to retain the right to choose whether to put such proposals before the House.'[20] This response underlines the reality of power within the House. Contrary to constitutional theory it is the executive that decides the manner and form through which it is held to account. And yet as the notions of risk taking and joined-up government take on priority it is clear they will have an impact upon the relationship between Parliament and the executive.

In launching its new public service agenda the government has simply put these issues aside, merely indicating the need to confront them at a later date.[21] Nevertheless, it is clear that hierarchical and organisationally defined forms of accountability will no longer hold where services are being delivered through collaborative forms of government. Individual ministerial responsibility will be further strained, as will parliamentary mechanisms that reflect the formal structure of Whitehall rather than the inter-organisational ties which now exist. The notion of risk and the pressures of joined up government demonstrate the constraints of extant forms of accountability. Reforms which may well benefit society as a whole are being restricted by the need to operationalise these goals within a framework of ministerial responsibility. That many of these reforms are being enacted without formal recognition that they fetter ministerial responsibility or a coherent account of how they will operate within its boundaries underlines the frailty of the convention.

9.3.3 The Development of Information Technology

Within the modernisation agenda for central government, alongside issues of risk and cross-departmentalism, is an appreciation of the opportunities and challenges of the information technology revolution.[22] Indeed, all public services – from tax returns to job vacancies – aim to be online by 2005. Within the Cabinet Office Tony Blair has demonstrated his commitment to realising the potential of IT through the appointment of an e-minister, Ian McCartney MP, and an e-envoy, Andrew Pinder. The latter enjoying the support of some 200 staff. While the debate regarding the capacity of IT has largely centred on operational aspects of service delivery it may increasingly challenge traditional models of representative government and political accountability. Tony Blair has repeatedly stressed his belief in the importance of his weekly webcast to the nation from No.10 as it provides him with a direct form of communication with a large section of the public.[23]

Although the benefits to a digitally empowered citizenry are currently the topic of a burgeoning literature it is clear that in future years the enforcement of ministerial responsibility will take place in a different technological environment.[24] The relationship between the governors and the governed will be both more complex and direct. All government departments now have internet sites that provide a mass of information. Technological developments will create new conduits and information flows. Evidence suggests that this process is underway and underlines the challenges such developments create. Dr Kim Howells, Minister of State for Consumer Affairs, has noted that the DTI's website receives 35,000 hits per week.[25] Hansard can be examined 24 hours a day. Electronic mail facilitates a direct form of communication between the public and ministers.[26]

The creation of electronic information libraries allows the public greater access to government information while negating the pathological organisational impacts of those demands. This, in turn, weakens ministerial arguments regarding the resource implications of greater disclosure. The dangers of too much information are reduced by the development of sophisticated search engines. Information technology not only supports increased public accountability but may also reinforce parliamentary accountability. MPs could use the internet to locate up-to-date and relevant information with which to enforce a greater and more exacting level of ministerial responsibility.

9.3.4 Innovations in Political Machinery

Technological advancement also creates the potential for a range of innovative forms of communication between the public and government. These innovations in political machinery are crucial as they challenge the position of ministerial responsibility as the source of political legitimacy for ministerial action between elections. The concept of a 'teleocracy' in which the public can express their opinions on an issue *en masse* without leaving their homes is increasingly feasible. For example, American senators often receive over a million emails a day on specific topics.[27] Such direct citizen involvement questions the role of, and potentially undermines, representative institutions like Parliament. Ministerial action may be legitimated via electronically communicated public instruction rather than parliamentary approval through ministerial responsibility. While this situation would appear to be some way off there are some notable examples of a more direct and complex relationship evolving between the public and ministers.[28]

In January 1998 the Cabinet Office established the People's Panel.[29] The Panel consists of 5000 members of the public who are regularly consulted to discover their views and opinions on government services and specific issues. Developments in information technology facilitate consultation on this scale. However, the People's Panel represents a refining of the concept of accountability in the modern state. It seeks to ensure the views of the public are taken into account before decisions are taken. In recent years a range of innovations have been employed, on varying scales, to increase the legitimacy of political decisions between elections. For example, citizens' juries, user panels, local referendums and public meetings. Technological advancement is likely to widen the scope and capacity of these mechanisms. In this environment decisions will carry a direct legitimacy which may well frustrate ministerial responsibility to Parliament.

9.3.5 The Constitutional Reform Agenda

Although Parliament fulfils a range of functions, perhaps its most important task is that of ensuring the legitimacy of government action.[30] The longevity of ministerial responsibility is very much linked to its role as the lynch pin between the government and Parliament. However, there is a clear paradox within the government's constitutional reform agenda. A critique can be proposed that focuses on the government's creation of alternative arenas of legitimate government while failing to address the obvious impact this will have on both parliamentary government and the convention of ministerial responsibility. As a result a sweeping programme of constitutional reform, which clearly challenges parliamentary sovereignty, has been introduced within a weak and confusing framework of ministerial responsibility. From a constitutional perspective what is most striking is the absence of a principled and coherent justification for the maintenance of ministerial responsibility. And yet the need to maintain ministerial responsibility at the centre of the British constitution creates a principled justification for the conflict between the government commitment to reform in *principle* and *practice*. But once established each part of this constitutional reform programme will further undermine the continuing validity of ministerial responsibility in its current form.

This tension can be seen in many areas. For example, incorporation of the European Convention of Human Rights will transfer significant powers to the judiciary and yet ministerial responsibility is maintained by the courts only being able to issue notes of incompatibility. The tension has arguably been seen at its crudest in relation to freedom of information. The planned legislation is significantly weaker than the original proposals due to the government's belief that this is necessary to protect ministerial responsibility and the conventions that underpin it. And yet at the same time the government has devolved power to institutions, like the Scottish Parliament, that are likely to introduce more liberal freedom of information regimes within their own framework of ministerial responsibility.

Devolution also challenges the role of ministerial responsibility in legitimating central government action, as the British Whitehall -

Westminster model is based on a presupposition that the final decision must remain with ministers. It also increases the likelihood of jurisdictional conflicts over spheres of ministerial responsibility. Most obviously, the creation of new institutions in Scotland and Wales creates anomalies for Westminster.[31] The fact that they have entirely different procedures and ways of working from Westminster is likely to highlight the flaws in Parliament over both legislation and government accountability.

The role of a reformed second chamber may also have important implications for ministerial responsibility. The Royal Commission in House of Lords reform suggested an elected component whose role would be to scrutinise the work of the executive.[32] The Commission noted,

> Our ambition for the reformed second chamber is that it should enhance the overall ability of Parliament as a whole to hold the government to account.[33]

There are already clear indications of a changing constitutional equilibrium within the Palace of Westminster. Since the 1999 House of Lords Reform Act, removing all but 92 of the hereditary peers, the second chamber has displayed a new and increasingly combative confidence. The government suffered 36 defeats in the Lords in the 1999-2000 session, a figure not significantly different from that in the previous two sessions. In February 2000 the Lords rejected a piece of delegated legislation for the first time since 1968. Before 1997, the Lords were constrained into passivity precisely because their composition was so irrational. The 'transitional' House of Lords, however, clearly feels it enjoys a greater constitution legitimacy than its predecessor. Not only does this raise questions about the Lords future relationship with the Commons but also the need for new forms of accountability to be placed on members of the Lords in light of their increased role and activity. For example, the Neill Committee on Standards in Public Life has suggested that the Lords move from a voluntary register of interests to a mandatory register of both financial and non-financial) interests.[34]

However, the Labour Party's control of the selection processes combined with the political appointment of the majority of the second chamber is likely to mellow the House of Lords' behaviour. In June 2000 the government announced the creation of a joint committee of both houses to examine the Royal Commission's proposals, but its members have yet to be appointed. In October 2000 a new sub-committee of the Consultative Committee between Labour and the Liberal Democrats was created to examine the issue. The two parties appear a long way apart in their views on the future composition of the Lords and press reports in February 2001 disclosed that discussions between the parties had collapsed in chaos.

The breakdown of the sub-committee on Lords reform was no doubt fuelled by numerous reports suggesting that the Prime Minister and senior members of the Cabinet have decided that the reformed chamber will have only 80 elected members. The suggested preference of the government for the 'minimalist' option has disappointed reformers and opposition parties. Lord Rogers, leader of the Liberal Democrats in the Lords, accused Mr Blair of going back on his word and of imposing his view undemocratically on both houses. He noted,

> It is a great pity that the reformed House of Lords will not command the widespread support that it deserves and as a result will be a less effective chamber than it is now and will seriously diminish Parliament's ability to hold the government to account.[35]

Mr Blair is well aware that a strengthened second chamber would threaten the executive's dominance of Parliament and create more obstacles for the government in getting its legislation into the statute book. An electoral mandate would empower those members of the second chamber with a legitimacy to play a greater role. Hence the executive's preference for appointed members based on the voting pattern of the previous election to ensure a government majority of supporters. Once more it is possible to identify a tension arising from the Labour government's commitment to 'Whig' principles of representative government and its reluctance to undermine the powerful position that the current constitutional configuration provides the executive.

There is, however, one constitutional reform that may remove the dominant position of the executive within the House and reinvigorate the convention of ministerial responsibility to Parliament. The Jenkins Commission on elections to the House of Commons has rekindled the debate on the desirability of a system of proportional representation which would better equate votes cast with seats in the House.[36] This reform has been adopted elsewhere in direct response to concerns regarding the practical effectiveness of ministerial responsibility to Parliament. For example, in 1993 New Zealand replaced single-member simple-plurality voting with a mixed-member proportional model based on the German system.[37] This change was introduced in the context of growing disillusionment with the unaccountability of single-party government. Electoral reform and coalition government were seen as a ways of restoring a degree of democratic accountability. Whilst proportional representation may alter the balance of power within the House and thereby reduce the dominant position of the executive it is not clear whether such a reform would necessarily increase Parliament's capacity to enforce ministerial responsibility. International research suggests that political accountability often becomes more opaque in multi-party states with coalition governments.[38] The benefit of strong majority governments bound by collective and individual ministerial responsibility is that they afford clarity at elections, which enables the public to enforce electoral accountability for past performance. A coalition government is rarely a homogenous entity, this breaks the transparent link between responsibility and action. Coalition bargaining undermines the connection between votes cast and policy preferences. Ministers may deflect responsibility on to other coalition members while the public's capacity to ascribe responsibility at elections becomes clouded.

It is clear, however, that on assuming office the Labour party has become markedly less enthusiastic about introducing electoral reform for Westminster. John Prescott, the Deputy Prime Minister, has said that plans for voting reform should be sent out to sea on a viking-style funeral barge. Lord Jenkins himself has conceded that Labour has abandoned its commitment to proportional representation. Labour's National Policy Forum has effectively ruled out adopting the 'AV-plus' system proposed by the Jenkins Commission. While Labour remains committed to a referendum on reform, the vote is expected to be on whether to adopt the Australian-style 'AV' system, which is not proportional. The issue is currently sidelined as the current Labour policy documents says any further electoral reform should be delayed until the new voting systems in Scotland and Wales have been 'thoroughly examined'.

Paradoxically, a Westminster government with a secure majority has legislated to surround itself with a new constitutional framework of checks and balances, while upholding the centrality of a convention that will become increasingly untenable in the light of these reforms. The British state is a parliamentary state. The actions of the executive are conceived of, executed and bounded within a parliamentary framework. However, the degree to which Britain remains a parliamentary state will become increasingly questionable. Jurisdictional arguments may limit the scope of ministerial activity, cloud responsibility and weaken the role of ministerial responsibility as the guarantor of legitimate government in the United Kingdom. Politicians need to recognise how these constitutional reforms relate to each other, and how they demand a reappraisal of the role and powers of Parliament within the new constitutional settlement.[39] If the constitutional reform programme is viewed as straining the convention from above it is probable that equal or greater challenges to ministerial responsibility will emerge from below as a result of the evolving state.

9.3.6 The Evolving State

Ministerial responsibility was designed to reflect the departmental structure of central government in the light of concerns regarding the accountability of appointed administrative boards. As earlier chapters have emphasised, the degree to which ministerial responsibility adequately reflected the structure of the state in reality is questionable. However, the increasing complexity of the state, a process which has accelerated markedly since the mid-1980s, has been increasingly difficult to reconcile with a coherent and credible model of ministerial responsibility. Devolved management has exhausted the flexibility of the convention. Consequently, the disparity between the *theory* and *practice* of the convention has become stark, thus increasing disquiet surrounding the continuing validity of the convention. It is suggested that the evolving state will move further and further away from the departmental configuration and in this context the convention of ministerial responsibility will become overstretched to the point where it is no longer possible to devise even the most tenuous framework of ministerial responsibility to legitimate the structure of the state.

As the state and society evolve, new challenges and responsibilities are placed at the door of ministers. However, these issues combined with the public expectations which accompany them place further pressure on the realistic scope of ministerial responsibility. The response is often to create new quasi-independent bodies to which ministers delegate responsibility for certain regulatory or monitoring functions. For example, in 1999 the Secretary of State for Health established the Commission for Health Improvement to oversee the performance of doctors and hospitals. At the same time the Secretary of State for the Environment, Transport and Regions was announcing plans to create a new Standards Board to scrutinise local government and a Strategic Railway Authority to coordinate the railway infrastructure. Consequently in many spheres of public policy it is regulators and not ministers who decide. Recent events validate this statement: the fate of the National Lottery, embryo research, interest rates, the future of television, the availability of drugs on prescription, and the level of the medium wage. Regulation is also one of the options in the Hunting Bill. A virtue has been made of 'depoliticising' sensitive decisions.[40] For example, the privatisation of the public utilities is based on the transfer of power from ministers to independent regulators to insulate the markets from political manipulation. This immediately reduces the scope of ministerial action and thereby fetters their responsibility for vital public services. This shift of power has taken place in a piecemeal manner and without a coherent debate surrounding the growth of regulatory bodies and their accountability.[41]

Moreover, the creation of these quasi-autonomous bodies is often a response to concerns regarding the operation of ministerial responsibility after incidents which have exposed or brought into question the adequacy of political accountability: for example, the transfer of responsibility for investigating miscarriages of justice from the Home Office to the Criminal Cases Review Commission and the establishment of the Food Standards Agency to take over functions previously conducted by the Ministry of Agriculture, Fisheries and Food.[42] Contrary to constitutional theory accountability and impartiality are thought to be increased by excluding certain functions from the constraints and influence of ministerial responsibility. As the institutional hybridity within the state increases the ability of ministerial responsibility to legitimate action will decrease. As power increasingly relocates upwards to supranational bodies, downwards to devolved bodies or horizontally to quasi-autonomous bodies, critical observers will become increasingly intolerant and resentful of the continuing centrality of the convention. At some stage the executive will have to respond.

Clearly it is possible to place this research within broader arguments regarding the usefulness of the concept of 'governance' as an analytical tool to reconceptualise the state. Governance, as an approach to the study of the state, facilitates the inclusion of a much broader range of bodies and relationships than would traditionally have been included within the 'governmental' framework. It therefore alerts us to the increasing complexity and fluidity of the state and the challenges this presents to the formulation and implementation of public policy. It also highlights the tensions and paradoxes involved in operating a 'governance' model of the state within a constitutional infrastructure which supports and champions a structure of 'government'. This study has examined just one aspect of this debate, namely accountability, and yet it has underlined the complexity of the issues under analysis, the restrictive influence of the existing constitutional framework and the value of the 'governance' perspective and literature to facilitate a wider and deeper appreciation of evolving constitutional and institutional relationships.

The fact that the evolution of alternative models of accountability has been constrained by the centrality of ministerial responsibility within the constitution places a weight on the convention which it is increasingly struggling to uphold. This section has suggested that the modernising government agenda, developments in information technology, innovations in political machinery, the constitutional reform agenda and the evolving state are likely to exacerbate the tensions and pressures that this book has highlighted. It is suggested that the British constitution is at a political and historical juncture in which the flexibility of the convention has now been exhausted. As a result the notion that central government can be justified through ministerial responsibility to Parliament will increasingly be subject to profound challenge. However, it is clear that the executive is committed to maintaining ministerial responsibility as the lynchpin of the constitution despite these challenges. It is in explaining this commitment that the politics of accountability becomes clear, there is an omnipotent link between the convention of ministerial responsibility and power in the modern state.

9.4 Conclusion: Labour, Parliament and Power in the Modern State

> I said that this place [Parliament] must never become the Prime Minister's poodle. Unfortunately, it has become so (Derek Foster MP, former Labour Chief Whip, January 1999).[43]

> The fire for strengthening Parliament burns brightly among some Government backbenchers, but not so brightly – indeed, it is flickering badly – among members of the executive (Nigel Evans MP, November 2000).[44]

> Parliament is a poodle posing as a rottweiler, which makes for an absurd spectacle. The myth of parliamentary sovereignty serves as a convenient substitute for real accountability (Tony Wright MP, Chairman, Public Administration Committee, 2000).[45]

Accountability is about relations of power and authority, it structures the giving of accounts in exchange for delegated powers and responsibilities and is dependent on the processes and institutions that enforce the production of accounts. This study has described how the concept covers a variety of relations and dimensions, largely because the configuration of the central state has changed dramatically in recent decades. As a result, whenever we talk about accountability we are, fundamentally, concerned with the (re)distribution of power. A claim for greater accountability is, essentially, a demand for a transfer of power between institutions or individuals. This research has demonstrated how ministerial responsibility in practice inverts the theoretical power relationship between Parliament and the executive. In addition it allows the executive to confine and restrict the development of alternative models of accountability. Therefore, the solution to concerns regarding the effectiveness of ministerial responsibility can only be resolved by making Parliament effective.

And yet there is a clear pattern in which opposition parties who support the 'Whig' view of ministerial responsibility and promise fundamental parliamentary reform to ensure increased accountability and scrutiny renege upon these commitments and actually embrace the 'Peelite' view of the convention, which prioritises strong government, on assuming office. The Conservative Party pledged to reform Parliament during the 1992 general election campaign but developments were minimal.[46] In the run up to the 1997 general election the Labour Party made parliamentary reform a central part of their platform. The shadow Leader of the House, Ann Taylor, made a far reaching 'New Labour, New Parliament' speech to Charter 88 in which she, echoing the damming report of the state of parliamentary democracy published 20 years earlier by the Procedure Committee, committed the Labour party to '...re-establish the proper balance between Parliament and the executive'.[47]

Yet, to date, substantial reform of the House of Commons has been notably absent from the government's constitutional reform programme. No white paper on reforming the House was published and the issue was notably absent from the 1988 Queen's speech. A Modernisation of the House select committee was established with a remit to '...look at the means by which the House holds ministers to account'.[48] The work of this committee has led to some practical reforms, for example minor changes in the parliamentary timetable. And yet although the achievements of the Modernisation Committee might have made the House of Commons a slightly more convenient place to work it has not tackled the fundamental issue of the balance of power between the executive and the legislature. As Hazell noted, 'Parliamentary reform started with a bang but has ended with a whimper. With no support from Downing Street, the initial momentum quickly dissipated'.[49] This fact led David Davis MP to put forward his Parliamentary Control of the Executive Bill in June 1998 which aimed to subject a range of executive decisions and appointments to parliamentary approval. Davis stated, 'If enacted this Bill will irrevocably alter the relationship between Parliament and the executive'. Executive support for his private members Bill was not forthcoming.

The Leader of the House between July 1998 to June 2001, Margaret Beckett, described herself as a 'small 'c'' conservative on these matters – an admission that did little to assuage concern both within and beyond Westminster. Riddell noted: 'Their [the Labour government] commitment to parliamentary reform often appears little more than mouthing conventional pieties'.[50] Accordingly, a number of commentators have raised concerns that the minor reforms are more to do with style than substance and that, in reality, the changes will not improve Parliament's ability to hold the executive to account. Gregory concludes, '...the government, despite its pre-election promises, appears to have no appetite for any tangible 'modernisation' of Parliament which will alter the balance of power'.[51]

The most recent and critical exposition of this issue was the Liaison Committee report 'Shifting the Balance: Select Committees and the Executive'.[52] The report states, '...in practice governmental power has always outstripped parliamentary control' and calls for further modernisation and reform of the House of Commons. Two key recommendations were made. First, that a new Select Committee Panel be established to replace the current Committee of Selection due to concerns that the latter is too heavily influenced by the whips. Second, that chairmen of select committees should be paid an additional salary in order to create an alternative career structure to ministerial office. The government's response to these recommendations, published on 18 May 2000, underlines the complexity and paradoxes of the politics of parliamentary reform.[53] 'The Government are not convinced that a change to the current system is needed.'[54] The Liaison Committee's official response, 'Independence or Control' (September 2000), was scathing: 'It [the government's reply] rejected virtually every recommendation we had made'. The committee went on to note:

> The reply was both disappointing and surprising...we found it surprising that a government which has made so much of its policy on modernising Parliament should apparently take so different a view when its own accountability and freedom of action are at issue.[55]

The government's response suggested that the Liberal view of the constitution is in fact reality, pointing out that the House may, in theory, refuse to accept the Committee of Selection's proposals. Moreover, reform is not necessary as no government would attempt to 'control' Parliament via tight party management:

> The Liaison Committee Report characterises the current system as one in which there is a danger that unfettered party management will exercise subversive control of select committee memberships to ensure, on the Government's part, a docile set of select committees. This Government does not accept that any government would desire such a state of affairs let alone manage to achieve it if it ever did.[56]

The paragon of the Liberal view of the constitution is held up as reality long after most observers have dispelled it as constitutional fiction. And yet the issue of selecting MPs to serve on select committees must also be set against the reality, rather than the theory, of power within Parliament. The role of the whips in the selection (and deselection) of MPs from select committees has frequently been a topic of complaint.[57] The downfall of Nicholas Winterton in 1992 crudely highlighted that even when a committee member becomes unexpectedly vexatious the executive can conspire to remould Parliament's procedures to remove them. The Liaison Committee's recommendation of a new Select Committee Panel reflects disquiet within the House that the whips have played a key role in designing the memberships of the committees under the Labour government. There is a groundswell of opinion within the House that it is quite simply wrong that those who are at the forefront of scrutinising the government should be chosen by the government of the day. The Commons debate on the report highlighted the extent of the whips' influence in select committee appointments. Sir Peter Emery concluded, '…it is about time that some people realised that when they [the government] say that the whips do not really interfere, that is a lot of baloney'.[58]

However, the executive's management of the Liaison Committee's report exemplifies the balance of power within the House.[59] The report was discussed at an opposition day debate in the Commons on 13 July 2000. In the debate the Prime Minister gave a unequivocal commitment that the 'Shifting the Balance' report would be timetabled for debate and with the reform proposals put to a free vote. Despite the fact that the report had been published unanimously by the Liaison Committee and an Early Day Motion supporting its recommendations had been signed by over 250 MPs the government reneged on its commitment to hold a free vote on the report's recommendations.[60] The government preferred to debate the report during an adjournment debate, involving no votes, on 9 November 2000 and refused to timetable future parliamentary time for the issue.[61] Margaret Beckett defended the government's position by emphasising the great implications of the recommendations and the need for caution in deciding upon them. Critics pointed out that the report had been published for over eight months and the government's reply for over six months. Moreover, the parliamentary interest fuelled by the report had been intense and MPs could hardly be accused of rushing to a judgement on the recommendations.

The government is also not persuaded by the Liaison Committee's idea of paying select committee chairs to create an alternative parliamentary career to ministerial office.[62] Judge is correct to state that internal reform of the House of Commons is thwarted by the fact that the '...normative system of the House, as with any other dominant value system, reflects the predilections of the most powerful actors'.[63] Any internal reforms risk being eviscerated by an executive who is unwilling to fetter their dominant position. The faith in strong opposition to strong government, as outlined famously by Crick, is flawed by the very political configuration to which reform is a response and the normative values of the executive mentality cannot be ignored.[64] Paying select committee chairmen to stimulate parliamentary independence has been recommended by a wide range of commentators.[65] However, research suggests that MPs are largely critical of this proposal, fearing that paying chairmen would reduce rather than increase the independent capacity of the committees. The majority of MPs surveyed thought that the executive mentality combined with the power of patronage would ensure that the government appointed compliant MPs and use the positions as rewards for service to the party.[66] One committee chairman noted (April 1998), 'It would achieve little more than the imposition of party hacks'. Therefore the *paradoxes* of the constitution have to be addressed, and cannot be resolved simply by asserting the *principles* of the parliamentary state.[67]

Similar concerns have been raised regarding the Liaison Committee's recommendation that a Select Committee Panel should replace the current Committee of Selection. A number of questions demand clarification: what criteria would the panel use to select people to serve on select committees? How would they ensure that fairness and equity is achieved? How will they ensure that the skills, preferences and time of MPs are properly allocated to a particular committee? The central issue is how would concentrating the power of appointment in three senior MPs necessarily produce and more transparent system, a system less open to the influence of patronage or party, or a system that would bring about a stronger select committee scrutiny process?[68] Nevertheless, the constitutional position is clear. The House, using the Liaison Committee as a conduit for its anxieties, has indicated its concern regarding the current balance of power between the executive and the legislature. Although needing further refinement, the Committee has put forward reforms which it believes would go some way towards allaying those concerns. These recommendations have received the support of the House through subsequent debates and early day motions. Contrary to constitutional theory, the supremacy of Parliament over the executive is thwarted by the latter's tight party management and procedural control of the House's timetable. In the face of executive obduracy the impotence of the House is unequivocal. Moreover, the government refuses to accept the issues that the Liaison Committee's recommendations are designed to address – 'The Government are not convinced that a change to the current system is needed'.[69] The Leader of the House noted, 'I do not accept that the House is as diminished, nor that it is as subservient, as it has become fashionable to allege'.[70] Several observers are confused by the Labour government's approach to parliamentary reform. Hazell noted, 'It is a puzzle why a government so committed to modernisation and reform has been so feeble when it comes to the House of Commons'.[71] There is no puzzle. Despite a wealth of largely prosaic literature lamenting its demise, Parliament remains the central locus of legitimate state power in Britain.

Internal parliamentary reform is therefore restricted by the executive's solicitous management of its majority within the House. The 'Norton view', that parliamentary control of the executive can be achieved through attitudinal change on the part of MPs, therefore flounders because Parliament is largely a creature of the executive and all the reforms that could be implemented to change the balance of power do not happen because of this fact.[72] As Hennessy noted before the Public Service Committee: '...we sit here and devise these improvements but in the end its really like expecting ministers not to behave like politicians'.[73]

But it is quite clear that a degree of modernisation has taken place within Parliament since 1997. It is, however, crucial to comprehend the difference between 'modernising Parliament' and 'parliamentary reform'. In December 1966 Richard Crossman explained that 'there is a difference between modernisation and parliamentary reform'.[74] For Crossman modernisation of the House involved practical and procedural changes to the day-to-day business of the House whereas parliamentary reform involved a conscious decision on the part of executive and legislature regarding the proper balance and distribution of power. Building on Crossman's distinction Tony Wright has outlined how the reforms implemented by Labour – more sensible hours, experiments with Westminster Hall, new rules to facilitate joint inquiries by committees, etc. – may be examples of modernisation but they do not amount to real parliamentary reform.[75] Indeed, the utility of such modernisation will be minimal and in many ways undermined by the lack of concomitant parliamentary reform. Moreover, without a change in the balance of power within the House many of the reforms introduced under the guise of 'modernisation' may well undermine the scrutiny capacity of the House. As one suspicious MP noted, 'We all know what modernisation means...It is a euphemism for streamlining the House so that a quantity of legislation can be got through as quickly as possible'.[76] Modernisation and parliamentary reform are, therefore, quite different processes, undertaken for quite different reasons and with quite different outcomes.

It could be suggested that the Labour party has shifted its allegiance from the 'Whig' to the 'Peelite', or the 'liberal' to the 'Whitehall', view of the constitution on assuming office. The antithesis of this shift is displayed by the Conservative party who have become vigorous proponents of parliamentary reform. On 29 July 1999 the Conservative party announced the creation of a Commission to Strengthen Parliament, chaired by Lord Norton of Louth, charged with developing recommendations to allow Parliament to scrutinise the government effectively. It duly published its final report, 'Strengthening Parliament', on the 10 July 2000.[77] Its recommendations were significant; often supporting the reforms advocated by the Liaison Committee and in many areas suggesting radical reform. William Hague immediately accepted two of the Commission's proposals: to return Prime Minister's Questions to a twice-weekly and extended slot, and to remove select committee appointments from the power of the whips. Hague also proposed to use the Norton report as a 'route' map to further parliamentary reform.[78] Not only have these commitments been included in the Conservative manifesto but a number of Conservative politicians have published their own critiques of the Labour government and proposals for reform.[79] Authoritative reports suggest that the Conservatives are planning to place parliamentary reform at the centre of the next general election campaign.[80] In November 2000 the Leader of the Opposition, William Hague, devoted a large section of his speech on the British constitution to the topic of parliamentary reform:

> The House of Commons is the keystone of democratic accountability in this country. It is what provides the crucial link between the citizen and government. Under this government, Parliament's decline has been accelerated rather than arrested. It is in renewing the House of Commons that we must concentrate our efforts.[81]

There is, of course, no guarantee that the Conservatives would not revert back to the Peelite attitude towards Parliament should they win the next election.

Parliament is not weak by accident. Suggestions of possible reforms have to be designed within an appreciation of the realities and not the theory of power in the Westminster model. Indeed it was over 20 years ago that the Procedure Committee stated that the balance of power was weighted so heavily in favour of the executive that it '...arouses widespread anxiety and is inimical to the proper working of democracy'.[82] The emphasis upon strong government within Britain has engendered an executive mentality that reflects the paradoxes of the parliamentary state.[83] Proposals for parliamentary reform, such as those currently being developed by the Hansard Society's Scrutiny Commission,[84] all seek to resolve these paradoxes, but are confronted in turn by the fact that the executive is unwilling to introduce meaningful reform.[85] The faith in strong opposition to strong government is flawed by the very political configuration to which reform is a response and the normative values of the executive mentality cannot be ignored.

Yet the degree to which the United Kingdom is a parliamentary state is increasingly questionable. Power within the state is becoming displaced, not least by the Labour government's constitutional reform agenda. The emerging agendas outlined above are largely beyond the control of ministers and will challenge traditional relationships. Within this environment it is unlikely that any amount of ministerial guile could satisfactorily legitimate the maintenance of the convention in anything like its current form. Two scenarios can be advanced as possible directions for the convention. The first involves the radical and formal deconstruction and revision of the convention in a manner that remoulds ministerial responsibility to reflect the fragmented state. This is likely to involve some kind of direct accountability to Parliament of named officials and a formal, probably legal, separation of agencies from a remaining small policy department. In the British context the design of such a coherent and formal blueprint would be highly unusual. More likely is the second scenario which speculates that the convention of ministerial responsibility will rapidly become a dignified element of the British constitution. The Osmotherly rules will 'wither on the vine' leading to the *de facto* direct accountability of officials. Moreover, the term 'civil servant' will become increasingly meaningless as individuals will increasingly associate themselves, and be viewed as, representatives of particular functional organisations. The challenge then will be to reconcile a complex and fragmented state based around a nexus of inter-organisational contacts with a coherent and workable framework of accountability. Most importantly there is a need for a clear acknowledgement that it is not, and has not been for some time, only ministers who make decisions. The accountability of non-ministerial decisionmakers will be facilitated by the removal of ministerial responsibility. This book has demonstrated how a range of accountability models exist and yet they have been applied in a largely ad hoc manner without any firm theoretical underpinning. Clarity will only be achieved with the creation and publication of an explicit constitutional framework which dictates the structure, procedures and accountability relationships that govern the reformed core executive. This, however, would mark a radical departure from the British constitutional tradition.

Notes

1. Tensions involving accountability and management are not exclusively British but are being confronted in a range of advanced liberal democracies. See: International Institute of Administrative Sciences (2000) *Accountability in Public Administration: Reconciling Democracy, Efficiency and Ethics* (Brussels : IIAS).
2. See Judge, D (1993) *The Parliamentary State* (London : Sage).
3. Norton, P (2000) 'Reforming Parliament in the United Kingdom' *Legislative Studies* Vol.6 No.3 p.8.
4. An exhaustive literature review on this topic uncovered only two relatively limited pieces of work on this topic. See: Andeweg, R & Nijzink, L (1995) 'Beyond the Two-Body Image: Relations Between Ministers and MPs in Western Europe' in Doring, H (ed.) *Parliament and Majority Rule in Western Europe* (Frankfurt : Campus-Verlag); King, A (1990) 'Modes of Executive/Legislative Relations: Great Britain, France and West Germany' in Norton, P (ed.) *Legislatures* (Oxford : OUP).
5. Interview with the author, March 1998.
6. Aucoin, P & Heintzman, R 'The Dialectic of Accountability for Performance in Public Management Reform' Paper to the International Institute of Administrative Sciences Conference, Civil Service College, Sunningdale, 12-15/5/99.

7   Pollitt, C 'Accountability and Democracy: Answering to Political Authority and Citizens' Needs' Paper to the International Institute of Administrative Sciences Conference, Civil Service College, Sunningdale, 12-15/5/99.

8   Gains, F (1999) *Resource Dependency Between Departments and Next Steps Agencies*, unpublished Ph.D. thesis, University of Sheffield.

9   See Rhodes, R (1997) *Understanding Governance: Policy Networks, Governance and Accountability* (Buckingham : Open University Press).

10 For example, the foiling of a major breakout from a high security prison in March 1998 received only the most cursory reporting. See 'Prison Escape Plot is Foiled' *The Times* 23/3/98.

11 Wilson, R 'The Role of the Public Servant in a Time of Change' speech to CIPFA, 14/6/00.

12 Cm 4310 (1999) *Modernising Government* HMSO, London. para.11.

13 Mulgan, R (1997) 'Contracting Out and Accountability' *Australian Journal of Public Administration* Vol.56 No.4 pp.106-116.

14 Wilson, R 'The Civil Service in the New Millennium' speech given at City University, London, 5/5/99.

15 See Flinders, M (2001) *Governance in Whitehall: Joining Up Government in a Fragmented State* (Sheffield : Department of Politics, University of Sheffield); Kavanagh, G & Richards, D (2001) 'Departmentalism and Joined-Up Government: Back to the Future?' *Parliamentary Affairs* Vol.64 No.1 pp.1-18.

16 In a presentation to the Prime Minister by the Performance and Innovation Unit as part of their 'Accountability and Incentives for Joined Up Government' project. Presentation received by the author 18/11/99.

17 Cabinet Office (2000) *Wiring It Up: Whitehall's Management of Cross-Cutting Policies and Services*, Performance & Innovation Unit, London.

18 HC 225 *Annual Reports for 1997 and 1998 on Strategic Export Controls*, Third Report of the Defence Committee/Second Report from the Foreign Affairs Committee/Third Report from the International Development Committee/Fourth Report from the Trade and Industry Committee, Session 1999/2000, London, HMSO.

19 HC 300 *Shifting the Balance: Select Committees and the Executive*, First Report of the Liaison Committee, Session 1999-2000, HMSO, London. paras. 64-67.

20 Cm 4737 (2000) *The Government's Response to the First Report from the Liaison Committee on Shifting the Balance: Select Committees and the Executive*, HMSO, London p.10.

21 Cm 4310 (1999) p.18.

22 See, Allan, A 'E-Democracy' Lecture to the Hansard Society, 22/5/00.

23 See Cockerill, M 'Trust me I'm the Prime Minister' Hugh Wheldon Memorial Lecture, 11/12/00 (Broadcast on BBC 2).
24 See: Coleman, M (1999) *Electronic Media, Parliament and the People: Making Democracy Visible* (London : Hansard Society); Hacker, K (2000) *Digital Democracy* (London : Sage); Margolis, M & Resnick, D (2000) *Politics as Usual: The Cyberspace Revolution* (London : Sage); Gibson, R & Ward, S (2000) *Reinvigorating Democracy: British Politics and the Internet* (London : Ashgate); Silcock, R (2001) 'What is E-Government?' *Parliamentary Affairs* Vol.54 No.1 pp.88-101.
25 HC 570-VII (1998/99) p.135 Q726. See also, Home Office (1999) *Code of Practice on Access to Government Information - 1998 Report*.
26 The Hansard Society has established an inquiry into the development and potential of 'e-democracy'. It is specifically concerned with the implications of information technology for Parliament and the role of MPs. The inquiry is directed by Steve Coleman.
27 Wilson, R 'The Civil Service in the New Millennium' speech given at City University, London, 5/5/99.
28 The publication of government 'Annual Reports' is an interesting development. See: Cm 4401 (1999) *The Government's Annual Report 1998/99* HMSO, London; Cm 3969 (1998) *The Government's Annual Report 1997/98* HMSO, London. These have been criticised for further undermining the political neutrality of the civil service. See, MacAskill, E 'PM's Rosy Round Up Omits Blunders' *The Guardian* 31/7/98 p.11; Pierce, A 'What do you think of the show so far? *The Times* 31/7/98 p.14.
29 Cabinet Office 'The Listening Government - Clarke Launches the People's Panel' Press Notice CAB 18/98 29/1/98.
30 Judge, D (1993) *The Parliamentary State* (London : Sage); Norton, P (1993) *Does Parliament Matter?* (Hemel Hempstead : Harvester Wheatsheaf); Smith, M (1999) *The Core Executive in Britain* (Basingstoke : Macmillan).
31 Hazell, R (2000) *The State and the Nations* (Thorverton : Imprint).
32 See 'Blueprint for a House of Lords with power to challenge Blair' *The Telegraph* 31/10/99. For a comparative analysis of the role of second chambers in relation to the executive see Russell, M (1999) *Reforming the House of Lords: Lessons from Overseas* (Oxford : Oxford University Press).
33 Cm 4534 (2000) *A House for the Future* HMSO, London. para.8.2.
34 Cm 4903 'Standards of Conduct in the House of Lords' Seventh Report of the Committee on Standards in Public Life, HMSO, London.
35 Webster, P 'Blair backs 80 elected peers' *The Times* 6/2/01 p.12.

36 Cm 4090 (1998) *The Report of the Independent Commission on the Voting System*, HMSO, London.
37 Mulgan, R (1995) 'The Democratic Failure of Single-Party Government: The New Zealand Experience' *Australian Journal of Political Science* Vol.30 pp.82-96.
38 Strom, K (1997) 'Democracy, Accountability and Coalition Bargaining' *European Journal of Political Research* Vol. 31 pp.47-62; Renaud, P & Winden, F van (1987) 'Political Accountability for Price Stability and Unemployment in a Multi-Party System with Coalition Governments' *Public Choice* Vol.53 pp.181-186; Narud, H (1996) 'Party Policies and Government Accountability' *Party Politics* Vol. 2 No.4 pp. 479-506. For a discussion of the possible impact of proportional representation on Parliament, see Johnson, N (1997) 'Opposition in the British Political System' *Government and Opposition* Vol.32 No.4 pp.487-511.
39 See Riddell, P (2000) *Parliament Under Blair* (London : Politicos).
40 Riddell, P 'Regulators turn up the heat' *The Times* 21/12/00.
41 Mather, G (2000) *Making Decision in Britain* (London : European Policy Forum).
42 Flinders, M & Cole, M (1999) 'Opening or Closing Pandora's Box? New Labour and the Quango State' *Talking Politics* Vol.12 No.1 pp.234-40.
43 Hansard, HC Debs. 13/1/99, Vol.323, col. 259.
44 Hansard, HC Debs. 9/11/00, col. 536.
45 Tony Wright (2000) *The British Political Process* (London : Routledge)
46 Conservative Party (1992) *The Best Future For Scotland* (Edinburgh : Conservative Party).
47 Taylor, A 'New Politics, New Parliament' Charter 88 seminar on the reform of Parliament 14/5/96.
48 Hansard, HC Debs. WA 22/7/97 Q10108.
49 Hazell, R (2001) 'Reforming the Constitution' *Political Quarterly* Vol.72 No.1 pp.43-44.
50 Riddell, P 'MPs should consider a move to a smaller House' *The Times* 31/3/98 p.10.
51 Gregory, D (1999) 'Style Over Substance? Labour and the Reform of Parliament' *Renewal* Vol.7 No.3 p.47.
52 HC 300 *Shifting the Balance: Select Committees and the Executive*, First Report of the Liaison Committee, Session 1999-2000, HMSO, London.
53 Cm 4737 (2000) *The Government's Response to the First Report from the Liaison Committee on Shifting the Balance: Select Committees and the Executive*, HMSO, London.
54 Cm 4737 (2000) p.2.

55 HC 748 *Independence or Control?* Second Report of the Liaison Committee, Session 1999-2000, HMSO, London. para.3.
56 Cm 4737 (2000) p.2 para.9.
57 HC 19 *The Working of the Select Committee System,* Second Report by the Committee on Procedure, Session 1989/90, HMSO, London; Cremin, M (1993) 'The setting up of the Departmental Select Committees after the 1992 election' *Parliamentary Affairs* Vol.46 No.3 pp.309-318; Judge, D (1992) 'The Effectiveness of the Post 1979 Select Committee System' *Political Quarterly* Vol. 63 No.1 pp.400-420.
58 Hansard, HC Debs. 9/11/00 col.515. A sentiment echoed in my own research within the House. One MP who had served on a select committee between 1992-1997 and had requested to remain on the committee during this parliament noted: There is a planned lack of continuity which means that the build up of expertise has been wasted. They have put on members who either have no experience or who are safe. They put on people who are ambitious and are not going to rock the boat and they have kept the nasties and the hard hitters away. They took off the old lags like me who would give ministers a hard time (interview with the author, April 1998). Another Labour MP noted: The whips have vast control over the membership of these committees and will decide the members in consultation with the departmental ministers. They will not appoint people who they know will be extremely troublesome; this has always been the case but sometimes people who think they will be safe will go native (May 1998).
59 House of Commons Library (2000) *Shifting Control? Aspects of the Executive-Parliamentary Relationship*, Research Paper 00/92.
60 EDM 1135, 8/11/00.
61 Margaret Beckett, the Leader of the House, was fiercely criticised for blocking proposals to strengthen the independence of select committees during January 2001. See Hansard, HC Debs. 30/01/01 cols.169-172.
62 Cm 4737 (2000) p.5.
63 Judge, D (1993) *The Parliamentary State* (London : Sage) p.93.
64 Crick, B (1968) *The Reform of Parliament* (London : Weidenfeld).
65 Keswick & Heathcoat-Amory, 1996; Dunleavy, 1995; Mandelson & Liddle, 1996; Cm 3330, 1996; Riddell, 1998.
66 A view supported in the work of Peter Riddell (2000), 'Many chairmen of select committees are themselves sceptical about being paid extra for this role. They believe it would create envy within the committees and would be another piece of patronage for the party whips to dangle and with draw'. *Parliament Under Pressure* p.243.
67 Judge, D (1993) *The Parliamentary State* (London : Sage) p.215.
68 See Hansard, HC Debs. 9/11/200, col.490 (Mr John Healey).

[69] Cm 4737 (2000) p.2, para7.
[70] Hansard, HC Debs. 9/11/00, col.43.
[71] Hazell, R (2001) 'Reforming the Constitution' *Political Quarterly* Vol.72 No.1 p.48.
[72] Norton, P (1978) 'Government Defeats in the House of Commons: Myths and Reality' *Public Law* pp.360-378; Norton, P. (1991) 'In Defence of the Constitution: A Riposte to the Radicals', in Norton, P (ed.) *New Directions in British Politics?* Aldershot : Edward Elgar, 145-173; Norton, P (1993) *Does Parliament Matter?* (Hemel Hempstead : Harvester Wheatsheaf); Norton, P & Wood, D (1993) *Back from Westminster: British Members of Parliament and their Constituents* (Lexington : University of Kentucky Press).
[73] HC 313 *Ministerial Accountability and Responsibility* Second Report of the Public Service Committee, Session 1996/97, HMSO. London, p.17.
[74] Hansard, HC. Debs. 14/12/66 vol.738 cols.479-480.
[75] Hansard, HC Debs. 9/11/00 col. 510.
[76] Hansard, HC. Debs. 9/11/00 col. 536 (Mr Nigel Evans). Tony Wright MP noted, 'Modernization can point in different and contrary directions. It can mean more efficiency in the way that parliament processes executive business, or more effectiveness in the way it holds the executive to account. While a little progress has been made with the former kind of modernization, the latter kind has so far been the absent guest at the political reform feast'. Wright, A (2000) *The British Political Process* (London : Routledge) p.341.
[77] Norton, P (2000) *Strengthening Parliament* The Report of the Commission to Strengthen Parliament (London : The Conservative Party).
[78] See the Opposition Day debate 'Parliament and Executive' Hansard, HC Debs. 13/7/00.
[79] See: The Conservative Party (2000) *Believing in Britain* (London : The Conservative Party) p.23; Tyrie, A (2000) *Mr Blair's Poodle: The Commons must Reform itself to deal with the reality of Presidential Power* (London : Centre for Policy Studies); Young, G (2000) 'Westminster: An Holistic Approach' *Crossbow,* summer, pp.6-7; Lord Strathclyde (2000) *New Frontiers for Reform* (London : Centre for Policy Studies); Lansley, A & Wilson, R (2000) *Conservatives and the Constitution* (London : The Conservative 2000 Foundation).
[80] Watson, R 'Tories get tough on ministers' *The Times* 22/3/99 p.2.
[81] Hague, W 'A Conservative View of Change' speech delivered at Magdalen College, Oxford, 13/11/00.
[82] HC 588 *Reports* First Report by the Committee on Procedure, Session 1977-78, HMSO, London. para.1.5.

[83] Judge, D (1993) *The Parliamentary State* (London : Sage) pp.212-213.
[84] See Brazier, A (2000) Systematic Scrutiny: Reforming the Select Committees (London : Hansard Society); Brazier, A (2000) Parliament and the Public Purse (London : Hansard Society); Power, G (2000) Under Pressure: Are we getting the most from our MPs? (London : Hansard Society); Power, G (2000) Creating a Working Parliament (London : Hansard).
[85] Beattie, A (1998) 'Why is the Case for Parliamentary Reform in Britain so Weak' *Legislative Studies* Vol.4 No.2 pp.1-16.

Methodology

There are a wide range of methodological techniques available to the social scientist (experiments, surveys, archival analysis, histories, case studies, etc.). Each is a different way of collecting and analysing evidence with which to test a research question. Each strategy has its advantages and disadvantages. This research employs a cross-comparative framework within a single case study to test its research question. This section justifies the selection of the method and sets out the research framework.

The research technique adopted depends largely on: the type of research question posed; the degree of control an investigator has over actual events; and the degree of focus on contemporary as opposed to historical events.[1] The most important issue for differentiating among the various research techniques is to identify the type of research question being asked. Descriptive 'what' questions may be exploratory (in which case any of the techniques might be used) or about prevalence (in which surveys, data analysis or archival records might be better suited). 'How' and 'why' questions are likely to favour the use of case studies, experiments and histories.

Assuming, as is the case here, that the focus of the study concerns 'how' and 'why' questions the chosen research technique will depend on the researcher's degree of control over behavioural events and the degree of focus on contemporary as opposed to historical events. Experiments are done when the investigator can manipulate behaviour precisely and systematically to prove or disprove a theory. This type of method is most common in scientific analysis where controlled experiments can control variables, the term 'social experiment' has emerged where social scientists approach different groups of people in different ways. Histories are the preferred strategy where there is virtually no access, contact or control of the topic under examination. They are employed as a specialist technique when no relevant individuals are alive to report, even retrospectively, what occurred. In this situation the researcher must focus on primary and secondary sources as the main source of evidence. The case study is preferred in examining contemporary events, but when the relevant actors cannot be manipulated. It utilises the primary and secondary resources but complements these with the collection of targeted empirical research through methods such as direct observation and systematic interviewing.[2]

The case study is particularly useful when there is a belief that the contextual conditions might be highly pertinent to the phenomenon being studied.[3] Case studies are often seen as a 'soft' form of research, a poor relation in the family of methodological techniques. Only recently has the value of case study analysis been emphasised.[4] One of the main problems associated with case studies is the lack of rigor of case study research. There have been concerns that investigators have set out to prove a predetermined conclusion or have allowed equivocal evidence or biased views to influence the findings and conclusions. But bias can enter any research technique, such as experiments,[5] designing questionnaires[6] or historical research.[7] The problem then is not specific to the case study technique but is a general issue, which emphasises the importance of a clear and coherent methodological framework whatever techniques are used. Another common criticism of case studies is that they provide little basis for generalisation.[8] Multiple case studies can be conducted but require a rigorous research design, especially where it is impossible to compare exactly like with like. Case studies are, however, useful in that their findings are generalisable to theoretical propositions. The investigator's aim is not to make universal claims but to expand and generalise theories (analytic generalisation) supported by the findings of their specific inquiry which can then be adopted and tested in future research.[9] As Lipset, Trow and Coleman describe in their classic single case study research, their aim was to do a 'generalizing' and not a 'particularizing' analysis.[10] A frequent complaint about case studies is that they take too long and result in voluminous unreadable documents. Some case studies may well support this criticism but case studies are not inherently unreadable.[11] Nor do they need to take a long time. It might be that case studies have been confused with techniques that involve long periods in the field or emphasise detailed evidence, ethnography or participant observation for example. Again, as with the criticism of bias, these complaints place a premium on planning and preparing both the case study itself and the form and type of report writing.

The importance of contextual conditions makes the case study a particularly attractive research method for this research. An experiment deliberately divorces a phenomenon from its context so that the effect of a specific variable can be assessed. A history might try and explore the relationship between events and context but is limited by its information sources. Surveys can attempt to include an appreciation of context but their ability is extremely limited. The survey designer must restrict the number of questions while also limiting the range of variables in the respondents' answers, to allow the completed surveys to be analysed. The case study allows contextual conditions to be examined and understood and combines multiple sources of qualitative and quantitative evidence that strengthen its internal validity.

A research design is the logic that links the data to be collected (and the conclusions to be drawn) to the initial questions of a study. Every empirical study has an implicit, if not explicit, research design. The research design guides the investigator in the process of collecting, analysing and interpreting observations. It is a logical model of proof that allows the researcher to draw inferences concerning causal relations among the variables under investigation. The research design also defines the domain of generalisability, that is, whether the obtained interpretations can be generalised to a larger population or to different situations.[12] The research design aims to maximise the construct validity; internal validity; external validity: and reliability of the research (see Table A1).[13]

Construct validity is especially problematic given the common criticisms of case studies that investigators fail to develop a sufficiently operational set of measures, that subjective judgements are used to collect data and that there is often no clear and coherent methodological framework. Chapter One introduces the scope, aims and background to the research. Chapters 2, 4 and 6 provide the background to the models. They represent a review of the literature and a discussion of the background and main debates. The purpose of these chapters is not to determine answers but to develop sharper and more insightful questions and develop pertinent hypotheses and propositions which will be explored in each of the followinging case study chapters (Chs. 3, 5 & 7). Chapter 8 examines the influence of extant forms of accountability on the design and implementation of Freedom of Information legislation. Chapter 9 concludes the book by re-examining its central question in light of empirical research and highlighting the overall findings of the research. It also outlines some emerging agendas that may have significant implications for this field of research.

Internal validity is a concern for causal or explanatory case studies. If the researcher incorrectly concludes that there is a causal relationship between 'x' and 'y' without knowing about the influence of 'y' the research design has failed to deal with a threat to internal validity. A

Table A1 Case Study Tactics for Four Design Tests[14]

Tests	Possible Case Study Tactics	Phase of Research in which Tactic occurs
Construct Validity	• use multiple sources of evidence • establish chain of evidence • have key informants review draft case study reports	data collection data collection composition
Internal Validity	• do pattern matching • do explanation building • do time series analysis	data analysis data analysis data analysis
External Validity	• use replication logic in multiple case studies	research design
Reliability	• use case study protocol • develop case study data base	data collection data collection

research design can build in techniques (pattern matching, explanation building, time series analysis) and questions (Have all the rival explanations and possibilities been considered? Is the evidence convergent?) to guard against this problem. The research design for this book ensures internal validity of the research by: designing and conducting an interview programme that secures information and viewpoints from a broad and appropriate range of individuals; highlighting and explaining converging/diverging views and opinions through subsequent research, for example official records (triangulation); while maintaining the scope of the research between realistic and specific boundaries.

External validity refers to whether a study's findings are generalisable beyond the immediate case study. Although case study typologies have been constructed, the simplest and most common distinction is between single and multiplecase studies.[15] Some fields, particularly political science and public administration, have attempted to delineate sharply between these two approaches and have developed the 'comparative case method' as a distinctive form of multiple case study.[16]

Critics suggest that single cases offer a poor basis for generalisations. Often researchers will fall into the trap of avoiding outliers and the atypical and try to select a 'representative' case or set of cases. The problem lies in the very notion of generalising findings rather than theories. The Home Office is a unique department. This fact does not undermine my research or its findings. My findings may not be found in other departments but that does not undermine their validity. Conversely, it might be possible cogently to suggest that certain aspects of my research results may be extrapolated beyond the Home Office. As Rhodes stressed: 'It is possible to generalise based on a single case study - the heuristic case method - if the case study sets out to test a theoretical proposition'.[17] What is generalisable is my theoretical framework, which would allow similar research to be conducted in other departments, and it is this future replication that may show correlations and differences between the Home Office and other departments.

The single case study *is* an appropriate design under several circumstances. One rationale for a single case is when it represents the *critical case* in testing a well-formulated theory. The theory has specified a clear set of propositions as well as circumstances within which the propositions are believed to be true. To confirm, challenge or extend the theory, there may exist a single case meeting all the conditions for testing the theory. The single case can then be used to determine whether a theory's propositions are correct or whether some alternative set of explanations might be more relevant. The single case study can, therefore, represent a significant contribution to knowledge and theory building.[18] A second rationale for a single case is one in which the case represents an *extreme* or *unique* case. A strong argument can be put forward that the Home Office is both a *critical* and *extreme* case. It has a number of features which make it an attractive arena in which to analyse each of the accountability models. For example, the Home Office attracts the highest number of judicial review cases; has been the centre of numerous debates about relationships between ministers, Parliament and civil servants; it attracts a substantial amount of parliamentary attention; and its bureaucratic structures contain the full range of both formal and informal quasi-contractual relationships and audit mechanisms.

A third rationale for a single case is the 'revelatory case'. This situation exists when the researcher has an opportunity to interview individuals and access documents that would be inaccessible to most researchers. Under such conditions, a single case study is justified due to its revelatory nature. The unrivalled and unique access to the Home Office, supported by the Cabinet Office, provided by my employment on two Economic and Social Research Council projects made the Home Office a 'revelatory' case demanding sole attention.[19] It provided unparalleled access to past and present ministers, senior civil servants, agency officials and MPs working on the Home Affairs select committee. Undertaking multiple case study research while keeping within realistic boundaries would have meant the under-utilisation of the unique opportunity afforded within the Home Office. In addition, the research might have become unbalanced as the degree of co-operation and access would have been unlikely within any other department.

A single case study can contain a comparative perspective, if sub-units of analysis are developed so that a more complex research design is developed. The sub-units can often add opportunities for extensive analysis enhancing the insights and overall value of the study. My research contains a comparative element as it is comparing and contrasting the utility of different models of accountability within one department. Mackie and Marsh have argued that: '...individual case studies are comparative if they use and assess the utility of concepts developed elsewhere; test some general theory or hypothesis; or generate concepts to be used elsewhere or hypothesis to be tested elsewhere'.[20] The constraints (time, financial, length, etc.) of the research will often dictate the most suitable research design. Inevitably, when deciding between a multiple or single case study a choice must be made between detail and generalisability.[21] Overall, 'the single-case study design is eminently justifiable under certain conditions - where the case represents a critical test of existing theory, where the case is a rare or unique event or where the case serves a revelatory purpose'.[22] This is a piece of research that explores the issue of accountability in the Home Office. It does not aim to make wider generalisations but that does not undermine the suggestion that the framework of analysis could not be applied to other departments, nor the intimation that some of the findings may be found, to a lesser or greater degree, in other departments.

Reliability refers to ensuring the academic propriety of the study and ensuring that the evidence collected in the course of the research is catalogued and stored and available for future analysis or replication by other researchers. In the past, case study research procedures have been poorly documented making external reviewers suspicious of the reliability of the case study. During the course of this research, a case study database has been established to catalogue and organise the data collected and utilised. This includes the transcripts of all the interviews given (confidentiality upheld where necessary), letters, documents, personal notes, parliamentary questions and a bibliography of all the books, articles and reports used in the research.

In total, 65 semi-structured elite interviews were conducted. Interviewees included former and present Home Office ministers, senior civil servants, members of the judiciary, members of the Home Affairs Committee, Prison Service officials and chief executives of companies managing private prisons. The interviews were supplemented with secondary material from a range of sources (Official Reports, Hansard, parliamentary papers, international and learned journals, bibliographies, etc.). Often interviewees would follow up our meeting in writing with further points or statistical information which they had subsequently collected. Parliamentary questions were tabled on my behalf by a local MP.[23] The Code of Access to government information was also employed to elicit information and documents, with varying degrees of success. Finally, a range of contacts with middle-ranking civil servants and parliamentary clerks provided me with a constant flow of information on which to draw.

Notes

[1] Yin, R (1994) *Case Study Research* (London : Sage) p.4.
[2] For an excellent discussion of the use of case studies in political science see: Eckstein, H (1975) 'Case Study and Theory in Political Science' in Greenstein, F & Polsby, N (eds.) *Handbook of Political Science Vol.7 Strategy of Inquiry* (Reading, Mass : Addison - Wesley) pp.79-137.
[3] See Agranoff, R & Radin, B (1991) 'The Comparative Case Study Approach in Public Administration' *Research in Public Administration* Vol.1 pp.203-231.
[4] For example see Rhodes, R (1994) 'State Building Without a Bureaucracy - The Case of the UK' in Budge, I & McKay (eds.) *Developing Democracy* (London : Sage) pp.165-189.
[5] Rosenthal, R (1966) *Experimenter Effects in Behavioural Research* (New York : Appleton).
[6] Sudman, S & Bradburn, N (1982) *Asking Questions: A Practical Guide to Questionnaire Design* (San Francisco : Jossey-Bass).

7   Gottschalk, L (1968) *Understanding History* (New York : Knopf).
8   Blondel noted that the case study: '...does not provide guidelines by which to abstract from reality the "critical" elements which would provide the material for comparisons on a large scale'. Blondel, J (1981) *The Discipline of Politics* (London : Butterworth) p.67.
9   See Eckstein, H (1975) 'Case Study and Theory in Political Science' in Greenstein, F & Polsby, N (eds.) *Handbook of Political Science. Vol. 7. Strategies of Inquiry* (Reading Mass. : Addison-Wesley).
10 Lipset, S, Trow, M & Coleman, J (1956) *Union Democracy: The Inside Politics of the International Typographic Union* (New York : Free Press).
11 For example see Feagin, J, Orum, A & Sjoberg, G eds. (1991) *A Case for the Case Study* (Chapel Hill : UNCP).
12 Nachmias, D & Nachmias, C (1992) *Research Methods in the Social Sciences* (New York : St Martin) pp.77-78.
13 See Kidder, L & Judd, C (1986) *Research Methods in social relations* (New York : Holt) pp.26-29.
14 Yin, R (1994) *Case Study Research* (London : Sage) p.33.
15 See Lijphart, A (1971) 'Comparative Politics and the Comparative Method' *American Political Science Review* Vol.65 pp.652-693; Eckstein, H (1975) 'Case Study and Theory in Political Science' in Greenstein, F & Polsby, N (eds.) *Handbook of Political Science Vol.7 Strategy of Inquiry* (Reading, Mass. : Addison Wesley) pp.79-137.
16 Agranoff, R & Radin, B (1991) 'The Comparative Case Study Approach in Public Administration' *Research in Public Administration* Vol.1 pp.203-231.
17 Rhodes, R (1994) 'State Building Without a Bureaucracy - The Case of the UK' in Budge, I & McKay (eds.) *Developing Democracy* (London : Sage) pp.56-57.
18 For example see Graham Allison's comparison of three theories of bureaucratic functioning and the Cuban missile crisis. Allison, G (1971) *Essence of Decision: Explaining the Cuban Missile Crisis* (Boston : Little Brown).
19 Firstly working on the ESRC 'Whitehall Programme' with Prof. Martin Smith, Prof. Dave Marsh and Dr Dave Richards on a project entitled 'The Fragmenting Governmental Framework: Central Government Departments in the Policy Process' and subsequently on an extension project entitled 'New Labour and the Reform of Whitehall: Inheritance, Transition and Accommodation'.
20 Mackie, T & Marsh, D (1995) 'The Comparative Method' in Marsh, D & Stoker, G (eds.) *Theory and Methods in Political Science* (Basingstoke : Macmillan) p.177.
21 For a fuller discussion of this, see Ragin, C (1987) *The Comparative Method: Moving Beyond Quantitative and Qualitative Strategies'* (Berkeley : UCP).
22 Yin, R (1994) *Case Study Research* (London : Sage) p.44.
23 Richard Allan MP (Sheffield Hallam).

Bibliography

Administrative Staff College (1963) *The Accountability of Government Departments* (Henley-on Thames : Administrative Staff College)

Agranoff, R & Radin, B (1991) 'The comparative case study approach in public administration' in Perry, J (ed.) *Research in Public Administration* (Greenwich : JAI Press) pp.203-231

Ahrens, T (1996) 'Styles of Accountability' *Accountability, Organisations and Society* Vol.21 No.2/3 pp.139-173

Alderman, R (1996) 'Prime Minister's Questions in the British House of Commons' *Parliamentarian* July Vol.LXXVII No.3 pp.290-292

Allison, G (1971) *Essence of Decision: Explaining the Cuban missile crisis* (Boston : Little Brown)

Anderson, B 'Derek Lewis: big job, little man, inaccurate book' *The Spectator* 1/3/97

Andrews, C & Kouzmin, A (1999) 'Re-legitimating 'voice' and 'loyalty' with economic theories of democracy and accountability' *International Review of Administrative Sciences* Vol.65 No.3 pp.395-409

Ashford, M (1993) *Detained without trial: a survey of immigrant detention* (JCWI : London)

Ashford, N (1985) 'The Bankruptcy of Collectivism' in Seldon, A (ed.) *The 'New Right' Enlightenment* (London : Economic and Literary Books)

Austin, R (1994) 'Freedom of Information: The Constitutional Impact' in Jowell, J & Oliver, D (ed.) *The Changing Constitution* (Oxford : Clarendon)

Bagehot, W (1867) *The English Constitution* (London : Collins)

Baldwin, R (1988) 'The Next Steps: Ministerial Responsibility and Government by Agency' *Modern Law Review* Vol.51 pp.622-628

Bale, T & Kopecky, P (1998) 'Can young pups teach an old dog new tricks?' *Legislative Studies* Vol.4 No.2 pp.149-170

Bamforth, N (1998) 'Parliamentary Sovereignty and the Human Rights Act 1998' *Public Law* pp.572-582

Banham, J (1994) *The Anatomy of Change* (London : Orion)

Barberis, P (1996) *The Whitehall Reader* (Buckingham : Open University Press)

Barberis, P (1996) *The elite of the elite: permanent secretaries in the British higher civil service* (Aldershot : Dartmouth)

Barberis, P (1997) *The civil service in an era of change* (Aldershot : Dartmouth)

Barberis, P (1998) 'The New Public Management and New Accountability' *Public Administration* Vol.76 pp.451-470

Barker, A (1996) *Myth versus Management: Individual Ministerial Responsibility in the New Whitehall* Essex Papers in Politics and Government No.105 (Colchester : University of Essex)

Barker, A (1996) *Political Responsibility for UK Prison Security: Ministers escape again* Essex Papers in Politics and Government No.106 (Colchester : University of Essex)

Barker, A (1996) 'The Impact of Judicial Review: Perspectives From Whitehall and the Courts' *Public Law* pp.612-621

Barker, A (1997) 'Practising to Deceive: Whitehall, Arms Exports and the Scott Inquiry' *Political Quarterly* Vol.68 No.1 pp.41-50

Barker, A (1998) *The Labour Government's Policy 'Reviews' and 'Task Forces': An Initial Listing and Analysis* Essex Papers in Politics and Government No. 126 (Colchester : University of Essex)

Barker, A (1998) 'Public Policy Inquiry and Advice as an Aspect of Constitutional Reform' *Journal of Legislative Studies* Vol.4 No.2 pp.107-127

Barker, A (1998) 'Political Responsibility for UK Prison Security - Ministers escape again' *Public Administration* Vol.76 No.1 pp.1-25

Barker, A & Wilson, G (1997) 'Whitehall's disobedient servants? Senior officials' potential resistance to ministers in British government departments' *British Journal of Political Science* Vol. 27 pp.223-46

Barnes, M (1997) 'British Ombudsmania' *The Stakeholder* Vol.1 No.1 pp.18-19

Barzelay, M (1997) 'Central audit institutions and performance auditing: a comparative analysis of organizational strategies in the OECD' *Governance* Vol.10 No.3 pp.235-260

Bayliss, R (1996) *Conflicting Modes of Accountability: A User Perspective* Newcastle Discussion Papers in Politics No.20, University of Newcastle

Beattie, A (1995) 'Ministerial Responsibility and the Theory of the British State' in Rhodes, R & Dunleavy, P (eds.) *Prime Minister, Cabinet and Core Executive* (Basingstoke : Macmillan)

Beattie, A (1998) 'Why is the case for Parliamentary Reform in Britain so Weak' *Legislative Studies* Vol.4 No.2 pp.1-16

Beer, S (1969) *Modern British Politics* (London : Faber)

Beetham, D (1994) *Defining and Measuring Democracy* (London : Sage)

Behn, R (1998) 'The New Public Management Paradigm and the Search for Democratic Accountability' *International Public Management Journal* Vol.1 No.2 pp.131-164

Bellone, C & Goerl, G (1992) 'Reconciling public entrepreneurship and democracy' *Public Administration Review* Vol.52 No.2 pp.130-134

Belsey, A (1985) 'The New Right, Social Order and Civil Liberties' in Levitas, R (ed.) *The Ideology of the New Right* (Oxford : Polity Press)

Benemy, F (1965) *The Elected Monarch* (London : Harrap)
Bennett, C (1997) 'Adoption of Policy Instruments for Bureaucratic Accountability' *Governance* Vol.10 No.3 pp.213-233
Berlins, M & Dyer, C (1994) *The Law Machine* (London : Penguin)
Beyn, R (1998) 'The New Public Management Paradigm and the Search for Democratic Accountability' *International Public Management Journal* Vol.1 No.2 pp.131-164
Birch, A (1964) *Representative and responsible government: an essay on the constitution* (London : Allen & Unwin)
Birch, A (1984) 'Overload, Ungovernability and Delegitimation: The Theories of the British Case' *British Journal of Political Science* Vol.14 pp.135-160
Bird, P (1973) *Accountability: Standards in Financial Reporting* (London : Haymarket)
Birkinshaw, P (1985) *Grievances, Remedies and the State* (London : Sweet & Maxwell)
Birkinshaw, P (1990) *Government and Information: The Law Relating to Access, Disclosure and Regulation* (London : Butterworths)
Birkinshaw, P (1991) *Freedom of Information: The US Experience* (Hull : Hull University Law School)
Birkinshaw, P (1993) 'I Only Ask For Information - The White Paper on Open Government' *Public Law* pp.557-568
Birkinshaw, P (1996) *Freedom of Information: the law, the practice and the ideal* (London : Butterworths)
Birkinshaw, P (1997) 'Freedom of Information' *Parliamentary Affairs* Vol.50 No.1 pp.164-182
Birkinshaw, P (1998) "An 'all singin' all dancin' affair: the new Labour government's proposals for Freedom of Information" *Public Law* pp.176-190
Birkinshaw, P & Parkin, A (1999) 'Freedom of Information' in Blackburn, R & Plant, R (eds.) *Constitutional Reform: The Labour Government's Constitutional Reform Agenda* (London : Longman)
Blackburn, R & Plant, R (eds.) (1999) *Constitutional Reform: The Labour Government's Constitutional Reform Agenda* (London : Longman)
Blake, C & Sunkin, M (1998) 'Immigration: appeals and judicial review' *Public Law* pp.583-591
Blom-Cooper, L (1984) 'Lawyers and Public Administrators: Separate and Unequal' *Public Law* pp.215-235
Blom-Cooper, L (1999) 'The Role and Functions of Tribunals of Inquiry - An Irish Perspective' *Public Law* pp.175-178
Blom-Cooper, L (2000) 'Tribunals Under Inquiry' *Public Law* pp.1-2
Bogdanor, V (1994) 'Ministers, Civil Servants and the Constitution' *Government & Opposition* Vol.29 pp.677-695

Bogdanor, V (1994) *Can government be run like a business?* (London : Chartered Institute of Public Finance and Accountancy)
Bogdanor, V (1996) *Politics and the constitution: essays on British government* (Aldershot : Dartmouth)
Bogdanor, V (1996) 'The Scott Report' *Public Administration* Vol.74 No.4 pp.593-611
Bogdanor, V (1997) 'Ministerial Accountability' *Parliamentary Affairs* Vol.50 No.1 pp.97-109
Borins, S (1995) 'The New Public Management is Here to Stay' *Canadian Public Administration* Vol.38 pp.122-132
Boston, J (1987) 'Transforming New Zealand's Public Sector: Labour' s Quest for Improved Efficiency and Accountability' *Public Administration* Vol.65 pp.423-442
Boston, J (1992) 'The Problems of Policy Co-ordination: The New Zealand Experience' *Governance* Vol.5 No.1 pp.88-103
Boston, J (1995) 'Lessons from the Antipodes' in O'Toole, B & Jordan, G (eds.) *The Next Steps - Improving Management in Government?* (Dartmouth : Aldershot) pp.161-177
Boston, J et al. (1997) *Public Management: The New Zealand Model* (Melbourne : Oxford University Press)
Bovens, M (1998) *The Quest for Responsibility: Accountability and Citizenship in Complex Organisations* (Cambridge, New York : Cambridge University Press)
Bovens, M (1998) 'The Social Steering of Complex Organisations' *British Journal of Political Science* Vol.20 pp.91-117
Bovens, M & Plug, P 'Accountability at a Distance. Reconciling political accountability and administrative autonomy' Paper to the International Institute of Administrative Sciences Conference, 12-15 May 1999, Civil Service College, Sunningdale
Boyle, A (1994) 'Sovereignty, Accountability and the Reform of Administrative Law' in Richardson, G & Genn, H (eds.) *Administrative Law and Government Action: the courts and alternative mechanisms of review* (Oxford : Clarendon) pp.81-104
Boynton, J (1986) 'Judicial Review of Administrative Decisions - A Background Paper' *Public Administration* Vol.64 No.3 pp.147-161
Bradley, A (1995) 'The Parliamentary Ombudsman again: a positive report' *Public Law* pp.345-50
Brazier, A (2000) *Systematic Scrutiny: Reforming the Select Committees* (London : Hansard Society)
Brazier, A (2000) *Parliament and the Public Purse* (London : Hansard Society)
Brazier, R (1989) 'Government and the Law: Ministerial Responsibility for Legal Affairs' *Public Law* pp.64-94

Brazier, R (1990) 'Post-Resignation Explanations' *Public Law* pp.300-307
Brazier, R (1994) 'It *Is* a Constitutional Issue: Fitness for Ministerial Office in the 1990s' *Public Law* pp.431-451
Bridges, L Meszaros, G & Sunkin, M (1995) *Judicial Review in Perspective* (London : Cavendish)
Bridges, L Meszaros, G & Sunkin, M (2000) 'Regulating the Judicial Review Case Load' *Public Law* pp.651-670
Broadbent, J & Laughlin, R (1997) 'Evaluating the 'New Public Management' reforms in the United Kingdom: a constitutional possibility?' *Public Administration* Vol.75 pp.487-507
Broadbent, J, Dietrich, M & Laughlin, R (1996) 'The Development of Principal-Agent, Contracting and Accountability Relationships in the Public Sector: Conceptual and Cultural Problems' *Critical Perspectives on Accounting* Vol.7 p.259-284
Brooks, J & Bates, P (1995) 'The problem of effecting change with the British Civil Service: a cultural perspective' *British Journal of Management* Vol.5 pp.123-138
Brown-Wilkinson, N (1988) 'The Independence of the Judiciary in 1988' *Public Law* pp.44-57
Bruce, A & McConnell, A (1996) 'Accountability in Local Government and the NHS' in Pyper, R (ed.) *Aspects of Accountability in the British System of Government* (Eastham : Tudor)
Bulpitt, J (1983) *Territory and Power in the UK* (Manchester : Manchester University Press)
Burton, P & Duncan, S (1996) 'Democracy and Accountability in Public Bodies: New Agendas in British Governance' *Policy and Politics* Vol.24 No.1 pp.5-17
Butler, D (1973) 'Ministerial Responsibility in Australia and the UK' *Public Administration* Vol.26 pp. 403-414
Butler, R (1988) *Government and Good Public Management - Are They Compatible?* (London : Institute for Personnel Management)
Butler, R (1992) 'The New Public Management: the contribution of Whitehall and Academia *Public Policy & Administration* Vol.7 No.3
Butler, R (1994) 'Reinventing British Government' *Public Administration* Vol.72 pp.263-270
Butt, R (1969) *The Power of Parliament* (London : Constable)
Cabinet Office (1987) *The Judge Over Your Shoulder*
Cabinet Office (1988) *Improving Management in Government: The Next Steps* [The Ibbs Report]
Cabinet Office (1992) *Questions of Procedure for Ministers*
Cabinet Office (1992) *Executive Agencies: A guide to setting targets and measuring performance* (London : HMSO)
Cabinet Office (1994) *Code of Practice on Access to Government Information*

Cabinet Office (1994) *Departmental Evidence and Response to Select Committees* [The Osmotherly Rules]
Cabinet Office (1995) *Judicial Review - Balancing the Scales*
Cabinet Office (1995) *Open Government - Code on Access to Government Information 1994 Report*
Cabinet Office (1996) *Open Government - Code on Access to Government Information 1995 Report*
Cabinet Office (1997) *Open Government - Code on Access to Government Information 1996 Report*
Cabinet Office (1997) *Openning Up Quangos*
Cabinet Office (1998) *Open Government - Code on Access to Government Information 1997 Report*
Cabinet Office (1998) *'Your Right to Know' - Background Material*
Cabinet Office (1998) *Annual Report. The Government's Strategy*
Cabinet Office (1998) *Quangos: Openning the Doors*
Cabinet Office (2000) *Wiring It Up: Whitehall's Management of Cross-Cutting Policies and Services*, Performance & Innovation Unit, London
Callaghan, J (1982) 'Cumber and Variableness' in RIPA *The Home Office: Perspectives on Policy and Administration* (London : RIPA) pp.9-23
Campbell, C (1975) 'Degrees of freedom and the case study' *Comparative Political Studies* Vol.8 pp.178-193
Campbell, C & Wilson, G (1995) *The End of Whitehall* (Oxford : Blackwell)
Campbell, E (1998) 'Investigating the Truth of Statements made in Parliament: The Australian Experience' *Public Law* pp. 125-136
Carter, N, Klein, K & Day, P (1992) *How Organisations Manage Success: the use of performance indicators in government* (London : Routledge)
Castles, F & Pierson, C (1996) 'A New Convergence? Recent Policy Developments in the United Kingdom , Australia and New Zealand' *Policy and Politics* Vol.24 No.3 pp.233-245
Chan, J (1994) 'The privatisation of punishment: a review of the key issues' in Moyle, P (ed.) *Private Prisons and Police: recent Australian trends* (Australia : NSW)
Chapman, R (1988) *Ethics in the Civil Service* (London : Routledge)
Chapman, R & Hunt, M (1987) *Open Government* (London : Routledge)
Chester, D & Bowring, N (1962) *Questions in Parliament* (Oxford : Clarendon)
Christiansen, P (1996) 'Accountability and New Public Management' *Politica* Vol. 28 No.3 pp.271-285
Clark, D (1996) 'Open Government in Britain: Discourse and Practice' *Public Money and Management* Vol.16 No.1 pp.23-31
Clements, L & Young, T (1999) 'Human Rights: Changing the Culture' *Journal of Law and Society* (Special Issue) Vol.26 No.1

Bibliography 389

Cm 5104 (1972) *Departmental Committee on Section 2 of the Official Secrets Act 1911*, HMSO, London. [The Franks Report]

Cm 9916 (1986) *The government's Response to the Fourth Report from the Defence Committee on 'Westland Plc: The Defence Implications for the Future of Westland Plc: The Government's Decision Making': Government Response to the Third and Fourth Reports from the Defence Committee, Session 1985/86*, HMSO, London

Cm 524 (1989) *Civil service Management Reform: the Next Steps: Government Reply to the Eighth Report from the Treasury and Civil Service Committee (1987-88)* HMSO, London

Cm 914 (1989) *The Financing and Accountability of Next Steps Agencies*, HMSO, London

Cm 1456 (1991) *Report of an Inquiry into Prison Disturbances*, HMSO, London. [The Woolf Report]

Cm 1532 (1991) *The Working of the Select Committee System*, HMSO, London

Cm 1599 (1991) *The Citizen's Charter. Raising the Standard*, HMSO, London

Cm 1647 (1991) *Custody, Care and Justice: the way ahead for the Prison Service in England and Wales*, HMSO, London

Cm 1730 (1991) *Competing for Quality*, HMSO, London

Cm 1761 (1991) *The Next Steps Initiative: Government Reply to the Seventh Report from the Treasury and Civil Service Committee*, HMSO, London

Cm 2101 (1992) *The Citizen's Charter. First Report*, HMSO, London

Cm 2540 (1992) *Citizen's Charter. Second Report*, HMSO, London

Cm 2290 (1993) *Open Government*, HMSO, London

Cm 2430 (1993) *Next Steps Review 1993*, HMSO, London

Cm 2626 (1994) *Better Accounting for Taxpayers Money. Resource Accounting and Budgeting in Government*, HMSO, London

Cm 2627 (1994) *The Civil Service. Continuity and Change*, HMSO, London

Cm 2508 (1995) *Home Office Annual Report 1994*

Cm 2748 (1995) *The Civil Service. Taking Forward Continuity and Change*, HMSO, London

Cm 2850 (1995) *First Report of the Committee on Standards in Public Life*, HMSO, London

Cm 2931 (1995) *The Government's Response to the First Report of the Committee on Standards in Public Life*, HMSO, London

Cm 3020 (1995) *Review of Prison Security in England and Wales and The escape from Parkhurst Prison on Tuesday 3rd January 1995*, HMSO, London. [The Learmont Report]

Cm 3164 (1996) *Next Steps Review 1995*, HMSO, London

Cm 3346 (1996) *The Government Reply to the First and Second Reports from the Home Affairs Committee, Session 1995/96 HC 111 and HC 412: Murder and the mandatory life sentence*

Cm 3208 (1997) *Home Office. Annual Report 1996*, HMSO, London
Cm 3687 (1997) *Prisons Ombudsman. Annual Report 1996*, HMSO, London
Cm 3782 (1997) *Home Office. Bringing Rights Home*, HMSO, London
Cm 3818 (1997) *Your Right To Know - The Government's Proposals for a Freedom of Information Act*, HMSO, London
Cm 3608 (1998) *Home Office. Annual Report 1997*, HMSO, London
Cm 3889 (1998) *Next Steps Review 1997*, HMSO, London
Cm 3908 (1998) *The Government's expenditure plans 1998/99 for the Home Office and Charity Commission*, HMSO, London
Cm 3920 (1998) *The government's expenditure plans 1998/99*, HMSO, London
Cm 3969 (1998) *The Government's Annual Report 1997/98*, HMSO, London
Cm 3984 (1998) *Prisons Ombudsman. Annual Report 1997*, HMSO, London
Cm 4011 (1998) *Modern Public Service for Britain: Investing in Reform* , HMSO, London
Cm 4014 (1998) *Modern Local Government. in touch with the people*, HMSO, London
Cm 4018 (1998) *Fairer, Faster, Firmer: a modern approach to immigration and asylum*
Cm 4090 (1998) *The Report of the Independent Commission on the Voting System*, HMSO, London [The Jenkins Report]
Cm 4174 (1998) *The Government Reply to the 3rd Report from the Home Affairs Committee, Session 1997-1998, HC 486: Alternatives to Prison Sentences*, HMSO, London
Cm 4181 (1998) *Public Services for the Future: Modernisation, Reform, Accountability*, HMSO, London
Cm 3908 (1999) *Home Office. Annual Report 1998*, HMSO, London
Cm 4205 (1999) *The Government's Expenditure Plans 1999-2000 to 2001-2002 for the Home Office and the Charity Commission*, HMSO, London
Cm 4273 (1999) *Next Steps Report 1998*, HMSO, London
Cm 4401 (1999) *The Government's Annual Report 1998/99*, HMSO, London
Cm 4310 (1999) *Modernising Government* , HMSO, London
Cm 4355 (1999) *Freedom of Information: Consultation on draft legislation*, HMSO, London
Cm 4376 (1999) *Scottish Prisons Commission Annual Report 1998*, HMSO, London
Cm 4534 (2000) *A House for the Future* HMSO, London.
Cm 4737 (2000) *The Government's Response to the First Report from the Liaison Committee on Shifting the Balance: Select Committees and the Executive*, HMSO, London
Cm 4864 (2000) *The Government's Reply to the Second Report from the Home Affairs Committee, Session 1999-2000, HC 95, Controls Over Firearms*, HMSO, London

Bibliography 391

Cm 4903 (2000) 'Standards of Conduct in the House of Lords' Seventh Report of the Committee on Standards in Public Life, HMSO, London

Cmnd 9230 (1918) *Report of the Machinery of Government Committee of the Ministry of Reconstruction* [The Haldane Report]

Cmnd 4060 (1932) *Report of the Committee on Ministers Powers* [The Donoughmore Committee]

Cmnd 2009 (1963) *Tribunal of Inquiry (Evidence) Act 1921 - Report of the Tribunal Appointed to inquire into the Vassall Case and related matters* Chairman: The Rt. Hon. Viscount Radcliffe

Cmnd 3121 (1966) *Royal Commission on Tribunals of Inquiry*

Cmnd 3638 (1968) *The Civil Service. Vol.1 Report of the Committee 1966-68*, HMSO, London. [The Fulton Report]

Cmnd 7520 (1979) *Open Government*, HMSO, London

Cmnd 8616 (1982) *The Financial Management Initiative*, HMSO, London

Cobbett, W (1966) *Rural Rides* (London : Everyman)

Coleman, M (1999) *Electronic Media, Parliament and the People: Making Democracy Visible* (London : Hansard Society).

Connolly, M (1994) 'Making the public sector more user friendly? A critical examination of the Citizen's Charter' *Parliamentary Affairs* Vol.47 No.1 pp.23-36

Constitution Unit (1998) *Checks and balances in single chamber parliaments - a comparative study* (London : The Constitution Unit)

Cooper, P (1995) 'Separating Policy from Operations in the Prison Service: A Case Study' *Public Policy & Administration* Vol.10 No.4 pp.4-19

Cormack, P (1996) 'Restoring Faith in Parliament' *The Journal of Legislative Studies* Vol.2 No.4 pp.277-283

Cornford, J (1988) 'Official Secrecy and Freedom of Information' in Holmes, R & Elliot, M (eds.) *1688-1988 Time For a New Constitution* (Basingstoke : Macmillan)

Council on Tribunals (1996) *Advice to the Lord Chancellor on the procedural issues arising in the conduct of public inquiries set up by ministers*

Cowley, P (1998) 'Unbridled Passions? Free votes, Issues of Conscience and the accountability of British members of Parliament' *Legislative Studies* Vol.4 No.2 pp.70-89

Craig, F W S (1990) *British General Election Manifestos 1959-1987* (London : Macmillan)

Craig, P & Walters, M (1999) 'The Courts, Devolution and Human Rights' *Public Law* pp.274-304

Craig, T (1994) 'Private sector and community involvement in the New Zealand prison system' in Moyle, P (ed.) *Private Prisons and Police: recent Australian trends* (Australia : NSW)

Cremin, M (1993) 'The setting up of the Departmental Select Committees after the 1992 election' *Parliamentary Affairs* Vol.46 No.3 pp.309-318

Crick, B (1968) *The Reform of Parliament* (London : Weidenfeld)

Crick, B (1989) 'Beyond Parliamentary Reform' *Political Quarterly* Vol.60 No.4 pp.121-138

Crow, D (1973) *The State of the Nation* (London : Granada Television)

Dahl, R (1956) *A preface to democratic theory* (Chicago : Chicago University Press)

Dahl, R (1961) *Who Governs?* (New Haven : Yale University Press)

Daintith, T (1997) *Constitutional Implications of Executive Self Regulation: The New Administrative Law* (London : Institute of Advanced Legal Studies, University of London)

Daintith, T & Page, A (1999) *The Executive in the Constitution: Structure, Autonomy and Internal Control* (Oxford : Oxford University Press)

Daniel, C 'Child-friendly but still straight laced' *New Statesman & Society* 20/3/98 pp.20-22

Day, P & Klein, R (1987) *Accountabilities: Five Public Services* (London : Tavistock)

Day, P & Klein, R (1990) *Inspecting the inspectorates* (London : Joseph Rowntree Foundation)

De Smith, S & Brazier, R (1994) *Constitutional and Administrative Law* (London : Penguin)

Deakin, N & Walsh, K (1996) 'The Enabling State: The Role of Markets and Contracts' *Public Administration* Vol.74 pp.33-48

Deleon, L (1998) 'Accountability in Reinvented Government' *Public Administration* Vol. 76 pp.539-558

Department for Education & Employment (1997) *Open Government: a guide for staff to the Code of Practice on Access to Government Information*

Dhavan, R (1985) 'Judges and Accountability' in Dhavan, R Sudarshan, R & Khurdshid, S (eds.) *Judges and Judicial Power* (London : Sweet & Maxwell)

Dicey, A (1885) *An Introduction to the Study of the Law of the Constitution* (London : Macmillan)

Dickson, B (1995) 'Judicial Review and National Security' in Hadfield, B (ed.) *Judicial Review - A Thematic Approach* (Dublin : Gill & Macmillan) pp.187-228

Doig, A (1996) 'From Lynskey to Nolan: The Corruption of British Politics and Public Service' *Journal of Law & Society* Vol.23 No.1 pp.36-56

Domberger, S & Hall, C (1996) 'Contracting for Public Services: A Review of the Antipodean Experience' *Public Administration* Vol.74 pp.129-147

Donahue, J (1989) *The Privatisation Decision: public ends, private means* (New York : Basic Books)

Donaldson, F (1962) *The Marconi Scandal* (London : Quality Book Club)
Dowding, K (1995) *The Civil Service* (London : Routledge)
Dowding, K & Kang, W (1998) 'Ministerial Resignations 1945-97' *Public Administration* Vol. 76 pp.411-429
Drewry, G (1975) 'Judges and political inquiries: Harnessing a myth?' *Political Studies* Vol.23 pp.49-61
Drewry, G (1986) 'Public Lawyers and Public Administrators: Prospects For An Alliance?' *Public Administration* Vol.64 No.3 pp.173-188
Drewry, G (1987) 'Judges and Justice' *Parliamentary Affairs* Vol.40 No.4 pp.542-544
Drewry, G (1989) 'The Home Affairs Committee' in Drewry, G (ed.) *The New Select Committees* (Oxford : Clarendon) pp.182-205
Drewry, G (1989) *The New Select Committees* (Oxford : Clarendon)
Drewry, G (1990) 'A Cutting Edge? The Parliamentary Commissioner and MPs' *The Modern Law Review* Vol.53 pp.745-769
Drewry, G (1990) 'Judicial Review - Quite Enough of a Fairly Good Thing?' *Public Policy and Administration* Vol.5 No.1 pp.20-32
Drewry, G (1992) 'Judicial Politics in Britain: Patrolling the Boundaries' *West European Politics* Vol.15 pp.9-29
Drewry, G (1994) 'The Civil Service: From the 1940s to Next Steps and Beyond' *Parliamentary Affairs*, Vol.47 No.4 pp.583-595
Drewry, G (1995) 'Public Law' *Public Administration* Vol.73 pp.41-57
Drewry, G (1996) 'Judicial Inquiries and Public Reassurance' *Public Law* pp.368-373
Dudley, G (1994) 'The Next Steps Agencies, Political Salience and the Arms Length Principle' *Public Administration* Vol.72 No.2 pp.219-240
Dunleavy, P (1989) 'The architecture of the British state, part one: framework for analysis' *Public Administration* Vol.67 pp.249-275
Dunleavy, P (1991) *Democracy, Bureaucracy and Public Choice* (London : Harvester)
Dunleavy, P (1994) 'The Globalization of Public Services Production: Can Government be 'Best in World'?' *Public Policy and Administration* Vol.9 No.2 pp.36-65
Dunleavy, P (1994) *Reinventing Parliament: Making the Commons more Effective* (London : Charter 88)
Dunleavy, P & Rhodes, R (1990) 'Core executive Studies in Britain' *Public Administration* Vol.68 No.1 pp.3-28
Dunleavy, P *et al.* (1993) 'Leaders, Politics and Institutional Change: the decline of Prime Ministerial accountability to the House of Commons' *British Journal of Political Science* Vol.23 pp.267-298
Dunleavy, P & Hood, C (1994) 'From Old Public Administration to New Public Management' *Public Money and Management* Vol.14 No.3 pp.9-17
Dynes, M & Walker, D (1995) *The New British State: The Government Machine in the 1990s* (London : The Times)

Eagles, I Taggart, M & Liddell, G (1992) *Freedom of Information in New Zealand* (Auckland : Oxford University Press)

Eckstein, H (1975) 'Case study and theory in political science' in Greenstein, F & Polsby, N (eds.) *Handbook of Political Science Vol.7 Strategy of Inquiry* (Reading, Mass : Addison Wesley)

Edley, C (1990) *Administrative Law: Rethinking Judicial Control of Bureaucracy* (London : Yale University Press)

Edwards, M & Hulme, D (1995) *Non-Governmental Organisation – Performance and Accountability* (London : Earthscan)

Efficiency Unit (1988) *Improving Management in Government: The Next Steps* (London : HMSO)

Efficiency Unit (1991) *Making the most of Next Steps: the management of ministers' departments and their executive agencies* [The Fraser Report]

Efficiency Unit (1993) *The Government's Guide to Market Testing*

Efficiency Unit (1993) *Career Management and Succession Planning Study* [The Oughton Report]

Efficiency Unit (1994) *Next Steps: Moving On* [The Trosa Report]

Efficiency Unit (1995) *After Next Steps* [The Massey Report]

Elcock, H (1998) 'The Changing Problem of Accountability in Modern Government: an analytical agenda for reformers' *Public Policy & Administration* Vol.13 No.3 pp.23-37

Elliott, M (1999) 'The demise of parliamentary sovereignty? The implications for justifying judicial review' *The Law Quarterly Review* Vol.115 pp.119-137

Elsenaar, M (1999) 'Law, accountability and the Private Finance Initiative in the National Health Service' *Public Law* pp.35-43

Errera, R (1986) 'Changes in Judicial Review: An Outsiders Reflections' *Public Administration* Vol.64 pp.189-195

Evans, H (1999) 'Parliament and Extra-Parliamentary Accountability Institutions' *Australian Journal of Public Administration* Vol.58 No.1 pp.87-89

Ewing, K (1999) 'The Human Rights Act and Parliamentary Democracy' *The Modern Law Review* Vol.62 No.1 pp.79-99

Falconer, P (1996) 'Charterism and Consumerism' in Pyper, R (ed.) *Aspects of Accountability in the British System of Government* (Eastham : Tudor)

Farmer, D (1995) *The Language of Public Administration* (London : The University of Alabama Press)

Farnham, S & Horton, S (1993) *Managing the New Public Services* (Basingstoke : Macmillan).

Fawcett, J (1985) 'Applications of the European Convention on Human Rights' in Vagg, J Morgan, R & Maquire, M (eds.) *Accountability and Prisons* (London : Tavistock)

Feagin, J, Orum, A & Sjoberg, G (1991) *A Case for the case study* (Chapel Hill : UNCP)

Feldman, D (1988) 'Judicial Review: A Way of Controlling Government?' *Public Administration* Vol.66 No.2 pp.21-34

Fell, B (1935) *The Nineteenth Century and After* Vol.118 (London)

Fenwick, H & Phillipson, G (2000) 'Public Protest, the Human Rights Act and Judicial Responses to Political Expression' *Public Law* pp.627-651

Finer, S (1952) 'Patronage and the Public Service' *Public Administration* Vol.30 pp.329-360

Finer, S (1956) 'The Individual Responsibility of Ministers' *Public Administration* Vol.34 pp.377-396

Finn, P (1993) 'Public Trust and Public Accountability' *Australian Quarterly* Vol.65 pp.50-59

First Division Association (1996) *Accountability in Government: A FDA Discussion Paper* (London : FDA)

Fitzgerald, E (1985) 'Prison discipline and the courts' in Vagg, J, Morgan, R & Maquire, M (eds.) *Accountability and Prisons* (London : Tavistock)

Flinders, M (1996) *Enforcing Ministerial 'Policy' Responsibility - The missing link in the chain?* (Sheffield : PERC)

Flinders, M (1997) 'Quangos: Why Do Governments Love Them?' in Flinders, M, Harden, I & Marquand, D (eds.) (1997) *How To Make Quangos Democratic* (London : Charter 88)

Flinders, M (1997) 'The Grey Zone- EGOs, NGOs and Quangos in Denmark' *The Stakeholder* Vol.2 No.5

Flinders, M (1997) 'Quangos: A Comparative Analysis - New Zealand' *The Stakeholder* Vol.1 No.3

Flinders, M (1998) 'Setting the Scene - quangos in context' in Flinders, M & Smith, M (eds.) *Quangos. Accountability and Reform: the politics of quasi-government* (London : Macmillan)

Flinders, M (1998) 'Squaring the Circle: parliamentary accountability and the Bank of England' *The Stakeholder* Vol.2 No.1

Flinders, M (1999) 'Britain's Quasi-Government' *Talking Politics* Vol.11 No.3 pp.176-182

Flinders, M (1999) 'Accounts and Accountability' *Fabian Review* Vol.111 No.1 pp.8-9

Flinders, M (2001) *Governance in Whitehall: Joining Up Government in a Fragmented State* (Sheffield : Department of Politics, University of Sheffield).

Flinders, M & Annesley, C (1998) 'Contrasting approached to quasi-government: the case of Germany and the UK' *The Stakeholder* Vol.2 No.2

Flinders, M & Cole, M (1999) 'Opening or Closing Pandora's Box? New Labour and the Quango State' *Talking Politics* Vol.12 No.1 pp.234-40

Flinders, M & McConnel, H (1997) 'Maybe Minister: Quangos and Accountability' in Flinders, M, Harden, I & Marquand, D (eds.) (1997) *How To Make Quangos Democratic* (London : Charter 88)

Flinders, M, Harden, I & Marquand, D (eds.) (1997) *How To Make Quangos Democratic* (London : Charter 88)

Flinders, M & Smith, M (1998) *Quangos, Accountability and Reform: the Politics of Quasi-Government* (London : Macmillan)

Flinders, M & Smith M.J (1998) 'Realising the democratic potential of quangos' in Flinders, M & Smith, M (eds.) *Quangos. Accountability and Reform: the politics of quasi-government* (London : Macmillan)

Flinders, M & Thiel, S van (1997) 'Going Dutch - Quangos in Holland' *The Stakeholder* Vol. 1 No.4

Flinders, M, Thiel, S van & Greve, C (1998) 'Quangos - What's in a Name? - Defining quangos from a comparative perspective' *Governance* Vol.12 No.2 pp.129-147

Flinders, M, Smith, M & Richards, D (1999) 'The Accountability of Public Bodies' memorandum of evidence to the Public Administration Committee Sixth Report *Quangos* (1998-99) HC 209-ll pp.196-205

Flynn, N (1990) *Public Sector Management* (London : Harvester Wheatsheaf)

Foreman, S (1986) *Shoes and Ships and sealing Wax: An Illustrated History of the Board of Trade* (London : HMSO)

Forsyth, C (1996) 'Of Fig Leaves and Fairy Tales: the *Ultra Vires* Doctrine, the Sovereignty of Parliament and Judicial Review' *Common Law Journal* Vol.122 pp.88-112

Foster, C (1996) 'Reflections on the true significance of the Scott Report for Government Accountability' *Public Administration* Vol.74 No.4 pp.567-592

Foster, C (1998) 'Interview with David Clark' *Parliamentary Brief* March pp.18-19

Foster, C & Plowden, F (1996) *The State Under Stress* (Buckingham : Open University Press)

Fox, C & Miller, H (1995) *Post-modern public administration: towards discourse* (London : Sage)

Fraser, P (1960) 'The Growth of Ministerial Control in the Nineteenth Century House of Commons' *English Historical Review* Vol.75 pp.444-463

Freedland, M (1994) 'Government by Contract and Public Law' *Public Law* pp.86-104

Freedland, M (1995) 'Privatising the *Carltona* Doctrine: Part II of the Deregulation and Contracting Out Act' *Public Law* pp.21-26

Freedland, M (1995) 'Contracting the Employment of Civil Servants - A Transparent Exercise' *Public Law* pp.224-234

Freedland, M (1996) 'The Rule Against Delegation and the *Carltona* Doctrine in an Agency Context' *Public Law* pp.19-31

Friedman, M & Friedman, R (1980) *Free to Choose* (Harmondsworth : Penguin)

Gains, F (1999) *Resource Dependency Between Departments and Next Steps Agencies*, unpublished Ph.D. thesis, University of Sheffield

Gagne, R (1996) 'Accountability and Public Administration' *Canadian Journal of Public Administration* Vol. 39 No.2 pp.213-223

Gamble, A (1986) 'The Political Economy of Freedom' in Levitas, R (ed.) *The Ideology of the New Right* (Oxford : Polity Press)

Gamble, A (1990) 'Theories of British Politics' *Political Studies* Vol.38 pp.404-420

Gamble, A (1996) *Hayek : The Iron Cage of Liberty* (Oxford : Polity Press)

Giddings, P (1994) 'Select Committees and Parliamentary Scrutiny: Plus Ca Change' *Parliamentary Affairs* Vol.47 No.4 pp.669-685

Giddings, P (1995) *Parliamentary Accountability: A study of Parliament and Executive Agencies* (Basingstoke : Macmillan)

Giddings, P (1995) 'Next steps to Where?' in Giddings, P (ed.) *Parliamentary Accountability: A study of Parliament and Executive Agencies* (Basingstoke : Macmillan)

Giddings, P (1995) 'Agencies and the Ombudsman' in Giddings, P (ed.) *Parliamentary Accountability: A study of Parliament and Executive Agencies* (Basingstoke : Macmillan)

Giddings, P (1997) 'Parliament and the Executive' *Parliamentary Affairs* Vol.50 No.1 pp.84-97

Gilmour, R & Jenson, L (1998) 'Reinventing Government Accountability: public functions, privatising and the meaning of state action' *Public Administration Review* Vol.58 No.3 pp.247-258

Gladstone, W (1879) *Gleanings from the Past Years* (London : John Murray)

Glor, E 'Do Generations Matter? The Effectiveness of Codes of Conduct with Different Generations of Public Servants' Paper to the International Institute of Administrative Sciences Conference, 12-15 May 1999, Civil Service College, Sunningdale

Glynn, J (1996) 'Performance auditing and performance improvement in government: public sector management reform, changing accountabilities and the role of performance audit' in *Performance Auditing and the Modernisation of Government* (OECD : Paris) pp.125-136

Glynn, J (1996) 'Public management: failing accountabilities and failing performance review' *International Journal of Public Sector Management* Vol.9 No.5/6 pp.125-137

Goldsworthy, D (1991) *Setting up next steps: a short account of the origins, launch and implementation of the Next Steps project in the British Civil Service* (London : HMSO)

Gottschalk, L (1968) *Understanding History* (New York : Knopf)

Gray, A & Jenkins, B (1985) *Administrative Politics in British Government* (Brighton : Wheatsheaf)

Gray, A & Jenkins, B (1993) 'Codes of Accountability in the New Public Sector' *Accounting, Auditing and Accountability* Vol.6/3 pp.52-68

Gray, A & Jenkins, B (1995) 'From Public Administration to Public Management' *Public Administration* Vol.73 pp.92-99

Gray, A & Jenkins, B (1998) 'New Labour, New Government? - Change and Continuity in Public Administration and Government 1997' *Parliamentary Affairs* Vol.31 No.2 pp.111-131

Gray, C (1994) *Government Beyond the Centre: Sub-National Politics in Britain* (Basingstoke : Macmillan)

Greene, J (1999) 'The inequalities of performance measurements' *Evaluation* Vol.5 No.2 pp.160-172

Greenleaf, W (1983) *The British Political Tradition: Vol.I The Rise of Collectivism* (London : Methuen)

Greenleaf, W (1987) *The British Political Tradition: Vol.III A Much Governed Nation* (London : Methuen)

Greer, P (1994) *Transforming Central Government: The Next Steps Initiative* (Milton Keynes : Open University)

Greer, S (1999) 'A Guide to the Human Rights Act 1998' *European Law Review* Vol.24 No.1 pp.3-22

Greer, S, Hedlund, R & Gibson, J (1978) *Accountability in Urban Society* (London : Sage)

Gregory, D (1999) 'Style over substance? Labour and the reform of Parliament' *Renewal* Vol.7 No.3 pp.42-50

Gregory, R (1991) 'The Attitudes of Senior Public Servants in Australia and New Zealand: Administrative Reform and Technocratic Consequence?' *Governance* Vol.4 No.3 pp.295-331

Gregory, R (1998) 'A New Zealand Tragedy: problems of political responsibility' *Governance* Vol.11 No.2 pp.231-40

Gregory, R & Pearson, J (1992) 'The Parliamentary Ombudsman After Twenty-Five Years' *Public Administration* Vol.70 No.4 pp.469-498

Griffiths, J (1979) 'The Political Constitution' *Modern Law Review* Vol.42 pp.1-21

Griffiths, J (1985) 'Judicial Decision Making in Public Law' *Public Law* pp.564-582

Griffiths, J (1985) 'Australian Administrative Law: Institutions, Reforms and Impact' *Public Administration* Vol.63 pp.445-463

Griffiths, J (1991) *The Politics of the Judiciary* (London : Fontana)

Griffiths, J (1995) 'The Study of Law and Politics' *The Journal of Legislative Studies* Vol.1 No.1 pp.3-16

Guida, R (1989) 'The Cost of Free Information' *The Public Interest* No.97 pp.87-95

HC 17 *Legal Aid - the Lord Chancellor's proposals*, Fifth Report of the Home Affairs Committee, Session 1992/93, HMSO, London

HC 18 *Right to Know Bill*, House of Commons, Session 1992/93, HMSO, London

Bibliography

HC 19 *The Working of the Select Committee System,* Second Report by the Committee on Procedure, Session 1989/90, HMSO, London

HC 21 *Representation of the People Acts*, First Report of the Home Affairs Select Committee, Session 1982/83, HMSO, London

HC 27 *The Role of the Civil Service* Fifth Report by the Treasury and Civil Service Committee, Session 1993/94, HMSO, London

HC 32 *Revised Immigration Rules,* Seventh Report of the Home Affairs Select Committee, Session 1981/82, HMSO, London

HC 35 *State and Use of Prisons* Third Report of the Home Affairs Committee, Session 1986/87, HMSO, London

HC 44 *Annual Report April 1995 - March 1996* HM Inspectorate of Prisons for England & Wales. HMSO, London

HC 46 *Racial Attacks*, Second Report of the Home Affairs Committee, Session 1981/82, HMSO, London

HC 57 *The Management of the Prison Service - Public and Private* Second Report of the Home Affairs Committee, Session 1996/97, HMSO, London

HC 60 *The Parliamentary Calendar: Initial Proposals* First Report of the Modernisation Committee, Session 1998/99, HMSO, London

HC 62 *Accountability of ministers and civil servants to select committees of the House of Commons* First Report of the Liaison Committee, Session 1986/87, HMSO, London

HC 67 *Government Response to the 2nd Report from the Committee (session 1995-96) on Ministerial Responsibility and Accountability* First Special Report by the Public Service Select Committee, Session 1996/97, HMSO, London

HC 75 *Government response to the 2nd report from the select committee on the Parliamentary Commissioner for Administration (Session 1995/96)* First Special Report by the Select Committee on the Parliamentary Commissioner for Administration, Session 1996/97, HMSO, London

HC 80 *Observations on the Second Report from the Home Affairs Committee, Session 1997/1998, Confidentiality of Police Settlements of Civil Claims* First Special Report from the Home Affairs Committee, Session 1998/99, HMSO, London

HC 82 *The Monetary Policy Committee of the Bank of England: Confirmation Hearings* Sixth Report by the Treasury Committee, Session 1997/98, HMSO, London

HC 84 *Open Government* Second Report by the Select Committee on the Parliamentary Commissioner for Administration, Session 1995/96, HMSO, London

HC 87 *Export Licensing and BMARC*, Third Report of the Trade & Industry Select Committee, Session 1995/96, HMSO, London

HC 92 *The Select Committee System* First Report of the Liaison Committee, Session 1982/83, HMSO, London

HC 92 *Civil Servants and Ministers: Duties and Responsibilities* Seventh Report by the Treasury and Civil Service Committee, Session 1985/86, HMSO, London

HC 111 *Murder - the mandatory life sentence*, First Report of the Home Affairs Select Committee, Session 1995/96, HMSO, London

HC 115 *Report of the Inquiry into the Export of Defence Equipment and Dual-Use Goods to Iraq and Related Prosecutions*, Session 1995/96, HMSO, London. [The Scott Report]

HC 126 *Computer Pornography*, First Report of the Home Affairs Select Committee, Session 1993/94, HMSO, London

HC 137 *Government Reply to the Fourth Report from the Home Affairs Select Committee, Session 1997/1998, Electoral Law and Administration* Second Special Report of the Home Affairs Committee, Session 1998/99, HMSO, London

HC 144 *The Operation and Performance of the Prison Service*, minutes of evidence, Home Affairs Committee, 18/1/95, Session 1994/95, HMSO, London

HC 155 *Pergau Hydro-electric Project* Seventeenth Report by the Public Accounts Committee, Session 1993/94, HMSO, London

HC 178 *Parliamentary Questions* Third Report by the Select Committee on Procedure, Session 1990/91, HMSO, London

HC 192 *Freemasonry in the Police and the Judiciary*, Third Report of the Home Affairs Select Committee, Session 1997/98, HMSO, London

HC 194 *Sittings of the House in Westminster Hall* Second Report of the Modernisation Committee, Session 1998/99, HMSO, London

HC 209 *Quangos* Sixth Report by the Public Administration Committee, Session 1998/99, HMSO, London

HC 225 *Annual Reports for 1997 and 1998 on Strategic Export Controls*, Third Report of the Defence Committee/Second Report from the Foreign Affairs Committee/Third Report from the International Development Committee/Fourth Report from the Trade and Industry Committee, Session 1999/2000, London, HMSO

HC 231 *Access to Official Information* First Report by the Parliamentary Commissioner for Administration, Session 1997/98, HMSO, London

HC 235 *The Ministerial Code: Improving the Rule Book*, Third Report of the Select Committee on Public Administration, Session 2000/01, HMSO, London

HC 258 *Police Discipline and Complaints Procedures*, First Report of the Home Affairs Select Committee, Session 1997/98, HMSO, London

HC 265 *Accountability of the Security Service*, First Report of the Home Affairs Committee, Session 1992/93, HMSO, London

HC 271 *Public expenditure: Pergau Hydro-electric Project, Malaysia, the Aid and Trade Provisions and Related Matters* Third Report of the Foreign Affairs Committee, Session 1993/94, HMSO, London

HC 274 *Prison Service Annual Reports and Accounts 1996/7* HM Prison Service 1997

HC 285 *Role and Responsibilities of the Head of the Home Civil Service* Minutes of Evidence for the 28/10/97 to the Public Administration Committee, Session 1997/98, HMSO, London

HC 291 *Contract Provision of Prisons* Fourth Report of the Home Affairs Committee, Session 1986/87, HMSO, London

HC 296 *Annual Report for 1995* Parliamentary Commissioner for Administration, HMSO, London

HC 300 *Shifting the Balance: Select Committees and the Executive*, First Report of the Liaison Committee, Session 1999-2000, HMSO, London

HC 301 *Funding of Political Parties*, Second Report of the Home Affairs Select Committee, Session 1993/94, HMSO, London

HC 307 *Annual Report for 1994* Parliamentary Commissioner for Administration, HMSO, London

HC 313 *Ministerial Accountability and Responsibility* Second Report of the Public Service Committee, Session 1996/97, HMSO. London

HC 323 *The Work of Select Committees* First Report of the Liaison Committee, Session 1996/97, HMSO, London

HC 364 (1972) *Tribunal of Inquiry (Evidence) Act 1921 - Report of the Tribunal Appointed to inquire into certain issues arising out of the operations of the Crown Agents as financiers on own account in the years 1967-74.* Chairman: Sir David Powell Croom-Johnson, HMSO, London

HC 367 *Government Response to the Fourth Report From the Select Committee on the Parliamentary Commissioner for Administration, Session 1995-6* Second Special Report by the Select Committee on the Parliamentary Commissioner for Administration, Session 1996/97, HMSO, London

HC 379 *Oral Questions*, First Report from the Select Committee on Procedure, Session 1989/90, HMSO, London

HC 380 *Report of the Parliamentary Ombudsman for 1995* Fourth Report by the Select Committee on the Parliamentary Commissioner for Administration, Session 1995/96, HMSO, London

HC 386 *Annual Report for 1996* Parliamentary Commissioner for Administration, HMSO, London

HC 398 *Your Right to Know: The Government's Proposals for a Freedom of Information Act* , Third Report of the Select Committee for Public Administration, Session 1997/98, HMSO, London

HC 421 *Miscarriages of Justice*, Sixth Report of the Home Affairs Select Committee, Session 1981/82, HMSO, London

HC 434 *Proposed New Immigration Rules and the European Convention of Human Rights*, First Report of the Home Affairs Select Committee, Session 1979/80, HMSO, London

HC 481 *Progress in the Next Steps Initiative*, Eighth report from the Select Committee on the Treasury and Civil Service, Session 1989-90, HMSO, London

HC 494 *Civil Service Management Reform: The Next Steps* Eighth Report by the Treasury and Civil Service Select Committee, Session 1987/8, HMSO, London

HC 496 *The Next Steps Initiative* Seventh Report by the Treasury and Civil Service Committee, Session 1990/91, HMSO, London

HC 499 *The PFI contracts for Brigend and Fazakerley Prisons* Fifty-Seventh Report by the Public Accounts Committee, Session 1997/98, HMSO, London

HC 517 *The Private Security Industry*, First Report of the Home Affairs Committee, Session 1994/95, HMSO, London

HC 519 *Westland Plc: Government Decision-Making* Fourth Report of the Defence Committee, Session 1985/86, HMSO, London

HC 535 *The Civil Service* Eleventh Report by the Expenditure Committee, Session 1976/77, HMSO, London

HC 555 *Prime Ministers Questions*, Seventh Report of the Select Committee on Procedure, Session 1994/95, HMSO, London

HC 570 *Freedom of Information Draft Bill* Third Report by the Public Administration Committee, Session 1998/99, HMSO, London

HC 572 *Annual Report for 1998-99* Parliamentary Commissioner for Administration, HMSO, London

HC 577 *Government Reply to the Third Report from the Home Affairs Select Committee, Session 1996/97: freemasonry in the police and the judiciary*, First Special Report of the Home Affairs Committee, Session 1997/98, HMSO, London

HC 588 *Reports*, First Report by the Committee on Procedure, Session 1977-8, HMSO, London

HC 669 *Administrative Law: Judicial Review and Statutory Appeals* The Law Commission, 1994, Law Commission Report No.226, HMSO, London

HC 683 *Government Reply to the Home Affairs Committee (1st Report) Police Disciplinary and Complaints Procedures*, Second Special Report of the Home Affairs Committee, Session 1997/98, HMSO, London

HC 719 *Thursday Sittings* Third Report of the Modernisation Committee, Session 1998/99, HMSO, London

HC 748 *Prison Service Annual Reports and Accounts 1998/9* HM Prison Service 1999

HC 748 *Independence or Control?* Second Report of the Liaison Committee, Session 1999-2000, HMSO, London

HC 760 *Sierra Leone: Exchanges of Correspondence with the Foreign Secretary*, First Report of the Foreign Affairs Select Committee, Session 1997/98, HMSO, London

HC 763 *Annual Report 1996-97* HM Inspectorate of Prisons for England & Wales, HMSO, London

HC 791 *The Scrutiny of European Business* Seventh Report of the Modernisation Committee, Session 1997/98, HMSO, London

HC 804 *Access to Official Information* Fourth Report by the Parliamentary Commissioner for Administration, Session 1997/98, HMSO, London

HC 820 *Ministerial Accountability and Parliamentary Questions* Fourth Report by the Public Administration Committee, Session 1997/98, HMSO, London

HC 831 *Government Response to the Third Report from the Select Committee on Public Administration (Session 1998/99) on the Freedom of Information Draft Bill* Fifth Special Report by the Public Administration Committee, Session 1998/99, HMSO, London

HC 845 *Annual Report for 1997-98* Parliamentary Commissioner for Administration, HMSO, London

HC 852 *Sierra Leone: Further Exchanges of Correspondence with the Foreign Secretary*, Second Special Report of the Foreign Affairs Select Committee, Session 1997/98, HMSO, London

HC 925 *Freedom of Information Draft Bill: The Committee's Response to the Home Office Reply*, Session 1998/99, HMSO, London

HC 998 *Prison Service Annual Reports and Accounts 1997/8* HM Prison Service 1998

HC 1016 *Return to an Address of the Honourable the House of Commons date 27th July 1998 for the Report of the Sierra Leone arms investigation* Foreign and Commonwealth Office, HMSO, London. [The Legg Report]

HC 1020 *Government Response to the Third Report from the Select Committee on Public Administration (Session 1997-98) on Your Right to Know: The Government's Proposals for a Freedom of Information Act* Fourth Special Report by the Public Administration Committee, Session 1997/98, HMSO, London

Hadfield, B (1995) *Judicial Review - A Thematic Approach* (Dublin : Gill & Macmillan)

Hadfield, B (2000) 'R v. Lord Saville of Newdigate, ex p. anonymous soldiers: What is the Purpose of a Tribunal of Inquiry?' *Public Law* pp.663-681

Hailsham, Lord (1978) *The Dilemma of Democracy* (London : Collins)

Hall, S (1983) 'The Great Moving Right Show' in Hall, S & Jacques, M (eds.) *The Politics of Thatcherism* (London : Lawrence & Wishart)

Hammond, A (1988) 'Judicial Review - the continuing interplay between law and policy' *Public Law* pp.34-43

Hanham, T (1969) *The Nineteenth Century Constitution* (Cambridge : Cambridge University Press)

Harden, I (1988) *The Noble Lie: The British Constitution and the Rule of Law* (London : Hutchinson)

Harden, I (1992) *The Contracting State* (Buckingham : Open University Press)

Harden, I, Donnelly, K & White, F (1994) *Should the NAO serve departmentally related select committees?* (Sheffield : PERC/Department of Law)

Harding, L (1997) *The Liar: The Fall of Jonathan Aitken* (London : Penguin)

Harding, R (1994) 'Models of accountability for the contract management of prisons' in Moyle, P (ed.) *Private Prisons and Police: recent Australian trends* (Australia : NSW)

Harding, R (1997) *Private Prisons and Public Accountability* (Buckingham : Open University Press)

Harlow, C (1999) 'Accountability, New Public Management and the Problems of the Child Support Agency' *Journal of Law & Society* Vol.26 No.2 pp.150-175

Harlow, C (2000) 'Disposing of Dicey?' *Political Studies* Vol.48 No.2 pp.356-369

Harmon, M (1995) *Responsibility as a Paradox: A Critique of Rational Discourse of Government* (London : Sage)

Harrigan, J (1995) 'Jamaica: mature democracy but questionable accountability' in Healey, J & Tordoff, W (eds.) *Voters and Budgets: comparative studies in Accountable Governance in the South* (Basingstoke : Macmillan)

Hawes, D (1993) *Power to the Backbenches?* (Bristol : School for Advanced Urban Studies, University of Bristol)

Hayek, F (1944) *The Road to Serfdom* (London : Ark)

Hazell, R (1989) 'Freedom of Information in Australia, Canada and New Zealand' *Public Administration* Vol.67 pp.189-210

Hazell, R (1995) 'Freedom of Information: The Implications for the Ombudsman' *Public Administration* Vol.75 pp.263-270

Hazell, R (1997) *Making the Civil Service More Accountable* (London : Charter 88)

Hazell, R (1998) 'Freedom of information takes time' *Review* No.1 May pp.13-14

Hazell, R (1999) *Constitutional Futures: A History of the Next Ten Years* (London : Oxford University Press)

Hazell, R (1999) 'Westminster: squeezed from above and below' in Hazell, R (ed.) *Constitutional Futures: A History of the Next Ten Years* (London : Oxford University Press)

Hazell, R (2000) *The State and the Nations* (Thorverton : Imprint)

Hazell, R (2001) 'Reforming the Constitution' *Political Quarterly* Vol.72 No.1 pp.39-50

Heald, D (1983) *Public Expenditure* (Oxford : Martin Robertson)

Hennessy, P (1989) *Whitehall* (London : Secker & Warburg)

Hennessy, P (1996) *Muddling Through* (London : Indigo)

Hennessy, P (1996) 'Teething the watchdogs: Parliament, government and accountability' in Hennessy, P *Muddling Through* (London : Indigo)

Hennessy, P (1996) *The Hidden Wiring: Unearthing the British Constitution* (London : Victor Gollanz)

Hennessy, P & Drewry, G (1996) 'Critics of the Osmotherly Rules' in Barberis, P (ed.) *The Whitehall Reader* (Milton Keynes : Open University Press) pp.230-234

Herman, F & Alt, J (1975) *Cabinet Studies - A Reader* (London : Macmillan)

Hewart, Lord (1929) *The New Despotism* (London)

Hill, A & Whichelow, A (1964) *What's Wrong With Parliament?* (London : Penguin)

Hinton, P & Wilson, E (1993) 'Accountability' in Wilson, J & Hinton, P (eds.) *Public Services and the 1990s: Issues in Public Service Finance and Management* (Sevenoaks : Tudor)

HM Prison Service (1993) *Framework Document*

HM Prison Service (1999) *Framework Document*

HM Prison Service (1996) *Corporate Plan 1996-99*

HM Prison Service (1997) *Prison Service Review*

Hodder-Williams, R (1996) *Judges and Politics in the Contemporary Age* (London : Bowerdean)

Hofmeister, A 'Restructuring ministries into holdings for managing accountability of agencies' Paper to the International Institute of Administrative Sciences Conference, 12-15 May 1999, Civil Service College, Sunningdale

Hogg, S & Jenkins, K (1999) 'Effective Government and Effective Accountability' *Political Quarterly* Vol.70 No.2 pp.139-145

Hoggett, P (1996) 'New Modes of Control in the Public Service' *Public Administration* Vol.74 pp.9-32

Hogwood, B (1987) 'Shaping Policy Through The Courts: (1) The British Courts' *Public Policy and Administration* Vol.2 No.1 pp.56-67

Hogwood, B (1994) 'A Reform Beyond Compare? The Next Steps Restructuring of British Central Government' *Journal of Public Policy* Vol.1 No.1 pp.71-94

Hogwood, B (1995) 'The growth of Quangos: Evidence and Explanations' in Ridley, E & Wilson, D (eds.) *The Quango Debate* (Oxford : Oxford University Press)

Hogwood, B 'UK Regulatory Institutions: explaining administrative forms' Workshop Conference on UK-North American Regulatory Institutions: Models and Issues for Reform, 9-10th April 1996, University of Exeter

Hogwood, B 'The quantitative analysis of agency accountability: what can it tell us and what does it miss out?' Paper presented at the Conference of the Structure and Organisation Group (SOG) of IPSA on Taking the Measure of Government, Pittsburgh, USA, 30th Oct. - 1st Nov. 1997

Hogwood, B (1997) 'The Machinery of Government 1979-97' *Political Studies* Vol.45 No.4 pp.704-715

Hogwood, B 'Bureaucratic autonomy and accountability in British Next Steps Agencies' paper presented to the Annual Conference of the American Political Science Association, Boston, September 1998

Hogwood, B (2000) 'UK Regulatory Institutions: increasing regulation in the shrinking state' in Doern, B & Wilkes, S (eds.) *Regulatory Institutions in North America and Britain* (Toronto : Toronto University Press)

Hogwood, B & McVicar, M *Agencies and Accountability* Paper given at the ESRC seminar on 'Theorizing Internal Public Sector Regulation' London School of Economics and Political Science 22-23rd March 1996

Hogwood, B & McVicar, M (1997) 'The 'Pondlife' of Executive Agencies: Parliament and 'Informatory' Accountability' *Public Policy & Administration* Vol.12 No.2 pp.95-115

Hogwood, B, Judge, D & McVicar, M 'Too much of a good thing? The Pathology of Accountability' paper presented to the Political Studies Association Annual Conference, University of Keele, 7-9th April 1998

Hollis, C (1949) *Can Parliament Survive?* (London)

Home Office (1982) *History of the Home Office 1782-1982*

Home Office (1982) *Prisons Over Two Centuries*

Home Office (1989) *Report on the practicality of private sector involvement in the remand system*

Home Office (1991) *The Management of the Prison Service* [The Lygo Report]

Home Office (1996) *Clarification of the law relating to the Bribery of Members of Parliament*

Home Office (1996) *The Victim's Charter*

Home Office (1997) *Managing Inquiries*

Home Office (1997) *The Prevention of Corruption (consolidation and amendment of the Prevention of Corruption Acts 1889-1916) - a Government statement*

Home Office (1997) *Managing Inquiries*

Home Office (1997) *The Prevention of Corruption: Consolidation and Amendment of the Prevention of Corruption Acts 1889-1916 - A Government Statement*

Home Office (1999) *Code of Practice on Access to Government Information - 1998 Report*

Home Office (1999) *Quinquennial Review of the Home Office: Prior Options Report*

Home Office (1999) *Quinquennial Review of the Home Office: Evaluation of Performance 1992-93 to 1997-98*

Hondeghen, A (1999) *Ethics and accountability in a context of governance and new public management* (Ohnsha : IOS Press)

Hood, C (1991) 'A Public Management for all Seasons?' *Public Administration* Vol.69 No.2 pp.3-19

Hood, C (1995) 'Contemporary Public Management: A New Global Paradigm' *Public Policy & Administration* Vol.10 No.2 pp.104-117

Hood, C (1997) 'Which Contract State? Four perspectives on over out-sourcing' *Australian Journal of Public Administration* Vol.56 No.3 pp.120-131

Hood, C (1998) 'Individualized contracts for top public servants: copying business. path dependent political re-engineering - or Trobriand cricket?' *Governance* Vol.11 No.4 pp.443-462

Hood, C (1998) *The Art of the State: Culture, Rhetoric and Public Management* (Oxford : Clarendon)

Hood, C & Wright, M (1981) *Big Government in Hard Times* (Oxford : Martin Robertson)

Hood, C et al. (1996) *Regulation Inside British Government: The Inner Face of the Regulatory State* Project Discussion Paper No.1 (London : LSE)

Hood, C et al. (1996) *Bureaucratic regulation and New Public Management in the UK: Mirror Image Developments* Project Discussion Paper No.2 (London : LSE)

Hood, C & James, O *Reconfiguring the UK Executive: From Public Bureaucracy State to Re-Regulated Public Service* Paper presented to ESRC conference 'Understanding Central Government: Theory into Practice' University of Birmingham 16-18th September 1996

Hood, C & Scott, C (1996) 'Bureaucratic Regulation and New Public Management in the UK: Mirror image developments? *Journal of Law & Society* Vol.23 No.1 pp.321-345

Hood, C & James, O *Watching the Custodians - The Regulation of Prisons in England and Wales* paper presented to the Annual Socio-Legal Studies Association Conference, Cardiff, April 1997

Hood, C et al. (1997) *Waste Watchers, Quality Checkers and Sleazebusters* (London : LSE)

Hood, C et al. (1998) 'Regulation inside government: where New Public Management meets the audit explosion' *Public Money & Management* Vol.18 No.2 pp.61-68

Hopwood, A & Miller, P (1994) *Accounting as Social and Institutional Practice* (Cambridge : Cambridge University Press)

Horn, M (1995) *The Political Economy of Public Administration* (Cambridge : Cambridge University Press)

House of Commons Library (1994) *Quangos and Non-Departmental Bodies* Research Paper 94/67

House of Commons Library (1996) *The Individual Responsibility of Ministers: An outline of the issues* Research Paper 96/27

House of Commons Library (1996) *Forms of Investigatory Inquiry & the Scott Inquiry* Research Paper 96/22
House of Commons Library (1996) *Public Interest Immunity* Research Paper 96/25
House of Commons Library (1997) *The Accountability Debate: Next Steps Agencies* Research Paper 97/4
House of Commons Library (1997) *The Accountability Debate: Codes of Guidance and Questions of Procedure for Ministers* Research Paper 97/5
House of Commons Library (1997) *The Code of Practice on Access to Official Information* Research Paper 97/69
House of Commons Library (1999) *Freedom of Information: The Continuing Debate* Research Paper 99/61
House of Commons Library (2000) *Shifting Control? Aspects of the Executive-Parliamentary Relationship*, Research Paper 00/92
House of Commons Public Information Office, Fact Sheet No.6 *The Post-1979 Departmental Select Committee Structure*
Howe, G (1999) 'The Management of Public Inquiries' *Political Quarterly* Vol.70 No.3 pp.294-304
Hughes, G, Mears, R & Winch, C (1997) 'An inspector calls? Regulation and accountability in three public services' *Policy and Politics* Vol.25 No.3 pp.299-313
Humphrey, C Miller, P & Scapens, R (1993) 'Accountability and Accountable Management in the UK Public Sector' *Accounting, Auditing & Accountability* Vol.6 No.3 pp.7-30
Hunt, M (1998) 'The 'Horizontal Effect' of the Human Rights Act' *Public Law* pp.423-444
Hurd, D (1997) 'The present usefulness of the House of Commons' *The Journal of Legislative Studies* Vol.3 No.3 pp.1-9
Hurwitz, L (1981) *The State as Defendant: Governmental Accountability and the Redress of Individual Grievances* (London : Aldwych Press)
Hyndman, N & Anderson, R (1997) 'A study of the use of targets in the planning documents of executive agencies' *Financial Accountability and Management* Vol.13 No.2 pp.139-164
Ilbert, C (1968) *Parliament: Its History, Constitution and Practice* (London: Oxford University Press)
Jabbra, J & Dwivedi, O (1988) *Public Service Accountability: A Comparative Study* (West Hartford : Kumarian Press)
Jack, M (1985) 'Parliament's Role as a Check on the Executive' *Parliamentary Affairs* Vol.38 No.3 pp.295-305
Jackson, M (1995) 'Democratic Accountability' *Canberra Bulletin of Public Administration* Vol.78 pp.86-88
Jacobs, F (1999) Public Law: The Importance of Europe' *Public Law* pp.232-246
Jacobs, M (1996) *The Politics of the Real World* (London : Earthscan)

James, A et al. (1997) *Privatising Prisons: Rhetoric and Reality* (London : Sage)
James, S (1996) 'The Political and Administrative Consequences of Judicial Review' *Public Administration* Vol.74 pp.613-637
James, S (1996) 'The Judges into Politics: The Rise of Judicial Review Since 1945' in James, S & Preston, V *Old Politics, New Politics and Post-war Britain* (London : Macmillan)
Jenkins, S (1995) *Accountable to None: The Tory Nationalization of Britain* (London : Hamish Hamilton)
Jennings, I (1934) *Parliamentary Reform* (London)
Johnson, N (1974) 'Defining Accountability' *Public Administration Bulletin* No.17 Dec. pp.3-14
Johnson, N (1977) *In Search of the Constitution* (Oxford : Pergamon Press)
Johnson, N (1982) 'Accountability, Control and Complexity: Moving Beyond Ministerial Responsibility' in Barker, A (ed.) *Quangos in Britain* (London : Macmillan)
Johnson, N (1997) 'Opposition in the British Political System' *Government & Opposition* Vol.32 No.4 pp.487-511
Johnson, T & Kaplan, R (1987) *Relevance Lost: The Rise and Fall of Management Accountancy* (Boston, Mass : Harvard Business School Press)
Jordan, G (1983) 'Individual Ministerial Responsibility : Absolute or Obsolete?' in McCrone, D (ed.) *Scottish Yearbook* (Edinburgh: Unit for the study of Government in Scotland)
Jordan, G (1994) *The British Administrative System: Principles versus Practice* (London : Routledge)
Jorgensen, T (1994) *Developments in Danish Public Administration: Agentification and De-Agentification* paper presented to the Public Service Seminar, London School of Economics, 9th December, 1994
Jorgensen, T & Hansen, C (1995) 'Agencification and De-Agencification in Danish Central Government contradictory developments - or is there an underlying logic?' *International Review of Administrative Sciences* Vol.61 pp.548-563
Joseph, K & Sumption, A (1979) *Equality* (London : Murray)
Jowell, J (1994) 'The Rule of Law Today' in Jowell, J & Oliver, D (eds.) *The Changing Constitution* (Oxford : Clarendon)
Jowell, J (2000) 'Beyond the Rule of Law: Towards Constitutional Judicial Review' *Public Law* 671-683
Jowell, J & Oliver, D (1994) *The Changing Constitution* (Oxford : Clarendon Press)
Judge, D (1984) *Ministerial Responsibility : Life in the Strawman Yet?* Strathclyde Papers on Government and Politics No.37 (Glasgow : University of Strathclyde)
Judge, D (1989) 'Parliament in the 1980s' *Political Quarterly* Vol.60 No.4 pp.400-412

Judge, D (1992) 'The Effectiveness of the Post 1979 Select Committee System' *Political Quarterly* Vol. 63 No.1 pp.400-420

Judge, D (1993) *The Parliamentary State* (London : Sage)

Judge, D, Hogwood, B & McVicar, M (1997) 'The Pondlife of Executive Agencies: Parliament and 'Informatory' Accountability' *Public Policy & Administration* Vol.12 No.2 pp.95-115

Kairys, D (1982) The Politics of Law: A Progressive Critique (New York : Pantheon Books)

Kavanagh, D & Seldon, A (1994) *The Major Effect* (London : Macmillan)

Kavanagh, G & Richards, D (2001) 'Departmentalism and Joined-Up Government: Back to the Future?' *Parliamentary Affairs* Vol.64 No.1 pp.1-18

Keeling, D (1972) *Management in Government* (London : Allen & Unwin)

Kellow, A (1990) 'Changing Conceptions of Responsibility' in Power, J (ed.) *Public Administration in Australia: A Watershed* (Sydney : Hale & Iremonger)

Kemp, P (1993) *Beyond Next Steps: A Civil Service for the 21st Century* (London : Social Market Foundation)

Kemp, P (1996) *A Better Machine: A Government for the 21st Century* (London : European Policy Forum)

Kemp, P (1996) 'Mr Blair, Don't be afraid of Sir Humphrey' *Parliamentary Brief* Vol.4 No.7 pp.30-32

Kemp, P (1996) 'Handling the Machine: a memo to Labour' *Political Quarterly* Vol.67 No.4 pp.303-310

Kemp, P (1996) 'Beyond Next Steps: Obstacles to Fulfilment' in Barberis, P (ed.) *The Whitehall Reader* (Buckingham : Open University Press)

Kernaghan, K & Langford, J (1990) *The Responsible Public Servant* (Halifax : IPPR)

Kerry, M (1986) 'Administrative Law and Judicial Review - The practical Effects of Developments Over the Last 25 Years on Administration in Central Government' *Public Administration* Vol.64 No.3 pp.163-172

Kettl, D (1993) *Sharing Power: Public governance and private markets* (Washington DC : The Brookings Institution)

Keynes, J (1936) *The General Theory of Employment, Interest and Money* (London : Macmillan)

Kickert, W (1995) 'Autonomizing Executive Tasks in Dutch Central Government' *International Review of Administrative Sciences* Vol.61 pp.531-548

Kickert, W (1997) 'Public Governance in the Netherlands: An alternative to Anglo-American managerialism' *Public Administration* Vol.75 No.4 pp.731-752

Kickert, W & Jorgensen, T (1995) 'Managerial Reform Trends in Western Europe' *International Review of Administrative Sciences* Vol.61 pp.499-510

Kickert, W & Stillman, R (1996) 'Changing European States: Changing Public Administration' *Public Administration Review* Vol.56 No.1 pp.65-101

Kidder, L & Judd, C (1986) *Research Methods in social relations* (New York : Holt)
King, A (1975) 'Overload: problems of governing in the 1970s' *Political Studies* Vol.23 pp.289-296
King, A (1976) *Why is Britain becoming harder to govern?* (London : BBC)
King, A (1976) 'Modes of Executive-Legislative Relations' *Legislative Studies Quarterly* Vol.1 pp.13-32
King, A (1996) *Is Britain a well governed country?* Paper given to the Lloyds TSB Forum 5th June 1996
King, D (1987) *The New Right: Politics, Markets and Citizenship* (Basingstoke : Macmillan)
King, T, Jenkin, P & MacGregor, J (1997) 'Ministers and Parliament' *The Journal of Legislative Studies* Vol.3 No.4 pp.1-24
Kirkpatrick, I & Martinez Lucio, M (1996) 'The Contract State and the Future of Public Management' *Public Administration* Vol.74 pp.1-8
Klug, F (1999) 'The Human Rights Act 1998: *Pepper versus Hart* and all that' *Public Law* pp.246-274
Labour Party (1997) *Because Britain Deserves Better* (London : Labour Party)
Landers, B (1998) 'Of Ministers, Mandarins and Managers' in Flinders, M V & Smith M J (eds.) *Quangos, Accountability and Reform: the politics of quasi-government* (London : Macmillan)
Landers, B (1999) 'Encounters with the Public Accounts Committee: A Personal Memoir' *Public Administration* Vol. 77 No.1 pp.195-213
Langford, J (1984) 'Responsibility in the senior public service: marching to several drummers' *Canadian Public Administration* Vol.27 No.4 pp.513-21
Laski, H (1938) *Parliamentary Government in England* (London : Allen & Unwin)
Laski, H (1951) *Reflections on the Constitution* (Manchester : Manchester University Press)
Laughlin, R (1993) *Rethinking Models of Accountability: The Influence of Professionalism and 'Higher' Principals on Actions and Reactions of Agents* Discussion Paper No.10 (Sheffield : SUMS)
Laughlin, R & Broadbent, J (1994) *Beyond Accountability: An Evaluation Model For the Public Sector Reforms in the UK* Discussion Paper No.8 (Sheffield : SUMS)
Lawrence-Lowell, A (1908) *The Government of England Vol.1* (London : Macmillan)
Laws, J (1993) 'Is the High Court the Guardian of fundamental Rights?' *Public Law* pp.59-79
Laws, J (1994) 'Judicial Remedies and the Constitution' *The Modern Law Review* Vol.57 pp.213-227
Laws, J (1995) 'Law and Democracy' *Public Law* pp.72-93

Lawson, N (1992) *The View From No.11* (London : Bantam)
Lawton, A & Rose, A (1994) *Organisation and Management in the Public Sector* (London : Pitman)
Le Sueur, A (1991) 'The Judges and the Intention of Parliament: Is Judicial Review Undemocratic' *Parliamentary Affairs* Vol.44 pp.283-297
Le Sueur, A (1996) 'The Judicial Review Debate: From Partnership to Friction' *Government and Opposition* Vol.31 No.1 pp.8-27
Le Sueur, A & Sunkin, M (1997) *Public Law* (London : Longman)
Leat, D (1988) *Voluntary Organisations and Accountability* (London : NCVO)
Leazes, F (1997) 'Public Accountability: Is it a private responsibility?' *Administration & Society* Vol.29 No.4 pp.395-411
Lee, S (1994) 'Law and the Constitution' in Kavanagh, D & Seldon, A (eds.) *The Major Effect* (London : Macmillan)
Legg, B (1994) *Civil Service Reform: The Case For More Radicalism* (London : European Policy Forum)
Leigh, D & Vulliamy, E (1997) *Sleaze: the corruption of Parliament* (London : Fourth Estate)
Leigh, I & Lustgarten, L (1996) 'Five Volumes in Search of Accountability: The Scott Report' *Modern Law Review* Vol.59 p.697
Lello, J (1993) *Accountability in Practice* (London : Cassell)
Lenman, B (1992) *The Eclipse of Parliament: Appearance and Reality in British Politics since 1914* (London : Edward Arnold)
Lester, A (1997) 'Acceptance of the Strasbourg jurisdiction: What really went on in Whitehall in 1965?' *Public Law* pp.237-265.
Levi, M & Nelken, D (1996) 'The Corruption of Politics and the Politics of Corruption' *Journal of Law & Society* Vol.23 No.1 pp.1-18
Levitas, R (1986) *The Ideology of the New Right* (Oxford : Polity Press)
Lewis, D (1997) *Hidden Agenda: Politics, Law and Order* (London : Hamilton Hamish)
Lewis, N (1989) 'The Case for a Standing Administrative Conference' *Political Quarterly* Vol.60 pp.421-432
Lewis, N (1990) *Happy and Glorious: The Constitution in Transition* (Buckingham : Open University Press)
Lewis, N (1993) 'The Citizen's Charter: A new way of governing?' *Political Quarterly* Vol.64 No.3 pp.316-326
Lewis, N (1994) 'Reviewing Change in Government: New Public Management and Next Steps' *Public Law* pp.105-113
Lewis, N (1995) 'Responsibility in Government: The strange case of the UK' *European Public Law* Vol.1 No.3 pp.371-93
Lewis, N & Longley, D (1996) 'Ministerial Responsibility: The Next Steps' *Public Law* pp.490-508

Liberal Democrat Party (1996) *A Parliament for the People: Proposals to reform the House of Commons* policy paper No.20 (London : Liberal Democrats)
Liberal Democrat Party (2000) *Reforming Governance in the UK* (London : Liberal Democrats)
Linders, S (1978) 'Administrative accountability: administrative discretion, accountability and external controls' in Greer, S *Accountability in Urban Society* (London : Sage)
Lipset, S, Trow, M & Coleman, J (1956) *Union Democracy: The Inside politics of the International Typographic Union* (New York : Free Press)
Livingstone, P (1994) 'The Changing Face of Prison Discipline' in Player, E & Jenkins, M (eds.) *Prisons After Woolf: Reform Through Riot* (London : Routledge)
Livingstone, S (1995) 'The Impact of Judicial Review on Prisons' in Hadfield, B (ed.) *The Impact of Judicial Review on Prisons* (Dublin : Gill & Macmillan)
Livingstone, S & Owen, T (1993) *Prison Law: text and materials* (Oxford : Oxford University Press)
Lock, G (1985) 'Parliamentary Privilege and the Courts: The Avoidance of Conflict' *Public Law* pp.64-92
Lord Beloff (1998) 'Amery on the constitution: Britain and the European Union' *Government & Opposition* Vol.33 No.2 pp.167-183
Lord Chancellor's Department (1994) *Disasters and the Law: Deciding the Form of Inquiry* (London : HMSO)
Lord Chancellor's Department (2000) *Review of the Crown Office List* (London : HMSO) [The Bowman Report]
Lord Irvine of Lairg (1996) 'Judges and Decision-Makers: The Theory and Practice of *Wednesbury* Review' *Public Law* pp.59-79
Lord Irvine of Lairg (1996) 'Response to Sir John Laws 1996' *Public Law* pp.636-639
Lord Nolan & Sedley, S (1997) *The Making and Remaking of the British Constitution* (London : Blackstone)
Lord Steyn *The weakest and the least dangerous department of government* Administrative Bar Assoc. Annual Lecture 27/11/96
Lord Strathclyde (2000) *New Frontiers for Reform* (London : Centre for Policy Studies)
Lord Woolf of Barnes (1995) 'Droit Public - English Style' *Public Law* pp.57-71
Loveland, I (1988) 'Housing Benefit: Administrative Law and Administrative Practice' *Public Administration* Vol.66 No.1
Loveland, I (1997) 'The War Against Judges' *Political Quarterly* Vol.68 No.2 pp.162-170
Lovell, A (1996) 'Notions of Accountability and State Audit: A UK Perspective' *Financial Accountability & Management* Vol.12 No.4 pp.261-280

Lovell, A & Hand, L (1999) 'Expanding the notion of organisational performance measurement to support joined up government' *Public Policy & Administration* Vol.14 No.2 pp.17-29

Lovell, R (1992) 'The Citizen's Charter: The Cultural Challenge' *Public Administration* Vol.70 pp.395-404

Low, S (1904) *The Governance of England* (London : Unwin)

Lundquist, L (1993) 'Freedom of Information and the Swedish Bureaucrat' in Chapman, R (ed.) *Ethics in the Public Service* (Edinburgh : Edinburgh University Press)

Lupia, A & McCubbins, M (1994) 'Designing Bureaucratic Accountability' *Law & Contemporary Problems* Vol.57/1 pp.91-95

McAuslan, P & McEldowney, J (1985) *Law, Legitimacy and the Constitution* (London: Sweet & Maxwell)

McAuslan, P & McEldowney, J (1985) 'Legitimacy and the Constitution: the dissonance between theory and practice' in McAuslan, P & McEldowney, J (eds.) *Law, Legitimacy and the Constitution* (London : Sweet & Maxwell)

McCallum, R (1946) *Considerations on Representative Government* (Oxford)

McDonald, A & Terrill, G (1998) 'Open Government in New Zealand' in McDonald, A & Terrill, G (eds.) *Open Government: Freedom of Information and Privacy* (Basingstoke : Macmillan)

McEldowney, J (1998) 'Legal Aspects of relations between the UK and the Scottish Parliament' in Oliver, D & Drewry, G (eds.) *The Law and Parliament* (London : Butterworths)

McHarg, A (1999) 'Reconciling Human Rights and the Public Interest: Conceptual Problems and Doctrinal Uncertainty in the Jurisprudence of the European Court of Human Rights' *The Modern Law Review* Vol.62 No.5 pp.671-696

McVicar, M, Judge, D & Hogwood, B (1998) 'Too much of a good thing?' *The Stakeholder* Vol.2 No.2 pp.10-11

MacIntosh, J (1962) *The British Cabinet* (London : Stevens)

MacKenzie, K (1950) *The English Parliament* (Harmondsworth : Penguin)

MacKenzie, W & Grove, J (1957) *Central Administration in Britain* (London : Longmans)

Mackie, T & Marsh, D (1995) 'The Comparative Method' in Marsh, D & Stoker, G (eds.) *Theory and Methods in Political Science* (Basingstoke : Macmillan) pp.173-187

Maitland, F (1908) *The Constitutional History of England* (Cambridge : Cambridge University Press)

Major, J (1999) *The Autobiography* (London : Harper Collins)

Mancini, G (1980) 'Politics and the Judges - The European Perspective' *The Modern Law Review* Vol.43 No.1 pp.1-17

Mandelson, P & Liddle, R (1996) *The Blair Revolution: can New Labour deliver?* (London : Faber & Faber)

Marquand, D *The State in Context: travails of an ancien regime* (Swindon : ESRC)
Marquand, D 'The Blair Paradox' *Prospect* May 1998 pp.19-24
Marquand, D (1998) *Must Labour Lose?* (Swindon : ESRC)
Marr, A 'The buck wanders round and round' *The Independent* 17/10/95 p.19
Marr, A (1995) *Ruling Britannia: The Failure and Future of British Democracy* (London : Michael Joseph)
Marshall, G (1986) *Constitutional Conventions: The Rules and Forms of Political Accountability* (Oxford : Clarendon)
Marshall, G (1989) *Ministerial Responsibility* (New York : Oxford University Press)
Marshall, G (1991) 'The Evolving Practice of Parliamentary Accountability: Writing Down the Rules' *Parliamentary Affairs* Vol.44 No.4 pp.460-468
Marshall, G (1996) 'OFCON: A Watchdog for Ministers' *Parliamentary Brief* Vol.4 No.6 p.7
Marston, G (1993) 'The United Kingdom's part in the preparation of the European Convention on Human Rights, 1950' *International and Comparative Law Quarterly* Vol.42 pp.796-827
Mascarenhas, R (1993) 'Building an Enterprise Culture in the Public Sector: Reform of the Public Sector in Australia, Britain and New Zealand' *Public Administration Review* Vol.53 No.4 pp.319-328
Massey, A (1993) *Managing the Public Sector: A Comparative Analysis of the United Kingdom and the United States* (Aldershot : Edward Elgar)
Massey, A (1995) 'Civil Service Reform and Accountability' *Public Policy and Administration* Vol.10 No.1 pp.16-33
Mather, G (1990) 'Management by Contract - Viewpoints' *Public Money and Management* Vol.10 No.3 p.1
Mather, G (1994) 'The Market, Accountability and the Civil Service' *Public Policy & Administration* Vol.10 No.1 pp.6-18
Mather, G (2000) *Making Decision in Britain* (London : European Policy Forum)
Matthews, R (1989) *Privatising Criminal Justice* (London : Sage)
Mayston, D (1993) 'Principals, Agents and the economics of accountability in the new public sector' *Accounting, Audit & Accountability* Vol.6 No.3 pp.68-96
Metcalfe, L & Richards, S (1990) *Improving Public Management* (London : Sage)
Miles, L (1997) 'Sweden - A Relevant or Redundant Parliament?' *Parliamentary Affairs* Vol.50 No.3 pp.423-437
Miller, P (1996) 'Dilemmas of Accountability: The Limits of Accounting' in Hirst, P & Kilhani, S (eds.) *Reinventing Democracy* (Oxford : Blackwell)
Mills, H 'Howard fires prison chief over debacle' *The Independent* 17/10/95 p.1
Minford, P (1987) 'The role of the Social Services: A View From the Right' in Loney, M (ed.) *The State of the Market: Politics and Welfare in Contemporary Britain* (London : Sage)

Moe, R (1994) 'The 'reinventing government' exercise: misinterpreting the problem, misjudging the consequences' *Public Administration Review* Vol.54 No.2 pp.111-122

Morgan, R (1985) 'Her Majesties Inspectorate of Prisons' in Maquire, M, Vagg, J & Morgan, R (eds.) *Accountability in Prisons* (London : Tavistock)

Morgan, R (1993) 'Prisons Accountability Revisited' *Public Law* pp.314-332

Morris, G (1999) 'Fragmenting the State: Implications for Accountability for Employment Practices in Public Services' *Public Law* pp.64-84

Mountfield, R (1997) 'Organisational reform within government: accountability and policy management' *Public Administration & Development* Vol.17 No.1 pp.71-76

Moyle, P (1992) 'Private Prisons - The Underlying Issues' *Alternative Law Journal* Vol.17 No.3 pp.114-119

Moyle, P (1994) 'Privatisation of prisons and the police: recent Australasian developments' in Moyle, P (ed.) *Private Prisons and Police: recent Australian trends* (Australia : NSW)

Muir, R (1930) *How Britain is Governed* (London)

Mulgan, R (1995) 'The Democratic Failure of Single-Party Government: The New Zealand Experience' *Australian Journal of Political Science* Vol.30 pp.82-96

Mulgan, R (1997) 'Contracting Out and Accountability' *Australian Journal of Public Administration* Vol.56 No.4 pp.106-116

Mulgan, R (1997) 'The Processes of Public Accountability' *Australian Journal of Public Administration* Vol.56 No.1 pp.25-36

Muller, W (1994) 'Political Traditions and the Role of the State' *West European Politics* Vol.17 No.3 pp.32-51

Muller, W & Wright, V (1994) 'Reshaping the State in Western Europe: The Limits of Retreat' *West European Politics* Vol.17 No.3 pp. 1-11

Mullin, C (1996) 'Miscarriages of Justice in the UK' *The Journal of Legislative Studies* Vol.2 No.2 pp.8-20

Mutahaba, G (1996) *Accountability in Public Service: Who answers what? when? and how?* (Brussels : IASIA)

Nachmias, D & Nachmias, C (1992) *Research Methods in the Social Sciences* (New York : St Martin)

Narud, H (1996) 'Party Policies and Government Accountability' *Party Politics* Vol. 2 No.4 pp. 479-506

Nicholson, I (1986) *The Mystery of Crichel Down* (Oxford : Clarendon)

Niskanen, W (1973 *Bureaucracy – Servant or Master?* (London : IEA)

Normanton, E (1966) *The Accountability and Audit of Government* (Manchester : Manchester University Press)

Norton, P (1978) 'Government Defeats in the House of Commons: Myths and Reality' *Public Law* pp.360-378

Norton, P (1981) *The Commons in Perspective* (Oxford : Robertson)

Norton, P. (1983) 'The Norton View', in Judge, D. (ed.) *The Politics of Parliamentary Reform.* London : Heinemann, 54-70

Norton, P (1985) *Parliament in the 1980's* (Oxford : Blackwell)

Norton, P. (1991) 'In Defence of the Constitution: A Riposte to the Radicals', in Norton, P (ed.) *New Directions in British Politics?* Aldershot : Edward Elgar, 145-173

Norton, P (1993) *Does Parliament Matter?* (Hemel Hempstead : Harvester Wheatsheaf)

Norton, P (2000) *Strengthening Parliament* The Report of the Commission to Strengthen Parliament (London : The Conservative Party)

Norton, P (2000) 'Reforming Parliament in the United Kingdom' *Legislative Studies* Vol.6 No.3 pp.1-15

Norton, P (2001) 'The Judiciary' in Jones, B *et al* (eds.) *Politics UK* (London : Longman)

Norton, P & Wood, D (1993) *Back from Westminster: British Members of Parliament and their Constituents* (Lexington : University of Kentucky Press)

Norton-Taylor, R (1995) *Truth is a difficult concept: inside the Scott Inquiry* (London : Fourth Estate)

Nozick, R (1975) *Anarchy, State and Utopia* (Oxford : Blackwell)

O'Donnell, A (1996) 'Legal and Quasi-Legal Accountability' in Pyper, R (ed.) *Aspects of Accountability in the British System of Government* (Eastham : Tudor)

O'Toole, B (1990) 'T H Green and the Ethics of Senior Officials in British Central Government' *Public Administration* Vol.68 No.3

O'Toole (1995) 'The Concept of Public Duty' in Barberis, P (ed.) *The Civil Service in an Era of Change* (Dartmouth : Aldershot)

O'Toole, B (1997) 'Ethics in Government' *Parliamentary Affairs* Vol.50 pp.130-142

O'Toole, B & Chapman, R (1995) 'Parliamentary Accountability' in O'Toole, B & Jordan, G (eds.) *The Next Steps: Improving Management in Government?* (London : Dartmouth)

OECD Public Management Papers *Ethics in the Public Service* Occasional Paper No. 14 (OECD : Paris)

Oliver, D (1989) 'The Judge Over Your Shoulder' *Parliamentary Affairs* Vol.42 pp.302-316

Oliver, D (1989) 'Law, Convention and the Abuse of Power' *Political Quarterly* Vol.60 pp.38-49

Oliver, D (1991) *Government in the UK: The Search for Accountability, Effectiveness and Accountability* Buckingham : Open University Press)

Oliver, D (1994) 'Parliament, Ministers and the Law' *Parliamentary Affairs* Vol.74 No.4 pp.630-646

Oliver, D (1994) 'The Judge Over Your Shoulder - Mark II' *Public Law* pp.514-515

Oliver, D (1994) 'Law, Politics and Public Accountability. The Search for a New Equilibrium' *Public Law* pp.238-253
Oliver, D (1996) 'Comment: The Scott Report' *Public Law* pp.357-368
Oliver, D (1998) 'Freedom of Information and ministerial accountability' *Public Law* pp.171-176
Oliver, D (2000) 'Democracy, Parliament and Constitutional Watchdogs' *Public Law* pp.553-555
Oliver, D (2000) 'The Frontiers of the State: Public Authorities and Public Functions under the Human Rights Act' *Public Law* pp. 476-494
Oliver, D & Drewry, G (1996) *Public Service Reforms: Issues of Accountability and Public Law* (London : Pinter)
Osbaldeston, G (1989) *Keeping Deputy Ministers Accountable* (Ontario: McGraw-Hill Ryerson)
Osborne, D & Gaebler, T (1992) *Re-Inventing Government* (London : Plume)
Ouchi, W (1987) 'Markets, Bureaucracies and Clans' *Administrative Science Quarterly* Vol.25/1 pp.129-141
Oughton, D (1995) 'Accountability versus Control - Rust never Sleeps' *Public Sector* Vol.17 No.3 pp.2-6
Page, A (1998) 'Controlling Government from Within: A Constitutional Analysis' *Public Policy & Administration* Vol.13 No.4 pp.85-95
Painter, C (1994) 'Public Service Reform: Re-Inventing or Abandoning Government' *Political Quarterly* Vol.65 No.3 pp.242-263
Painter, C (1995) 'The Next Steps Reforms and Current Orthodoxies' in O'Toole, B & Jordan, G (eds.) *The Next Steps: Improving Management in Government?* (Dartmouth : Aldershot)
Pannick, D (1992) 'Who Is Subject To Judicial Review and In Respect of What?' *Public Law* pp.1-7
Pannick, D (1998) 'Principles of interpretation of convention rights under the Human Rights Act and the discretionary area of judgement' *Public Law* pp.545-552
Parris, H (1969) *Constitutional Bureaucracy* (London : Allen & Unwin)
Parsons, W (1998) 'Fuzzy in theory and getting fuzzier in practice: post-modern reflections on responsibility in public administration and management' in Hondeghen, A (ed.) *Ethics and accountability in a context of governance and new public management* (Ohnsha : IOS Press)
Parsons, W (1998) *Redesigning Public Policy* (London : Edward Elgar)
Patton, J (1992) 'Accountability and Government Financial Reporting' *Financial Accountability and Management* Vol.8 No.3 pp.163-180
Paul, S (1992) 'Accountability in Public Services: Exit, Voice and Control' *World Development*, Vol.20 No.7 pp.1047-1060
Peach, L (1997) 'Top Jobs: How the system works' *The Stakeholder* Vol.1 No.1 pp.11-13

Pendlebury, M & Karbhari, Y (1997) 'Management and Accounting Developments in Executive Agencies' *Financial Accountability & Management* Vol.13 No.2 pp.117-138

Peters, B & Savoie, D (1994) 'Civil Service Reform: misdiagnosing the patient' *Public Administration Review* Vol.54 No.5 pp.418-425

Piper, J (1991) 'British Backbench Rebellion and Government Appointments' *Legislative Studies Quarterly* Vol.26 No.2

Pirie, M (1988) *Privatisation* (Aldershot : Wildwood House)

Plowden, W (1994) *Ministers and Mandarins* (London : IPPR)

Plummer, J (1996) *How are Charities Accountable?* (London : Demos)

Polidano, C (1997) 'The Bureaucrat who fell under a bus: Ministerial responsibility, executive agencies and the Derek Lewis Affair' *Governance* Vol.12 No.2 pp.201-231

Polidano, C (1998) 'Why bureaucrats can't always do what ministers want: multiple accountabilities in Westminster democracies' *Public Policy & Administration* Vol.13 No. 1 pp. 35-50

Political Studies (1999) 'Sovereignty at the Millennium' (Special Issue) Vol.47 No.3

Pollitt, C (1993) *Managerialism and the Public Services: Cuts or cultural Change in the 1990s?* (Oxford : Blackwell)

Pollitt, C (1994) 'The Citizens Charter: A Preliminary Analysis' *Public Money and Management* April/June p.13

Pollitt, C 'Accountability and democracy: answering to political authority and citizen's needs' Paper to the International Institute of Administrative Sciences Conference, Civil Service College, Sunningdale, 12-15 May 1999

Power, G (2000) *Under Pressure: Are we getting the most from our MPs?* (London : Hansard Society)

Power, G (2000) *Creating a Working Parliament* (London : Hansard)

Power, M (1994) *The Audit Explosion* (London : Demos)

Power, M (1996) 'Making things auditable' *Accounting, Organizations and Society* Vol.21 No.2/3 pp.289-315

Power, M (1997) *The Audit Society* (Oxford : Oxford University Press)

Premfors, R (1991) 'The Swedish Model and Public Sector Reform' *West European Politics* Vol.14 pp.83-95

Premfors, R (1996) *Reshaping the Democratic State: Swedish Experiences in a Comparative Perspective* (Stockholm : Stockholm Centre for Organizational Research, University of Stockholm)

Prosser, T (1979) 'Politics and Judicial Review: The Atkinson Case and its Aftermath' *Public Law* pp.59-83

Prosser, T (1986) *Nationalised Industries and Public Control* (Oxford : Blackwell)

Puddephatt, A (1997) *The Scott Report and Ministerial Accountability* (London : Charter 88)

Pyper, R (1984) 'The F.O. Resignations: Individual Ministerial Responsibility Revived?' in L.Robbins (ed.) *Updating British Politics* (London : Politics Assoc.)

Pyper, R (1995) *The British Civil Service* (Hemel Hempstead : Harvester Wheatsheaf)

Quirk, B (1997) 'Accountable to Everyone: Post-modern Pressures on Public Managers' *Public Administration* Vol.75 pp.569-586

Radford, M & Kerr, A (1997) 'Acquiring Rights - Losing Power: A Case study in ministerial resistance to the impact of European Community Law' *Modern Law Review* Vol.60 No.1 pp.23-43

Ragin, C (1987) *The comparative method: moving beyond quantitative and qualitative strategies'* (Berkeley : UCP)

Raison, T (1979) *Power and Parliament* (London : Blackwell)

Ransom, S & Stewart, J (1994) *Management for the Public Domain* (Basingstoke : Macmillan)

Rasmussen, K & Yeates, N 'Performance Management and the divided worlds of accountability' Paper to the International Institute of Administrative Sciences Conference, 12-15 May 1999, Civil Service College, Sunningdale

Rawlings, H (1986) 'Judicial Review and the Control of Government' *Public Administration* Vol.64 pp.135-145

Raynard, P (2000) *Mapping Accountability in Humanitarian Assistance* (London : ALNAP)

Redlich, J & Ilbert, C (1908) *Procedure of the House of Commons* (London : Archibald Constable)

Rees, M (1987) 'The parameters of politics' in Chapman, R & Hunt, M (eds.) *Open Government* (London : Routledge) pp.31-39

Rees, R (1985) 'The Theory of Principal and Agent' *Bulletin of Economic Research* part 1: pp.3-26, part 2: pp.77-95

Reid, G (1984) 'The Westminster Model and Ministerial Responsibility' *Current Affairs Bulletin* Vol. 61 pp.4-16

Renaud, P & Winden, F van (1987) 'Political accountability for price stability and unemployment in a multi-party system with coalition governments' *Public Choice* Vol.53 pp.181-186

Rhodes, R (1981) *Inspectorates in British Government* (London : Allen & Unwin)

Rhodes, R (1988) *Beyond Westminster and Whitehall* (London : Unwin-Hyman)

Rhodes, R (1994) 'State building without a bureaucracy - the case of the UK' in Budge, I & McKay (eds.) *Developing Democracy* (London : Sage) pp.165-189

Rhodes, R (1994) 'Reinventing Excellence: or how best sellers thwart the search for lessons to transform the public sector' *Public Administration* Vol.72 No.2 pp.281-288

Rhodes, R (1995) 'The Institutional Approach' in Marsh, D & Stoker, D (eds.) *Theory and Methods in Political Science* Basingstoke : Macmillan) pp.42-58

Rhodes, R (1995) *'Reinventing Whitehall 1979-1994: evolving the hollow state?'* Newcastle Discussion Papers in Politics No.11, University of Newcastle

Rhodes, R *Towards a Post-Modern Public Administration: Epoch, Epistemology or Narrative* paper given to the ESRC Whitehall Programme Conference on 'Understanding Central Government: Theory into Practice' University of Birmingham 16-18th Sept. 1996

Rhodes, R (1996) 'The New Governance: governing without government' *Political Studies* Vol.44 No.4 pp.652-667

Rhodes, R (1997) *Understanding Governance: policy networks, governance and accountability* (Buckingham : Open University Press)

Richards, D & Smith, M J (1998) 'The Gatekeepers of the Common Good: power and the public service ethos' in Hondeghen, A (ed.) *Ethics and accountability in a context of governance and new public management* (Ohnsha : IOS Press)

Richards, S 'Interview: Jack Straw' *The New Statesman* 23/5/97 pp.16-17

Richards, S (1997) 'New Labour - New Civil Service' *Political Quarterly* Vol.67 No.4 pp.311-320

Richards, S 'The irrelevance of backbenchers is a myth' *The New Statesman* 16/1/98 p.7

Richards, S 'Interview: Jack Straw' *The New Statesman* 3/4/98 pp.14-16

Richardson, G (1985) 'Judicial intervention in prison life' in Vagg, J, Morgan, R & Maquire, M (eds.) *Accountability and Prisons* (London : Tavistock)

Richardson, G & Sunkin, M (1996) 'Judicial Review: Questions of Impact' *Public Law* pp.79-104

Richardson, J & Jordan, A (1979) *Governing Under Pressure: The Policy Process in a Post Parliamentary Democracy* (Oxford : Blackwell)

Riddell, P (1998) *Parliament Under Pressure* (London : Victor Gollancz)

Riddell, P (1999) 'A Shift of Power – and Influence' *British Journalism Review* Vol.10 No.3 pp.26-33

Riddell, P (2000) *Parliament Under Blair* (London : Politicos)

Ridley, F (1995) 'Re-Inventing British Government' *Parliamentary Affairs* Vol.48 No.3 pp.375-401

Ridley, F (1996) 'The New Public Management in Europe: Comparative Perspectives' *Public Policy and Administration* Vol.11 No.1 pp.16-29

Ridley, F & Doig, A (1995) *Sleaze: politicians private interests and public reaction* (Oxford : Oxford University Press)

Rist, R (1989) 'Management Accountability: The signals sent by auditing and evaluation' *Journal of Public Policy* Vol.9 No.3 pp.355-369

Ritzer, G (1993) *The McDonaldization of Society* (California : Thousand Oaks)

Roberts, J (1991) 'The Possibilities of Accountability' *Accounting, Organizations and Society* Vol.16, No.4 pp.355-68

Roberts, S (1997) 'The Implementation of Dutch Public Management Reforms 1980-96' in Ministry of Finance *Public Management Reforms: Five Country Studies* (Helsinki, Finland : Ministry of Finance)

Robertson, G (1996) *Freedom of Information: The Cure for the British Disease* (London : Charter 88)

Robertson, G 'A triumph for Sir Humphrey' *New Statesman* 6/3/98 pp.24-25

Robinson, A (1987) 'Symposium on Ministerial Responsibility' *Public Administration* Vol.65 pp.61-91

Romzek, B & Dubnick, M (1987) 'Accountability in the public sector: lessons from the Challenger tragedy' *Public Administration Review* May/June Vol.47 No.3 pp.227-239

Rose, N & Miller, P (1992) 'Political Power Beyond the State: Problematics of Government' *British Journal of Sociology* Vol. 43 pp.173-205

Rose, R (1982) *The Role of Laws in Comparative Perspective* (Glasgow : Centre for the Study of Public Policy)

Rose, R & Peters, G (1977) *Can Government go Bankrupt?* (New York : Basic Books)

Rosenbloom, D (1978) 'Accountability in the Administrative State' in Greer, S (ed.) *Accountability in Urban Society* (London : Sage)

Rosenthal, R (1966) *Experimenter Effects in Behavioural Research* (New York : Appleton)

Ross, J (1943) *Parliamentary Representation* (London)

Roth, D (1996) 'Finding the Balance: Achieving a Synthesis Between Improved Performance and Enhanced Accountability' in *Performance Auditing and the Modernisation of Government* (Paris : OECD) pp.249-259

Rowe, M (1999) 'Joined up government: bringing the citizen back in' *Public Policy & Administration* Vol.14 No.2 pp.91-102

Rozenberg, J (1997) *Trial of Strength* (London : Richard Cohen)

Rutherford, B (1996) 'The Structure and Content of Executive Agency financial statements' *Financial Accountability and Management* Vol.12 pp.30-57

Rush, M (1990) *Parliament and Pressure Politics* (Oxford : Clarendon)

Rush, M (1997) 'Damming the Sleaze: The New Code of Conduct and Outside Interests of MPs in the British House of Commons' *The Journal of Legislative Studies* Vol.3 No.3 pp.10-28

Russell, M (1999) *Reform of the House of Lords: Lessons from Overseas* (Oxford : Oxford University Press)

Ryan, M (1994) 'Private prisons in the UK: radical change and opposition' in Moyle, P (ed.) *Private Prisons and Police: recent Australian trends* (Australia : NSW)

Ryan, M & Ward, T (1989) 'Privatization and the Penal System: Britain Misinterprets the American Experience' *Criminal Justice Review* Vol.14 No.1 pp.1-12

Sappington, D (1991) 'Incentives in Principal - Agent Relationships' *Journal of Economic Perspectives* Vol. 5 No.2 pp.45-66

Savage, S & Robins, L (1990) *Public Policy Under Thatcher* (London : Macmillan)

Savoie, D (1994) *Thatcher, Reagan, Mulroney: In Search of a New Bureaucracy* (Toronto : University of Toronto Press)

Schaffer, B (1957) 'The idea of the ministerial department: Bentham. Mill and Bagehot' *The Australian Journal of Politics and History* Vol.3 No.1 pp.60-78

Schichor, D (1995) *Punishment for Profit: Private Prisons/Public Concerns* (London : Sage)

Schwartz, H (1994) 'Small States in Big Trouble - State Reorganization in Australia, Denmark, New Zealand, and Sweden in the 1980s' *World Politics* Vol.46 pp.527-555

Schwartz, H (1994) 'Public Choice Theory and Public Choices - Bureaucrats and State Reorganization in Australia, Denmark, New Zealand and Sweden in the 1980s' *Administration & Society* Vol.26 No.1 pp.48-77

Schumpeter, J (1952) *Capitalism, Socialism and Democracy* (London : Allen & Unwin)

Scott, R (1996) 'Ministerial Accountability' *Public Law* pp.410-427

Scott, R, Barbuk, I & Ecclestone, A (1996) *Is Public Access to Civil Service Policy Advice Possible?* (London : Campaign for Freedom of Information)

Scruton, R (1980) *The Meaning of Conservatism* (London : Penguin)

Sedley, J (1994) 'Governments, Constitutions and Judges' in Richardson, G & Genn, H (eds.) *Administrative Law and Government Action: the courts and alternative mechanisms of review* (Oxford : Clarendon) pp.35-45

Sedley, S (1989) 'Public Inquiries: A Cure or a Disease' *The Modern Law Review* Vol.52 pp.469-479

Sedley, S (1990) 'Law and State Power - a time for reconstruction' *Journal of Law and Society* Vol. 17 No.2 pp.234-241

Sedley, S (1994) 'Public Law and Contractual Employment' *Industrial Law Journal* Vol.23 No.3 pp.201-208

Sedley, S (1994) 'The sound of silence: constitutional law without a constitution' *Law Quarterly Review* Vol.110 pp.270-291

Sedley, S (1995) 'Human Rights - a Twenty First Century Agenda' *Public Law* pp.386-400

Sedley, S (1997) 'The Common Law and the Constitution' in Lord Nolan & Sedley, S *The Making and Remaking of the British Constitution* (London : Blackstone)

Sedley, S (1997) 'Law and Public Life' in Lord Nolan & Sedley, S *The Making and Remaking of the British Constitution* (London : Blackstone)

Sedley, S (1997) 'The Constitution in the Twenty First Century' in Lord Nolan & Sedley, S *The Making and Remaking of the British Constitution* (London : Blackstone)

Segal, Z (1984) 'Tribunals of Inquiry: A British Invention Ignored in Britain' *Public Law* pp.206-214

Seldon, A (1984) *Hayek's Serfdom Revisited* (London : Institute of Economic Affairs)

Self, P (1993) *Government by the Market?* (Basingstoke : Macmillan)

Shichor, D (1995) *Punishment for Profit* (London : Sage)

Sikka, P Willmott, H & Lowe, T (1989) 'Guardians of Knowledge and Public Interest: evidence and issues of accountability in the UK accountancy profession' *Accounting, Audit & Accountability* Vol. 2 No.2 pp.47-66

Sikka, P Willmott, H & Lowe, T (1991) 'Guardians of Knowledge and Public Interest: a reply to our critics' *Accounting, Audit & Accountability* Vol.4 No.4 pp.14-22

Silcock, R (2001) 'What is E-Government?' *Parliamentary Affairs* Vol.54 No.1 pp.88-101

Simm, M (1999) 'Models of Political Accountability and Concepts of Australian Government' *Australian Journal of Public Administration* Vol.58 No.1 pp.48-57

Sinclair, A (1995) 'The Chameleon of Accountability - forms and discourses' *Accounting, Oranizations and Society* Vol.20 No.2/3 pp.219-237

Skelcher, C (1998) *The Appointed State: Quasi-governmental Organizations and Democracy* (Buckingham : Open University Press)

Smith, B & Hague, D (1971) *The Dilemma of Accountability in Modern Government: Independence versus Control* (London : Macmillan)

Smith, M *Theoretical and Empirical Challenges to British Central Government* paper presented to the ESRC conference 'Understanding Central Government: Theory Into Practice' 16/18/96

Smith, M (1996) 'Reforming the State' in Ludlam, S & Smith, J (eds.) *Contemporary British Conservatism* (London : Macmillan)

Smith, T (1994) 'Post-Modern Politics and the Case for Constitutional Renewal' *Political Quarterly* Vol.65 pp. 128-137

Smith-Green, P (1995) *Accountability in Development Organisations* (London : Sage)

Spiro, H (1969) *Responsibility in government: theory and practice* (New York : Van Nostrand Rheinhold)

Stanyer, J (1974) 'Divided Responsibilities: Accountabilities in Decentralised Government' *Public Administration Bulletin* No.17 Dec. pp.14-31

Stephen, L (1900) *The English Utilitarian* (London)

Stephens, R (1993) *The Independence of the Judiciary: The View from the Lord Chancellor's Office* (Oxford : Clarendon)

Sterett, S (1992) 'Legality in Administration in Britain and the United States - Towards an Institutional Explanation' *Comparative Political Studies* Vol.25 No.2 pp.195-228

Stewart, J (1984) 'The Role of Information in Public Accountability' in Hopwood, A & Tomkins, C (eds.) *Issues in Public Sector Accounting* (Oxford : Philip Allan)

Stewart, J (1993) 'The Limitations of Government by Contract' *Public Money and Management* Vol.13 No.3 pp.7-13

Stewart, J (1993) 'Defending Public Accountability' *Demos Quarterly* Winter pp.5-10

Stewart, J (1994) 'Management in the Public Domain' in McKevitt, D & Ransom, S (eds.) *Public Sector Management: Theory, Critique and Practice* (London : Sage)

Stewart, J (1994) 'Reply to William Waldegrave' in Flynn, N (ed.) *A Reader: Change in the Civil Service* (London : Public Finance Foundation)

Stewart, J (1994) 'The Rebuilding of Public Accountability' in Flynn, N (ed.) *A Reader: Change in the Civil Service* (London : Public Finance Foundation)

Stewart, J (1998) 'Advance or Retreat? From the traditions of public administration to the new public management and beyond' *Public Policy & Administration* Vol.13 No.4 pp.12-28

Stewart, J & Walsh, K (1992) 'Change in the Management of Public Services' *Public Administration* Vol.70 No.4 pp.499-518

Stewart, J & Walsh, K (1994) 'Performance Management when performance can never be finally defined' *Public Policy & Management* Vol.14 No.2 pp.45-50

Stone, B (1995) 'Administrative Accountability in the Westminster Democracies: Towards a New Conceptual Framework' *Governance* Vol.8 No.1 pp.505-525

Straw, J & Boateng, P (1996) *Bringing Rights Home* (London : The Labour Party)

Strom, K (1997) 'Democracy, accountability and coalition bargaining' *European Journal of Political Research* Vol. 31 pp.47-62

Sudman, S & Bradburn, N (1982) *Asking Questions: A Practical Guide to Questionnaire Design* (San Francisco : Jossey-Bass)

Sunkin, M (1987) 'What is happening to applications for judicial review?' *Modern Law Review* vol.50 p.432-467

Sunkin, M & Le Sueur, A (1991) 'Can Government Control Judicial Review' *Current Legal Problems* Vol.161

Sunkin, M, Bridges, L & Mesmoros, G (1993) 'Trends in Judicial Review' *Public Law* pp.443-446

Sutherland, S (1991) 'Responsible Government and Ministerial Responsibility: Every Reform Is Its Own Problem' *Canadian Journal of Political Science* Vol.24 No.1 pp.91-120

Sutherland, S (1991) 'The Al-Mashat Affair: administrative responsibility in parliamentary institutions' *Canadian Public Administration* Vol.30 No.4 pp.573-603

Swinhoe, K (1971) *A study of the opinion about the reform of the House of Commons Procedure 1945-1968* Unpublished PhD. Thesis, University of Leeds

Talbot, C (1995) 'The Prison Service - A framework of irresponsibility' *Public Finance Foundation Review* No.8 pp.16-19

Tant, A (1990) 'The Campaign for Freedom of Information: a participatory challenge to elitist British government' *Public Administration* Vol.68 pp.477-491

Taylor, A 'New Politics, New Parliament' speech to the Charter 88 seminar on the reform of Parliament 14/5/96

Taylor, M (1996) 'Between Public and Private: Accountability in Voluntary Organisations', *Policy & Politics*, Vol.24, No.1 pp.26-38

Theakston, K (1992) *The Labour Party and Whitehall* (London : Routledge)

Theakston, K (1995) *The Civil Service Since 1945* (Oxford : Blackwell)

Theakston, K (1997) 'Comparative Biography and Leadership in Whitehall' *Public Administration* Vol.75 pp.651-677

Theakston, K (1998) *Leadership in Whitehall* (New York : St Martin's Press)

Thomas, P (1998) 'The Changing Nature of Accountability' in Peters, G & Savoie, D (eds.) *Taking Stock: Assessing Public Sector Reforms* (Montreal : McGill)

Thompson, B (1997) 'Judges as Troubleshooters' *Parliamentary Affairs* Vol.50 No.1 pp.182-189

Thompson, E & Tillotsen, G (1999) 'Caught in the Act: The smoking gun view of ministerial responsibility' *Australian Journal of Public Administration* Vol.58 No.1 pp.48-57

Thynne, I & Goldring, J (1987) *Accountability and Control: Government Officials and the Exercise of Power* (Sydney : Law Book Co.)

Tomkins, A (1996) 'The Scott Report: The Hope and Failure of Parliament' *Political Quarterly* Vol.67 No.4 pp.349-353

Tomkins, A (1996) 'Government Information and Parliament: Misleading by Design or by Default?' *Public Law* pp.472-489

Tomkins, A (1998) *The Constitution After Scott* (Oxford : Clarendon)

Travis, A 'Lawyer in jail release row named' *The Guardian* 31/3/06

Tritter, J (1994) 'The Citizen's Charter: Opportunities for User Perspectives' *Political Quarterly* Vol.65 No.4 pp.397-414

Truman, D (1951) *The Governmental Process* (New York : Knopf)

Turpin, T (1994) 'Ministerial Responsibility' in Jowell, J & Oliver, D (eds.) *The Changing Constitution* (Oxford : Clarendon) pp.109-151

Twigg, J (2000) 'The Age of Accountability?' *Australian Journal of Emergency Management*, Vol.14 No.4 pp.51-58

Tyrie, A (2000) *Mr Blair's Poodle: The Commons must Reform itself to deal with the reality of Presidential Power* (London : Centre for Policy Studies)

Uhr, J (1999) 'Three Accountability Anxieties' *Australian Journal of Public Administration* Vol.58 No.1 pp.98-101

Vagg, J (1994) *Prison Systems - A comparative study of accountability in England, France, Germany and The Netherlands* (Oxford : Clarendon)

Vinten, G (ed.) (1995) *Whistleblowing: subversion or corporate citizenship?* (London : Paul Chapman)

Wadham, J (1997) 'Bringing Rights Home: Labour's plans to incorporate the European Convention on Human Rights into UK Law' *Public Law* pp.75-79

Waldegrave, W (1993) *The Reality of Reform and Accountability in Today's Public Service* Lecture to the Public Finance Foundation 5th July 1993

Waldegrave, W (1993) *Public Service and the Future: Reforming Britain's Bureaucracies* (London : Conservative Political Centre)

Waldegrave, W (1995) 'The Future of Parliamentary Government' *The Journal of Legislative Studies* Vol.1 No.2 pp.173-177

Waldron, J (1990) *The Law* (London : Routledge)

Walkland, S & Ryle, M (1981) *The Commons Today* (London : Fontana)

Wall, A (1996) 'Mine, Yours or Theirs? Accountability and the New NHS' *Policy and Politics* Vol.24 No.1 pp.73-85

Walsh, D (1997) *The Bloody Sunday Tribunal of Inquiry: A Resounding Defeat for Truth, Justice and the Rule of Law* (London : British-Irish Rights Watch)

Walsh, K (1995) *Public Services and Market Mechanisms* (Basingstoke : Macmillan)

Wass, D (1983) 'The Public Service in Modern Society' *Public Administration* Vol.61 No.1 pp.7-20

Wass, D (1984) *Government and the Governed* (London : Routledge)

Wass, D (1996) 'Scott and Whitehall' *Public Law* pp.461-472

Webb, S (1986) *The difficulty of individualism* Fabian Tract No. 69 (London)

Webb S & Webb, B (1920) *A Constitution for the Socialist Commonwealth of Britain* (London : Longmans, Green & Co.)

Weber, E (1999) 'The question of accountability in historical perspective' *Administration & Society* Vol.31 No.4 pp.451-494

Weir, S & Beetham, D (1998) *Political Power and Democratic Control in Britain* (London : Routledge)

Weir, S & Hall, W (1994) *Extra-Governmental Organisation in the United Kingdom and their accountability* Democratic Audit Paper No.2 (London : Charter 88)

Weir, S & Wright, A (1997) *Power to the backbenches?* Democratic Audit paper No.9 (London : Scarman Trust)

Westcott, C (1992) *The Last Right? Open Government, Freedom of Information and the Right to Know* Strathclyde Papers in Politics and Government No.12 (Glasgow : Strathclyde University)

White, F Harden, I & Donnelly, K (1994) *The changing Constitutional Role of the Public Sector Audit- A Framework for Comparative Analysis* (Sheffield : PERC/Dept of Law)

Wicks, E (2000) 'The United Kingdom Government's Perceptions of the European Convention on Human Rights at the Time of Entry' *Public Law* pp.438-455

Wilensky, H (1967) *Organizational Intelligence* (New York : Basic Books)

Willson, F (1955) 'Ministries and Boards: Some Aspects of Administrative Development Since 1832' *Public Administration* Vol.33 pp.43-58

Wilson, D 'What ever happened to Freedom of Information Legislation' *New Statesman & Society* 25/7/97 p.27

Wilson, D 'The fact that Britain is finally getting a freedom of information act is almost entirely due to the single mindedness of one great reformer' *New Statesman & Society* 24/4/98 p.19

Wilson, G (1997) 'The Courts, Law and Convention' in Lord Nolan & Sedley, S *The Making and Remaking of the British Constitution* (London : Blackstone)

Wilson, J & Hinton, P *Public Services and the 1990s: Issues in Public Sector Finance and Management* (Sevenoaks : Tudor)

Wilson, W (1887) 'The Study of Administration' *Political Science Quarterly* Vol.2 pp. 197-222

Winetrobe, B (1997) 'Inquiries after Scott: the return of the tribunal of inquiry' *Public Law* pp. 61-75

Wiseman, H (1966) *Parliament and the Executive* London : Routledge

Wistrich, E (1992) 'Restructuring Government New Zealand Style' *Public Administration* Vol.70 pp.119-135

Wolf, A 'Accountability in public administration: reconciling democracy, efficiency and ethics' Paper to the International Institute of Administrative Sciences Conference, 12-15 May 1999, Civil Service College, Sunningdale

Wood, S (1999) 'Constitutional Reform - living with the consequences' *Renewal* Vol.7 No.3 pp.1-10

Woodhouse, D (1993) 'Ministerial Responsibility: the abdication of responsibility through the receipt of legal advice' *Public Law* pp.412-419

Woodhouse, D (1994) *Ministers and Parliament: Accountability in Theory and Practice* (Oxford : Clarendon)

Woodhouse, D (1994) 'Matrix Churchill: A Case Study in Judicial Inquiries' *Parliamentary Affairs* Vol.48 No.1 pp.24-40

Woodhouse, D (1995) 'Politicians and the Judiciary: A Changing Relationship' *Parliamentary Affairs* Vol.48 No.3 pp.401-417

Woodhouse, D (1996) 'Politicians and Judges: A Conflict of Interest' *Parliamentary Affairs* Vol.49 No.3 pp.423-441

Woodhouse, D (1997) 'The Attorney General' *Parliamentary Affairs* Vol.50 No.1 pp.97-109

Woodhouse, D (1997) *In pursuit of good administration; ministers, civil servants and judges* (Oxford : Oxford University Press)

Woodhouse, D (1997) 'Ministerial Responsibility: Something Old, Something New' *Public Law* pp.262-282

Woodhouse, D (1998) 'A Code of Good Administration: A Parliamentary Response to Judicial/Executive Tension' *Legislative Studies* Vol.4 No.2 pp.89-106

Woodhouse, D (1998) 'The office of the Lord Chancellor' *Public Law* pp.617-633

Woodrow, W (1887) *The Study of Administration* (Princeton : Princeton University Press)

Wright, A (1995) *Beyond the patronage state* Fabian Society pamphlet No. 569 (London : Fabian Society)

Wright, A (2000) *The British Political Process* (London : Routledge)

Wright, V (1994) 'Reshaping the State: The Implications for Public Administration' *West European Politics* Vol.17 No.3 pp.102-135

Yin, R (1980) 'Creeping Federalism: The Federal Impact on the structure and function of local government' in Glickman, N (ed.) *The Urban Impacts of federal Policies* (Baltimore : JHUP)

Yin, R (1994) *Case Study Research* (London : Sage)

Young, D (1969) 'The Colonial Office in the early 19th Century' in Parris, H (ed.) *Constitutional Bureaucracy* (London : Allen & Unwin)

Young, G (2000) 'Westminster: An Holistic Approach' *Crossbow,* summer, pp.6-7

Young, H & Sloman, A (1982) *No, Minister* (London : BBC)

Zellick, G (1985) 'Government Beyond the Law' *Public Law* pp.283-308

Zifcak, S (1994) *New Managerialism : Administrative Reform in Whitehall and Canberra* (Buckingham : Open University Press)

Index

Accountability
    And responsibility 11-12, 47-52
    Circuits of 21-25
    Codes of accountability 14-15
    Definitions 9-16
    Directions 13-14
    Formal-informal 14
    Fuzzy accountability 17
    Judicial accountability 131-228
    Legal advice 167-169, 217-218
    Mechanisms of 16-27
    Multi-layers 12-13
    Party accountability 115-119
    Pathological impact 275-276
    Policy 47-52
    Relationships 8
    Responsibility 'gap' 16, 41
    Versus efficiency 287-294
Agencies 52-55
Attlee, C. 57
Attorney General 167, 218, 328
Australia 16, 314

Backbenchers
    Culture 57-60
    Informal influence 115-119
    Parliamentary reform 120, 364-365
Bagehot, W. 2, 5, 45
Baker, K. 48
Baker, N. 73
Barberis, P. 21
Barker, A. 63
Beattie, A. 5
Beckett, M. 360, 362
Beetham, D. 8

Benemy, F. 7
Bentham, J. 2, 3, 5
Bermingham, G. 105, 118
Bingham, Lord. 138
Birch, H. 5
Bogdanor, V. 66, 69, 246
Bridges, E. 48
Brittan, L. 168
Brixton Prison 48
Brown, Lord. 169
BSE 208-209
Bureauratic reform and the law 136-137
Butler, R. 47, 53
Butt, R. 115

Campaign for Freedom of Information 315
Canada 16, 314
Carltona doctrine 55, 136-137
Child Support Agency 74
Civil Service Commissioner 60
Clark, D. 313, 315
Clarke, K. 272
Cobbett, W. 43
Code of Access on Government Information 188, 310-312
Codification of convention 60-64
Commercial confidentiality 292
Comptroller & Auditor General 4
Constitutional Reform in the UK 169, 352-356
Contracting-Out 236-251, 287-294
Corbett, R. 99, 103, 106, 110
Corruption 1
Crichel Down 44, 47

Crick, B. 7
Criminal Cases Review
    Commission 357
Crossman, R. 64
Crown Prerogative 55-56

'declaration of incompatibility' 156
Department for Education &
    Employment 188
Department of Social Security 188
Department of Trade & Industry 43,
    188
Devolution 352-353
Dicey, A. 45, 134
Disability Rights Commission 157
Donoughmore Committee 135
Drewry, G. 60, 65
Dugdale, T. 47

Eden, J. 114
Efficiency Unit 52, 71
Environment Select Committee 58
Equal Opportunities Commission
    157
European Convention on Human
    Rights 155-159, 212-217, 352
'evolving state' 379-381, 356-359
Executive
    Domination within Parliament
        42-47
    ECHR 155-160
    Legal regulation of behaviour
        142-145
    Mentality 56-59
    Relationship with the judiciary
        137-140

Faulkner, D. 18
Fell, B. 7
Financial Management Initiative 52
Finer, S. 43
First Division Association 10, 49,
    60, 69, 322

Food Standards Agency 357
Foreign Affairs Select Committee
    120
Framework documents 62, 278-287
Frankel, M. 329
'Fraser Figure' 283-284
Freedland, M. 56
Freedom of Information
    and 'Open Government' 319-320
    Code of Access 310-312
    Draft Bill on FOI 315-318
    Politics of 309-327
    rationale underpinning FOI Act
        320-327
    Your Right to Know 312-315
Freeman, R. 66

Garnier, J. 157
Giddings, P. 57
'governance' 237, 358
Griffiths, J. 139
Griffiths, N. 75

Hague, W. 365
Haldane Report 4
Hall, S. 323-233
Hansard Society 10, 366
Harden, I. 131, 242
Hartington, Lord. 44
Hazell, R. 319, 360
Heath, E. 231
Hennessy, P. 59, 61, 70, 364
Heseltine, M. 168
Hewart, Lord. 7
Hollis, C. 7
Home Affairs Select Committee
    Appointments to the HAC
        109-110
    History of 101-102
    Membership 102-105
    Parliamentary reform 114-115
    Party accountability 115-119
    Politics of 101-115

Questions 107-109
Relationship with the Labour government 112-114
Reports 110-113
Role of chairman 110-113
Scope of the committee's remit 114
Time constraints of members 102-103
Home Office
Audit 278-287
contracting-out 287-294
ECHR 155-160, 212-217
Information asymmetries 278-282
Inquiries 203-212
Internal-external accountability 273-278
'joined-up government' 348-350
Judicial accountability 187-229
Judicial review 188-203
Managerial accountability 229-265
Parliamentary accountability 93-131
Policy-operations 285-286
Prison Service Monitoring Unit 282-283
Hood, C. 250
House of Lords reform 353-354
Howard, M. 48, 139, 199-200, 201, 207, 282
Howe, Lord. 67, 74
Howells, K. 326, 327, 350
Hughes, B. 95, 103
Human Rights Act 1998 155-160, 212-217
Human Rights Commission 157
Hurd, D. 106, 109, 117
Hutton, W. 138

Ibbs, R. 52
Information Commissioner 314-315
Information Technology 350-351

Irvine, Lord. 145, 156

Jennings, I. 7
Johnson, N. 11
'joined-up government' 285-286, 348-350
Judge, D. 64
Judicial accountability
and the Home Office 187-229
European influence 155-160, 212-217
Politics of 131-187
Rule of law 134-136
Judicial Inquiries
'borrowed authority' 161-162
Definition of 160-161
Establishment 160
Executive control 163-166
Home Office 203-212
Politics of 160-167
Publication of the report 165-166
reform proposals 166
relationship with Parliament 166-167
resources 162
Judicial Review
Administrative response 147-148, 154-155
Continued deference 152-153
Grounds for 146-147
Growth of 145-146
Home Office 188-203
Impact of 147-149
'leave to appeal' 151-152
Media reporting 151
Methodological issues 150
Obstacles to 146-148
Politics of 145-155
Public Interest Immunity Certificates 153
Judiciary
Accountability of 158
History of 137-140
Home Office 187-229

Protection of fundamental rights 140-142

Kemp, P. 10, 50, 53, 68
Key Performance Indicators 278-284
'Keynesianism' 230-233

Labour Party 69
Landers, B. 108, 109, 280
Law Commission 110-111, 143
Lawrence, I. 102, 106, 107, 114
Laws, J. 141
Lawton, A. 19
Le Sueuer, A.151
Leader of the House 105, 360
Learmont Report 97, 207
Lee, S. 168
Legal advice to ministers 167-169, 217-218
Legal regulation of ministerial action 142-145
Lello, J. 11
Lewis, D. 63, 107, 209, 269-271
Liaison Committee 42, 361-364
Low, S. 7
Lowell, A. 7

Mackay, Lord. 140, 146
Major, J. 163, 168
Managerial Accountability
   Audit 249-251
   Downward accountability 239-242
   High-low accountability 242-243
   Information asymmetries 278-287
   Internal-external accountability 273-278
   Policy/operations dichotomy 244-246
   Politics of 229-265
   Relationship with Parliament 294-309
   Tensions of 236-251
   Versus efficiency 287-294
'Managing Inquiries' 204-206
Marconi 160
Massey, A. 234-235
Mather, G. 238-239
Maxwell-Fife, D. 47
Maze Prison 48
Methodology 26, 375-382
Mill, J. 2
MINIS 52
Ministerial Responsibility
   Abdication on legal advice 167-169, 217-218
   and Freedom of Information 309-339
   Importance of 2-9
   Origins 42-47
   'Whig' and 'Peelite' views 5-9
Ministry of Agriculture, Fisheries & Food 357
'Modernising Government' 347
'Modernising Parliament' 364-365
'Monetarism' 232
Monetary Policy Committee 120
Muir, R. 7
Mullin, C. 103, 104, 105, 106, 107

National Audit Office 70
National Debt Commission 3
New Public Management 1, 16, 230-236, 285
'New Right' 54, 230-233,
New Zealand 16, 324
'Next Steps' 52-58
Niskanen, W. 232
Nolan, Lord. 41, 57, 61, 69
Northcote-Trevelyan Reforms 55
Northern Ireland Human Rights Commission 157
Norton, P. 58, 70, 365

O'Brien, M. 214
Oliver, D. 19, 143
Omand, D. 273
Open Government 319-320
'Overload thesis' 231-232

Page, G. 114
Parliament
   Contracting-out 287-294
   'declaration of incompatibility' 155-160
   Fundamental rights 140-142
   Information technology 350-351
   'Next Steps' Agencies 52-55
   Party accountability 115-119
   Politics of 56-60
   Power of 359-375
   PQs 71-76, 94-101
   Reform of 359-375
   Relationship with the judiciary 137-140
   role of 1-9, 41-52
   select committees 64-71, 101-115
Parliamentary correspondence 97
Parliamentary Questions
   'as a game' 94-100
   Cost of 74
   Home Office 94-101
   Ministerial perception 99-101
   Oral PQs 71-76
   Organisational impact 70-71
Parliamentary reform under Labour 359-375
Party accountability 115-119
Peel, R. 6-7
Performance & Innovation Unit 348-350
Pergau Dam 67
Phillips, Lord. 165
Policy-Operations dichotomy 47-52, 55

Political parties (development of) 42-47
Poor Law Commission 2-3
Post-decisional disclosure 324
Power, M. 249-250
Prime Minister 58, 61, 348
Principal-Agent Theory 244-251
Prior, J. 48
Prior Options Scheme 234
Prison Service
   Contracting-out 287-294
   Inquiries 203-212
   Judicial review 188-203
   Media Relations Unit 270
   Oral PQs 99-100
   Parliamentary Unit 97-98
   Prison Service Monitoring Unit 282-284
Procedure Committee 66-67
Proportional Representation 377-378
Public Accounts Committee 4, 70, 113
Public Administration Select Committee 74, 334, 337
Public Immunity Interest Certificates 11, 231-232
Public Service Select Committee 18, 49, 66, 69, 324
Publication
   Blocking by the executive 62
   Codes, documents, etc. 61-66
Public Choice Theory 232
Pyper, R. 9, 19

Quangos 360-362
Questions of Procedure for Ministers 47, 61, 63
Quinlan, M. 59

Reform Act 1832 44
Regulators 360-361
Rhodes, R. 26
Riddell, P. 18, 363

Risk 347-348
Rose, R. 72
Ross, J. 7
Rossi, H. 58
Royal Commission on Tribunals 161
Rule of Law 134-135

Salmon, Lord. 161
Saville, Lord. 165
Scott, R. 51, 58, 68, 71, 121, 161, 165, 166, 204, 210-11, 322
Select committees
    And agencies 66-68
    And 'joined-up government' 348-350
    Appointments to select committees 105-106
    Paradox of reform 96-97
    Politics of 71-76
    Power of 75
    Statistics 95
    Syndication 75
    Continuity of membership 103-104
    History 64-66
Separation of powers 134-136
'spectrum of autonomy' 234
St John-Stevas, N. 65
Stone, B. 19, 27
Straw, J. 73, 100, 156, 165, 208, 269, 283, 315, 321, 322, 323, 326

Taylor, A. 69, 105
Taylor, H. 5
Tebbitt, N. 202
'teleocracy' 351
Thatcher, M. 52, 71, 233, 288
Toulmin-Smith, J. 2
Treasury and Civil Service Select Committee 11, 18, 49, 53, 68
Tribunals of Inquiry (Evidence) Act 1921 160
Trosa, S. 248

Waddington, D. 199, 201
Waldegrave, W. 48, 235-236
Warner, N. 283-284
Weir, S. 8, 152
Westland Affair 168
Wheeler, J. 114
'Whig' view 5-7, 326-327, 365
Whips Office 105
Widdecombe, A. 100, 109, 116, 117, 119, 195, 200, 207, 271, 280, 281
Wilson, H. 64, 155
Wilson, R. 283, 348
Woodhouse, D. 11, 46, 59, 66, 139, 146, 161, 167
Woolf, Lord. 141
Wright, T. 105

Young, D. 43
'Your Right to Know' 312-315